To Elaine,
Thomas & Jenny
with lots of love

Marie Antoinette as a young girl

THERE WERE THREE OF US IN THE RELATIONSHIP: THE SECRET LETTERS OF MARIE ANTOINETTE (Vol 1)
by

MARGARET ANNE MACLEOD

Selected extracts from

MARIE ANTOINETTE
CORRESPONDANCE SECRETE
entre
MARIE-THERESE ET LE COMTE DE MERCY-ARGENTEAU
AVEC LES LETTRES DE MARIE-THERESE ET
MARIE ANTOINETTE (PARIS, 1874)

Published by Isaac MacDonald

Published by Isaac MacDonald

Copyright © 2008 by Margaret Anne MacLeod

ISBN 978-0-9559991-0-9

Printed by Paterson Print Ltd., 1 Ailsa Road, Irvine KA12 8LL, Scotland

1

Dedicated to my loving parents Margaret Anne and Donald John, Donna, Derek, and my loving and beautiful children.

The writer acknowledges her gratitude to Glasgow University Library, the Mitchell Reference Library of Glasgow, the National Library of Scotland, Edinburgh, the British Library, London and the Bibliotheque Nationale, Paris.

CONTENTS

INTRODUCTION

In 1770, the fourteen year old Marie Antoinette was sent to France as bride for the fifteen year old dauphin. Four years later, in 1774, she became a much loved queen. Yet only fifteen years after she became queen, in 1789, the Revolution began, and by then she was widely hated.

What went wrong?

Only months after Marie Antoinette's arrival in France, Mercy, Maria Theresa's ambassador to France, was writing to the Austrian empress telling her how her daughter's instinctive kindness to a postilion injured at a hunt, was "making her adored" (December 1770). He further wrote of how her "kindness and attention" to all those presented to her at court, "enchanted" everyone (January 1771). It was no surprise therefore that when the old king died, "everyone in France was ecstatic at the new king of nineteen, and his eighteen year old queen" (June 1774).

However the new queen quickly "abandoned herself to entertainments which disturbed Paris" (May 1775). Moreover the "people soon knew of her debts from excessive cardplay" (September 1776), caused simply because she was "afraid to be bored" (November 1777), and that "her desire for jewellery was still not satisfied" (July 1776). Furthermore it was clear to all that, given a choice "between two options, that of influencing the king through kindness, or of dominating him through intimidation," the queen "inclined to the latter" (July 1775). Maria Theresa wrote to Mercy, "She is rushing headlong to her ruin" (July 1775).

What had changed and distorted the initial promise of the beautiful young princess?

The French court itself was malicious and dangerous. Only a few weeks after Marie Antoinette's arrival in France, Mercy was writing "they are using duplicity and lies in an attempt to decrease the king's liking for Marie Antoinette" (June 1770). Maria Theresa wrote to Mercy in May 1771 about "the situation of my daughter and that of the court of France; the one is as delicate as the other is frightening." While still dauphiness, Marie Antoinette complained to Mercy, "if my mother saw all that happened here she would pardon me; no one could tolerate it" (November 1771). After she became queen, Mercy wrote of how he suspected that a former minister, d'Aiguillon, "was involved in anonymous writings against the government, which are especially trying to harm the queen" (September 1774). Everything Marie Antoinette did was written about in the fledgling press, who happily exaggerated every incident, as in March 1776, when it was claimed that at the Opera Ball in Paris, Marie Antoinette had been "left alone by Monsieur for two or three hours, and then talked without distinction to different masked men who each in turn took her arm." Again in March 1779, the queen was once more at the Opera Ball in Paris, (again with her husband's blessing), and initially accompanied only by a courtier, when her carriage broke down, obliging her to hail a passing hackney coach. Despite her mask, and presumed anonymity, the press again heard of this escapade, and was then full of fanciful reports of assignations with lovers and so on. Maria Theresa time and again referred to the treacherous nature of the French court, writing in August 1774 of the "poor innocent queen" who was "surrounded by traitors and scoundrels." She added in October 1776, "I pity my daughter."

And what of Louis XVI himself, the husband of Marie Antoinette, of whom Mercy wrote dismissively in June 1777, "He loves her as much as he is capable." Why was Marie Antoinette so keen to escape from his plodding embrace to the heady excitement of the Opera Balls in Paris? Was it to meet with the succession of lovers (of both sexes) which the newssheets claimed she had? Yet her brother, the stern emperor

Joseph, wrote in a private letter to his brother Leopold in June 1777, while he was visiting their sister in France, that she was "truly honourable and virtuous and living a respectable life." No, Marie Antoinette engaged in pleasure seeking, at least initially, in order to lessen the agony of her childlessness. She endured this childlessness for seven excrutiatingly long years until Joseph visited her husband, and finally persuaded the reluctant spouse to have a simple remedial operation which permitted him to ejaculate, whilst engaged in intercourse. During these seven long years, Marie Antoinette was often to be found in tears (for example in July 1772, August 1775 and September 1776), as she endured the admonitions of her mother to use all her graces to encourage the king to complete the sexual act. She also endured the constant sneering and whisperings of a vindictive court, and the torment of witnessing her sister-in-law give birth to an heir to the throne.

But Louis was not just inept in a marital sense. He was inept as a man, for example telling his wife in August 1770, that he associated with his grandfather's mistress "for the sake of peace." His weakness was obvious to all, including his wife, and these letters abound with instances of this. This lack of authority exposed his wife, his crown and his country to the excesses of the French Revolution, as Louis for some years underestimated the depths of feeling in France, and then refused to exercise control over events, instead preferring to wait for his allies to rescue him from his position, whilst duplicitously assuring the French people that he was happy with the changes which they had wrested from him.

It was Marie Antoinette's great misfortune to be married to an irresolute man and king ("as a woman she is united to an inert being, as a queen she is seated on a teetering throne," La Marck, January 1791), at a time when the great philosophers of the time were questioning the accepted wisdom that it was in the natural scheme of things for the poor to be downtrodden and overtaxed; the aristocracy was questioning the absolute power of the king and looking enviously at their neighbours in Britain, where the aristocracy enjoyed some power in the parliaments; the press was beginning to enjoy freedom to commentate on state affairs (largely through the incompetence of the ministers); many French had participated in the American War of Independence, and had returned to France, enthused with ideas of their rights; and the harvests failed or were insufficient, for several years in succession.

What then of Marie Antoinette's personal contribution to the distressing state of affairs? Queen at eighteen, she was undoubtedly thoughtless, pleasure seeking and heedless of the dire warnings of her mother (like most eighteen year olds!). However can she be damned for not being able to look ahead to her future, as her mother often implored her (for example in February 1777) to do? After all, as Louis was wont to say during the Revolution, "No one has ever been in our position before" (February 1792). That is, absolute power had been the norm in European royal families, until then. The population of Europe mostly lived on the land and endured almost feudal, cowed lives, scarcely daring to question the overarching authority of the crown, the aristocracy and the church. This was at the dawn of the age of revolutions. How could the giddy Marie Antoinette anticipate the great social upheaval which was about to disturb not only France, but all of Europe?

However the story of Marie Antoinette does not finish with the last of these letters. The next chapter in the life of this foolish, but tremendously brave young woman, was just about to begin. To regard these letters as a final judgement on Marie Antoinette, is to do her a disservice.

Because during the Revolution, the queen changed.

The pleasure seeking young girl was replaced by the exhausted and desperate woman, writing frantic letters deep into the night, to all the neighbouring powers, beseeching them to intervene in France; meeting with ministers in an attempt to use their influence to appease the ever increasing revolutionary fervour of the people; trying distractedly to compensate for her husband's deficiencies and apathy with her own energy – it was little wonder that she should write to Fersen, her lover, several months before the overthrow of the throne, "I no longer know myself" (December 1791).

But her efforts were in vain. The monarchy was overthrown and the royals were incarcerated. Just as the moving account of Maria Theresa's last days, by her daughter, (which is included in this volume), renders justice to the humanity and dignity of the woman Maria Theresa, as opposed to the empress Maria Theresa (if such a simplistic differentiation can be made), so the moving account of Marie Antoinette's end, by her own daughter (and others), renders justice to the humanity and dignity of the woman Marie Antoinette, who endured heartbreakingly harrowing cruelties in the days, weeks and months before her trial, until her execution put an end to her agony. They form part of the second volume of this set.

The letters in both volumes testify to the integrity of the comte de Mercy. Nonetheless, both volumes are incomplete, if one wants to do justice to Marie Antoinette, without further reading, especially if considered without reading the 'Memoirs of Madame Campan.' Mercy, despite his extensive spies and contacts, still only had the perspective of one person, moreover the perspective of a man, who at times simply did not appreciate the emotional life of the young queen. Campan's account, although at times rather overblown, (a natural romance writer, manquée!) is nonetheless a fascinating and almost totally reliable account of many of the same events and incidents, but with a slightly different perspective (available as a free download on the internet http://campanmemoirs.blogspot.com).

The final judgement on Marie Antoinette is not the cruel but understandable judgement delivered by the Revolutionary Tribunal as foreign armies fought on French soil, but rather that delivered by the reader.

CHRONOLOGICAL TABLE (PARTIAL)

1754. The dauphin is born – Marie Antoinette's future
husband – the future Louis XVI.
1755. Axel von Fersen (Marie Antoinette's future lover) born.
November 2nd: Marie Antoinette is born
1765. December: The future Louis XVI's father dies
1767. March: The future Louis XVI's mother dies
1770. May: Marriage ceremony at Versailles between Marie
Antoinette and the dauphin.

[For a fuller chronology, see p. 408]

In April 1770, the fourteen year old Marie Antoinette,
daughter of Maria Theresa, empress of Austria, was sent to France in
an arranged marriage with the fifteen year old dauphin, crown prince
of France….

1770

MARIA THERESA TO MARIE ANTOINETTE, 21 APRIL 1770, DAY OF YOUR DEPARTURE. RULES TO BE READ EVERY MONTH

When you waken, on rising, immediately go down on your knees and say your morning prayers. Then do a little religious reading, even if only for ten minutes or so without being distracted by anything or having spoken to anyone. Everything depends on a good beginning to the day and on the intention with which you begin. This can transform even indifferent actions into good and worthy ones. This is a point you must be quite firm about; its execution depends only on you, and it can influence your spiritual and temporal happiness. It is the same with evening prayers and examining your conscience; but I repeat, your morning prayers and a little religious reading are the most important matters to remember.

Always tell me what books you are reading. Pray as often as you can during the day, especially at Holy Mass. I hope that you will listen to it and learn from it every day, and go twice on Sundays and feast days, if that is the custom at your court. However much I would like you to occupy yourself in praying and with good reading, I would not however wish you to think of introducing something which is not customary in France: you must not claim that something is exceptional, nor cite what is customary here, nor ask for it to be imitated; on the contrary you must conform totally to what is the custom at your court.

Go after dinner if possible and especially on Sundays, to Vespers. Pray in the evening and when you pass in front of a church or a cross, but behave normally while doing so, as this does not prevent your heart concentrating on inner prayers, the presence of God being all that is necessary for this whatever the occasion; your incomparable father had that quality to perfection.

10

On entering a church, allow yourself to feel only great respect and do not let your curiosity run away with you, as this will lead to distractions. All eyes will be fixed on you; therefore do not give rise to talk. In France people behave in a very respectable way while in church and also while in public; you do not find, as you do here, oratories which are too comfortable, and which often give rise to carelessness in people's bearing and talk, which scandalizes many in France. Remain on your knees for as long as possible, that is the best way to give an example. Do not allow yourself to assume overly serious expressions as they can seem hypocritical; in that country especially, you must avoid that reproach.

Do not read any book, however indifferent it may be, without your confessor's approval: this is even more necessary in France than elsewhere, because there are always books being published there which seem pleasant and erudite, but behind this respectable facade they are pernicious with regard to religion and morals. I therefore beg you my daughter not to read any book, not even a pamphlet, without your confessor's permission; I expect you, my dear daughter, to behave thus as a very real proof of your love for your good mother, and respect for my advice, as I wish only for your salvation and happiness. Never forget the anniversary of your late dear father's death and mine when the time comes: until then you can pray for me on my birthday.

PRIVATE INSTRUCTION

Do not undertake any recommendations; listen to no one if you would be at peace. Have no curiosity; that is a point which I fear very much in respect to you. Avoid any familiarity with the lower classes. Ask M. and Madame de Noailles and even exact of them, that they advise you as to what, as a stranger and being desirous of pleasing the nation, you should do, and that they tell you frankly if there is something to be corrected in your bearing, your speech or other points. Reply pleasantly to everyone, with grace and dignity: you can do it if you wish. You must also learn to refuse. In my states and in the empire you cannot refuse to accept petitions, but will give them all to Starhemberg [Edit: one of Maria Theresa's advisers].

After Strasbourg accept nothing without asking for the advice of M. and Madame de Noailles [Edit: Madame de Noailles was to be Marie Antoinette's lady of honour], and you should refer to them anyone who speaks to you of their business, telling them honestly that being a stranger yourself, you cannot undertake to recommend someone to the King. Do not be ashamed to ask advice of anyone and do nothing of your own volition.

At the beginning of every month I will send a courier to Paris: while waiting, you can write your letters in order to send them off immediately the courier arrives. Mercy [Edit: Maria Theresa's ambassador in France] has orders to attend to this. You can even write to me by post, but only on trivial matters, which anyone can hear about. I do not think you need to write to your family, except for specific reasons, and as for the emperor [Edit: Marie Antoinette's brother, Joseph, who ruled jointly with her mother Maria Theresa, since the death of their father], you can make arrangements with him yourself on this matter. You can still write to your uncle and aunt and even prince Albert if you wish.

The Queen of Naples [Edit: Marie Antoinette's sister] wants you to write; I see no problem in that. She will tell you nothing unless it is reasonable and useful. Her example should serve as a model and will encourage you, as her situation was and still is much more difficult than yours. Through her intelligence and deference she has overcome all her considerable problems; she is my consolation and has also won public approval: so you can write to her, but be careful to write only what can be read by all. Tear up my letters, as this will enable me to write to you more openly; I will do the same with yours. [Edit: Maria Theresa did not do this]

Do not bother about domestic matters here; they only consist of boring and uninteresting facts. Speak truthfully but tactfully about your family: although I am not always entirely pleased with them, you may find others even worse, and that while there is only childishness and jealousy over trivialities here, elsewhere quarrels may be more serious.

MARIA THERESA TO MERCY, 1 MAY 1770

Comte de Mercy, I authorise you to furnish to my daughter the dauphine, as required, up to one thousand louis for the expenses which she may incur from time to time.

MARIA THERESA TO MARIE ANTOINETTE, 4 MAY 1770

My dear daughter, now you are settled where Providence has destined you to live. If only in relation to your impressive situation, you are the luckiest of your sisters and of all princesses. You will find a loving father, who at the same time will be your friend, if you so deserve. [Edit: Louis XV was Marie Antoinette's husband's grandfather but was often referred to as father] Trust him totally; you will risk nothing by it. Love him, be submissive to him, try to guess his thoughts, you cannot do enough for him now I have lost you. This father and friend, alone consoles me and relieves my despair. I hope that you will follow my advice of only listening to him and awaiting his orders and directions.

As for the dauphin, I will say nothing about him; you know my delicacy on this point; the wife must submit to her husband in everything and must have no other occupation but to please him and do his will. The only true happiness in this world lies in a happy marriage; I know this. For this everything depends on the wife being obliging, gentle and amusing.

People have been saying only one thing about you all the way to Gunzbourg. The first and last things they notice are your attentions and affability, and also your gentle expression which enchants all. Do not be familiar, because that only flatters, as it is too obvious, kindness however is what attracts and reassures everyone. I recommend my dear daughter that you reread my letter on the 21st of every month. Please be faithful to me on this point; I only fear that you will neglect your prayers and your reading, and a lack of concern for one's faith often follows negligence. Fight against this, for it is more dangerous than a more reprehensible, even wicked state; one can overcome that more easily.

13

Love your family; be affectionate to them, to your aunts as well as your brothers and sisters-in-law. Do not allow any unpleasantness to develop; you can either silence people, or else avoid them, by withdrawing from them. If you want peace of mind, avoid this from the beginning, as it is a pitfall I fear for you, knowing your curiosity.

Give the enclosed letter to the King and talk about me to him as often as you can. You can never say too much about my feelings for him. Give the other letter to Madame Adelaide [Edit: the dauphin's aunt]. These princesses are full of virtues and talents; you are very fortunate; I hope you will merit their friendship.

The Choiseuls [Edit: the duc de Choiseul was Louis XV's foreign minister] will be aware that I have asked you to be especially kind to them. Do not forget the Durforts [Edit: M. de Durfort had been the French ambassador to Vienna when Marie Antoinette's marriage had been arranged] and the abbe de Vermond [Edit: her reader].

Remember your mother as, although far from you, I will be concerned about you until I draw my last breath. I give you my blessing and will always be your faithful mother.

MARIA THERESA TO MERCY, 24 MAY 1770

[Send two reports - one private one for me, and the other to be seen by others if necessary]…I fear my daughter's youthfulness, that she will respond to flattery, her idleness and lack of desire to apply herself. I would like you to watch over her and ensure she does not fall under any malign influence. [Edit: with these words possibly ringing in his ears, Mercy made desperate attempts, after her husband was executed, to persuade Austrian forces to march on Paris to save the life of the Queen.][1]

---

[1] See for example in volume II of these letters, Mercy's letter of October 1793, "I tremble for the Queen…When one reads the journals, can one refrain from a feeling of terror?"

I went to Versailles on the evening of the 8th and arrived while cavagnol was being played; as soon as Madame la dauphine saw me come in, she signalled to me to approach and told me she wanted to talk to me. I begged her to finish her game; as soon as she did, she stood up and seeing a paper in my hand, realized then it was from Your Majesty [Y.M.]. She seized it eagerly saying: "Gott sei dank!" and read it joyfully on the spot.

[Edit: Mercy in a letter to baron Neny of 14th of May wrote: "In her debut at Strasbourg, our archiduchesse dauphine behaved in a way which surpassed all my hopes, as much by her bearing as by the appropriateness and grace of her words. The meeting this afternoon in the forest of Compiegne (where Marie Antoinette first met her husband and the rest of the French royal family) crowned her achievement; it would be impossible to appear under happier auspices than those of our dauphine. They are still threatening that Mme du Barry (Louis XV's mistress, some claim a former courtesan) will sup tomorrow at La Muette with the royal family; I cannot believe it; but whatever happens, Madame la dauphine will certainly be pleasant."]

When I was leaving, the comtesse de Noailles told me she had important matters to discuss with me. When I went to her room I learned that the duc de la Vauguyon' s cabal [Edit: the duc de la Vauguyon had been the dauphin's governor] was trying urgently to have the abbe de Vermond dismissed, on the pretext that, not fulfilling his duty as a reader, he was becoming useless at court and that apart from that they were using duplicity and lies in an attempt to decrease the King's liking for Madame la dauphine; that someone had told His Majesty [H.M.] that the princess had declared she did not want to accompany the King on his weekly trips to his country houses, that the duc de la Vauguyon wanted Madame la dauphine to have a confessor who indulged in intrigue and was suspect in every possible way, and a femme de chambre who was the comtesse de Marsan's creature, that in sum they were creating all sorts of bother for the comtesse de Noailles, and that she would not be able to withstand them in the long run, and that she would rather resign than be subject to such persecution.

I tried to calm her by saying everything I could think of; I agreed that we were in truth dealing with wicked people, but that they were neither clever enough nor powerful enough to frighten us, that my advice was that the very next day the comtesse de Noailles should obtain an audience with the King and tell him what she knew of concerning Madame la dauphine's service and the proprieties of that service and that in this conversation she would deny the words falsely attributed to the princess. This was carried out as I had proposed; the King said he still wanted the abbe de Vermond to remain as a reader, and that he also agreed that I should have access to Madame la dauphine in order to acquit myself of what Y.M. ordered me to say.

The comtesse de Noailles spoke quite skilfully of Madame la dauphine's great desire to please the King, and she added amongst other things that this princess would be charmed to accompany H.M. "on the little trips he was in the habit of taking." The King smiled at this but did not reply; he spoke of the dauphin's cold expression, saying, "that he would have to be left to himself for a while," that he was extremely "timid and unsociable," and that finally he was "different from other men." Moreover the King not only treated the comtesse de Noailles quite well, he also told her that he depended on her for Madame la dauphine's service and that he would help her in the future if she had further suggestions to make to him about this matter.

Now it only remains for me to think of means of engaging Madame la dauphine to cooperate to make our steps successful. Despite promises she made to the prince de Starhemberg, there has been no reading up till now. I suggested to the abbe de Vermond to insist energetically on this and even to speak of leaving. [Then] I saw Mme l'archiduchesse in her rooms alone with the comtesse de Noailles, who retired to a corner of the room, leaving me free to talk. I profited from this to tell Madame la dauphine that I was extremely embarrassed at being obliged to ask Y.M. to dismiss the abbe de Vermond

16

in the next few days as he was not carrying out his functions as a reader, and therefore he could not remain at court without his stay appearing to be due to intrigue. [I told Madame la dauphine]…that this had already been dangerously implied, and that…[his remaining] was not desirable therefore, either for Y.M. or for herself, and that it was necessary to act. H.R.H. seemed slightly embarrassed at what I had said. She told me that nothing in the world would induce her to agree to the abbe de Vermond leaving and that if this depended on her reading, she would start that very day, which in fact she did.

H.R.H. told me she was pleased with the dauphin, that she attributed his timidity and coldness to the type of education he had received, but that nonetheless he appeared to be of good character, that she was firmly convinced that the dauphin was attached to the duc de la Vauguyon only from habit and fear, but was not fond of him and did not trust him, that apart from that, the dauphin was so reserved about the people around him, that, despite little tentatives, she had not been able to draw from him one word to clarify her misgivings.

I begged Madame la dauphine not to show animosity towards the duc de la Vauguyon nor his son, the duc de Saint-Megrin, both quite badly treated up till now by H.R.H.; that it was sufficient to know them for what they were, but that, whilst remaining on guard against them, good politics demanded secrecy and that she did not appear to be partisan, which would only give them more of an excuse to continue with their behaviour. I believe this to be very important.

With reference to Madame la dauphine's confessor, the prince de Starhemberg, the duc de Choiseul, the bishop of Orleans and the comtesse de Noailles all agree that the King's confessor, a priest of known probity and piety, who adheres to no party and refrains from intrigue, would be the best person to choose for Mme la dauphine. I spoke of this to the princess, who intends to seize the first available opportunity to ask the King for the priest in question and thus prevent any other choice suggested by a dangerous cabal.

All I have reported above, has been arranged in concert with the duc de Choiseul, who, deeply affected by the trust which Y.M. deigns to have in him, has promised me that he is

17

prepared to speak to the King every time it is necessary to protect Mme la dauphine from the manoeuvres of intriguers and thereby prevent possible unpleasantness which could result for the princess. This minister will shortly have an audience with H.R.H. and will tell her all that he thinks for the best. I believe therefore that for the moment everything is fine.

According to what I have observed, it is certain that for some days Mme l'archiduchesse has made some progress in pleasing the dauphin; he told Madame Adelaide that he found his wife very attractive, that her face and her character pleased him and "that he was very content;" however he keeps his feelings locked away inside him. Until now there has not been very extensive intimacy when they have been alone, but there is no reason to worry for the future, and considering the youthfulness of these two august spouses, it is perhaps better that their liaison forms a slow progression, and will thus be more assured.

The King is still very pleased with Mme la dauphine; she is affectionate when fitting, and in a very touching and delicate way. The King, as he did me the honour of telling me the other day, finds her "lively and quite childish," but, he added, "that is fine at her age." Mesdames de France [Edit: the collective term for the King's unmarried daughters] are delighted with Mme la dauphine; she is praised by both the court and the public for her affability and her custom of always being gracious to everyone who approaches her. They find her full of grace, and I can assure Y.M. that this is not just flattery, but a very firmly held conviction which is almost universal here.

However as it has pleased Y.M. to order me to tell her all my thoughts, I must obey with as much frankness as zeal, and tell you that, without letting myself be dazzled by the justly merited success of Mme la dauphine, I believe that, in the midst of such a lively and capricious nation, and at such a stormy court, it is easier at the beginning to win popularity than to keep it for long. In order to succeed in this, Mme la dauphine must watch herself in regard to several little points, one of the most essential is her bearing, and H.R.H. sometimes forgets this when sitting at her meals or at cavagnol. Often her clothes become dishevelled by her little amusements during the day; however I must also say that at church Mme l'archiduchesse maintains the most seemly and most appropriate bearing.

H.R.H. simply from fun and without bad intentions sometimes lets herself joke about those whom she perceives to be ridiculous; that has already been noticed here, and could become much more dangerous as the princess knows how to add to her remarks all the wit and sarcasm necessary to make them more cutting; but above all else the most important point is to encourage H.R.H. to overcome her extreme repugnance for serious occupations, especially reading: these are the only means by which this princess can keep herself safe from the dangers attached to her position.

When I have occasion to talk to her, she shows so much love for Y.M., also respect and desire to please you, that I am convinced that if Y.M. thought it appropriate to insist on the three points indicated above, in your private letters, that would achieve much more than all the representations which could come from anyone else.

The prince de Starhemberg left me a paper written by Y.M. enclosed within his seal to give to Mme la dauphine whenever she asked me, and H.R.H. has ordered me to give it to her on the 21st of every month. The princess is pleased with her lady of honour, who until now has shown attentiveness and zeal in her service. She has declared herself totally opposed to the duc de la Vauguyon's party and favourably disposed to that of the duc de Choiseul; I am quite busy trying to bring them together, because that would result in great advantages when intrigues, which are so common at this court, occur.

Judging from what Mme la dauphine has told me, I can see that she has fathomed the character and qualities of the people around her, with a wisdom which is quite astonishing for her age. She understands the comtesse de Noailles totally; I would prefer that the latter were not quite so obliging and flattering towards her mistress. I have not concealed these observations from the comtesse, but I am far from obtaining what would be desirable in the circumstances. As for the others in Mme la dauphine's service, up till now there has been no

19

problem. Her ladies are all equally well treated; they are all pleased and show great zeal and attachment to their mistress.

I have learned from the abbe de Vermond that Mme la dauphine has read twice since Saturday and that she appeared decided to continue doing so.

Mme du Barry felt she should pay court one morning to H.R.H.; the princess received her without affectation; it all took place in a dignified fashion and displeased no one.

MARIE ANTOINETTE TO MARIA THERESA, 9 JULY 1770

My dear mother, tomorrow, the 10th, we are leaving for Choisy, and will come back on the 13th to go to Bellevue on the 17th and on the 18th to Compiegne, where we will remain until the 28th of August, and from there we will go for a few days to Chantilly [Edit: different palaces belonging to the French royal family]. The King is exceptionally kind to me and I love him very much, but his weakness for Mme du Barry is to be pitied, as she is the most foolish and impertinent creature imaginable. She played cards with us at Marly every evening; she was beside me twice, but she did not talk to me and I felt justified in not entering into a conversation with her; however when it was necessary, I spoke to her.

As for my dear husband, he has greatly changed, and all to his advantage. He is very friendly to me and has even begun to show trust in me. He certainly does not like the duc de la Vauguyon, but is afraid of him. The other day a strange thing happened. I was alone with my husband, when the duc de la Vauguyon rushed up to the door to eavesdrop. A valet who is either a stupid or very honest man opened the door, and M. le duc was then left stuck like a pole unable to move. Later I remarked to my husband that it was inconvenient to have people eavesdropping and he took it very well.

I forgot to tell you that yesterday I wrote for the first time to the King; I was really worried, knowing that Mme du Barry reads all his letters, but you can rest assured, my very dear mother, that they will never be able to fault me by finding me either for or against her.

I have the honour of being the most loving, submissive and respectful of daughters.

MARIE ANTOINETTE TO MARIA THERESA, 12 JULY 1770

Choisy. My dear mother, I cannot tell you how touched I am by the kindness Y.M. shows me, and I assure you that I have not yet received one of your precious letters without tears of regret forming at being separated from such a good and loving mother, and although things are fine here, I would however dearly love to be able to go back and see my beloved and very precious family if only for a moment.

As you ask about my devotions, I can reply that I have only taken communion once. Our trip to Choisy was delayed by a day, as my husband had a cold and some fever, but that passed in a day, as he slept for twelve and a half hours and was then quite well and able to leave. We therefore came here yesterday - and here we stay from one in the afternoon when we dine, until one in the morning, without going back to our rooms - which really displeases me because after dinner we play cards until six o'clock, then go to a play until half past nine, and then to supper, from there we play cards again until one o'clock and sometimes even until half past one. Yesterday the King, seeing I could go on no longer, was kind enough to send me away at eleven o'clock, which really pleased me and I slept very well until half past ten, although I was alone; my husband, still following a strict regime, went to bed in his own room and slept immediately, which is not the normal procedure.

Y.M. is very kind to be so interested in me and to want to know how I spend my day. Therefore I will tell you that I rise at ten or at nine, or half past nine and, having dressed, I say my morning prayers, then I have breakfast, and afterwards I go to my aunts, where I usually find the King. We stay there until half past ten; then at eleven o'clock I have my hair dressed. At midday the chamber is announced and anyone can enter, if they are not of the common people. I put on rouge and wash my hands in front of everyone, then the men go out and the women stay and I change into court dress in front of them.

Mass is at midday; if the King is at Versailles, I go with him, my husband and aunts to mass; if he is not here, I go alone with M le dauphin, but always at the same time. After mass we both dine in front of everyone, but that is over by half past one because we both eat quickly. Then I go to M le dauphin's rooms, and if he is busy, I go back to my own room, read, write or do some handwork because I am making a waistcoat for the King, which is not progressing very well, but I hope that, God willing, it will be finished in a few years.

At three o'clock I go again to my aunts and the King comes at that time too; at four o'clock the priest [Vermond] comes to me and at five o'clock every day a teacher of harpsichord or singing comes until six o'clock. At half past six I almost always go to my aunts, if I am not going for a walk; you will probably be interested in knowing that my husband nearly always goes with me to my aunts.

At seven o'clock we play cards until nine, but when the weather is fine, I go for a walk and then there is no card play in my rooms, but in my aunts. At nine we have supper, and when the King is not there, my aunts have supper with us, but when the King is there, we go after supper to my aunts, where we wait for the King, who usually comes at a quarter to eleven. While waiting I lie on a sofa and sleep until the King arrives, but when he is not there, we go to bed at eleven o'clock.

I beg you my very dear mother, to excuse me if my letter is too long, but my only pleasure is to talk to you. I also beg your pardon if the letter is dirty, but I had to write it two days in succession at the time of my toilette, having no other time to myself, and if I do not reply exactly, believe me that it is only because I burn your letter immediately. I must finish now in order to dress and go to the King's mass; I am honoured to be the most submissive of daughters.

I am sending you a list of the gifts I have received, because I think you will find them amusing.[2]

---

[2] Unlike the present Charlie Windsor, it is not believed that Marie Antoinette sold off her unwanted gifts.

MERCY TO MARIA THERESA, 14 JULY 1770

Mme la dauphine received your letters with great joy. I told her that Y.M. did not want her letters shown to anyone except the King, and only when Mme la dauphine thought it appropriate.

In my last letter I told you that the duc de la Vauguyon was trying to interfere in Mme la dauphine's household, in order to procure enough authority to have direct influence over the princess, and thus make her dependent on him. To achieve this, the duc de la Vauguyon felt firstly that it would suit him to have M le dauphin behaving in a kind manner to the comtesse du Barry.

For some time this prince has wanted to be included in the supper parties at Saint-Hubert, a place the King frequents when hunting. The duc de Saint-Megrin was charged by his father with informing the comtesse du Barry of the dauphin's wishes; this woman quickly passed the request on to the King, who consented, so that from then on, M le dauphin has been at all the little trips, has remained to supper and consequently has found himself in some way initiated into the pleasure parties where the favourite reigns and where decency is not always scrupulously observed.

However this arrangement has had a contrary effect to that intended, because Mesdames de France, alarmed at the danger M le dauphin was running, decided to tell him everything about the favourite, the most striking details about her life, and above all about the disorder occasioned by her presence at court. This made such a strong impression on the dauphin, that since then he has shown marked aversion towards the comtesse du Barry, who will certainly never be the same in his eyes again.

The duc de la Vauguyon did not succeed any better in gaining the entrees familieres at Mme la dauphine's because the comtesse de Noailles prevented him; this has led to such a violent dispute and such harsh words that both now hate each other unreservedly.

The intrigue formed to give a confessor to Mme la dauphine having been discovered in time, H.R.H. was advised to ask the King if she could share his confessor, and this request was made so well and with such good grace, and at the same time was so well received, that on the same day, the 24th of last month, the King ordered his grand almoner to present to Mme la dauphine the aforementioned ecclesiastic, who is in every respect a good person, full of piety and leads a secluded life at court. The choice of this confessor was of great importance and has kept away several dangerous people whom it had been proposed to establish with Mme la dauphine. As a result of these circumstances the duc de la Vauguyon has until now failed in his projects. He still intends placing the duchesse de Saint Megrin, his daughter-in-law, as dame d'atours with Mme la dauphine, and giving her a first lady of the bedchamber, but I hope that there will be means to prevent both, the people in question being only too suspect.

H.R.H. has been quite good at continuing her reading, followed always by a little serious conversation with the abbe de Vermond on the day's happenings, and this is all to the good, because Mme la dauphine, though naturally high spirited, forgets nothing that is said to her; she listens quietly and it is certain that she pays attention to everything reasonable which is said to her. On several occasions, I have taken the liberty of telling her that it is necessary to watch her expressions and not to allow little jokes at the expense of others. H.R.H. has always listened kindly and she is changing for the better.

The recent trip to Marly was quite a difficult and delicate occasion for Mme la dauphine; she behaved there with all possible prudence. Obliged to play lansquenet [a card game] every evening with the comtesse du Barry, and even finding herself sitting next to that woman, still H.R.H. did not make the slightest gesture which could have given rise to remarks, nor to talk that she had treated the favourite well or badly. Mme l'archiduchesse told me that she herself gave an account to Y.M. of what happened at Marly.

The King continues to be perfectly satisfied with Mme la dauphine and shows it with all sorts of attentions and signs of affection. I never stop asking H.R.H. to be always very loving towards the King; it is the surest way of captivating him and must not be neglected. If Y.M. deigned to mention this point, it would certainly have the desired effect. It has seemed for the past few days that Mme la dauphine has been a little less bothered to please the King, and more timid in speaking to him. This could be as a result of the example of Mesdames de France, who are now very close to Mme la dauphine and this has its advantages, but also a few minor drawbacks as they are not always circumspect in their talk, and also because of the little intrigues which Mesdames always want to meddle in and which would be dangerous if they involved Mme la dauphine.

Until now, H.R.H. has been inaccessible to recommendations; she constantly refuses to be charged with them. I am very careful to remind her of the importance of this, but I am sometimes contradicted by Mesdames and even by the comtesse de Noailles. This latter fulfils her position quite well in some respects, but I cannot prevail on her to change her tone of obligingness and flattery, through which she thinks she will procure credit, but she is wrong. In fact Mme la dauphine treats her well but has no trust in her and does not believe her in a position to give good advice.

Of all those around Mme la dauphine, the abbe de Vermond is the only really useful one because of his way of telling her the truth and making her feel it. On Mme la dauphine's arrival, all of her household received presents, except for the abbe de Vermond, and even the expenses of his trip from Strasbourg to here have not been reimbursed. [Edit: the abbe de Vermond had been sent by the French court to Vienna to improve Marie Antoinette's French shortly before she had come to France] I begged H.R.H. to speak of it to the duc de la Vrilliere in order to regulate the abbe de Vermond's position, as he was becoming affected by it all.

What is most satisfying for Mme l'archiduchesse, is that each day she gains more ascendancy over M le dauphin. She behaves with so much gaiety and grace with him that he is subjugated; he speaks to her trustingly of matters he has never spoken of to anyone. His dour and reserved character had made him impenetrable up till now, but Mme la dauphine can make him talk on any subject, and she discovered that he did not have a good opinion of the duc de la Vauguyon. I told Mme la dauphine that it was very important she never spoke to anyone, especially Mesdames, of what M le dauphin told her, in order to keep his trust; H.R.H. agreed.

I always discuss with the duc de Choiseul what regards H.R.H. and I tell her myself, or through the abbe de Vermond, the minister's advice. In the present critical situation he believes he should not appear often at Mme la dauphine's. However Y.M. has every reason to be content with the continuation of this august princess' success and she tells me on every occasion of her desire for you to be content with her and in essence, she does everything to merit this.

SECRET LETTER

Sacred Majesty, on Sunday the 8th of this month, M le dauphin and Mme la dauphine had a very animated discussion; I do not know how it started, but the result was that M le dauphin told Mme l'archiduchesse that he understood everything about the state of marriage, that in the beginning he had formed a plan, from which he did not wish to deviate, that now the time had come and that at Compiegne he would live with Mme la dauphine in all the intimacy demanded by their union.

This outpouring of heart did not stop there; Mme la dauphine said: "As we must live together in close friendship, we must talk openly together on all matters;" and the talk then fell on the comtesse du Barry. Then M le dauphin, for the first time in his life, spoke of those at court. He told Mme la dauphine that he knew of and saw many things, but he had never allowed himself to speak of them to anyone. Mme l'archiduchesse remarked that it was quite annoying that the King had been led into the liaisons he was in from motives of personal intrigue, as they occasioned such disorder at court and it could all lead to the fall of the duc de Choiseul. The dauphin replied that Mme la dauphine did not know what the duc de Choiseul had done to obtain his position, nor how he had intrigued with the marquise de Pompadour [Edit: a former mistress of Louis XV] and helped at that time to increase this favourite's credit.

Mme la dauphine's reply did not betray too much partiality for the duc de Choiseul. She simply replied that it was claimed that he had talents and that she had heard he was esteemed abroad and that even if he had intrigued with the marquise de Pompadour, it could not be compared to the horrors practised now by the ducs d'Aiguillon, de la Vauguyon and their cabal.

This conversation remained there and here is how I was informed: when I saw the agitation occasioned in Mme la dauphine by Mesdames' words, I became worried and thought I should charge the abbe de Vermond with trying to calm Mme la dauphine in their private conversations. I even suggested to him the language which seemed to me most likely to succeed in this. The abbe did so and it was then that Mme l'archiduchesse, with a gesture of liveliness and joy, told him what I have just related. I agreed with the abbe that he would make Mme la dauphine appreciate the importance of keeping such a matter secret, and not make exceptions for Mesdames nor anyone else; and it was also decided between the abbe and I to say nothing to the duc de Choiseul, in order to prevent any indiscretion.

I imagine that Y.M. will be of the opinion that it is best not to let Mme la dauphine know that Y.M. knows these details, because if Mme l'archiduchesse were to suspect that I had reported them, she could start mistrusting the abbe de Vermond, and that would deprive us of the great advantage of being able to remedy different circumstances with our representations.

Y.M. will judge by this how much Mme l'archiduchesse has won over the dauphin. It is not to be doubted that with a little prudence, she will be able to subjugate him entirely and I base this hope on the rare and natural talents of this princess, who understands matters marvellously and lends herself to the advice given her, when she sees that it is dictated by reason and by care for her wellbeing.

MARIA THERESA TO MERCY, 1 AUGUST 1770

Comte de Mercy, the news you continue to send me on the conduct of my daughter pleases me; but I am still a little worried that she will become too involved, and that by throwing herself into one of the two parties (or a third of Madame de Noailles and the aunts) in the end it will only result in unpleasantness for her in her delicate situation, young as she is and obsessed by dangerous people, with little experience of the world. I depend therefore on your prudent advice to prevent her from making wrong moves.

It is essential for my daughter to be prudent and reserved in lending herself to recommendations, in order not to increase the King's expenses. She was inclined to it before; but I always dissuaded her, and I only allowed her to start making recommendations just a few months before she left, and I was even obliged to set limits, because she wanted them to be too extensive.

The dauphin's indisposition makes me worry, and I fear that he will not last long. Here are the letters for my daughter; I scarcely touch on anything except general matters, trusting you entirely, as I am afraid of saying too much or too little.

MARIA THERESA TO MERCY, 1 AUGUST 1770

Comte de Mercy, I remember that while still here, my daughter was inclined to be careless of her expressions and to joke; I therefore charge you to tell Madame de Noailles and the abbe de Vermond that I am assured of their attachment to my daughter by their care to warn her about these faults if she ever lets herself be tempted to behave thus.

MERCY TO MARIA THERESA, 4 AUGUST 1770

Sacred Majesty, the King had plays given at Choisy in a little theatre. The ladies of the palace took the front seats, and refused to move for the comtesse du Barry and her two friends, the duchesse de Mirepoix and the comtesse de Valentinois. This led to harsh words and one of Mme la dauphine's ladies, the comtesse de Gramont, was identified as the leader in this dispute. [Edit: Gramont was related to the sister of the duc de Choiseul and was therefore perhaps instrumental in his later fall] The three ladies complained to the King and asked him to exile the comtesse de Gramont. Her exile has caused a great sensation; Mme la dauphine was begged to intercede for her and I suggested suitable language which would not compromise her.

Mme l'archiduchesse therefore told the King that she was pained by the fault committed by a lady in her service and that she did not want to know the King's motives in punishing this lady, but that she was slightly upset that a woman attached to her was exiled without a word being said to her about the King's wishes. The King, as I had foreseen, was embarrassed and said that the duc de la Vrilliere should have warned H.R.H. about the comtesse de Gramont's imminent exile, but had forgotten, but that it would not happen again. Then the King added a few loving and friendly words and matters remained like that.

However Mme la dauphine's step was neither inappropriate nor useless because it is necessary that she is in the habit of speaking directly to the King on all the matters which concern her personally, or the people in her service. This is an absolutely crucial point when one considers the present state of this court, the intrigues which reign there, the type of people who organise them and how these same people succeed in governing the King. As a result, if an intrigue takes hold, it would be weakness in Mme la dauphine not to use a tone of assurance and ease in talking to the King, as this would certainly succeed with the King and would make Mme l'archiduchesse respected by her associates.

In recounting this to Mme l'archiduchesse, at the same time I told her of the drawbacks of never having opinions except those of her aunts. These princesses although totally respectable, have never had the talent to conduct themselves according to circumstances. I notice clearly that they are inspiring these same principles in Mme la dauphine, that they are making her timid and remote from the King; also Mesdames often permit themselves talk which is at best indiscreet, sometimes even too impassioned. Mme la dauphine joins in, repeats what has been said, and I know it is certain that the King has been told of this, with the intention of thus harming H.R.H. This is of such great consequence for the present and the future that I had to inform Y.M. of the situation and submit to your insight whether you consider it appropriate to touch on this point in your letters to Mme l'archiduchesse.

At the same time it would be desirable that she did not suspect that I had reported this to Y.M., as that would make her more reserved with me, while at present she allows me to talk to her both frankly and zealously, and this has almost never been unsuccessful. The points on which I have been most successful have been those of her expressions, and the slightly mocking words. Mme l'archiduchesse has considerably reformed on those two articles; she is also continuing her reading reasonably assiduously.

During the week H.R.H. remained at Versailles alone with M le dauphin, she behaved marvellously, carrying out all the little tasks demanded by the indisposition of her husband with grace and care, and he seemed very moved and grateful. Mme la dauphine also treats the ladies in her service very well and all who come to pay court to her; on that point there is nothing to desire, and H.R.H. continues to enchant everyone. She is only harsh to the duc de la Vauguyon and his friends. I would like her to be more restrained with them. At least now H.R.H. no longer jokes in public about them.

The comtesse de Noailles told me that the last few days at Versailles had gone well, that Mme la dauphine had been charming and that M le dauphin was acquiring more and more liking for her, despite Vauguyon's efforts. The comtesse de Noailles added that I could see Mme la dauphine in private in her apartments, when that princess had some order to give me.

On the 1st of August at card play, Mme l'archiduchesse told me she was upset as the King had just named the comtesse de Valentinois as the dame d'atours of the future comtesse de Provence. Mme la dauphine had hoped that this position would fall to the duchesse de Saint-Megrin, whom H.R.H. with reason, did not want in her service, especially in such an intimate position as that of dame d'atours.

I told H.R.H. that, in order to avoid compromising herself in this situation, it was necessary to know: what promises the King had made to the duc de la Vauguyon about this; if M le dauphin was interested; when Mme la duchesse de Villars intended leaving her position; then it would be appropriate to take steps, always directly to the King, but with modifications indicated by circumstances.

There was a hunt and M le dauphin rode with it in his usual reckless fashion. This prince had given himself indigestion several days beforehand from eating too many cakes: at supper that night, Mme la dauphine had the plates with that kind of food removed from the table, and said they were not to be served again until ordered; the dauphin smiled and took this mark of attention very well.

The comtesse de Noailles told me that she could not prevail on Mme la dauphine to wear a corset, that as a result this princess' waist was becoming visibly misshapen, that her right shoulder was put out, which indeed is quite true and demands the most prompt precautions. The comtesse de Noailles added that she had mentioned it to the King, but he had said nothing and would never say anything to Mme la dauphine so she begged me to inform Y.M. of all these points, you alone being able to rectify them, that she, the comtesse de Noailles, did not have enough authority to make herself heard, although she often took the liberty of raising the matter with Mme la dauphine.

What the comtesse de Noailles says is partly true; everyone knows that the King has never been able to take it on himself to advise his children or correct them on any point and he is the same with regard to Mme la dauphine; but, on the other hand, the comtesse de Noailles is not correct in saying she often raises this matter with Mme l'archiduchesse; as she is very obliging to her mistress in the hope of gaining ascendancy over her, but she is wrong because I can see that Mme l'archiduchesse prefers those who tell her the truth and dislikes flattery. I tried to explain this to the comtesse de Noailles.

The abbe de Vermond's salary has been settled now. I have pressed for this for more than six weeks because he is beyond recompense.

MERCY TO MARIA THERESA, 20 AUGUST 1770

On the morning of the 4th, Mme la dauphine went to the King's room, where he embraced her and gave her a very affectionate reception. It was noticeable on this occasion, that the King always receives Mme la dauphine in a more friendly manner when she comes to see him alone, unaccompanied by her aunts. After midday H.R.H. went for a drive in the forest; there she met the duchesse de Choiseul and the duc de Praslin; she stopped her carriage to talk to them. Mme la dauphine never misses these opportunities to show kindness; she always acquits herself with as much judgement as grace, and that has even more effect here as people are unaccustomed to such behaviour.

I spoke to the duc de Noailles, brother in law of the lady of honour. He is perhaps the most intelligent man in France and he best knows his King and the court. He told me that he was convinced by his experience and by Mme la dauphine's qualities, that she would one day govern the King's soul; that the King's passing tastes were diminishing with age, and he would return to find happiness in the bosom of his family and then Mme la dauphine's charms would acquire the requisite influence.

I gave Mme la dauphine a letter from the comtesse de Brandis. [Edit: Mme la dauphine's former governess in Austria] Mme l'archiduchesse joked a little about this correspondence and did not seem bothered therefore I suggested that she should not bother replying.

On the 6th I learned that Mme la dauphine had gone to see M le dauphin, who, on seeing her, stretched out his arms and said he wanted to talk to her. He suggested going into her rooms as they would not be disturbed there by the gentlemen who were incessantly in and out of his rooms. Mme la dauphine often has these talks with M le dauphin, and on these occasions she talks to him openly and trustingly and is always listened to, with no attempt at contradiction. She told the prince her husband that the duc de la Vauguyon and his son the duc de Saint-Megrin were two scoundrels who could never be sufficiently mistrusted. She cited some new petty intrigues as proof. M le dauphin shook his head without answering, but it seems he is already much enlightened about his governor.

Mme la dauphine asked the King when supping with him, to grant her a woman called Thierry, wife of M le dauphin's valet, as one of her chief maids. The King granted this immediately. These Thierrys are creatures of the duc de la Vauguyon and therefore not suitable for Mme la dauphine. H.R.H. appeared convinced of this after my representations. But Mesdames tormented her to have this woman given a place, and also they have an attractive, lively four year old and H.R.H. enjoys this child's company because of her passion for children. Unfortunately there is already a boy, son of the first femme de chambre, named Misery; this little boy, aged 5, is always in Mme la dauphine's rooms and causes some disorder, especially too much distraction when it is time for reading and serious occupations. The abbe de Vermond and I cannot prevail on Mme la dauphine to send him away, even for a few hours. However this is not really important except for the worry that M le dauphin will be troubled by this amusement.

On the 8th there was a hunt. Mme la dauphine was there with Mesdames. M le dauphin was overcome with such tiredness that after the hunt he could barely stand.

Mme la dauphine told me that she was pained that M le dauphin went to the hunting suppers, that it looked as if they wanted to come between them and introduce him into unsuitable company, that M le dauphin agreed and regretted being at these pleasure parties; that the comtesse de Noailles had advised Mme la dauphine to ask to be admitted to these suppers and that she did not know what to do as she felt it was not an appropriate request. I told Mme la dauphine that it would be useful to consult the duc de Choiseul and I begged H.R.H. to authorise me to tell this minister she wanted to speak to him…Firstly I saw the duc de Choiseul and suggested several matters which I felt it was essential he should mention.

The abbe de Vermond told me that Mme la dauphine had told Mme Adelaide everything that M le dauphin had told her about this minister. Mme Adelaide and the comtesse de Narbonne [Edit: Mme Adelaide's lady in waiting] had then abused this confidence and the duc de Choiseul had been instructed of this, which I wished he had not.

H.R.H. spoke with all possible intelligence and grace when she saw the duc de Choiseul who told her, on his part, some general maxims that it would be a good idea to follow. He said that everything centred on two subjects, the King and M le dauphin, that the conduct to follow to please both depended on their tastes and characters; that with regard to the King, eagerness, gaiety and artless assurance in talking to him were necessary, with neither embarrassment nor fear, when talking of the reasonable matters which concerned Mme la dauphine.

The duc de Choiseul advised that H.R.H. should not ask to be at the suppers at the chateau, but that if the King asked her, she must go with an appearance of pleasure; further that when the duchesse de Villars retired, Mme la dauphine must not hesitate to ask the King not to give the position to anyone disagreeable or suspect to H.R.H., that with regard to M le dauphin, friendship, discretion, trust and patience were needed, and to be on good terms with Mesdames without being dominated by them. Also Mme la dauphine should not involve herself in intrigues at court and as a result all France would be at her feet. He went into detail on the current intrigues at court, their aim, the means used to succeed with the King, the characters of those at court, and Mme la dauphine questioned him with a wisdom which astonished the minister. Later the duc de Choiseul told me, "I am only now beginning to know Madame. I am overwhelmed with her. I have never seen her like at her age and I beg you to tell her that I am hers in life and death."

I can honestly tell Y.M. that Mme la dauphine has this effect on everyone who has the honour of knowing her, and it is quite certain that she will reach a position no other dauphine has.

On the 13th, Mme la dauphine heard mass in the parish church. I gave Mme la dauphine the letter from Y.M. just when she was sitting down to eat with M le dauphin. Because of her impatience to read it, she only ate for ten minutes. M le dauphin had a great appetite as he had just returned from the hunt, and did not have much time to eat but he did not become impatient, and laughed as Mme la dauphine had the plates taken away almost as soon as they were put on the table.

On the 14th, Mme la dauphine did not go out; she bathed in the evening, went to the King's rooms at half past nine, returned to M le dauphin's rooms and then went to the comtesse de Noailles' rooms at eleven o'clock. These rooms communicate with Mme la dauphine's via a terrace. On this terrace H.R.H. spoke to me of her conversation with the duc de Choiseul, in a way which showed she had not forgotten one essential word.

She then spoke to me of the dauphin, telling me she was pleased with him, that all the little faults in his manners were due to the negligent education he had received, but that he was basically a very good person, that he was the best of the family and had the best character; these are the actual words Mme la dauphine used and she said them movingly. She added that she found no difficulty in talking to the dauphin, that he showed trust in her and pleasure in listening to her; that although he was quite reserved about the people in his service, she was now quite sure that he knew the duc de la Vauguyon and his son and that he neither liked them nor esteemed them; that he was scornful of the comtesse du Barry and the people in her cabal; that when she asked him why he let himself be involved with these people, M le dauphin had replied that it was necessary to be prudent and to conform for the sake of peace. [3]

Mme la dauphine told me that everything was going quite well at present, but that in the midst of the unpleasantness and cabals which desolated this court, she was worried for the future.

SECRET LETTER

Since the last indisposition of M le dauphin, he has not slept again in Mme la dauphine's rooms as before. However there is nothing to be alarmed about in that, nor any reason for it except that nature is very slow to act in M le dauphin,

---

[3] Unfortunately, when King, Louis XV1 continued to practise this policy.

probably because his physique has been weakened by his sudden growth; but his constitution reveals nothing which would oppose his acquiring good, robust health, provided he is careful in his reckless exercise which could become very harmful.

This prince finds Mme l'archiduchesse charming; he is pleased with her and shows her an obligingness and gentleness which were not thought to be in his character. Mme la dauphine governs him in minor matters, without him opposing the slightest resistance; thus it is only a question of being patient and waiting for this influence to be established in everything; but, as in this country they want to move matters ahead before their time, the King and Mesdames say things which only agitate Mme la dauphine and make her worry [Edit: they were discussing the dauphin's lack of libido]. I use the abbe de Vermond to calm her down and that has succeeded quite well so far in restraining Mme la dauphine's language which, in the long run, could have resulted in more harm than good.

MARIA THERESA TO MERCY, 22 AUGUST 1770

Comte de Mercy, the duc d'Arenberg has told me of his desire to have his son enter the service of France. His family is distinguished in my states. I charge you with seconding the duc d'Arenberg's views at your court. [Edit: his son was known as the comte de la Marck and his correspondence with the comte de Mirabeau, the most famous deputy in the new National Assembly,[4] nearly twenty years later, provides a fascinating insight into the revolution. Some of his observations are included in this work.]

MARIA THERESA TO MERCY, 1 SEPTEMBER 1770

Comte de Mercy...[my daughter] has always greatly enjoyed being with children, and I know perfectly well that that sort of amusement (and her dislike of reading and applying

---

[4] See volume II of these letters.

herself) is capable of distracting her during the time she should be reading with the abbe de Vermond. Therefore in order to concentrate her mind on this point, I think I will have her send me each month, with your correspondence, a sort of journal of her reading with the priest. I think it best not to mention him, and I will not even name him in my letters, in order not to give my daughter the slightest suspicion of some secret intelligence between us.

I see the difficulties which could result from the closeness between my daughter and her aunts; but as I only wish her good health, and do not want her to have anything to do with politics, I am far from wanting to break up her friendships, and provided my daughter does not involve herself in the protections and recommendations granted by her aunts, I will leave the rest to Providence.

I must warn you to be reserved with my daughter about the funds which remain at her disposal, which you hold. Inclined as she is to expense, she could go too far (and make it a custom).

They are writing from Spaa that Choiseul will be disgraced, or at least will be allowed to retire, the duc d'Aiguillon will take his place, Broglie will be at the head of the military…I do not believe it, but the rumours astound me; I am warning you for your information only.

MARIA THERESA TO MERCY, 1 SEPTEMBER 1770

I am pained that most of the time I cannot persuade the emperor to share my opinions; he often has others: it makes business very difficult for me and makes life insupportable. I will not be able to relax until after peace is concluded; try to make them think the same where you are; the good Muslims are the sacrifice. The plague, famine, all will come and no one will be worse off than us. [Edit: Maria Theresa is referring to the war between Turkey and Russia. Joseph was trying to exploit this to gain territory for Austria]

P.S. What you have told me confidentially does not surprise me, let us hope that will change with time. According

37

to the gossip, there is nothing more to hope for: it would be fatal; tell me if there is any change in their state.

MERCY TO MARIA THERESA, 19 SEPTEMBER 1770

Mme la dauphine has for some time had a great desire to ride and I have tried all sorts of ways to discourage her because of the very great risks of this exercise. I spoke of this to the comtesse de Noailles and the duc de Choiseul, talking of Mme la dauphine's tender age and her possible future circumstances. The duc de Choiseul agreed to speak to the King about this. Therefore when Mme la dauphine spoke to him, the King declined, but said she could ride a donkey. This did not displease Mme l'archiduchesse and now H.R.H. and some of her ladies have been on these mounts. Everyone crowded into the forest to see Mme la dauphine, who as usual spoke with kindness and grace.

H.R.H. told me she wanted to send to Vienna for a lap dog called Mops. Mme la dauphine loves dogs; she has two which unfortunately are quite grubby but this amusement is very innocent.

I asked the duc de Choiseul to be attentive to events… [especially involving Mme du Barry, on the visit to Chantilly], and to give Mme l'archiduchesse any necessary advice. I told H.R.H. she could approach him if she experienced the slightest problem. At the same time I begged her to be careful she did not give rise to remarks on her expressions, with regard to the favourite.

I went to Versailles and found the comtesse de Noailles piqued and discouraged. She complained at length that, despite her care and zeal, she had no credit with Mme la dauphine and she had resolved to retire. Finally I calmed the comtesse de Noailles down.

[Later] I took the liberty of telling Mme la dauphine that if the comtesse de Noailles retired, her position could be given to someone from the comtesse du Barry's party, especially the marechale de Mirepoix or the duchesse d'Aiguillon; that besides, if the comtesse de Noailles retired, it would remove from Mme la dauphine all the related attentions of this numerous family who are well considered here.

I also touched on the fact that Mme la dauphine becomes bored holding court in the evening and she does not do so a little too often; Mesdames take over on these occasions, although this is contrary to etiquette and custom. Besides when the comtesse de Provence [Edit: the future wife of the dauphin's brother] arrives, she will seize the upper hand over Mesdames. They are already occupied with means of giving her the greatest possible eclat, because the duc de la Vauguyon's party and that of the comtesse du Barry count on her protection. As a result if Mme la dauphine refuses to hold court, Madame la comtesse de Provence will and will therefore attract people to her, in which case Mme la dauphine's role will not be the correct one.

This all seemed to make an impression on H.R.H. She replied directly and kindly that she agreed she had been led into making false moves in relation to the comtesse de Noailles, but she would repair them, both for the present and for the future. She acknowledged that the game of cavagnol bored her, however she would behave according to the reflections I had made to her, whose truth she herself recognised. However I think it is important for Y.M. to insist that Mme la dauphine holds court.

If one considers the form of this court, the King's custom of never expressing his wishes to his children, nor using the slightest authority with them, it is as a result inconceivable that such a young and high spirited princess as Mme la dauphine will not sometimes do foolish things. However I cannot sufficiently repeat that Mme la dauphine is gifted with such an excellent character and such just intelligence, that Y.M. can be assured she will never commit great faults.

She is never taken unawares, because she notices what is happening very clearly and this is shown in the way she judged the steps which the comtesse de Marsan, the duc de la Vauguyon and others took with her in the beginning. Thus it is not to be feared that H.R.H. will let herself be drawn into dangerous cabals, especially when she has been warned not to trust them. It is true that amusements have a great hold over her; but that does not prevent her appreciating the people who try to amuse her, and who, by this means alone, succeed with difficulty in winning her over.

Mme la dauphine said nothing to me of Y.M.'s request to send you a journal of her reading; I felt I should not appear to know this, as Mme l'archiduchesse appeared a little embarrassed, to judge by the eagerness with which she immediately consulted the abbe de Vermond in order to satisfy you. This will make Mme la dauphine more attentive to her reading, which she does regularly, but not for long enough.

Mesdames, by their education, are timid and lacking in all the charms which please, and they want to be imitated by Mme la dauphine. I will cite a very recent proof. A few days ago, the municipality of Paris and the estates of Languedoc wished to make a speech to the royal family. Mesdames, consulted by Mme la dauphine, tried to persuade her that on such occasions it was not necessary to reply and that this is what they did. The abbe de Vermond had to insist again and again before Mme la dauphine would agree not to behave in this way, of which all France complains. H.R.H. let herself be persuaded and replied charmingly to the municipality and to the estates and this delighted the public.

Besides Mme Adelaide, respectable as is her character, is entirely subjugated and governed in everything by her dame d'atours, the comtesse de Narbonne, and therefore the latter governs Mme la dauphine as a result. Madame de Narbonne has some good qualities but she is an intriguer and could easily involve Mme la dauphine, without her realizing she was being dominated by her.

Mme la dauphine has made no use so far of any monies available from you, but I am sure she will be careful. H.R.H. proposes to have a bureau made for you but I am supposed to keep this secret.

It is certain that if Y.M. sends the bust of H.R.H. to the King, it will please him. They are working on a marble bust of Mme la dauphine and I believe it is for you.

Mme la dauphine has all the gazettes brought to her but reads only about Vienna. H.R.H told me she reproached herself for a wicked thought…having heard that the plague was in Poland, she would not be upset if it reached Austria because this danger would oblige Y.M. to move to Flanders and therefore she would enjoy the greatest possible pleasure, that of seeing her mother again.

SECRET LETTER

Whatever the intrigues and bitterness of those who wish to make Choiseul fall, it seems that this minister will however be kept in place. His principal enemies, that is the chancellor and the duc d'Aiguillon, are people discredited and lost in the view of the public. The King knows this; he does not esteem them, because he knows their dangerous character and distrusts them, but he uses them partly from weakness for their protector, the comtesse du Barry, and partly because he believes he needs them to tame the parlements, which cause him the greatest annoyance. [5]

Whether from personal reasons, or in the hope of finding support in Mme la dauphine, or from naturally good sentiments, for some time I have seen the duc de Choiseul's attachment to Y.M. and the present system [Edit: the alliance between France and Austria, guaranteed by the marriage between Marie Antoinette and the dauphin] increasing each day. He is becoming more amenable and reasonable in foreign affairs. I cannot disguise the fact he has faults, especially irresponsibility and a little thoughtlessness, but essentially I feel he is the best minister for Y.M.

Y.M.'s great soul inclines you always towards good, and with the superior qualities with which H.M. the emperor is gifted, it would be impossible for him not to change his views to those of his august mother eventually.[6]

---

[5] The parlements were occasional gatherings of the aristocracy, whose discontent rumbled on for years, and was one of the factors contributing to the Revolution.
[6] The diplomatic and rather fawning phraseology of Mercy, de rigueur in the 18th century, can jar with modern ears.

MARIA THERESA TO MERCY, 2 OCTOBER 1770

Your two private letters were very important and reassured me on the health of the dauphin, but this is still quite a disagreeable matter. I preach patience to my daughter, and that there is nothing lost, but to redouble her caresses. I speak to her very firmly about her figure and her waist, telling her, which is true anyway, that I saw a letter from someone in Brussels who found her badly dressed and her waist misshapen. I even tell her that I charge you to take care to warn her and to write to me about it.

My second point is on card play and holding court. I tell her that, on this point, you wrote to me and that she must not neglect either and must follow your good advice. I enclose her letter which you can burn and do not disclose that you saw it. I send it to you to let you see why I wish that she would apply herself a little to writing better, especially with regard to spelling. I also mention in passing that if she had asked me for permission to mount a horse, I would never have approved, even a donkey, and that I see that the King spoils her. I did not find it appropriate to mention Mesdames again.

MERCY TO MARIA THERESA, 20 OCTOBER 1770

Sacred Majesty, Mme la dauphine is now treating the comtesse de Noailles better than in the past and everything is now as it should be. It is not the same with holding court. Mme la dauphine still finds this boring and unfortunately Mesdames encourage this. It is more convenient for them to have the card play in their apartments; besides they gain in prestige, at Mme la dauphine's expense. Already all the court has noticed Mme la dauphine's too marked dependence on Mesdames and the manifest abuse which they make of this. The duc de Choiseul is the first to agree; although he is very attached to Mesdames and assured of their support.

Although it is a question of a period still in the future, I feel it is good for Y.M. to be informed in advance of the ideas which they are giving Mme la dauphine on the way to behave with Mme la comtesse de Provence. H.R.H. seems determined to treat her coldly; she believes that Mesdames will do the same, and that thus, Mme de Provence will experience sufficient bother that her debut will be blighted. I have not yet openly combated this system, which seems to me quite wicked, dangerous and useless; it will certainly lead to a war in the heart of the royal family, and a deluge of unpleasantness and intrigues amongst the courtiers.

I am not concerned that Mme la dauphine will not give up this idea, which certainly was not thought up by her and could only come from bad advice; even if she listened to it initially, her benevolent character and good heart, of which she is always giving proofs, would make her reject such advice once she thought about it. H.R.H. does not need to use such harsh means to maintain her superiority; it is assured to her by her rank, but even more so by her intelligence and grace. There is nothing left to desire of these two qualities and provided that Mme l'archiduchesse continues to use them, as she has done up to the present, no one can be put on an equal footing with her, nor cast the slightest shadow over her.

Mme la dauphine's figure is filling out; this is attributed to her constant exercise either on foot or on a donkey.[7] She prefers riding and does it three or four times a week. What is only exercise to Mme la dauphine is tiring to her ladies; but they are so attached to her that they do whatever pleases H.R.H., who, on her part, recompenses them by kind and truly charming treatment.

Despite Mesdame's advice and example, Mme la dauphine still maintains the habit of talking to people of distinction who come to pay court. However I think it best if Y.M. deigns to encourage this, as it has succeeded so well with her and I have recently noticed a slight diminution in this behaviour. [Recently three men]…who form part of the King's daily society, were presented at Mme la dauphine's dinner and card play. She did not talk to them, and this caused a sensation. The duc de Choiseul warned me, telling me that Mme la dauphine must always base her behaviour on means of attaching the people to her and she had an infallible method –

---

[7] An inversion of what we consider to be the truth nowadays.

that of letting everyone experience her kindness and attentions, which charmed especially as it was unusual at this court, where the princes receive all who approach them in an offhand manner.

[In relation to your request for a list of Mme la dauphine's reading, there is a problem for the abbe de Vermond in that]…the time necessary for this, spent in Mme la dauphine's room, could give rise to speculation and to supposition that Mme la dauphine is dictating letters, or anything in fact, rather than a journal of her occupations. On the other hand, if the priest wrote it out in his own rooms, it would not achieve its object of compelling Mme la dauphine to give more attention and time to her reading. It cannot be said that H.R.H. neglects her reading, she grasps and retains what she has read, but she does not do it for long enough. The perpetual movement of the court and the dissipation caused by the trips, have created obstacles to more serious occupations. Winter will be a more appropriate time for this. Mme l'archiduchesse has finally agreed to wear a corset regularly.

For some time the King has been increasing his care, attention and affectionate behaviour to Mme la dauphine, and she is treated now as in the first days after her arrival. H.R.H. is lodged here [Edit: Fontainebleau] in the rooms of the former Queen, adjoining those of the King; if this monarch would adopt the habit of going to Mme la dauphine's rooms during the day, there could be very good results, and I begged H.R.H. to try to procure this, and especially to be as cheerful and relaxed as possible, on these occasions. I am convinced that no more is needed to distract the King from his disordered society, and I do not despair that one day Mme la dauphine will render this important service to France; but in order to succeed it is absolutely necessary that she adopts the opposite conduct and bearing to that of Mesdames her aunts.

The abbe de Vermond said he would concentrate on Mme la dauphine's spelling, but that her writing could only be improved up to a point. He told me the reason for Mme la dauphine's bad handwriting, especially when writing to Y.M., was that she did not feel that what she wrote was safe, and therefore she waited until the courier was about to leave before writing, and as a result her letter was full of careless mistakes caused by her precipitation. I told the abbe de Vermond that it was necessary to reassure Mme la dauphine about a suspicion which I did not believe was well founded [Edit: Mercy felt that her associates were trustworthy], as long as she took care to keep the key…[for her bureau] on her person.

[I told Mme l'archiduchesse]…that it was necessary to avoid forming parties opposed to one another in the family, that the royal family must have common interests, and that to act otherwise would encourage intrigues. I had good reasons for saying all of this, because I have known for a long time that Mme Adelaide and Mme Sophie have been trying to inspire Mme l'archiduchesse with dislike for Mme Victoire, although she is unquestionably the best of the three sisters. I also know of Mme Adelaide's dangerous advice in relation to Mme de Provence. Mme la dauphine who had listened [to me] with more attention than her natural liveliness usually allows, told me that she would follow my advice as she realized that the advice given her was not always the best. I conclude therefore that Mme la dauphine is beginning to open her eyes and that if Y.M. reinforces this with a word or two, I feel H.R.H. will reduce her liaison with Mesdames to a more suitable friendship.

Mme la dauphine, to whom the royal treasury must give 6000 francs a month, has in reality not a penny to dispose of herself, without someone else's agreement. The reason for this is the scandalous abuse here in the matter of handling of money. Mme la dauphine's money goes first, by right of position, to her treasurer called Pomeri; he retains 2,500 livres each month for the former pensions of the late Queen, and therefore Mme la dauphine is charged for them without knowing why. Her garcons de chambre receive 100 louis a month for Mme la dauphine's expenses at card play, and whether she wins or loses, she sees nothing of this sum; the ladies of the bedchamber take the rest, which most of the time is distributed in gifts suggested by the comtesse de Noailles, and for which she extorts Mme la dauphine's consent and therefore H.R.H. has nothing left for herself.

Fortunately she is very far from being inclined to expensive whims; the little money she can dispose of is spent carefully on alms and I feel sure that Mme la dauphine will always be discreet and careful with Y.M.'s money.

On the 15 th, Mme l'archiduchesse spent the morning in pious duties, knowing she could not better celebrate Y.M.'s name day, a day on which all your faithful subjects must call upon God to preserve a sovereign so necessary to our happiness.

It is true that Mme la dauphine is not dressed to advantage; but the fault lies with her dame d'atours, who pays little attention to the matter.

I lose no opportunity to combat the little prejudices which they inspire in Mme la dauphine about different people. I must say that H.R.H. conducts herself with some circumspection in relation to the favourite; and it would be even better if Mme l'archiduchesse's associates were more prudent and less rash in their speech.

THE ABBE DE VERMOND TO MARIA THERESA

The need and desire to talk about a thousand matters whose character and novelty render them interesting to Mme la dauphine, have prevented her from settling to reading for some time. Apart from the lack of exactness still in Mme la dauphine's language, each day she acquires ideas which one neither could nor would have given her in Vienna. They appear quite pleased with Mme la dauphine's speech, even in her household, where she speaks in a livelier and less attentive way; she expresses herself easily, pleasantly and very nobly on exceptional occasions.

Mme la dauphine said to me: "My mother is asking what I read – What shall I reply?" – "Only the truth madame." Mme la dauphine's age and character mean she needs to be scolded into studying.

I am hardly ever with Mme l'archiduchesse when she writes. Sometimes she calls me when she is finished. Sometimes she tells me: "They say you dictate my letters." I cannot risk writing in her presence or under her dictation, nor even tell her what I would have said. Sometimes Monsieur le dauphin finds me in Mme la dauphine's room; he always enters unannounced. Other times a woman or boy of the bedchamber comes in on an errand from Mesdames; Y.E. knows our court: what stories would they tell if they saw me reading papers?

A little thoughtlessness and natural laziness suffice to ensure Mme la dauphine never finds the time to do a task which is not pressing. She fears duplicate keys. She wanted to reread your last letter and felt she could not keep it another night, except in her bed. If Mme la dauphine wrote about her reading, she would be afraid people would see her papers. Would she not blush if it were known that she was still receiving lessons? At [almost] 15 years old she cannot yet withstand certain pleasantries. When Mme la dauphine first came here, Mesdames often spoke to her of her education and of theirs; they let her see they felt the education of archduchesses to be too strict.

Y.E. knows how unfortunate our princes and princesses are; once their education is finished, they no longer want occupation or advice. People often work at subjugating them, rarely at enlightening and advising them. Five months of experience and continual attention persuade me that this example will not spoil Mme la dauphine in any essential way. Her great respect for Y.M. and her well disposed character guarantee it. Y.E. knows how she listens and gradually loses her scorn. Every day I admire her gentleness and I dare say her docility. She permits me respectful truths in the presence of her lady of honour. Is it not astonishing that Mme la dauphine has the courage to maintain a troublesome counsellor by her side, in the midst of homage and adulation?

SECRET LETTER

[With regard to]…the article in which H.R.H. had said that Monsieur le dauphin had promised to sleep in her room two days later, Mme l'archiduchesse, quite pleased with this promise, had nothing more urgent to do than to confide this to Mesdames Adelaide and Sophie, and the comtesse de Narbonne. They, in turn, confided in so many people that it

47

became the news of the day. Furthermore, Mme Adelaide wanted to add to this indiscretion by exhorting Monsieur le dauphin, and he was so alarmed, that he simply failed to keep his word to Mme la dauphine. He renewed a similar promise for the 10th of this month; it was confided to Mesdames just as the first, and Monsieur le dauphin did not keep this promise either.

Foreseeing that as long as these sorts of confidences took place, they would only succeed in scaring Monsieur le dauphin, and not knowing how to broach such a delicate matter with Mme la dauphine…[I decided anyhow] to tell H.R.H. that I had real worries about her because of the news spread all over Paris that she had quarrelled with Monsieur le dauphin, that this rumour had arisen because the public claimed to know of a certain promise made by Monsieur le dauphin to sleep on a certain day in Mme la dauphine's room, a promise which he had failed to keep, and therefore people concluded there had been a very serious quarrel.

H.R.H. seemed embarrassed at this, but without evasion she told me: "What you have just said is only too well founded and comes from my imprudence in making the confidence in question to the comtesse de Narbonne; but how could I know that there are people who are sufficiently chatty and indiscreet to talk of such things?" I tried to make her understand that what concerned the intimacy of a marriage was a sacred secret, whose violation could be excused by no motive, that eventually an indiscretion about this could easily destroy all trust between two spouses for ever and, considering the timid and reserved character of Monsieur le dauphin, he could remain distant from Mme la dauphine for a long time, if he was apprehensive that what happened between them could become known. I noticed that I had succeeded in frightening H.R.H. She assured me that henceforth she would make no more confidences; I am quite sure she will keep her word in relation to the comtesse de Narbonne, but I fear that she will not do the same with Mesdames.

The King reproached Monsieur le dauphin on his coldness and questioned him. The young prince replied that he found Mme l'archiduchesse charming, and loved her, but that he needed more time to conquer his timidity.

MARIA THERESA TO MERCY, 30 OCTOBER 1770

They are saying a lot of unfavourable things about my daughter here. They say the King has become reserved and awkward with her, that she clashes head on with the favourite, that the dauphin is worse than ever and more than indifferent to my daughter.

MARIA THERESA TO MERCY, 1 NOVEMBER 1770

Your letter has reassured me on the rumours going around here. I only fear Mesdames and her indiscretion. I enclose her letter and my reply; I am ashamed to do so, but you serve me too well for me not to inform you of everything and to find out if you approve of the line I take with my daughter. In order not to cite anything which you tell me and therefore diminish her trust in you, I would like you to send these copies back to me every month

MARIA THERESA TO MARIE ANTOINETTE, 1 NOVEMBER 1770

My dear daughter, thank God your health remains good, according to the courier, who was in your suite; he found you had grown and put on weight. I beg you, do not be negligent about your person; at your age that is not suitable, and even less in your position; it brings in its train grubbiness, negligence and indifference which spreads to other actions, and that would harm you; that is why I torment you. I cannot sufficiently warn you about these circumstances to prevent you sharing in the same defects of all the French royal family over the years: they are good, virtuous in themselves, but incapable of appearing to advantage, setting the tone or amusing themselves in simple ways, and that has been the usual reason for their menfolk being led astray, as, finding no pleasure within their families, they looked for it elsewhere.

It is possible to be virtuous, cheerful and also knowledgeable; but when people are secluded to the point where they only see a few people, (I must tell you this to my great regret, as you have seen this lately here), [Edit: after the death of her husband, Maria Theresa had spent some time in mourning], it leads to discontent, jealousy, envy, unpleasantness; but in associating with society, as happened here fifteen or twenty years ago, all these drawbacks are avoided, and your soul and body are strengthened. I ask you therefore as a friend, and as your loving mother, speaking from experience, do not give in to carelessness about your appearance or about holding court. You will regret it, if you do not take my advice, but it will be too late. It is up to you to set the tone at Versailles; you have succeeded in doing so; God has blessed you with so many charms, with so much sweetness and docility, that no one can fail to be charmed by you.

With regard to your reading with the abbe, in future if you would send me a list every month I would be pleased, and in order to save you the bother of writing it, perhaps the abbe could put it in a separate note which could be enclosed with your letter.

Windischgraetz told me that you neglected yourself a lot and did not even brush your teeth; that is an important point, as is the matter of your waist, which she also found worsened. You are now at the stage where your body is being developed; it is a most critical stage; she also added that you are badly dressed and that she dared to say so to your ladies.

My dear daughter! Tomorrow is a day of great consolation for me, a day which, for fifteen years, has only given me satisfaction. May God grant you long life both for your happiness and for that of your families and peoples. Mercy tells me you spent the morning of the 15th praying. This charming attention touched me greatly; you are indeed capable of such actions. With love and my blessing, my dear daughter. Always your faithful mother.

On the 19th, Mme la dauphine told me she had just received a letter from the comtesse de Gramont, saying she was ill and needed treatment and could she please come back to Paris. Mme la dauphine wanted to talk to the King and I suggested some advice. After card play, Mme l'archiduchesse, who supped with the King, took the opportunity to tell him in a sweet and graceful way, of the request made by the comtesse de Gramont, and the reasons for it. The King seemed a bit embarrassed and told Mme la dauphine, in a friendly way, that he would think about it and would shortly give her an answer. At this juncture, I did not delay in telling the duc de Choiseul of what was going on, and I asked him to be ready to intervene in this matter if circumstances permitted.

On the 20th, Mme la dauphine, as we had agreed the evening before, sent for the duc de la Vrilliere, and, telling him of what she had said to the King, she charged this minister (whose department includes such matters) to ascertain the King's orders and not to leave him unaware that it was Mme la dauphine who had sent him.

The duc de la Vrilliere acquitted himself of this commission and the King told him that first it would have to be verified that the comtesse de Gramont was really ill, and that therefore a courier would have to be dispatched to her doctor to obtain attestation, that apart from that it would also be necessary to warn the comtesse du Barry, whose consent to the return of someone who was only exiled because of offending her, was necessary. The duc de la Vrilliere obeyed, and after sending the courier, he went to tell the favourite, who at first wanted to oppose Mme la dauphine's wishes. That day, Choiseul spoke to the King about this, and told him in the strongest terms that his kindness and humanity would be shamefully compromised, if he rejected the prayer of Gramont; however the King still would not decide.

On the 21st, after supper, Mme la dauphine spoke to the King again about the comtesse de Gramont. H.M., with a serious expression replied: "Madame, I thought I had told you I would give you a reply at the appropriate time." Mme la dauphine, without the slightest unease, replied: "But papa, apart from motives of humanity and justice, think how upset I would be if a woman in my service were to die disgraced in your eyes." These words, spoken in a charming way, had the best possible effect on the King: he smiled, and again adopting a tone of friendship, he assured Mme la dauphine that she would soon be satisfied. [Edit: Mercy had suggested to Marie Antoinette how she should proceed, at every stage of this matter]

On the 23rd, the courier sent to the comtesse de Gramont's doctor came back with the necessary attestations. The King, before going to the play, ordered the duc de la Vrilliere to send the comtesse de Gramont permission to come back immediately to Paris, and this was sent without the comtesse du Barry knowing; but also, whether from ill will or tactlessness, the duc de la Vrilliere did not tell Mme la dauphine of the success of her request, nor did the King and she only found out next day from public rumour.

On the 24th, H.R.H. sent for the duc de la Vrilliere and told him in a dignified way: "I charged you with a request, concerning a woman in my service. I should have been first to be informed, and by you, of the resolution the King had made about this affair; but I see sir, that you treat me like a child, and I am obliged to tell you that I will not forget this." The duc de la Vrilliere, very confused, wanted to reply with some bad excuses, to which Mme la dauphine would not listen. As soon as she saw the King, she thanked him for granting her request and the King told her laughingly: "Madame, I carried out your orders."

Y.M. cannot sufficiently understand the favourable impression this has produced in people's minds about Mme l'archiduchesse, who behaved in this matter with all the judgement and dignity possible. The little rebuke given to the duc de la Vrilliere has let the public see that H.R.H. knows how to appreciate behaviour, and how to elicit the respect she is due, and to judge faults which could be committed against her. Mesdames her aunts, while complimenting her on what had happened, acknowledged that they would not have dared to be so firm, and Mme Adelaide said, "It is easy to see that you are not of our blood."

[Later] I begged Mme la dauphine never to make requests unless they were just and she had a right to be interested in them, but also to make it understood that she was neither of the character nor the temperament to easily forget faults committed against her.

The 27th was wet. Monsieur le dauphin spent about three hours with Mme la dauphine. He told her he thought he knew the people in his service well, that the duc de Saint-Megrin and the comte de Montmorin[8] planned to dominate him, that the marquis de Choiseul and the marquis de Bourbon-Busset were indiscreet and gossipy, that the comtes de Beaumont and de Laroche-Aymon were nonentities and very limited. These six people are the young gentlemen presently in service and it would appear that Monsieur le dauphin's assessment of them is very just.

I learned that Mme Adelaide had again suggested going on horseback to Mme la dauphine and that she had even taken it upon herself to negotiate this with the King. She did so, and the King was embarrassed, but as he refuses nothing, he agreed, although reluctantly.

Mme la dauphine was overjoyed at horse-riding and the court that evening was crowded with well wishers. When H.R.H. went out riding, I did not go that day, as she had remarked to someone that it would be interesting to see my expression. When Mme la dauphine [saw me, she told me]…that everyone had congratulated her. I replied that I was pained by the displeasure Y.M. would feel. Then Mme la dauphine's expression changed and she said with charming naivety and in an emotional way: "You will make me despair in saying I will upset the empress. I tell you I am really worried."

Formal opposition to horse-riding could compromise Y.M.'s authority; besides Monsieur le dauphin really likes having her on horseback.

---

[8] Montmorin was a minister during the Revolution, whose fidelity to Marie Antoinette and Louis XV1, resulted in his very cruel death.

[I told Mme la dauphine I thought it best]…if she never went hunting on horseback, to ride moderately and not gallop; not to ride at all when there could be doubts about her condition.

On the 3rd, Mme la dauphine held court in the evening and I notice that she has done this for a month now and has resisted Mesdames' insinuations on this matter.

For a long time Mme la dauphine has been urging Monsieur le dauphin not to stay so late at the hunt and she asked him on the 6th to come back at a reasonable time, so that he could be dressed and not delay the play. Monsieur le dauphin came back late, according to his custom, long after the King. He found Mme la dauphine in her room; he went up to her, a little awkwardly, and said: "You see, I am back in time." Mme la dauphine replied drily: "Yes, this is a fine time!" They went to the play, where Monsieur le dauphin sulked all the time. On returning from the theatre he tried to have a discussion; then Mme la dauphine made a very forceful speech in which she told him sharply of all the drawbacks of his undisciplined life. She made him see that no one in his suite could tolerate this type of life, and that furthermore his behaviour and rough manners did not compensate those who were attached to him, and that if he continued thus he would end up destroying his health and making himself detested.

Monsieur le dauphin listened quietly and submissively; he agreed he was at fault, promised to make amends and apologised to Mme l'archiduchesse. This was remarkable, and even more so as on the next day, Monsieur le dauphin showed his wife much more eager attention and friendship than usual.

On the 8th, there was a play at court and at the end, the actors sang some lines in praise of Mme la dauphine. All the spectators were so moved at this that they clapped their hands throughout the theatre, despite the strict prohibition against making a noise in the court theatre. This event is without example here and testifies to the feelings for Mme la dauphine.

Mme la dauphine hardly ever sees the favourite, who is not present either when court is being held, or at Mesdames, and in the very rare cases where this woman and Mme l'archiduchesse have been together, H.R.H. has never treated her haughtily.

SECRET LETTER

I am not at all surprised that sometimes rumours detrimental to Mme la dauphine are spread about. [As I have already maintained]… the duc de la Vauguyon and the comtesse du Barry are counting on her protection [Edit: the future comtesse de Provence]. They believe they have nothing to hope for from Mme la dauphine. As a result this cabal tries to dissect H.R.H.'s behaviour to discover faults in her, and to spread lies in order to lead the public astray, but fortunately they have no other effect than that of showing the impudence and ill will of their authors.

I have made sure of three people in Mme la dauphine's service, one of her waiting women and two of her lackeys who give me an exact account of what happens in her rooms; I am informed every day of the conversations between Mme la dauphine and the abbe de Vermond, from whom she conceals nothing; I learn from the marquise de Durfort the slightest detail of what is said in Mesdames' apartments and I have more people and yet more means to find out what happens when Mme la dauphine is with the King. To this I add my own observations such that there is not an hour of the day when I cannot tell Y.M. what Mme la dauphine said or did or heard, and I do this to ensure Y.M.'s repose.

I can therefore affirm on my faith and fidelity to Y.M. that it is absolutely false that the King is becoming reserved and ill at ease with Mme la dauphine, who on the contrary gains daily in friendship with this monarch, and in his consideration. They accused H.R.H. of clashing head on with the favourite, with just such little reason; there have only ever been a few words spoken against this woman, and Mesdames have always initiated them; at present Mme la dauphine is more reserved on this, to the extent that weeks have passed without anyone being able to cite one word. Finally Mme la dauphine is making herself adored by her associates and by the public

MARIA THERESA TO MERCY, 1 DECEMBER 1770

It would be better for my daughter not to speak to him…
[Monsieur le dauphin] of his grandfather's behaviour as I do not trust
this dissimulating prince.

P.S. I must admit that I do not approve at all [Edit: of horse
riding] and I know my daughter well enough to be convinced that she
will succeed in her wishes and will take risks to do so. That is why I
am careful to conserve my credit with her, mingling remonstrances
with a lot of love. I especially fear Mesdames and see no remedy. I
enclose her letter; she says nothing about her reading. I fear there is
not a lot to say. I did not want to insist again this time, but I would
like to know if you want me to repeat this and to insist.

MARIA THERESA TO MARIE ANTOINETTE,
2 DECEMBER 1770

People are still very pleased with you; how happy you
make me, my dear child! Now I have reached the point to which
you have already probably rushed on: it is about your horse-riding.
You are right to believe that being only fifteen years old I could not
possibly approve of it; your aunts, whom you cite, started at thirty.
They were Mesdames and not the dauphine. I am a little annoyed
that they encouraged you, but you tell me the King approves and the
dauphin, so nothing more remains to be said. Riding will spoil your
complexion and your shape. I must say, that if you ride in the way a
man rides, which I suspect, it is very dangerous if you are pregnant,
and that is your duty: that is where your happiness lies. Accidents
cannot be foreseen; that of the Queen of Portugal and of several
others, who have not been able to have children after miscarriages,
are not reassuring.

I will take you at your word; a great princess must keep
her promises. You have said these words in your promise: "I will
never ride to the hunt." I accept this promise, and because of
it I will try not to worry; I saw in a private letter that for several
days at the beginning of November, you were riding for two
or three hours; that is too long, you will agree one day, but

it will be too late. What reason could I have to deprive you of something which gives you pleasure, if not from fear of the consequences? You will agree that at all times I have given my children all the freedom and pleasure possible; so why should I suddenly want to deprive you, especially when you are such a consolation to me?

MERCY TO MARIA THERESA, 17 DECEMBER 1770

Recently the comtesse de Noailles was in a bad temper as Mme la dauphine dispenses with her a little too often when she follows the hunt, and seems to prefer being accompanied by the ladies of the palace who are younger and more lively. When the lady of honour complained to me, I said it was up to her not to accept this dispensation and that if she seemed determined to follow H.R.H. all the time, I was convinced that she would not be contradicted. In fact it is important that Mme l'archiduchesse always has some person with her who, from bearing and age, will be able to impose, and suppress the inclination which Frenchmen have of being only too relaxed and casual.

When Mme la dauphine accompanies the King to the hunt, two or three times a week, H.R.H. usually brings in her carriage all sorts of cold meats and refreshments, which she enjoys distributing to the courtiers who follow the hunt. This results only from her natural kindness, and would not be a problem anywhere else, but unfortunately it causes problems in this country, because it so happens that, during the hunt, all the young people in the King's suite gather around Mme la dauphine's carriage, and because there are so many, there are always some thoughtless enough not to show the circumspection and respect which is owed to the young princess. Up till now this has not caused a problem but as it is better to prevent any abuse, I took the liberty of warning Mme la dauphine that she must guard against the familiarity and ease which they sometimes dared to adopt with her, and this has led me to insist that the comtesse de Noailles always accompanies her, especially to the hunt.

On the 29th of November, Mme l'archiduchesse left the hunt. While coming back and crossing over a bridge, the postilion of her carriage fell and was very unfortunate in that four of the horses went over him. He was moved out of danger and found to be covered with blood and unconscious. Mme la dauphine waited with him for more than an hour; she sent in all directions looking for a physician; while waiting, an officer of the guard, who accompanied her, dismounted and bandaged the injured man with all possible zeal and care. They wanted to take the injured man away in a carriage; Mme la dauphine objected, pointing out very correctly the risks of jolting someone who was so badly injured; finally a stretcher was brought, on which the injured man was carried to Versailles, accompanied by two physicians and several people from Mme la dauphine's retinue.

When H.R.H., returned, she had never before been received with so much respect and admiration. She sent for the doctors to find out about the injured man's condition, and was overjoyed on learning that he might not die. She ordered her senior physician to take care of him and tell her every day how he was. She thanked the officer of the bodyguard, who had helped the injured man in the first few moments. When Mme l'archiduchesse recounted the details of this accident in front of the whole court, she added: "I addressed everyone as friend, pages, grooms, postilions. I said to them: My friend, go and find a doctor! My friend, run quickly for a stretcher; see if he can talk, if he is conscious." When they heard this, everyone was moved with admiration for Mme la dauphine, and the talk in Versailles was "that Maria Theresa would recognise her daughter by such behaviour."

At the time of this accident, nothing escaped Mme la dauphine which could affect a sensitive person. The coachman who was driving her was the father in law of the injured postilion; the brother of the injured man was driving one of the King's carriages and was even obliged to go by while seeing his brother on a stretcher; Mme la dauphine pondered these points and seemed quite upset at them. They wanted to reassure her by saying that the people who worked in the stables had hard hearts.

The next day, in front of many people, she spoke to the abbe de Vermond about these grounds for reassurance, which she did not consider to be just. The abbe was furious that they had so little regard for Mme la dauphine's sensitivity that they could dare to say such things to her. He told her that the people who said this were very wrong; that poor people lived closer together, were less dissolute, and must love each other at least as much as more fortunate people did.

By such means Mme la dauphine is making herself adored here and public opinion is so decided in this respect that, a few days ago, when the price of bread decreased, the people of Paris said openly in the streets and in the markets, "that it was surely Mme la dauphine who had requested and obtained this decrease for the poor people."

The dauphin seems to have redoubled his friendship and attentiveness towards Mme la dauphine; he lends himself to everything which could please her. H.R.H. likes dancing; Monsieur le dauphin, who does not, has been the first to ask for balls and there is one every Monday in Mme la dauphine's rooms. H.R.H. likes to give, preferably to the poor; but she does not give haphazardly and the multiplied proofs of her discernment in this regard have had the good effect they deserved, in this place. H.R.H. took communion on the 8th and spent that day quietly.

I took Y.M.'s letter to Mme la dauphine who asked me in her lively way if I brought good news and if she could relax. I replied that Y.M., out of kindness and love would perhaps not show how upset she was about the horse rides and that I hoped Mme la dauphine would take measures to tranquilize Y.M.

I cannot fathom the impressions being created in a prince as taciturn and reclusive as Monsieur le dauphin. I had flattered myself that by seeing the abbe de Vermond constantly, he would become accustomed to talk to him and certainly the conversation of this ecclesiastic could be very useful to him; but up till now Monsieur le dauphin has not addressed a word to him. This is not due to any prejudice against the abbe, but simply to embarrassment or indifference.

Please insist on a journal of reading [otherwise] serious subjects will be more and more neglected and soon will be forgotten altogether.

H.R.H. rides a horse sidesaddle; for some time she has been taking care of her appearance and is more neatly dressed.

SECRET LETTER

The King's extreme and marked indifference to all kinds of business, his disgust for work, his style of life which does not leave him one hour in the day to occupy himself with serious matters... [leave one perplexed].

1771

MARIA THERESA TO MERCY, 4 JANUARY 1771

I was very pleased by the way my daughter's sensitivity was revealed in her actions for the poor wounded postilion, and if any such revealing behaviour occurs again, you would please me by letting me know.

I must admit that Choiseul's fall has affected me, and I fear that we will feel it only too much. It is certain that Vermond will be sent away, I regard that as being infallible, as is the future fall from grace of my daughter. You will no longer be able to approach her so easily, nor will they dare to inform you of what is happening. That abominable clique will harm my daughter and will make her regard those who would give her good advice, as suspect or inconvenient. I tell you I feel this blow is decisive for my daughter, but not for the alliance, which suits France as much as us.

I beg you to tell me all the private details, especially the words and expressions of the dauphin, whom I do not think so foolish, but entirely devoted to and led by this clique, and thus false and hypocritical. If you learn anything from time to time about the Choiseuls and the cause of their disgrace, as their thoughtlessness and impertinence have been tolerated for so many years that they cannot be the reason for their fall, I beg you to tell me. I cannot help pitying them and if I can be useful to them once, it would give me pleasure; they can count on me. Our situation is becoming more delicate; it is fortunate for us to have you there; believe in my trust and thanks. [Edit: on the 24th of December 1770, Choiseul had been dismissed from the ministry.]

MARIA THERESA TO MARIE ANTOINETTE,
6 JANUARY 1771

I must admit I was really upset when I heard about it [Edit: Choiseul's disgrace]; I saw in their conduct only fairness, humanity and attachment to the alliance; apart from that I will not enter into the reasons which the King had for this, and you will do so even less. I hope that the King will find a suitable successor and that he will also merit our trust. Never forget that your marriage was the work of the Choiseuls and that you owe them gratitude.

Now more than ever, my girl, you need the advice of Mercy and the abbe, who, I fear, knowing his honesty, will be greatly weakened by this move; but do not let yourself be allied to any faction, remain neutral in all things; attend to religious matters, keep the King happy, do what your husband wishes. Try to furnish your mind with a little good reading, that is more necessary for you than others. I have been waiting for two months for the list from the abbe, and I fear that you have scarcely bothered; the donkeys and horses filled the time necessary for reading; but now, in the winter, do not neglect that occupation, which is more necessary to you than to any other, as you have no other acquirements, not in music, nor drawing, nor dance, nor painting or other pleasant accomplishments. So I am back once again to your reading and charge you to have the abbe send me every month a list of what you have completed and what you intend beginning.

I advise you to be even more reserved than before about what is happening, to give no confidences and to show no curiosity if you wish to preserve your peace of mind, and maintain the general approval which you have kept so well up till now, only, you must agree, because you followed good advice. I am sorry to have to say this, but do not even make confidences to your aunts, even though I greatly esteem them: I know why I am saying this. Perhaps Mercy is not similarly informed, but I have my reasons. I am delighted at the balls which are taking place in your rooms and which will be very good for the dauphin.

MERCY TO MARIA THERESA, 23 JANUARY 1771

The very day the duc de Choiseul was exiled, and one hour after I heard (being unable to go to Versailles at such a critical moment), my first thought was to send Mme l'archiduchesse, via the abbe de Vermond, a note on what seemed most important to me concerning the conduct and language which it would be advisable for H.R.H. to maintain in circumstances where she would, without doubt, be closely observed.

I begged her to be careful that her expressions did not show the displeasure which she must feel at the dismissal of a minister whom everyone knew to have been honoured with the kindness and confidence of Y.M., and who besides was fundamentally important in arranging Mme la dauphine's marriage, and that these two reasons for her interest could be alleged by H.R.H. whenever people spoke to her about the exiled minister, [Edit: ministers were usually exiled to their estates, far from Versailles] but that it was necessary to avoid trying to justify him, and to confine herself to pitying him for the misfortune of having displeased the King his master, and especially to make no mention of his enemies nor of the means which they used to make him fall.

[Mme la dauphine took the measures I had advised]…and it resulted in the good effect for which I had hoped. All Versailles and Paris greatly praised H.R.H.'s behaviour and even the cabal was forced to applaud. However a few days later some little problems were caused by Mesdames, when Mme la dauphine let herself be led into making some indiscreet statements, which she would not have lent herself to without being incited by bad example.

Mme Adelaide has neither coherence nor system in her way of thinking; she had openly declared herself the patron of the duc de Choiseul and the duchesse de Gramont. The day after the dismissal of the minister, she was first to attack his conduct and accuse his sister, which scandalized the public. This inconsistency in her conduct is echoed by the same inconsistency in her advice.

The comtesse de Narbonne would like to rule Mme la dauphine through Mme Adelaide, but the presence of the abbe de Vermond presents an obstacle to the success of her project. Although Mme la dauphine trusts him [Edit: Vermond] implicity, they have however succeeded in making H.R.H. a little timid and uncertain in her opinions, such that, against her will, it is not inconceivable that she could let herself be persuaded to have the abbe de Vermond dismissed, if Mesdames were forceful and inspired doubts in her about the usefulness of keeping this ecclesiastic in her service. All of the cabal would be delighted to be rid of him. They are already eager to make common cause with the comtesse de Narbonne in this, and she seems already to be drawing closer to the duc de Choiseul's enemies.

As this was so important, I told Mme la dauphine, that losing the abbe de Vermond would deprive H.R.H. of the only really useful and trustworthy person she had; it would be extremely difficult for me, as I would lose a safe means of sending Mme la dauphine all I thought it necessary for her to know, and I do this several times a week. Besides it is not known what will happen here when the new ministry is formed. The intrigues are already becoming more intense and dangerous, and therefore more prudence and circumspection are needed to avoid the traps which could form around Mme la dauphine. I cannot appear at Versailles too often without causing problems, and even when I do, H.R.H. hardly ever has time to talk to me, usually because of Mesdames.

Perhaps Y.M. would write to Mme l'archiduchesse emphasizing the importance of keeping the abbe de Vermond, that it is best to let me see her often so that I can be useful to her, and that it is dangerous to let herself be led by the advice and example of Mesdames.

[You sent a physician]…to examine Mme la dauphine's state of health, that of Monsieur le dauphin and the rest of the royal family. Mme l'archiduchesse claimed that doctor Ingenhouse did not have the entrees de la chambre. I charged the abbe de Vermond to tell H.R.H. that if Y.M. sends someone for whatever reason, he is not subject to rules of etiquette. I later discovered that Mme Adelaide had suggested this. Y.M.

65

will please note that you cannot say this without Mme l'archiduchesse becoming annoyed with the abbe de Vermond and I.

When the balls which occur every Monday at Versailles [Edit: during carnival time] are taking place, Mme la dauphine shows every attention and kindness to those who attend. No one is forgotten, everyone is enchanted. The King has shown his pleasure in this by increasing the kindness and friendship which he shows Mme l'archiduchesse; he wants her to amuse herself, and arranges matters to this effect. He has just ordered that there should be two comedies a week at Versailles, only because it was suggested to him that Mme la dauphine would be pleased at this.

Her progress in captivating Monsieur le dauphin continues, and this young prince is changing almost visibly, to his advantage. Recently a woman of the palace said to him that with such a good figure, Mme la dauphine would dance very well, if she wished. Monsieur le dauphin replied: "She has so much grace that everything she tries is successful; it must be agreed that she is charming." For some time Monsieur le dauphin has been saying such things, which are very important from a young prince who is naturally taciturn and timid and who until now has said nothing even vaguely similar.

Mme la dauphine's liking for riding continues, but H.R.H. also reads more, sometimes even for one hour and a quarter.

The marquise de Durfort, seeing that the comtesse de Narbonne, through Mme Adelaide, was preventing Mme la dauphine from extending her protection to her, used her credit with Mme Victoire and persuaded Mme Victoire that she should not ask for the bishop of Gap to be her first almoner. (He is the brother in law of the comtesse de Narbonne and has wanted this position for a long time). As a result the two dames d'atours decided they both needed one another. Both capitulated, and it was agreed that the comtesse de Narbonne would have Mme Adelaide talk to Mme la dauphine in favour of the marquise de Durfort. [Later] the bishop of Gap was requested and named first almoner to Mesdames Victoire and

Sophie. [Then] H.R.H. spoke to the King…[and the King agreed to make the marquis de Durfort a duke].

I had the abbe de Vermond explain to Mme l'archiduchesse how she had been used without realizing. H.R.H. understood and seemed slightly ashamed. I think it would be a good idea to compliment Mme la dauphine on having had the courage to talk to the King, but say you could not understand what could be delaying the execution of a move you had long been expecting from Mme la dauphine. [Edit: Maria Theresa had asked Marie Antoinette some months before, to grant some favour to the marquis de Durfort who had been French ambassador in Vienna when Marie Antoinette's marriage had been arranged]

H.R.H. told me: "H.M. the empress talks to me of my aunts; I do not know who gives her her information." These words full of sincerity and judgement pleased me; I replied that Y.M. got to hear of everything eventually.

SECRET LETTER

Mme la dauphine already has considerable influence here and the dismissal of the duc de Choiseul can only affect this up to a point. I also feel sure that I will not be forbidden my usual access to H.R.H., provided she wishes this, and it is the same with regard to the abbe de Vermond. This would be very simple for her to ensure. In keeping with the way in which things happen here and the King's manner of thinking and acting, Y.M. must be assured that no one would successfully attempt to attack the abbe de Vermond and I, so long as it was noticed that Mme l'archiduchesse wished to oppose this. I only fear Mme Adelaide's suggestions, as I have already said in my very humble report.

Monsieur le dauphin showed neither pleasure nor pain at the dismissal of the duc de Choiseul. According to what he has said to Mme la dauphine, it is possible that he doubts all he has heard said about this minister, whether good or bad. Moreover he seems not to have any interest in anyone at court, not even those who have looked after him since infancy. The duc de la Vauguyon is as indifferent in his eyes as the others, and that is what seems to have decided the duke, and the rest of the cabal, to go to the comte de Provence in the hope of finding support in him. Until now, Monsieur le dauphin has only shown real signs of trust in Mme la dauphine.

Although Mme la dauphine's position is delicate, even dangerous in some ways, either because of her associates, or other reasons, I believe nothing serious will happen, and that with a little more experience Mme l'archiduchesse will certainly govern her husband, whose indifference comes from a bad education and great natural timidity rather than a deceitful character.

[Implicated in the duc de Choiseul's fall was]…the open struggle against the favourite into which he had been drawn, the bold things he had dared to say to his master about that woman, and even more the cutting jokes that he made in public about her, all that had for a long time established in the King a seed of disgust for the minister; the latter's enemies fomented and poisoned these dispositions even more; finally they profited from them to persuade the King that the duc de Choiseul was inciting the parlements to be disobedient, and that an uprising in the country could ensue, if the minister were not promptly dismissed. False witnesses were produced, they persuaded the prince de Conde to interfere; the chancellor declared he would resign; finally the King, pressed on all sides by the favourite, several of his ministers and a little apprehensive of the danger represented to him as being very near, decided to dismiss the minister.

The latter learned of his disgrace from the duc de la Vrilliere with the greatest sang-froid. For the duke's sake and my own, I could not see him before he left. He knew it was impossible and begged me, as did the duchesse, to let Y.M. know of their inviolable and very respectful attachment to your sacred person, and begged you to deign to maintain your protection. I had them told verbally, that Y.M. would continue to accord her favour, while pitying them for having displeased their sovereign.

Since this event, the King has shown no resentment against the duc de Choiseul; there have even been moments when it was thought that he felt he had been deceived about the minister, and that he regretted him.

MARIA THERESA TO MARIE ANTOINETTE, 10 FEBRUARY 1771

My dear daughter, I am delighted that you anticipated my wishes in the rather delicate case of the Choiseuls' exile. Please continue in the same way and do not belie your kindly character. Do not let yourself be led astray by contrary examples; do not adopt the French thoughtlessness, remain a good German and glory in being so and in being a friend to your friends.

I compliment you on having finally found the courage to speak to the King of the commission I charged you with for Durfort; I no longer knew what could be causing that long delay! Ingenhouse tells me he found you very well and that you had grown, that he saw the whole family and found all in good health, that for a moment he was not able to approach you because of etiquette, but the ambassador procured for him means of seeing you. I cannot believe that a man of our court would not have access in yours; you have found a way round so many other etiquettes – do not let this one continue.

I beg you to tell me if you dance better than when you were here, especially the contre-danses: they say lots of good things about these balls, and especially about the dauphin, which pleases me even more, and they attribute this change to you; how happy you must be.

I am beginning to worry because you are not dauphine. I am afraid that the future comtesse de Provence will be pregnant before you: they talk well of her, mentioning her excellent character and sweetness, although she is not beautiful, but she has interesting features and a shapely figure.

I am waiting impatiently for the return of this courier to hear of your reading and studies; it is permitted, especially at your age, to have a good time, but to do so all the time and to do nothing solid or useful, and to only kill time between walks and visits, eventually you will see the emptiness in all that and will regret not having better used your time.

I am consoled by what you tell me of the King's continuing care and kindliness to you: try to merit their continuation and believe me all yours.

MARIA THERESA TO MERCY, 11 FEBRUARY 1771

Although the dauphin continues in his insensitivity, I am however reassured by what you tell me about his conduct vis-a-vis my daughter; we will have to wait for the result. In the meantime I will be tranquil so long as I can depend on the union of the two spouses; but I must admit that, amidst the unsettled situation of the court of France, my daughter's position causes me a great deal of anxiety. Her nonchalance, her lack of taste for serious study, her indiscretion (because of her youth and high spirits), her liaison with the aunts and especially Mme Adelaide (who is perhaps the most worldly and inclined to intrigue of the sisters), give me more than one reason to worry.

I will write to my daughter in the way you advise, but I prefer to trust your zeal and insight. Apart from that I am pleased that my daughter thinks I receive news from other sources [such as] my sister in law, princess Charlotte.

I am pleased that my daughter finally succeeded in securing a mark of favour for Durfort, but the way that affair was conducted seems fantastic to me; fortunately I do not see such plots at my court.

I very much fear for my daughter the arrival of the princess of Savoy [Edit: the comte de Provence's future wife]. You will see in my letter that I am trying to warn her little by little; I fear jealousy, quarrels, factions. The best would be perfect union between them; I would hope for this if not for the presence of the aunts.

MERCY TO MARIA THERESA, 25 FEBRUARY 1771

[Mme la dauphine told me]…she had thought about what I had said at Fontainebleau concerning the comtesse de Provence's arrival and that she was resolved to treat her well, and to encourage her friendship and thus disconcert the plans the cabal had formed around Mme de Provence, and that she would occupy herself with means of maintaining union in the royal family.

Every Monday during carnival, Mme la dauphine has been charmingly gracious to the ladies admitted…[to the balls]. For his part, Monsieur le dauphin has been totally different to what was expected; he has greatly enjoyed dancing, and spoke to everyone in a kindly way which was not known in him till now. Such a favourable change is attributed with great reason to Mme la dauphine, and gives her even greater right to public homage. Apart from the balls in Mme la dauphine's rooms, the comtesse de Noailles has given several in her rooms, which H.R.H. honoured with her presence.

She arrived on the first occasion with Monsieur le dauphin, who held her arm; he said on entering, to the comtesse de Noailles: "I hope madame, that you will welcome both husband and wife; we have not come to cause bother, but to share in your amusements." [Then] Monsieur le dauphin spent the whole evening dancing, talking and showing kindness and attention to all who presented themselves to him. This conduct caused a great sensation, and gave rise to hopes which until now there had not seemed great reason to hold.

As this young prince changes to his advantage, he is less inclined to conceal his thoughts about the duc de la Vauguyon. The latter has recently had a quite serious illness which lasted for three weeks. Monsieur le dauphin did not go to see him and one day, at Mesdames his aunts, he spoke of his former governor with some contempt, complaining of the bad education he had received. All these instances show the effects of the influence which Mme la dauphine has been able to acquire over her husband.

Mme l'archiduchesse is always gracious, but it is noticeable that she speaks less to people of distinction who have the honour of paying their court to her in the morning, or at her dinner; during the ball or at other amusements, H.R.H. seems more disposed to talk, and these are precisely the occasions when people of a certain age and importance tend not to come.

71

He [Edit: the King] is very friendly to her and very often kisses her hands. When H.R.H. is at ease and forgets Mesdames' lessons in timidity, the King is enchanted and shows a gaiety he has with none of his children.

I have been reminding Mme la dauphine of possible surprises being planned for her with regard to the abbe de Vermond. H.R.H. understood the importance of this, and decided to give the abbe a token of her kindness and protection which will keep him safe from the enterprises possibly being meditated against him. Mme la dauphine asked the King to grant…[Vermond] a vacant abbey, and that was agreed.

The person who was most intent on persecuting the duc de Choiseul [Edit: the duc de la Vauguyon], is mortally ill, and this could well free France from one of the most dangerous subjects she has ever produced. All Paris continues enthusiastically to show signs of esteem and regret in public for the exiled minister.

SECRET LETTER

Nothing has yet happened relative to the projects which Monsieur le dauphin seemed to have formed to live with Mme la dauphine in the intimacy demanded by their union. This conduct is inexplicable and annoying. I use all possible means to distract Mme l'archiduchesse and to prevent her from dwelling on this, by emphasizing the advantages of her position, that is, the certainty she is loved by her husband and has his trust. H.R.H.'s health is perfect, and her face is becoming more beautiful.

MARIA THERESA TO MERCY, 15 MARCH 1771

Despite the little problems I still find in the dauphine's conduct, there does not seem a remedy. I will again mention them, but I will have to be careful. I know my children: if I preach to them too much, it makes them worse rather than better. I see with pleasure that the dauphin seems to be changing to his advantage, but I do not understand his conduct vis-a-vis his wife; is it perhaps as a consequence of the bad principles which were inspired in him while he was being educated?

The death of the duc de la Vauguyon would surely not be regretted, but does the King's goodheartedness extend to the point where he is unable to dismiss this dangerous man from his post? (Is it true that the King is drinking?)

MERCY TO MARIA THERESA, 17 MARCH 1771

For some time Mme la dauphine has felt special affection for the princesse de Lamballe, born princesse de Carignan [an Italian] and widow of the prince de Lamballe, son of the duc de Penthievre. This young princess [is] sweet and gentle. [9]

For almost two months the change in the conduct and feelings of Monsieur le dauphin about what is happening at court has become so obvious, that it has resulted in the members of the cabal becoming anxious and making it the object of all their attention.

Monsieur le dauphin, who until recently seemed unaware of, and indifferent to, the current intrigues, has suddenly shown disdain towards his governor, the duc de la Vauguyon and a great contempt for the comtesse du Barry, the chancellor of France and those in their party. This young prince who had so much desired and requested so often to be admitted to the suppers with the King's close friends, no longer goes, and even affectedly avoids them. They did not fail to point this out to the King and to suggest that Mme la dauphine had encouraged the change.

I was informed that the King was persuaded of the truth of this, that he was annoyed and that he proposed to tell Mme l'archiduchesse so. I foresaw that the King would not talk to H.R.H. himself, because of his timidity, but to the comtesse de Noailles, therefore I informed Mme la dauphine of all I knew

---

[9] Lamballe remained with the Queen throughout most of the Revolution, even returning from the safety of England to be at the Queen's side in the later stages of the Revolution, and suffered an infamous and barbaric death in 1792, in the September Massacres. (See volume II of these letters)

and insisted that at the first word said to her on behalf of the King, she should go to the monarch and explain herself to him, and I told her at the same time what to say in such a case. I also alerted the comtesse de Noailles and told her that her duty and attachment to Mme la dauphine must inspire her to try to protect H.R.H. from the King's displeasure. The comtesse promised to follow the advice I gave her in this matter and she soon had reason to use it.

The King sent for the comtesse de Noailles; he told her that for a long time he had wanted to have a talk with her about Mme la dauphine; first he praised her character and grace but he added that he feared the effects of her high spirits; that he found it appropriate that, in private, Mme la dauphine should be naturally cheerful, but that in public, and when she held court, more reserve was necessary. The King added that he disapproved of Mme la dauphine's habit of taking foodstuffs to the hunt, and distributing them to all these around her carriage, that it caused too much familiarity, especially with the young people and that this displeased him. He also said that Mme la dauphine allowed herself to talk too freely "of what she saw or thought she saw, that her thoughtless remarks could occasion unpleasantness within the family."

With regard to these complaints, the first is less well founded than before, as Mme la dauphine's high spirits have moderated, and her behaviour in public is better than it ever was, therefore what the King was saying, was only a pretext to embark on a list of complaints. Concerning the second point, I have already mentioned it in my reports. With regard to the third complaint, Mme l'archiduchesse in her private conversations with Monsieur le dauphin, has opened his eyes, whether with regard to her former governor, the favourite or the rest of the cabal, but she cannot be reproached with any open step nor any words to draw Monsieur le dauphin away from the King; while Mesdames have not ceased talking publicly to this young prince in a most imprudent way, likely to dissuade him from finding opportunities to be with the King.

The comtesse de Noailles replied to the King that she could assure him that Mme la dauphine had a great desire to please him in everything, that the basic character of this princess showed only desirable qualities, but that her age and her high spirits sometimes led her into little faults which it would be very easy to rectify, if the King wanted to alert her or authorise her, the comtesse de Noailles, to warn Mme l'archiduchesse.

The King favoured this last method; he questioned the comtesse about the advice given to Mme la dauphine, and added that she did not always receive good advice. The lady of honour agreed; she said that the King must know more than she did on this matter and that, from respect for the source of this advice, she could not discuss it. The King replied: "I know the source and I am very displeased." The implication of this response bears directly on Mesdames and the comtesse de Narbonne.

The King asked the comtesse de Noailles if I spoke frequently to Mme la dauphine. The countess replied that it did not happen as often as could be desired. The King kindly replied that he knew my zeal and probity, and that he would be pleased to see me often with Mme l'archiduchesse to tell her my thoughts on what concerned her. Finally the King told the countess to let H.R.H. know of the conversation. The lady of honour did so; Mme la dauphine then consulted Mesdames, who did not hesitate to advise imprudent behaviour...[However I persuaded H.R.H. to be more careful when she spoke to the King, and advised her on what to say to him]

She spoke to the King that very evening, and told him she was very upset that her papa did not sufficiently like her or trust her, to talk directly to her about what was agreeable or disagreeable to him. H.R.H. seasoned her words with all the grace natural to her. The King seemed extremely embarrassed; he would enter into no details, assured Mme l'archiduchesse that he found her charming and that he loved her with all his heart; he kissed her hands, embraced her and agreed with all H.R.H. had just said. This behaviour of the King's is the result of his character, and the way he never contradicts his children in anything, and tolerates what displeases him rather than remedying it by a direct approach.[10]

MARIE ANTOINETTE TO MARIA THERESA, 16 APRIL 1771

My dear mother, I am delighted that Lent has not harmed your health; mine is still very good.

I would be really upset if the Germans were dissatisfied with me; I admit that I would have spoken more to M. de Paar and the young Starhemberg if they had a better reputation here. However when it was the season for balls, I sent for M. de Lamberg and Starhemberg, and as soon as I saw that they danced, I had them dance with me.

There is a lot happening here just now; on Saturday there was a lit de justice [Edit: a formal occasion in which the King imposes his will, usually on a parlement] to affirm the dissolution of the former parlement and install a new one; the princes of the blood [Edit: princes quite closely related to the King] refused to come and protested against the King's wishes; they wrote a very impertinent letter to him, signed by all, except for the comte de la Marche, who behaved very well on that occasion.[11]

What is most astonishing in the conduct of the princes, is that M. le prince de Conde had his son, who is not yet fifteen years old and has always been brought up here [Edit: Versailles], sign. The King had him told to leave, as with the other princes, whom he forbade to appear before him or before us. The dukes, although they attended, have protested, and it is said that twelve of them have been exiled.

One month from today I will be able to give Y.M. news of the comtesse de Provence, as the marriage is on the 14th of

---

[10] This was an unfortunate character trait adopted also by his grandson, Louis XVl

[11] The aristocracy rebelled against the absolute power of the French King, and, it is said, taught the French people to rebel, by example. See the letter of Fersen, Marie Antoinette's lover, in the second volume of these letters, of 1st of February 1790.

May; they had arranged many celebrations for this wedding, but there will not be so many because of the lack of money.

Y.M. can be reassured about my conduct with the comtesse de Provence, and I will certainly try to win her friendship and her trust, without however going too far. But I am afraid that, if she is not very intelligent and is not forewarned, she will be in Mme du Barry's party. They are doing all they can to win her over, as her dame d'atours, who is Mme de Valentinois, is in that party.

I greatly regret the comtesse de Paar, whom I respected and loved with all my heart. I share your regret at losing faithful old servants. The book you sent me is very precious, as is all that comes from you.

MERCY TO MARIA THERESA, 16 APRIL 1771

Sacred Majesty, in the midst of the intrigues of this court and the disorder they cause, Mme la dauphine's position often causes me worry...

People are totally appalled at all that happens here, and the public is no longer guarded in its speech. Matters of government have become almost the only subject of conversation at court, in town, throughout the whole kingdom, and even amongst the royal family. As a result, in the little committees which are held daily at Mesdames, they have discussed in depth the conduct of the princes of the blood, the ministers, and all the actors on the present scene, and they have proposed to receive them more or less favourably according to the judgement which has been brought against each of them.

Mesdames felt that the prince de Conde was one of the most reprehensible characters. When he was presented to pay court to Mesdames and to Mme la dauphine, he was given a bad reception. The prince de Conde addressed himself to me via an intermediary, and said that, of all the princes of the blood, he was the one who most tried to please Mme la dauphine. I assured the prince de Conde's intermediary that Mme l'archiduchesse, from principle and character, was inclined to treat those who approached her, well, and that princes of the blood were more entitled to this than others

77

[therefore] he must be mistaken, and this was perhaps due to distraction or chance, and…[I would tell Mme la dauphine what he had said].

I observed to her that in the present critical situation, the only way to remain tranquil was in inaction, and not to permit herself examination, nor talk, nor enquiry into what was happening, that Mme la dauphine knew very well that she was not in a position to remedy anything; that adopting a particular position would attract the ill will of the opposing party, and she would run the risk of compromising herself. I also recalled the history of this country and proved that the more or less favourable position of a dauphine or Queen of France often depended on the degree of opinion and affection that she had attracted from the nation and the princes; that it was especially necessary to take care of the princes of the blood, or a seed of dislike could grow.

Mme la dauphine replied that she was never the first to talk of current affairs, nor of those involved in them, but that in the privacy of the family, when everyone was stating their opinion, it was difficult not to state hers. I told her that no one was interested in Mesdames' opinions but only in hers, and that consequently, the risks were hers alone. H.R.H. agreed and promised she would try. It is certain that it was the example which made her act thus, and if Mme la dauphine was not encouraged to speak on these matters at Mesdames, she would easily refrain from doing so.

I see Mme l'archiduchesse once or twice a week and then only for a few moments as she fears that people will remark on these audiences. However I believe she honours me with her confidence and always seems eager to see me, but at the same time, she tells me she fears to be observed and I have reason to believe that this fear is inspired by Mesdames. Nonetheless when I have something important to say, I find means and I am always kindly listened to.

Against all expectations, the duc de la Vauguyon has recovered. The continued existence of this dangerous man is a great misfortune. His intrigues are to be dreaded as he will use any means to achieve his aims, therefore I have asked Mme la dauphine to conceal her opinion of this person.

[The former parlement has been dismissed and the country is in ferment therefore]…I told Mme la dauphine not to show approval or disapproval about what had happened. H.R.H. promised me this and this relieved my anxiety as Mme l'archiduchesse holds almost exactly to what she promises.

SECRET LETTER

Despite my ministerial dispatches, it is almost impossible for Y.M. to form an exact idea of the dreadful confusion which reigns here in everything. The throne is debased because of indecency, the extensive credit of the favourite, and the malice of her partisans. The nation is producing seditious words, indecent writings in which the person of the monarch is not spared; Versailles has become the centre of treachery, hatreds and vengeance; everything happens through intrigues and personalities and it seems that all feelings of decency have been renounced. I did not hesitate to tell this to Mme la dauphine.

When Mme la dauphine heard of the death of…[two of your friends] she was worried about the grief which Y.M. would feel at this and spoke of it to me with some emotion.

Relative to Mme la dauphine, my duty prescribes as law that I write the most exact truth in my very humble reports. I would never tranquilize Y.M. at the expense of the truth therefore believe me when I say that although Mme l'archiduchesse's situation is delicate, her basic conduct is such that it will prevent any great problems and nothing will ever be sufficiently serious to worry Y.M.

Y.M. asks me if the King is drinking. The rumour which is going around is not well founded and could be as a result of the absences of spirit which are often remarked in this monarch, which resemble the effects of drunkenness, although they are not. It is true that the King's interest is fading more and more, and to that is added the weariness caused in the monarch by the general disorder which surrounds him on all sides. This is recounted in my ministerial dispatches.[12]

MARIA THERESA TO MERCY, 7 MAY 1771

There is nothing I can add to your reflections on the situation of my daughter and that of the court of France; the one is as delicate as the other is frightening.

Here is my letter for my daughter; I hope you are pleased with it; there is much repetition; I wrote it on several occasions.

MARIA THERESA TO MARIE ANTOINETTE, 8 MAY 1771

I am writing now in front of the portrait of my very dear daughter; but I do not find the look of youth which you had eleven months ago, and unfortunately a change in your condition is not the reason; I am anxiously awaiting that news and flatter myself that the marriage which will soon take place will accelerate my wishes; however I cannot repeat too often: show no ill temper about this; sweetness and patience are the only means you can use. There is nothing lost, you are both so young: on the contrary it is better for the health of both of you, as you are both becoming stronger; but it is natural to us old parents to wish for consummation, scarcely being able to flatter ourselves with the hope of seeing our grandchildren and great grandchildren.

You will greatly please me, my dear daughter, by telling me how you find your sister in law; according to Rosenberg's account, you will have no reason to be jealous, but lots of reason to pity her and busy yourself with her: that will honour you and will be appropriate. Do not try to govern her, that is as unsuitable as jealousy, but prevent her embarrassment if you can, because they say she is not pretty, is very timid, not good with people, but nonetheless well brought up; with time

---

[12] Mercy wrote a ministerial dispatch to the Austrian court, every month, as well as these letters.

that could become a suitably friendly relationship. Avoid people who will bring you reports and stories both for and against her: people are wicked; they will try to ingratiate themselves with you by flattering your self love and piquing it.

Be careful to maintain and try to daily increase the great trust which you tell me the dauphin shows you, and by behaving respectfully and affectionately try to meet with the King's approval in everything. I would very much like you to see him more often in your rooms; it is important. He saw your mother in law every day in her rooms, and to my great astonishment I have learned that he never comes to your rooms except on ceremonial days: it is a custom and may decide for or against you with the public; try therefore to secure this in the future; I will mention something to Mercy, it is very important.

What you tell me of the two ladies who have been given to the comtesse de Provence must convince you of how careful you must be; what a difference between Mme de Noailles and those two! I grant you that she annoys you because she is concerned about your welfare, but nonetheless she is said to be honest and is attached to you; that is an important point, and as she is from one of the best families, where else would you find a perfect lady who was not an intriguer and not irritating?

My dear daughter, they say in great astonishment that you rarely see my ambassador, that you only speak to him in passing, and even that you seem to show embarrassment when with him rather than trust. They cite the example of the Queen your grandmother, and of your mother in law, both of whom regularly saw their family ministers in their own rooms, twice a week. Also they spoke to them and treated them with distinction at all times. If they advise you not to behave in this way, I fear that it is not for your own good. Moreover Mercy is esteemed by every reasonable person and it can only honour you and benefit you if you listen to him often.

I must admit that what you told me about Paar and Starhemberg, claiming they did not have good reputations, truly pained me. I can see from that, all that they dare to say to you, and if you had shown more liking for your nation and had at least said that you did not want to hear ill spoken of them in front of you, they would have been more guarded. Give a suitable welcome to the distinguished and show kindness to all Germans, especially my subjects and those from important families: to the least, that is to say those who do not have the entrees to our court, show kindness, affection and protection. You will not be censured for this, but rather esteemed, unlike those who have never had the happiness of attracting love from anyone. It is the sole resource and happiness to be gained from our position. You have so perfectly acquired this; do not lose it from neglect of what procured it for you: it was not your beauty, which in fact is not so great, nor your talents and knowledge (you know very well you have neither); it was your kind heart, your candour and your skilfully employed attentiveness, which attracted people.

They say you neglect to talk to and distinguish important people; that at card play, you only talk to your young ladies, whispering to them and laughing with them. I am not so unjust as to wish to forbid you conversing with the young people you know, which is only natural, in favour of those whom you only see in public, but it is essential to distinguish people who must not be neglected. Let us have no negligence on this point, and do not imitate anyone: do what you saw and learned here.

They still talk of how you amused yourself last winter. Do not let yourself be tempted to make fun of others: you are a little inclined to that; if this weakness is noticed, you will be provided with only too many opportunities for it, and you will lose the esteem and trust of the public which are so necessary and so pleasant, and which you still possess so perfectly.

My love causes me to repeat myself unendingly; but I regard these qualities as the foundation for your happiness, therefore you can judge how concerned I am. Do not think that Mercy wrote to me about this, but I must repeat that what is known here is astonishing; I have no correspondence, but there are several here who do and who know the slightest details. Everyone, knowing my love for you, brings me their news to console me, but for some time there has been a decrease in favourable reports, which is attributed to the advice given to you. I felt I could not make too much of this point, and even charged Mercy to keep me informed and to assist you more than ever with his advice.

The turmoil in France pains me both for the King and for you. Mercy assures me that you conduct yourself in such a way as to attract the esteem of everyone, and even increase by your measured, good and Christian conduct, the esteem people have for you. Therefore follow Mercy's advice as he is only concerned with you, and do not become involved with any party; if you could even feign lack of awareness, that would be for the better. It is at such a time as this that I prefer the horse rides, the trips in a carriage, the balls, plays and all kinds of pleasure seeking, even childish things, in order to cut short opportunities to gossip.

MERCY TO MARIA THERESA, 22 MAY 1771

The letter which Y.M. wrote to Mme l'archiduchesse at the beginning of April, has had such a good effect that, ever since, I have watched most of the little problems which furnished material in my previous very humble reports, diminish in a very remarkable way. This favourable change is particularly obvious in two essential points: in that of the talk about the critical situation here at present, and in the kind welcome suitable for those who pay court to Mme la dauphine.

I let Mme l'archiduchesse see that it was not appropriate to a great princess' dignity to pointlessly criticise matters which could not be remedied, that in such cases cold silence was the only suitable repudiation; that such an expression showed majesty of soul, while words only indicated a powerless weakness; that to openly combat a cabal, was in a sense to place herself on the same level as those who composed it and expose herself to possible compromise.

I noticed that this portrayal of the situation struck Mme la dauphine; I told her that the people in the comtesse du Barry's party boasted of being badly treated by H.R.H., and that it was necessary not to give them the impertinent satisfaction of believing that Mme l'archiduchesse was bothered with them, that the best means of punishing them was to talk to them from time to time with a relaxed and polite expression, and that if Mme la dauphine had just once addressed the comtesse du Barry herself, I was quite sure that this step would very quickly have disconcerted this wicked cabal, which luxuriates in its reputation gained from withstanding the futile efforts employed against them by the royal family.

Mme la dauphine told me naively that fear of displeasing her aunts would always prevent her from talking to the favourite, but that she would speak to the others, and in fact, the very next day. H.R.H. spoke to the comtesse de Valentinois and to the duc d'Aiguillon. This caused a sensation at court, and the members of the cabal, having mentioned it to me as an extraordinary piece of news, I seized the opportunity to reproach them for the inaccuracy and lack of restraint in their talk about Mme la dauphine's bias towards a specific party (having waited a long time for this opportunity), and I emphasized as best as I could, the proofs of H.R.H.'s impartiality in matters which did not concern her personally.

Matters could be maintained like this if not for Mesdames' opposition; but it is always as a result of their inept political judgement that I have the pain of seeing partially destroyed, what the judgement and good sense of Mme la dauphine makes her adopt as reasonable.

H.R.H.'s ideas are becoming clearer and although she is still high spirited, nonetheless she is gaining in dignity when in public. Her language is better; she knows how to use her intelligence and grace in a way which enchants, and if this charming princess only followed her own instincts and was not distracted by bad examples, there would surely never be the slightest comment to make on her conduct.

Mme la dauphine still enjoys riding, and a fortnight ago a slight accident occurred, which I heard about despite the precautions taken to conceal the matter from me. H.R.H. was riding, when an equerry's horse reared, striking Mme la dauphine's foot, although she did not show any pain. She continued her ride and when she returned her foot was swollen. When her ladies said that she should immediately have said she was in pain, H.R.H. replied that she had concealed her pain in order to spare the equerry any upset. Next day her foot was as normal. This kindness made an impression on all, and it illuminates perfectly Mme la dauphine's character.

H.R.H. failed slightly to keep her promise not to follow the hunt on horseback [Edit: she pretended she had come across the hunt by chance]. Mme l'archiduchesse tried to keep this secret, especially from me. She thinks I know nothing about this, and if it pleases Y.M. to mention it to Mme la dauphine, this will make her more exact in holding to a promise.

On the 11th, the court went to Fontainebleau; Mme la dauphine seemed preoccupied with the object of this trip; it was noticed that she was more attentive and affectionate to the King, who was enchanted as a result. Next day the royal family met Mme la comtesse de Provence. The King embraced her affectionately; she was welcomed by her husband who showed great joy; Mme la dauphine received her warmly and graciously but without affectation; she seemed preoccupied with the new wife, showing her all possible consideration, and combined with this behaviour a lot of hugs for the King, which had a great effect.

On returning to Fontainebleau, during supper, although those first moments seemed to have been set aside for Mme la comtesse de Provence, the King was much less bothered with her than with Mme la dauphine. She had never seemed so charming and her triumph has never been as complete as on this occasion. The King hugged her a thousand times and told her he wanted to see her at breakfast time next day. The King even took his coffee at Mme la dauphine's…[next day] and remained there for two hours, seeming more cheerful and content than usual.

I took the liberty of telling H.R.H. of the necessity of maintaining the visible progress in her influence over the King. She assured me that this was her intention. I must say that although H.R.H. is aware of her superiority over the comtesse de Provence, she has not prided herself on it, and in this the natural kindness of her character has triumphed over her pleasure in a public victory over a princess whom the cabal had proposed to set up as a rival to Mme l'archiduchesse.

85

As for Mme la comtesse de Provence, her face is not pretty and her bearing not very pleasant; she has no graces, she speaks little and not well. The King said at first sight, "that he found her quite ugly" and the public agree. I see that they even take pleasure in saying this and only because of their affection for Mme la dauphine.

MARIA THERESA TO MERCY, 6 JUNE 1771

The more the dauphin's coldness is extraordinary, the more my daughter needs to maintain very measured conduct. Van Swieten [Edit: Maria Theresa's physician] is of the opinion that if a young girl with the appearance of the dauphine cannot arouse the dauphin, nothing can be done, and that it is best therefore not to try and hope that time will effect a change in such strange conduct.

I have every reason to be pleased with my daughter's behaviour when the comtesse de Provence arrived, but I am not without worry for the future. The ostentation of forming the comtesse de Provence's court only with people from that party, and making it much more numerous than that of the dauphine, is already a proof [Edit: of the cabal's power]. The intrigues, cabals, jealousies and quarrels will finally merge and render my daughter's situation even more difficult so that she may abandon herself in consequence to her aunts, with her head bowed.

I would therefore like you to approach my daughter as often as possible to observe what is happening in her household and to counsel her in consequence; the abbe de Vermond will no doubt be a great help to you. Apart from that I would be grateful for news from time to time about the comtesse de Provence, informing me of how she behaves with the King, her husband, my daughter and the aunts, and if she has the approval of the court and the nation...

The cabal will surely gain in strength now that the comtesse de Provence has arrived.

MARIA THERESA TO MARIE ANTOINETTE,
9 JUNE 1771

Thank God your health is still so good; I do not disapprove of your exercise, but use moderation, especially in your riding. I was upset to learn that you did not keep your word and that you rode with the hunt. I agreed to you continuing riding on that condition only, although I was still very worried, so your silence on this point upset me twice over.

All the letters from Paris and Versailles mention only your wise and kind behaviour with your sister in law, but what means even more to me is what Mercy tells me about your behaviour. They do not talk a lot about that princess and they even dare to make comparisons; continue as you are doing, my dear daughter, and you will soon realize that our advice is useful to you. Do not be bad tempered or jealous, and they will finally tire of trying to provoke you, once they see you firm and tranquil. The scene you painted for me of the wedding day made me weep and only increased my hopes for you. [Edit: this letter by Marie Antoinette is not in the collection, like many others which are missing] Do not be discouraged, retain your charming gaiety more than ever and believe in God: all will go well.

EXTRACT FROM MME. CAMPAN 'MEMOIRS' [13]

Once only, when tired out with the misplaced remonstrances of an old lady attached to her person, who wished to dissuade her from riding on horseback, under the impression that it would prevent her producing heirs to the crown, "Mademoiselle," said she, "in God's name, leave me in peace; be assured that I can put no heir in danger."

---

[13] Extract from Campan, 'Memoirs of the Court of Marie Antoinette Queen of France,' (1904), vol I, p.117

MARIE ANTOINETTE TO MARIA THERESA, 21 JUNE 1771

My dear mother, I received your dear letter the day before yesterday, telling me that Y.M. is well. As for me I am in really good health; my dear husband took medicine today, having had a little indigestion for two nights but he is fine now and he has promised me that he will certainly not be long in coming back to sleep with me.

My husband and I are still getting on well together with my brother and sister: I hope it will always be so. My sister is very sweet, obliging and cheerful. She likes me a lot and also trusts me. She is not at all biased in favour of Mme du Barry or of M. de la Vauguyon, as we had feared; she spoke to me very reasonably about it and behaved very well at Marly when the favourite sat beside her one day.

I am in despair that Y.M. can think that I broke my word about riding with the hunt, having only been once, to a deer hunt, and I did not even follow it very closely.

I will not talk to you, my dear mother, of the nomination of M. d'Aiguillon, as I do not involve myself in politics. [Edit: M. d'Aiguillon had become prime minister]

MERCY TO MARIA THERESA, 22 JUNE 1771

Mme la comtesse de Provence's expression is cold, constrained; she speaks little, without grace, and she has nothing of what is essential to please this nation; nonetheless Mesdames cannot prevent themselves feeling jealous and I see that they wish to inspire Mme la dauphine with these feelings. Fortunately H.R.H.'s heart and character are too disinclined to hatred for her to lend herself easily to this, and I am careful to try to prevent this.

Mesdames, on the comtesse de Narbonne's advice, took Mme la dauphine to the dame d'atour's rooms for a few evenings but did not invite the comtesse de Provence. I was surprised and afflicted at the liking Mme la dauphine has acquired for this comtesse de Narbonne, who, without intelligence and insight, has however subjugated Mme

Adelaide and makes her behave pitiably on all occasions. I dared to tell Mme la dauphine this. H.R.H. is usually disposed to agree with me; but the need to look for little amusements, and the ease of finding them at Mesdames, often prevents any other reflection, and she abandons herself from boredom to occupations which her judgement would otherwise reject.

The subject which has most excited Mesdames' jealousy, is the sumptuous household created for M. le comte and Mme la comtesse de Provence. It is certain that this luxury passes the bounds of reason. The public is shocked at it. M le dauphin has seemed displeased and as he is not unaware that this arrangement results from the intriguing ways of the duc de la Vauguyon, and his eagerness to make money from the sale of these offices, it is certain that this conduct will add to the scorn which M le dauphin has already conceived for his former governor.

The duc de Duras, knowing how much Mme la dauphine liked dancing, suggested having balls while the court was at Fontainebleau in the autumn. Mme l'archiduchesse replied that she would like this very much, but that as an increase in expenses would result, she did not want people to say that money was found for amusements, but not to pay the salaries of members of her household,[14] therefore she did not think that the amusements were a good idea. Everyone heard of this reply and it caused general admiration, especially as it is not common in this court for people to care about those with problems.

Recently Mme la dauphine has once again resumed her custom of playing with children, and unfortunately her premiere femme de chambre has two children, both of whom are very annoying. Mme l'archiduchesse spends a lot of her day with these children, who spoil her clothes, tear and break the furniture and leave the rooms in the greatest disorder. But worst of all is that because of this amusement, Mme la

---

[14] Marie Antoinette has been censured for contributing to the financial distress of the French government, which was one of the contributory factors leading to the French Revolution, but in fact the French government was financially embarrassed even before Marie Antoinette became Queen.

dauphine does not have time to read and this has been so neglected, that it might be suppressed altogether, if Y.M. does not write severely about this. When H.R.H. gives herself up to a few hours of pleasure, it is afterwards impossible to fix her attention on anything. [However] when I speak to her immediately after her reading, she is disposed to listen and to reason very sensibly.

When the duc d'Aiguillon was presented to the royal family as a minister, it was noticed, to my great regret, that Mme la dauphine said nothing to him, while Mesdames and especially M. and Mme la comtesse de Provence, spoke kindly to the new minister. I had however asked Mme l'archiduchesse in advance to be careful on this occasion. I hope to engage her at least to repair this omission, which will in the long run have a bad effect.

SECRET LETTER

The duc d'Aiguillon praised H.R.H.'s character, grace and judgement, then spoke of the vagaries in her conduct and said that the King had asked him to speak to me about this as he observed with displeasure in Mme la dauphine, signs of a too marked aversion towards the people who formed the King's society. Also that Mme l'archiduchesse did not limit herself to refusing to give them the treatment they deserved, but that she also employed sarcasm and hatred in her talk, and that this worsened the party spirit at court; that besides Mme la dauphine acted in a manner which was too lively and childish; that all this was combining to deaden the King's liking and affection for Mme l'archiduchesse.

[I told the duc d'Aiguillon]…(realising that I risked compromising myself, but it was important to remove Mme la dauphine from attack) of the principles of conduct which had been given to Mme l'archiduchesse in Vienna and which H.R.H. had practised on her arrival here; I entered into detail on her kindness, her character and her intentions; I observed that as long as she was guided by herself, there was nothing with which to reproach her, but that others had spoken to Mme la dauphine of things she should neither see nor know of, and had even gone to the point of giving her poisonous advice which had led to problems, and that it was not difficult to discover the source [but I added that]…because of the gentleness of character of Mme la dauphine, the slightest loving and friendly hints by the King would produce a certain effect, but if he never explained anything, it could only be assumed that he was pleased with the family.

I also said that if there were complaints about her high spirits, it was nonetheless certain that Mme la dauphine was visibly correcting this; that it was not her, but those around her that it was necessary to reprimand; that it would besides be unjust to demand of a princess of fifteen years, a composed and serious being, that her innocent gaiety showed a good and sincere heart and that thus there was not too much to complain of in the state of affairs which existed.

The duc d'Aiguillon understood very well that in speaking of the entourage of Mme la dauphine, I meant Mesdames, and he named them quite plainly, while adding quite rash statements about them. He insisted that I should talk to Mme la dauphine often in private, that the King wanted it and that he, the duc d'Aiguillon, had been ordered to tell me so. He mentioned lightly the cold reception he had received from Mme l'archiduchesse on the day of his presentation as minister, while protesting his respectful attachment for H.R.H. and his desire to merit her kindness. I replied that I would use every care for the best; but that if my advice was incessantly contradicted by other advice, it would be difficult for it to be wholly effective.

It remains to be seen whether the use the duc d'Aiguillon makes of what I told him, will not result in compromising me with Mme la dauphine herself. It is clear that the duc d'Aiguillon's step was decided in the comtesse du Barry's council and that it has as aim that of leading Mme la dauphine step by step to treating this favourite better.

MARIA THERESA TO MERCY, 8 JULY 1771

Despite my daughter's good disposition, I always tremble when thinking of the wicked nature of her associates and how she is obsessed with them. Among them there are only too many of Mme de Narbonne's type. I am further disturbed by her dislike of useful, sound occupations therefore I will again emphasize the need for steady reading. You will see in the enclosed copy of her last letter, how laconic she is in replying to the different points in my long letter, especially to that relative to her passion for horse riding.

It is true that I would never approve of her according the dominant party a too marked reception, which would approach baseness, but that she treats them well, without affectation, as people whom the King wishes to distinguish and about whom she must ignore anything to be despised in their character and conduct.

I recognize my daughter in her refusal to host the balls [Edit: because of the expense], but what the duc d' Aiguillon said to you about her, merits your attention, and hers even more; it is especially remarkable that the duc d'Aiguillon repeated what Mme de Noailles had already said about the faults which the King found in my daughter's conduct.

MERCY TO MARIA THERESA, 24 JULY 1771

I charged the abbe de Vermond to warn H.R.H that the dominant party was complaining of being badly treated [and] that it was a serious matter…[but I told the abbe de Vermond to give her no details]. That same evening, Mme la dauphine was playing cards with the King and all the royal family, and, finding herself sitting beside the comtesse du Barry, H.R.H. adopted a relaxed expression which betrayed neither disgust nor temper; she spoke to the favourite when required to by the game, with good grace, no affectation and without either too much or too little being said.

Next day, the duc d'Aiguillon presented himself at Mme la dauphine's card game and was treated marvellously; H.R.H. spoke to him with charming gaiety; the duke seemed slightly embarrassed and only replied in monosyllables. However this had the good effect I had hoped for.

That day H.R.H. wanted to return from Marly on foot; the people lined her route and seemed overcome with admiration. When she arrived at the gates of Versailles Park, Mme la dauphine, noticing a huge crowd, slipped away like a flash. [Later I asked H.R.H.]…why she had disappeared and she replied, "Because there were too many people." I recognised Mesdames in this and I hazarded some reflections on the usefulness of attracting the love and attachment of the people, by showing herself to them with kindness and no repugnance. Then I told Mme la dauphine all that the duc d'Aiguillon had told me. H.R.H. listened attentively although she had heard it all before, so I tried to make it more striking.

She spoke to me of the different people in favour, with an astonishing accuracy, but, at the same time she agreed on the necessity of being careful with them and indeed she told me she was resolved to this, and I would see the results soon. Since then Mme l'archiduchesse has observed this carefully.

When the duc d'Aiguillon presented the ambassador, [Edit: Rohan], Mme la dauphine treated the minister kindly and said a few polite words to the ambassador. These circumstances had all the success desirable and, in my last two conversations with the duc d'Aiguillon, I found him very pleased with the treatment he was receiving from Mme la dauphine; he asked me "to direct him" (those were his words) "in how to earn H.R.H.'s trust."

Mme la dauphine had a slight fever and during her indisposition, M le dauphin showed her much loving care; the King went to see her several times a day and stayed for quite a long time with H.R.H., adopting a tone of friendship and ease which proves his liking for her.

The progress which this princess is making on M le dauphin's soul is daily becoming more remarkable. On Monday, in the presence of M. and Mme la comtesse de Provence, Mme la dauphine rebuked M le dauphin on his immoderate taste for the hunt, which was destroying his health, and on the rough and neglected look he was acquiring as a result. M le dauphin thought he would cut short this reproach by retiring to his rooms, but Mme la dauphine followed him, and continued to tell him quite forcefully of the drawbacks in his way of life. This resulted in M le dauphin becoming so

93

upset that he began to cry. Mme la dauphine then began to cry too and the reconciliation was very loving.

Mme l'archiduchesse did not forget that the quarrel had begun in Mme la comtesse de Provence's rooms; she took M le dauphin back there. M. and Mme de Provence asked if peace had been made; M le dauphin replied gallantly that lovers' quarrels never lasted long.

The friendship between Mme la dauphine and Mme de Provence is becoming stronger; Mme la dauphine is naturally cheerful and friendly with her; Mme de Provence responds with consideration, goodwill and trust. Because of her quite cold and reserved manner, she has disconcerted all the plans which the comtesse du Barry had formed for her. The cabal seems embarrassed by this miscalculation, and that is what has determined these people to make new attempts to attract Mme la dauphine's good will. For some days the comtesse du Barry has been praising Mme l'archiduchesse's face and her natural graces, and speaking unfavourably about Mme la comtesse de Provence.

It has always struck me that Mesdames, while encouraging Mme la dauphine to be severe and silent [Edit: to the comtesse du Barry], act in a measured way themselves in their behaviour to the comtesse du Barry, and this conduct is all the more strange as it would appear that they wish to use Mme la dauphine as an instrument of a hatred they themselves dare not admit.

MARIA THERESA TO MARIE ANTOINETTE, 17 AUGUST 1771

I received your portrait, it is very like you; it has delighted me and all the family; it is in my office where I work, and the miniature is in my bedroom where I work in the evening; thus I have you always with me, always before my eyes; you are of course always in my heart.

Mercy tells me you have already begun to act on his advice, by treating the dominant party politely. I will not say anything else about this matter; Mercy is charged to speak plainly to you about it. I am always sure of your success when

94

you undertake something, the good Lord having blessed you with a lovely face and so much charm, in addition to your kindness, that all hearts belong to you, when you wish; however they claim that you are beginning to ridicule people, that will justly rebound on you. In trying to please five or six young people you will alienate everyone else. This fault in a princess, my dear daughter, is a serious one; it will be imitated by all the courtiers, and it will drive away the decent people, who will not wish to be ridiculed, or angered, so that finally all that will be left will be bad company, who will draw you gradually into every vice.[15]

Everything I hear about how you four get on so well together gives me great pleasure: you are much better looking than your sister in law but her character is more sound and she knows more; you can only gain therefore from always remaining friends, and naturally you will spend many years together. It is necessary to have a good relationship with her, both for your personal reasons as well as for those of the state. So long as you are friends, there will be few people who will dare to make trouble; but the slightest coolness would leave the field open and you would feel the repercussions only too well in lack of peace of mind and a dulling of your happiness.

Mercy told me that the little writing desk that I sent you gave you great pleasure; that you immediately said the sweetest and most touching things. Imagine what effect that had on me; therefore do not neglect these resources of love and kindness which you possess. I want you to be happy and avoid the traps you cannot see because of your youth.

MERCY TO MARIA THERESA, 2 SEPTEMBER 1771

Sacred Majesty, on the 25th, [I saw Mme la dauphine]... and I recalled the interview I had had with the duc

---

[15] Maria Theresa and Mercy both tended to exaggerate when trying to guide Marie Antoinette's behaviour. As a result, in later years when they truly had good reason to threaten dire consequences from her behaviour, there was in effect nothing left to say.

d'Aiguillon. I firmly insisted on the necessity of talking to the King.

Mme l'archiduchesse showed a lot of repugnance to making this step, which, according to her, would produce no other effect than that of embarrassing the King, and make him assume a cold manner without explaining himself. H.R.H. cited as proof what had happened to her, a few months before, when she had complained to the King of charging the comtesse de Noailles with talking to her, instead of telling her directly himself. On that occasion, without replying, the King had changed the subject, and Mme la dauphine believed he would do the same again this time.

I told her that neither the King's embarrassment nor his silence should prevent Mme l'archiduchesse from talking to him when it was a question of enlightening him on her conduct, as indirect explanations were always subject to doubt, apart from the possible abuse of this method by those charged to employ it. H.R.H. replied that she would think about it, and in the meantime she would be so careful in her conduct and her speech, that there would surely be no reason to complain.

The duc d'Aiguillon told me that the King wished to talk to me privately, the day after next, in the comtesse du Barry's rooms. Two days later, the duc d'Aiguillon took me to the comtesse du Barry's rooms, where the comtesse du Barry received me with most marked attentions. She begged me to sit beside her.

The favourite told me that she knew that for a long time they had been trying to destroy her in Mme la dauphine's eyes and that to do so, they had had recourse to the most atrocious calumnies, daring to attribute to her, du Barry, disrespectful words about H.R.H., that, far from having to reproach herself with such a fault, she had always joined those who justifiably praised Mme l'archiduchesse's charms, that, although this princess had always treated her harshly and with a sort of contempt, she had never allowed herself complaints against H.R.H., but only against those who inspired this aversion in her; that when it had been a question of some things which Mme la dauphine seemed to wish, (as lately, the salaries for members of her household), she, du Barry…[had urged the

King to grant this, and when the King came, I could confirm this].

I replied to the favourite, claiming ignorance of the aversion and coldness she had felt from Mme la dauphine.[16] I assured her that the character of this princess was not compatible with sentiments of hatred and that such conjectures were based on vague words rather than realities. Then the King arrived by a little stairway, one end of which terminated in the room I was in. The comtesse du Barry retired.

The King, while coming up to me, said to me: "Until now you have been the empress' ambassador, but I would like you to be my ambassador now, at least for some time." After this beginning the King became embarrassed; he told me that he had wanted to talk to me in private about Mme la dauphine, that he loved her with all his heart, and found her charming, but that, being young and lively, and "having a husband who was not capable of guiding her," it was impossible for Mme l'archiduchesse to avoid the traps which were set for her by intriguers; and that, knowing that Y.M. trusted me, the King had decided to trust me also in this matter, involving as it did his happiness and that of the royal family.

I replied "that if the King would discuss his wishes with Mme l'archiduchesse himself, he would certainly find her eager to obey him and to please him." The King replied that he disliked reprimanding his children, that he begged me to do so; he then told me that he noted with displeasure that Mme la dauphine was allowing others to inspire her with prejudices and hatreds and that she treated those whom the King admitted into his private circle badly, and affectedly so; that, without thinking of controlling Mme l'archiduchesse's preferences for this or that person, she was only being asked to treat each person presented to her as they had a right to expect and that if she did not do so, her conduct could lead to scenes at court and encourage intrigue and party spirit.

The King repeated to me several times: "See Mme la dauphine often; I authorise you to tell her all you wish as

---

[16] The spin doctors of Tony Blair and Gordon Brown's 'New Labour' would surely have regarded Mercy as one of their own.

coming from me; bad advice is given to Mme la dauphine, it is necessary that she does not follow it." After these words the King immediately added: "You see how I trust you, since I tell you what I think about what is happening in my family." This seems to me to refer to the advice given by Mme Adelaide...[The King told me]: "I will see you from time to time; you may say whatever you consider appropriate."

On the 1st of August, Mme la dauphine followed the hunt in a carriage. It was necessary to cross a field of wheat to reach the stag but Mme l'archiduchesse refused, saying those who farmed the land were not sufficiently compensated on these occasions. This display of kindness and humanity had a marvellous effect and was the subject of conversation throughout Compiegne. During this hunt, the King came to see Mme la dauphine several times; he took her on his knees and hugged her a thousand times.[17]

[Later] H.R.H. told me she had come to a decision and she would talk to the comtesse du Barry on one occasion only, that M. le dauphin approved, but that Mme Adelaide was opposed to the plan of talking to the King, as the monarch would only become embarrassed and besides would explain nothing.

I pointed out all the weakness in this argument. H.R.H., who rapidly agrees with everything that is reasonable, promised to talk... [to the King]. I added that the King was disheartened by the restraint and embarrassment with which his children greeted him, that, never having found sweetness nor enjoyable company with them, he had looked for it elsewhere, which was unfortunate for the state and more so for the royal family.

[A few days later]...H.R.H told me in good faith that "her courage was completely lacking" and that she did not feel herself strong enough to talk to the King, as she had promised before. It was not possible for me to persuade her to change her mind.

On the 10th, I learned that the comtesse du Barry intended going to court next day. I informed Mme la dauphine

---

[17] Louis XV had an infamous liking for young girls

of this. H.R.H. assured me that she would say a few words to the favourite, but that she wanted me there; that at the end of the card game I was to approach the favourite and talk to her; that Mme l'archiduchesse, while walking round, would stop beside me, and as if by chance, address a word to the comtesse du Barry. H.R.H. added that this arrangement was necessary to reassure her as she felt very nervous.

I observed that it was only necessary to make a firm resolution to carry out this plan, because, without that resolution, my role would appear to have been to induce Mme la dauphine to talk to the favourite, and that I would only be ridiculed if H.R.H. showed invincible repugnance of a sudden, to that step. Mme l'archiduchesse was distressed that I had the slightest doubt about the firmness of her resolution; I begged her not to confide this arrangement to Mesdames; she promised, but unfortunately the secret was not kept.

On the evening of the 11th, I went to court; the comtesse du Barry was there with her friends; Mme la dauphine called me over to tell me she was nervous, but that the arrangements were still the same. Towards the end of card play, H.R.H. sent me to stand beside the favourite, with whom I engaged in conversation. At that moment all eyes turned towards me; Mme la dauphine began to talk to the ladies, she came closer and was only a couple of steps away when Mme Adelaide, who had not lost sight of her, raised her voice and said: "It is time to leave, let's go, we will wait for the King at my sister Victoire's." Then Mme la dauphine left and the arrangement came to nothing.

This little scene was followed by much talk at Mesdames; they criticised my advice a great deal; Mme la dauphine however was good enough to defend me, especially after M. le dauphin said calmly: "As for me, I think Mercy is right and you are wrong."

After supper, the King came up to me looking embarrassed; finally, having almost pushed me into a corner, he asked if I had seen Mme la dauphine and immediately added: "Your advice did not bear fruit; I will have to help you!" I was about to reply, but the King [walked away]...I very much doubt that the King will talk to Mme la dauphine, as he will be too embarrassed; but that is unfortunate as the King, while remaining silent, has recourse to showing his discontent in sulkiness and coldness. The royal family is sure the King will say nothing, therefore feel they can dispense with caution.

After what happened on the 11th, Mme la dauphine told me most kindly that she was very sorry to have compromised me, that if her aunts had not opposed it, she would have followed my advice; then H.R.H. admitted that she believed my advice was good but she was afraid to displease Mme Adelaide, and besides felt sure that the King would say nothing.

Mme l'archiduchesse read your letter and exclaimed over the inexactitude of the reports, especially that concerning her mockery of people.

MARIE ANTOINETTE TO MARIA THERESA, 2 SEPTEMBER 1771

Mercy has spoken to me of what Y.M. instructed him to say; I believe that he will be pleased with the results, and I hope you are persuaded that my greatest pleasure consists in pleasing you. I will also try to treat Broglie well, although he was lacking in respect to me. [Edit: this relates to a reply which Mme la dauphine had sent to Broglie, dictated by the comtesse de Narbonne. Maria Theresa was worried because she knew Broglie was very powerful, as he controlled Louis XV's secret correspondence]

I am in despair that you believe them when they tell you that I do not talk to people any more; you must trust me very little to believe that I am so unreasonable that I amuse myself with five or six young people, and do not bother with those I must honour.

I pity my brother Ferdinand as the moment of his departure approaches, knowing from my own experience how much it costs to live far from one's family. I can well believe his marriage will be fruitful: as for me, I continue to live in hope, and the love which M. le dauphin shows me more and more every day, does not leave me in doubt, although I would prefer that the waiting was over. We four live in harmony. The comtesse de Provence is very gentle and gay in private, although not in public. I will not mention the unpleasantness here; M. de Mercy will surely tell you what is necessary; as for me, I become involved as little as possible.

MARIA THERESA TO MARIE ANTOINETTE, 30 SEPTEMBER 1771

This fear of, and embarrassment at talking to the King, the best of fathers, or to people to whom you are advised to talk! Admit that this embarrassment, this fear of even saying good day; a word about their clothes, about a triviality, which cost you so much, is mere posturing, or worse! You have let yourself be drawn into such subjugation that reason, even your duty, are no longer sufficient to persuade you. I can no longer remain silent after Mercy's letter, and all he told you that the King wished and that your duty demanded, but you still dared to fail him; what good reason do you have? None. You must neither know nor see Barry in any way other than that of being a woman admitted to court and the society of the King. You failed him because of a shameful obligingness towards people who have subjugated you by treating you as a child, procuring you rides on horseback, on donkeys, the company of children, dogs; these are the important reasons which attach you to them rather than to your master, and which will eventually render you ridiculous, neither loved nor esteemed.

You started off so well. Your expressions, your judgement, when not directed by others, are always appropriate and for the best. You are afraid to talk to the King, but not to disobey him or offend him.

You tell me that, because you love me, you treat the Broglies well, although they did not show respect for you; here is something else amiss, again from the same source: how is it that a little Broglie can be disrespectful to you? I do not understand that; no one has ever been disrespectful to me, nor to any of your ten brothers and sisters. It is sufficient for you to know that the Broglies are esteemed by the King, and that consequently you must not listen, nor act, nor even think otherwise.

I delayed the courier in order to calm myself down, and I cannot hide from you that I was so overwhelmed with his news that I needed time to recover. Just imagine how upset I am, and how much I would like, at the cost of my own life, to be useful to you and withdraw you from your self induced abandonment.

After letting you see the drawbacks, you would be inexcusable if you did not remedy the situation. I want you to begin to act independently. Excessive obligingness is weakness or baseness; it is necessary for you to know how to act your part in order to be esteemed; you can do this if you can be bothered to stir yourself a little and follow the advice you are given; if you cannot be bothered, I foresee great misfortune for you: nothing but petty problems and petty cabals, which will make you deeply unhappy. I would like to prevent that and beg you to accept the advice of a mother who knows the world and idolises her children, and only wants to spend her sad days being useful to them. With all my love; do not think I am angry, but upset and concerned with your well being.

MARIA THERESA TO MERCY, SEPTEMBER 1771

You will find the enclosed letter to my daughter quite severe, but having failed you so strikingly, it is necessary to shake her from the dependency into which she has sunk. If you find it too severe, you can keep it and tell her that I have charged you to give her my excuses but I was not able to write her. Tell the abbe de Vermond I can never sufficiently thank him for his attachment and his advice, and ask him to please continue in the same way for some time, that the happiness of my daughter depends on his advice and yours.

MARIE ANTOINETTE TO MARIA THERESA, 13 OCTOBER 1771

You will permit me to justify myself on all the points you made to me. Firstly I am desperately sorry that you believe all the lies they tell you about what is happening here, rather than what Mercy or I can tell you. Do you really believe that we wish to deceive you?[18] I have good reason to believe that the King himself does not want me to talk to Barry, apart from the fact he has never spoken of her to me. He has been even friendlier to me since learning that I did not talk to her, and if you were able to see, as I do, all that goes on here, you would see that that woman and her clique would not be satisfied with a word, it would have to be done repeatedly over and over again.

You can be assured that I have no need to be directed by anyone in matters relating to courtesy. As for the Broglies, if you were better informed, my dear mother, you would know that it is possible for a little Broglie to be lacking in respect here, but not in Vienna.

The death of Mme de Villars caused me a lot of trouble. I asked him [Edit: the King] to agree to one of my ladies having the position of dame d'atours, but he refused because of Mme du Barry. I have been given the duchesse de Cosse. She has a very good reputation; the King asked me to tell her of her appointment telling me he would not tell anyone; however, the day before, M. d'Aiguillon had announced it to Mme de Cosse and fifty people knew of it. I complained to the King that the indiscretion of his friends was making me ridiculous; he received me well and said he was sorry.

You will surely know, my very dear mother, of the misfortune of Mme la duchesse de Chartres who has just had a stillborn child; although that is appalling, I wish it were me, but there are still no signs of it [Edit: pregnancy].

In order to let you see the injustice of Barry's friends, I must tell you that I spoke to her at Marly; I will not say that I will never talk to her again, but I cannot agree to talk to her on a specific day and at a specific time, so that she can tell everyone in advance and boast about it. I beg your pardon for writing so forcefully on this matter; if you could have seen the anguish your dear letter caused me, you would pardon the agitation in my language and you would believe that, now as

---

[18] Marie Antoinette's reply to her mother indicates, at best, naivety, although she certainly had some justification for her resentment of du Barry

103

throughout my life, I am deeply penetrated by most loving and most respectful submission to my dear mother.

MERCY TO MARIA THERESA, 15 OCTOBER 1771

In my audience of the 30th of August, I found H.R.H. more penetrated than ever with the impressions which her aunts give her; but she agreed at the same time that she followed their advice less from persuasion, than from indulgence and obligingness. I cited what had happened when the marquise de Pompadour was alive. Mme Adelaide, having shown a lot of hatred towards her, had finally thrown herself completely into her arms to the point of asking the favourite about the choice of a confessor.

[Mme du Barry sent for me and told me she had written to the King saying she no longer wished to be present on the occasions when Mesdames were present]…and had received a satisfactory reply from the monarch. I decided that it would be a good idea to see the King's letter, therefore I feigned not to fully understand her and made objections so that, although reluctantly, she showed me the letter which I read through completely.

The King told her in the letter that he loved her very much. The King then continued that if he ordered Mesdames to treat her better, they would do so, but with bad grace; that he attributed their coolness to the comtesse du Barry less to party spirit favouring the duc de Choiseul, than to religious principles and scruples; that the late Queen, although very pious, had never behaved thus, that the King was tired with the dreariness and trouble which Mesdames occasioned on the little trips...

I was struck by this letter. The King usually writes to his children, his ministers and his mistresses from timidity, embarrassment or any other reason, what he finds repugnant to say. I suggested to her [Edit: Mme du Barry] that from reasons of prudence, she should be careful with regard to Mme la dauphine, and think of the present and the future. She understood and received all this very well [Edit: Louis XV was not a young man].

Y.M. will recall that…[Mme la dauphine did not want the duc de la Vauguyon's daughter in law as her dame d'atours] but the King had agreed to this. The duc de la Vauguyon had been promised this, and had it in writing. He had M. le dauphin write to the duc d'Aiguillon…[about this]. Immediately afterwards M. le dauphin excused himself to Mme la dauphine by saying that he had only written the letter because he wanted to stop the duc de la Vauguyon pestering him[19], but that, apart from that, he was neither interested in his governor, nor his business. The King did not know what to do and therefore asked me through the duc d'Aiguillon what he should do. I replied that the King's promise to Mme la dauphine was clear and precise and seemed to annul any preceding engagement, that besides the duchesse de Saint-Megrin was very young and this could serve as reason but that it would also be difficult to have such a person in a position so close to Mme la dauphine if she felt distant from her. Matters remained at this point.

SECRET LETTER

Although Y.M. deigned to authorise me to suppress your letter to Mme la dauphine, I thought it best to give it to her, as there was no time to lose in remedying a fault which has already taken such deep root that I fear Y.M. will be obliged to maintain for some time yet a tone of authority, which alone can make Mme la dauphine reject the harmful prejudices inspired in her by Mme Adelaide.

Mme la dauphine, who was at her toilette, opened your letter. She read it quickly and I noticed that she was struck by it; but, as I have learned to know what her initial expressions indicate, I was not very satisfied by these I noticed on this occasion.

H.R.H. said very little to me, in a tone which showed impatience rather than docility or conviction of being in error: as a result I can guess how she will reply. I do not doubt that she will be reticent to Y.M. about the favourite; Mme

---

[19] When the dauphin became King, his weakness was fatal for his family, and indeed for all France, especially during the Revolution.

l'archiduchesse will probably say that the King has not shown displeasure about all this; that what the monarch instructed me to say was only due to the cabal's nagging, but that, at heart, the King is quite indifferent as to how the favourite is treated; that is what Mme Adelaide never stops telling Mme la dauphine.

Apart from this, whatever Mme la dauphine's response, it is certain that Y.M. 's letter will have a profound effect on her and I only have to wait for a moment of reflection to successfully reinforce all the points which Y.M. mentioned.

MARIA THERESA TO MARIE ANTOINETTE, 31 OCTOBER 1771

This letter will arrive much too late for your birthday; but you can be sure that I am thinking of it and that I daily thank God for you.

I did not think it wrong for you to forcefully defend yourself on the subject of my last letter. Everything which shows me your sensitivity and your candour is dear to me; but consider a little if your reaction was not impatience rather than distress at my remonstrances; but what hurt me, and convinced me that you do not really want to correct yourself, was your total silence about your aunts, even though they formed the main point in my letter and are the cause of all your mistakes.

Do my advice and love merit less attention than theirs? I admit, that reflection pierces my heart. Consider their role in this world and the approval they have earned, with, it costs me to say this, the role I have played in comparison. You should prefer to believe me, when I warn you or advise you to do the opposite of what they do. Due to their kindness and habit of letting themselves be governed by others, they have rendered themselves odious, disagreeable and boring even to themselves, and the subject of cabals and vexations. I see you taking the same path therefore should I be silent? I love you too much to do so or wish to do so and your affected silence on this point gave me a lot of pain and little hope of change.

The good news from your dear sister the Queen of Naples is overwhelming me with joy, and that of Ferdinand, who is delighted with his wife. All their news, which should have filled me with contentment, was spoiled by reflections on your dangerous situation, which is even more so, as it seems you do not realize it or do not wish to do so, as you are not using the necessary means or the advice you are given, to extricate yourself from the danger.

For months now I have heard nothing about your reading. All that makes me tremble: I see you going astray at the very least, and at worst, moving calmly and nonchalantly towards your ruin. You do not realize what pain and effort will be required to return to the right path again. If you would only believe what I say now, it would not cost you so much.

You tell me you spoke to the King; that should be a daily occurrence and not something you do only when you have requests to make. You will waste your time if you write to him; neither your writing nor the message will succeed, on the other hand there is something so touching about you that it is difficult to refuse you in person; that is a gift from God, for which you should be grateful, and use it for his glory or for the good of others.

MARIE ANTOINETTE TO MARIA THERESA, 15 NOVEMBER 1771

My dear mother, I was touched by what you said about my birthday. I want above all to profit from your good advice, my dear mother. The letter from my brother [Edit: Ferdinand] gave me such pleasure that I cannot describe it; it seems to me that I love him even more for it; he will certainly be a good husband, and will make his wife happy.

I do not believe I was wrong to give in to my immediate thought and tell M. le dauphin the little secret! [Edit: Maria Theresa believed that Ferdinand's wife would soon be pregnant] I did not speak reproachfully, however he was a little embarrassed. I am still hopeful; he loves me a great deal and does all I want and will succeed when he is less awkward.

I can certainly assure you that, although I showed you my sensitivity quite vividly, it was only sensitivity. The friends of that creature cannot complain that I treat them badly.

When I wrote to you, my dear mother, that I did not need advice on how to be polite, I meant that I had not consulted my aunts. No matter how much friendship I feel for them, I will never compare them to my loving and respectable mother; I do not believe I am blind to their faults, but I believe people exaggerate them to you.

Although the Queen's condition often makes me think of mine, I still share my dear sister's joy [Edit: Caroline in Naples was pregnant].

Since summer the trips and hunting have prevented me from doing regular reading; however I have read something almost every day.

I cannot tell you, my dear mother, how much I desire and hope to give you as much satisfaction as my brother and sister [Edit: that is, become pregnant].

MERCY TO MARIA THERESA, 16 NOVEMBER 1771
SECRET LETTER

For some weeks, M. le dauphin has no longer been recognisable because of the advantageous change in his manner towards Mme l'archiduchesse, as he is attentive to her to the point of gallantry and shows her exceptional care. [For example]…he hugs her, shows eagerness to be with Mme la dauphine as much as possible, and to inform her about everything, in fact he shows his love in every possible way and it seems to grow from day to day.

The King was recently in the bosom of the family, and said jokingly that he could hope for a successor only from M. le comte d'Artois [Edit: the younger brother of the dauphin and the comte de Provence]. M. le dauphin turned towards Mme Victoire and said laughingly: "My father has little opinion of me, but he will soon be disabused." Meanwhile Mme la dauphine is calm and tranquil on the subject and has stopped making confidences about this.

MARIE ANTOINETTE TO MARIA THERESA, 18 DECEMBER 1771

My dear mother, please accept my respects and good wishes for the New Year; your children wish only to give you satisfaction, and this is my wish as much as any of the others. If you could only have seen the joy I felt when I received your last letter and how relieved I was to see you were not displeased with me! It would have persuaded you that I will never be happy, dear mother, unless I am pleasing you.

I enclose my measurements and these of M. le dauphin; mine were taken without shoes or a high hairstyle. Although I have grown a lot, I have not become thinner; as for M. le dauphin, his complexion is clearing and his health becoming stronger; every day he becomes more pleasing to me and the only thing lacking to make my happiness complete is to be [pregnant] like the Queen; I hope it will happen soon.

When I wrote to you about Barry, my dear mother, it was for your eyes only, and you may be sure that I am too prudent to talk in that way with the people here.

Today I was present while M. le dauphin was shooting; he shoots very well. He killed about forty birds; this proves that he is not as short sighted as is believed.

I am delighted that the news from Milan is still good; my new sister in law makes me jealous, her marriage is so wonderful. Although I am quite content, I envy my sister Marie's happiness in seeing you often; I dare say that I would be equally worthy of this, because of the respectful and deep love I feel for my dear mother.

MERCY TO MARIA THERESA, 19 DECEMBER 1771

Mme la dauphine told me she appreciated Y.M.'s love, shown in your concern to warn her about what was necessary for wise and good conduct. She spoke with admirable candour of all the little failings due to high spirits and thoughtlessness that she had to reproach herself with; "but" she added, "if the empress saw all that happened here, she would pardon me; no one could tolerate it."

Mme l'archiduchesse, speaking about Mesdames, said she knew their faults and their weak characters; but however they were her only company; that she sometimes felt fleeting displeasure with them, but that it was necessary to ignore some weaknesses in those with whom she was obliged to live. She talked very well about the intriguing and dangerous character of the comtesse de Narbonne; I could see that H.R.H. was beginning to make very just and sound judgements about her associates.

I spoke about the favourite; but I found Mme l'archiduchesse as little disposed as usual to listen to talk about this matter. She only replied in a vague and indecisive way.

The ascendancy which the comtesse du Barry has over the King has hardly any limit; it influences everything concerning the royal family, and in a very visible way, and the more the favourite is embarrassed by bad treatment, the more she tries to assert her momentary powers in order to show her resentment. As a result, every favour requested by Mesdames is refused, they incessantly experience unpleasantness of all kinds, and the King is detaching himself gradually from his children. This is leading to irritating scandal.

Until now I have succeeded in separating Mme la dauphine's cause from that of Mesdames, by blaming them for everything; but eventually it would be almost impossible for Mme l'archiduchesse not to be involved, and, taking into consideration the principles and maxims of the dominant party at this court, and the inclination of its members to look at everything from the viewpoint of their personal interests, it is not inconceivable that fear of Mme la dauphine's unremitting hatred could lead them to make errors of judgement, which in turn could even influence in very important and serious matters. However strange this reflection may sound, the disorder of this court seems to warrant it, as does the suspect character of those who have most credit in it.

While waiting for Mme la dauphine to adopt rather more politic behaviour, my sole concern has been to pacify the favourite and inspire in her, hope for a future more in conformity with her wishes. Thus I maintain myself in her confidence; I am instructed of her fears, of her ways; they have decreased the observation and spying which they employed in relation to Mme la dauphine and I feel I have obtained in this way, an essential advantage.

Lately M. le comte d'Artois told H.R.H. that when praising her to the duc de la Vauguyon, the latter had contradicted him with some bitterness and expressed himself unfavourably about Mme la dauphine, that the comtesse de Marsan went even further in displaying bad will, and that she was as malicious and venomous as possible about Mme l'archiduchesse.

H.R.H. spoke to me about this with some emotion and I had no difficulty in making her realize that it was beneath her to fret over such trifles, which could only be despised, and merited no attention other than that of being careful in the future in the presence of these people, and not furnishing them with matter to exercise their misplaced impertinence. Mme la dauphine seemed to adopt this sentiment and did not treat the duc de la Vauguyon nor the comtesse de Marsan any different to usual.

It is not so easy for me to persuade Mme la dauphine to act as I advise on the question of M. le comte de Provence, whom she distrusts and, truth be told, with reason. This young prince appears to be totally false and his minor political trickery seems beyond his age. He has extensive ambition[20] , he attracts the dominant party to him by every means and is trying to establish himself as the focus of this party; this behaviour greatly shocks Mme la dauphine, and despite the strongest representations, it is not always possible to prevent her showing her resentment.

Recently, [at a fete]…the favourite received a very distinguished reception from Mme la comtesse de Provence,

---

[20] The falsity and ambition of Provence was amply demonstrated after June 1791, when he escaped from France to Belgium, while Marie Antoinette and her husband failed in their escape attempt, and were dragged back to Paris by the National Guard and a threatening rag tag army. Then, as Louis XVl continued to pretend to the French people that he was happy with his situation, whilst secretly appealing to his allies to invade France and 'free' him, Provence undermined every statement he made, by proclaiming that his brother was lying – as he was.

who received her in her private rooms. No more was necessary to invite disgust at Versailles. Four days later Mme la dauphine went to see Mme de Provence at la Muette [Edit: one of the royal family's residences]; the fete was mentioned and Mme la comtesse de Provence was embarrassed but excused herself by saying she had only behaved as M. le comte de Provence had wanted. When Mme l'archiduchesse returned to Versailles, she found the prince at the aunts and rowed him severely on the duplicity of his character and on different points of conduct in which she recalled what he had done with a bitter jokiness which totally disconcerted M. le comte de Provence.

Later Mme la dauphine impetuously ran to M. le dauphin, threw her arms round his neck and hugging him tenderly, told him: "I feel, my dear husband, that I love you more each day. Your honesty and frankness charm me; the more I compare you with the others [Edit: his brothers], the more I know how much you are worth more than them."

[Mme la dauphine]…told me this with her usual kindness and trust. I told her that it was necessary in such cases to be guarded and reserved and not to give him the opportunity to harm Mme la dauphine; that besides, by causing discord in the royal family, it could lead to very regrettable consequences in the present and the future; that finally, at such a critical time, patience and prudence were the only remedies as they let one gain time and [that it was not a good idea]…to push people to their limit. H.R.H. listened to me attentively, but it was impossible for me to shift her from her indecision as to what to do on these occasions.

SECRET LETTER

The King, although not old in years, is very much so in the way of life he leads; he is weakening; he could fail in a few years. The dominant party cannot envisage this happening without trembling. They can see that Mme la dauphine is acquiring a decided influence over M le dauphin, and consequently their future will one day be in the hands of this princess. These reflections are based on the fear which a bad conscience always occasions, and this fear could provoke these wicked people to extremes.

I have tried to demonstrate these truths to Mme la dauphine, telling her that the best way to preserve herself, is to let these people see that there is a possibility they will be pardoned, when they merit it, by better behaviour. This method calms the spirits and stops them from going to extremes. H.R.H., because of her high spirits and her extreme dislike of thinking for a minute about matters which displease her, was not sufficiently convinced by my representations, as, in all that concerns politic conduct, I cannot succeed in fixing her attention.

The duchesse de Brancas, lady of honour to Mme la comtesse de Provence, is about to lose her post because of her marked opposition to the favourite. Such events are becoming more and more frequent here: they cause scandal and lead to arguments within the royal family.

H.R.H. told me of her embarrassment in talking to you about Mesdames. It is true, as you say, that it is because Mme l'archiduchesse dislikes occupations which entail repose, that she is so laconic in her letters. She always plans to tell you a thousand things; but when she has to sit down at her desk, her high spirits put obstacles in the way and this means that she often attaches to a short phrase a much more extensive sense than it is possible to remark. Sometimes she talks like that, and it is only from habit and reflection that I succeed in losing nothing of what H.R.H. wishes to tell me.

1772

MARIA THERESA TO MERCY, 4 JANUARY 1772

The contents [of your letters] show me how you strive to be useful to my daughter, as well as letting me see the critical situation she is in. I realize the danger with anguish. Your task is in truth a painful one, especially considering the nonchalance and thoughtlessness of my daughter (and some stubborness), accustomed to content herself with fleeting amusements without thinking of the consequences: but that is a further reason to encourage you to redouble your efforts.

MARIE ANTOINETTE TO MARIA THERESA, 21 JANUARY 1772

I am sure that Mercy will have told you about my behaviour on New Year's Day, and I hope you are pleased. You may well believe that I will always abandon any prejudices and dislikes I have, so long as no one suggests anything ostentatious or dishonourable, to me. If a quarrel arose between my two families, I would be disconsolate; my heart will always incline towards Austria, which would make my duties here very hard to fulfil. The idea alone makes me tremble; I hope it will never happen, or that at least I will not be the cause. I am delighted that the news from Naples and Florence remains the same: I have a feeling that, when mine begin [Edit: pregnancies], they will follow one after another, and will bring joy to my dear mother.

I was very wrong in what I told you about the comte de Provence; he has greatly dishonoured himself in the affair of Mme de Brancas [Edit: dismissed from Mme de Provence's service, because of antagonism to Mme de. Barry]: his wife follows his lead in everything, but that is only from fear and stupidity, being, I believe, quite unhappy. Apart from that, I am

115

quite friendly with them, although I do not trust them as they are not as sincere as I am.

As for the comte d'Artois, although he is still being educated, he shows signs of honesty, which he cannot have acquired from his governor [Edit: the duc de la Vauguyon] He also has the approval of his older brother, who showed, in the business with Brancas, that he felt more friendship for and trust in his wife, than in the comte de Provence.

MERCY TO MARIA THERESA, 23 JANUARY 1772

Sacred Majesty, Mme l 'archiduchesse was overjoyed when she received your letter. "For once I am not scolded and the empress is beginning to see that I cannot change my behaviour vis-a-vis the favourite," she said. H.R.H. added that she had told you that harmony reigned between herself, Mme la comtesse and M. le comte de Provence, and that although some serious faults were attributed to the latter, she did not feel them to be well founded. Mme la dauphine told me she had said this to reassure Y.M., but that, in fact, she had very strong suspicions about M. le comte de Provence's character, and she was quite displeased with him.

I said that in relation to the comtesse du Barry, I feared that Mme l'archiduchesse read her own ideas into the thoughts of Y.M. H.R.H. did not seem pleased with this remark.

Mme la comtesse de Provence plays a suspect role; she sometimes complains of the necessity of conforming to her husband's requests, she would like it to seem that she dislikes doing so; however I am certain that this young princess is not acting in good faith and without saying too much to Mme la dauphine, I have begged her not to make very extensive confidences to Mme la comtesse de Provence in the course of their all too necessary association.

In relation to Mesdames, Y.M.'s advice has had some effect, and I see with great satisfaction that Mme l'archiduchesse (at least in some situations), is trying to free herself from Mme Adelaide's influence. I have a very recent proof in what happened on New Year's Day.

It is customary on that day for all the women presented to pay court to the royal family. I was informed that the comtesse du Barry intended doing so on New Year's Eve. I obtained an audience with Mme la dauphine, in which I used all possible means to persuade H.R.H. not to treat the favourite badly. It was only with great difficulty that I extracted a promise that she would not do so. It was essential that Mesdames were not consulted and fortunately that is what happened.

Next morning the comtesse du Barry appeared at Mme l'archiduchesse's; she had come with the duchesse d'Aiguillon and the marechale de Mirepoix. Mme la dauphine spoke firstly to the former; then passing in front of the favourite and looking at her without irritation or affectation, she said to her: "There are a lot of people here today at Versailles," after which H.R.H. spoke immediately to marechale de Mirepoix.

I went along to Mme l'archiduchesse's dinner, and after leaving the table she sent for me and told me: "I followed your advice, and Monsieur le dauphin is my witness." The prince began to smile, but said nothing; then Mme l'archiduchesse told me herself what had happened and finished by saying: "I have spoken once, but I have decided to leave things as they stand, and that woman will never again hear the sound of my voice."

This was the first time I found myself able to talk in front of M le dauphin and I decided to use this opportunity. First of all I complimented Mme l'archiduchesse on her reasonable behaviour in the morning; I permitted myself to make some plain remarks on the present situation of the royal family, on the drawbacks it must try to avoid, and finally on the necessity for prudent conduct which would not upset the King.

I saw that M le dauphin appreciated what I was saying; he marked approval with some gestures and nods of the head, without however saying a word. Mme l'archiduchesse took what I said a little more lightly, without however contradicting my reasoning. I feel that, since this audience, M le dauphin, (who has always treated me quite well), has shown me more kindness than usual, and I am the only foreign ambassador to whom he speaks now and again.

That evening, Mesdames reproached Mme la dauphine. The comtesse de Narbonne became carried away when talking about it and H.R.H. almost regretted what had happened.

H.R.H. is continuing to read regularly. She reads well written letters, historical anecdotes, sometimes plays but never novels or frivolous books for which she shows no curiosity. She has the ability of talking to a whole court in such a way that everyone can believe she is talking to each individually. Despite this ability, which makes Mme l'archiduchesse charming, it is nonetheless true that she does not talk enough to distinguished people and never talks to strangers.

There will be balls in the comtesse de Noailles' apartments, and I know they wish to exclude Mme la comtesse de Provence and that this plan was hatched in Mesdames' rooms. I am trying to prevent this.

Monsieur le dauphin persists in his kindness towards Mme la dauphine; but the point essential to their marriage remains the same. M. le comte de Provence is in the same situation and there is reason to believe that he will remain so longer than Monsieur le dauphin.

SECRET LETTER

Mme l'archiduchesse is bored with the King and does not always take the trouble to hide it; however it is certain that the King has the most decided inclination for Mme la dauphine, but she does not want to take advantage of it and I have little success in trying to persuade her to do so.

MARIA THERESA TO MERCY, 10 FEBRUARY 1772

I am pained at the King's decline; if he were to die just now, when the kingdom is in the greatest turmoil and at a crisis point, it would be the worst possible time.

MARIA THERESA TO MARIE ANTOINETTE, 13 FEBRUARY 1772

You tell me how you followed my advice on New Year's Day. The results have shown that this advice was good, and it made me laugh that you could imagine that either I or my minister would ever give you dishonourable or unworthy advice. You can see by this how much other people's prejudices and bad advice have captured your soul.

Your agitation after saying a few words, vowing not to do so again, all this makes me tremble for you; what interest could I have except in your welfare and even that of your country, your happiness and that of the dauphin, taking into consideration the critical situation in which you, the family and all the kingdom are placed, because of the intrigues and the factions.

Who is better placed to advise you and merit your trust, than my minister, who knows the country thoroughly and all its workings? He has nothing else to absorb him apart from your happiness. His attachment to you and his abilities must reassure you and you must use them as a resource in all the different situations in which you find yourself. But it is not enough only to converse with him: you must follow all his advice without exception: you must act formally and consistently in order to be in a position to cope with any occurrence. The King is old, the sickness he suffers from is not without cause: changes for good or ill could happen in relation to Barry, the ministers.

The comte de Provence's behaviour merits circumspection and your attention. You will find many people who will report what he has done and try to turn you against him; but be careful, they may be doing the same with him. Avoid any discord in the family; hide your feelings, do not respond to vexations and remain kind; that is the only way to maintain peace in the home. I repeat my dear daughter, if you love me follow my advice by doing what Mercy recommends, unhesitatingly and with trust.

I am sending you this separately, so that you can give it back to Mercy, as I do not want it to fall into the hands of others. If you want to see it again, you can ask him to bring it so you can go over it, and remind yourself of my loving advice, which will end only with my life, which you can make more or less happy.

MERCY TO MARIA THERESA, 29 FEBRUARY 1772

[Recently Mme la dauphine heard from the duc d'Aiguillon that you had been unwell]...From the first word he spoke, Mme la dauphine was so upset that she heard nothing else. The comtesse de Noailles [discovered that]...the indisposition had almost entirely ceased, however H.R.H. asked for a rosary which she had received from Y.M. and began to pray; M. le dauphin, who did not leave her, seemed to share his wife's grief and spoke to me later in a way which showed his respectful attachment to the sacred person of Y.M. [Later the duc d'Aiguillon complained to me]...about Mme la dauphine's reaction. Next day at Versailles, I succeeded in persuading Mme la dauphine that the duc d'Aiguillon had only acted with good intentions, and I also succeeded in persuading the minister that H.R.H. recognised the truth of this.

I found Mme la dauphine troubled by the contents of Y.M.'s last letter; she was greatly struck by the possibility of coolness developing between the two courts and what could cause this. She told me: "This is much more serious than I had imagined. You were right to tell me. I will tell the empress that I would never forgive myself if my conduct were to cause a rupture, and that rather than risk that, I am resolved to overcome my dislike of the favourite, that on all occasions my heart inclines me towards my family, and if there were quarrels, my duties here would become very difficult. [Mme la dauphine added]... "When M. le dauphin becomes King, there will be no quarelling [Edit: between the two countries]." This was said in a very touching way, which perfectly expressed Mme l'archiduchesse's feelings.

The balls which the comtesse de Noailles has been giving for Mme la dauphine have succeeded without occasioning trouble. It had firstly been thought to exclude M. le comte and Mme la comtesse de Provence but I vehemently opposed this so they limited themselves to inviting no one and

M. le comte and Mme la comtesse de Provence came without an entourage and these occasions passed with gaiety and simplicity.

There are 120,000 livres assigned to Mme la dauphine's wardrobe each year. When the duchesse de Villars was in position, her age and infirmity led to pillage in that department. When the duchesse de Cosse took over, she thought…[the excess expenditure] was due to Mme la dauphine's extravagance. On examining the accounts, I found outstanding depredations. [For example]…the wardrobe women claimed money for four pairs of shoes for Mme la dauphine each week, three ells of ribbon every day for Mme l'archiduchesse's hair. It was the same with an infinity of other articles. I urged Mme l'archiduchesse to thwart this abuse, with her dame d'atours, and I am sure that the original amount will now be sufficient.

Mme la dauphine is neither inclined to parsimony nor to extravagant expense. She has only used a fraction of the 1000 louis Y.M. gave me for her needs, and the little she has used has been spent on some presents and on alms.

No one governs her [Edit: Mme la dauphine]; she is treating the comtesse de Noailles better and everything is as desired.

In considering the events which could possibly occur, the death of the duc de la Vauguyon has been one of the most favourable to Mme l'archiduchesse. This former governor was not esteemed by M. le dauphin, however retained an ascendancy over him, which was very dangerous in such a malicious man. The demonstrations of the public have been punishment for his faults. The general joy was almost indecent when he died. M. le dauphin would not go to see him once. I asked Mme l'archiduchesse to try to engage him to carry out this act of propriety, but she could not. The King himself showed great indifference to the death of this courtier.

When doctor Ingenhouse was here again, I made several observations to him so that he could see things clearly, and he will give you an account of this.

M. le dauphin treats me daily with more and more kindness; he is so used to me that he comes to talk to me whenever he sees me, which until now he has done with no one, having taken as maxim not to talk to people except when he sees them in his rooms.

SECRET LETTER

The chancellor, with the aid of the archbishop of Paris, has been quite successful in involving Mme Louise [Edit: the King's other daughter, who had become a nun] in intrigues which this princess perhaps does not fully understand.

[Edit: In a letter from the baron de Pichler to Mercy, dated 4th of December 1771, Pichler wrote: "They say that the King and the duc d'Aiguillon have frequent discussions with Mme Louise, the Carmellite nun, who is supposed to be working hard to engage the pope to dissolve the marriage of Mme du Barry in order to place her in a position to be able to marry the King. The success of this negotiation is quite indifferent to the empress, she even knows only too well that it is the only way to pacify the King's conscience. H.M. wishes to know however if this rumour is based in truth."]

MARIA THERESA TO MERCY, 18 MARCH 1772

The prince de Rohan [Edit: French ambassador to Vienna] displeases me more and more. Truth to tell, the emperor likes to talk to him, but only to make him make inept, gossipy statements. Kaunitz also seems to like him because he does not disturb him and is submissive to him. [Edit: at this moment, the treaty to dismember Poland was being negotiated. Austria had decided to take part, without informing France.]

MARIA THERESA TO MERCY, 31 MARCH 1772

I see with pleasure the progress you are making over my daughter's spirit. In order to let her see my satisfaction, I will take a gay tone with her.

The amusements for carnival time are now over, and the sober lifestyle of Lent leaves me little to tell Y.M. about Mme la dauphine's daily occupations.

Mme la dauphine is participating in serious occupations more often and the abbe de Vermond has noticed a great improvement. She reads almost daily, often for several hours and has instructive conversations.

For some weeks, Mme la dauphine has decided to establish good and sincere harmony between herself and M. le comte and Mme la comtesse de Provence. The comte de Provence, for his part, has been more eager to please Mme l'archiduchesse; he spoke to her of the advice given to him by the late duc de la Vauguyon and spoke in such a way as to make it seem that he believed he had been led into error and that he was convinced it did not suit him. I am inclined to think that there is more skill than good faith in M. le comte de Provence's overture, but in any case, Mme l'archiduchesse listened and said nothing which could compromise her, and this has soothed the bitterness.

H.R.H. is still perfectly well treated by the King; the favourite has not appeared at court since New Year's Day, but she is content and does not complain. I made her realize that after the good reception she had been given once by Mme la dauphine, it would be wise and appropriate to leave things as they were for some time and that gradually the party spirit would weaken around the royal family and that then, everything which at present was causing little problems, would not have the same effect. The favourite agreed.

H.R.H told me she was pleased and encouraged that Y.M. was content with her conduct.

SECRET LETTER

[The struggle between the two factions at court]…is favourable to Y.M. in that, as the movements of intrigue absorb everyone here and distract them from external matters, there is less to fear from the moves which the French ministry would have made at other times, to disturb the operations relating to Poland, which will in the near future lead to the ending of the war.

[Edit: Mercy to the baron Neny, 15th of June 1772: "The chancellor (Maupeou) and M. d'Aiguillon are fighting with equal arms. The King does not esteem them much and seems decided to let them continue in opposition for a long time, without choosing between them. The director of finances (Terray) maintains himself by pillaging from the public; despite his extortion, no one is paid and everyone complains as loudly as possible. The favourite and her family are enriching themselves as much as possible. Nothing satisfies their avidity."]

MARIA THERESA TO MERCY, 1 MAY 1772

The weakness of the present ministry in France would be inopportune if we did not benefit because of the slight attention they pay to more worthwhile affairs. It is essential to act in concert with Spain to restrain France, if possible, from the false moves it may make, in its torpor.

MERCY TO MARIA THERESA, 15 MAY 1772

Recently Mme la dauphine has neglected no useful or agreeable occupation. Despite this, she still has moments of boredom, which lead her to Mesdames, and these are the occasions I most dread.

For a while, and always at Mesdames' instigation, Mme la dauphine has let herself be persuaded to grant protections and make recommendations which are often inappropriate and unjust and therefore the ministers cannot grant them. I showed Mme l'archiduchesse that this could only seriously compromise her credit and even the natural justice of her character.

H.R.H. finds it difficult to overcome or conceal her dislike of the duc d'Aiguillon. She never asks him for anything and refuses all solicitations for his department. It is only with great difficulty that I have succeeded in persuading H.R.H. to conceal her aversion towards this minister; at present he has no reason to complain, he is not badly treated, but he could be better, and I believe that good politics requires it.

Everything seems to indicate that M. le comte and Mme la comtesse de Provence have truly abandoned the party of the favourite and the duc d'Aiguillon.

H.R.H. has Mme de Misery as her premiere femme de chambre. She is an intriguer, and Mme la dauphine realizes this, however her obligingness, or the fear of being exposed to importunities, have often led H.R.H. to give in to Misery's requests, and I had to intervene on several occasions to reprimand this woman for her indiscretion.

Lately I learned that she had induced Mme la dauphine to grant audiences to certain women who solicited favours, in Misery's room. This abuse and the possible danger it could cause led me to tell Mme l'archiduchesse that Misery had failed in her duties and that the lady of honour could complain about her to the King and demand her expulsion. H.R.H., who with her usual thoughtlessness had not envisaged this as being a serious matter, seemed taken aback by my remarks and agreed with her usual good faith that I was right. Mme l'archiduchesse later reprimanded Misery and forbade her to become involved in future solicitations.

SECRET LETTER

Y.M. will have learned in my last [Edit: official] dispatch of the sensation produced here by news of the arrangements which are on the point of being concluded in Poland. The King believes that Y.M. could not avoid becoming involved [Edit: because Russia and Prussia had already determined on this partition], and that the situation is an inevitable consequence of the circumstances. The only thing which would pain the King, would be to believe that Y.M.'s friendship for him had cooled; but the remedy for this would be for Y.M. to give the King a direct and purely personal token of her trust, either by letter, or by ordering me to say something flattering on the appropriate occasion.

[Edit: Maria Theresa to Joseph, 25th of January, 1772: "We wanted to act like the Prussians, and at the same time, to appear honest. Even if we gain the Valachie district, even Belgrade, I will always regard them as bought too dearly, being at the expense of honour, of the glory of the monarchy, of good faith and religion. Since my unfortunate reign started, we have attracted the trust, I dare say even the admiration of Europe, the respect and veneration of our enemies; for a year now all that has been lost.]

MARIA THERESA TO MERCY, 1 JUNE 1772

The comte de Rosenberg's mission in Parma was unsuccessful; my daughter completely refused all my suggestions. I have ceased all correspondence with my daughter and have ordered my family, whether here or in Florence or Milan to do the same, and to return all letters to her, unopened. It remains to be seen what effect this will have. [Edit: another of Maria Theresa's daughters was married in Parma. Her behaviour was displeasing the Spanish court and her mother]

MARIE ANTOINETTE TO MARIA THERESA, 13 JUNE 1772

I am waiting impatiently for news of the delivery of the Queen [Edit: of Naples]. I am annoyed at those who have made her prejudiced against male midwives. I would gladly abandon myself to anyone they wanted, if I could only be in the same position.

As we now have fine weather here, I hope that the harvest will be a good one because it is sorely needed.

I have just received a letter from Bohme [Edit: in Naples]. The Queen is very happy and I am too now that she is safely delivered; although it is only a girl, I believe that she will still be pleased, because next time it may be a boy.

You are very kind in thinking of my name day: all I want from God is that He makes me worthy of my dear mother and maintains her friendship for me. [Edit: Maria Theresa had just ordered her family to cease all correspondence with her sister in Parma.]

MERCY TO MARIA THERESA, 15 JUNE 1772

I have recently witnessed the charming spectacle of Mme l'archiduchesse's compassion for Y.M. H.R.H. read me your last letter several times.

All Y.M.'s letters have been received with respect, but with at least as much fear. The inappropriate conduct of those around her, the fact that she does not receive reprimands, contradiction or even advice from the King, far less from M. le dauphin, added to her distance from you, are probably the reasons why the stricter letters did not always have the desired effect. In any case, no mother has ever had as much right as Y.M., to speak with authority. I made this point several times when the letters distressed her: Mme la dauphine agreed in principle, but she concluded she was not loved very much, and that she would always be treated severely. The recent letters finally destroyed that idea, and Y.M. can be more and more certain of guiding Mme l'archiduchesse as to what is necessary conduct in her position, considering her duties.

Mme la dauphine continues to learn dance steps. M. le dauphin has decided to take lessons with her. He seems keener to seize opportunities to be alone with Mme la dauphine. Her influence over him is increasing visibly; she speaks quite naturally to him about his faults; he takes what is said to him about this very well. As a result, the young prince's bearing and language are improving, and this is certainly Mme l'archiduchesse's work. Finally, the union of these two spouses would be perfect if only their marital relationship was satisfactory; but as regards this essential article, there exists only hopes, which have not yet been realized. Meanwhile Mme la dauphine's conduct in this matter is as wise and prudent as is possible to wish; there is no talk, no impatience, no temper shown, and she no longer permits people to talk about a subject which neither talk nor advice can help.

Although Mesdames' influence still operates in many circumstances, no problems have arisen as a result. [The two young couples]…sometimes spend the evenings with each other, although previously they spent them with Mesdames. I took the liberty of suggesting this idea.

Mme la dauphine has for a long time wanted to see Paris [however] they convinced her that she would be afraid to meet so many people. If Mme la dauphine went to Paris, she would be received with joy and enthusiasm, which is the only reason why they have persuaded the King not to let her go there, as the usual custom is for this to happen immediately after the marriage.

M. le comte de Provence had an object made from beautifully worked porcelain on the fireplace in his room, and when M. le dauphin was in his room, he usually picked it up and looked at it. This seemed to worry M. le comte de Provence and, just as Mme la dauphine was teasing him about this, at that very moment, M. le dauphin dropped it and it smashed into pieces. M. le comte de Provence, in his immediate reaction of anger, went up to M. le dauphin; they grappled with one another and punched one another. Mme la dauphine, who was very embarrassed at this behaviour, had the presence of mind to separate them. Reconciliation followed immediately; no one witnessed the quarrel and nothing happened as a result.

Mme l'archiduchesse told me later that she was about to call for help and I told her that that would have caused lots of problems for M. le comte de Provence because of the difference in ranks between them.

SECRET LETTER

It is quite certain that the King is quite equitable and moderate about Poland [however] the duc d'Aiguillon is personally piqued at the sad role he is playing at the start of his ministry. I flatter myself that there are effective means I can use to bring him round; the good dispositions of the favourite must not be neglected, and I believe that, taking these considerations into account, it would be useful if Mme la dauphine, during the trip to Compiegne, received the comtesse du Barry in a sufficiently favourable way for me to use this woman's ascendancy over the King and the minister. The slightest caution from Y.M. would produce the desired effect on Mme la dauphine.

MARIA THERESA TO MERCY, 18 JUNE 1772

The happy and consoling news from Naples [Edit: the Queen's delivery], has overwhelmed me with joy. I will write a brief note to my daughter about the dauphin; the situation is incomprehensible, and I am totally astonished that matters are allowed to continue thus, and no one bothers.

MARIA THERESA TO MERCY, 2 JULY 1772

I am pleased my daughter enjoys music and dancing; she needs something to occupy herself. The scene between the comte de Provence and the dauphin was a little extreme; it is fortunate it ended without consequences or fuss. My daughter behaved well in this.

I have put your request concerning my daughter's behaviour at Compiegne, in a separate paper…[for you to use at your discretion]. I have told my daughter that I have charged you with a specific commission for her, which interests me greatly, as sovereign and mother. [I feel we have]…wronged our allies.

We know it is a fact that England and Prussia are trying to win over Barry. The King is constant, but he is weak, his entourage does not allow him time to think and follow his own inclinations. If France treated with Prussia, I would regretfully have to change the alliance. To prevent this, [our only resource is]…my daughter, aided by you. She must cultivate the King and treat the favourite well. I do not want baseness, even less intimacy, but attention due to her grandfather.

MARIE ANTOINETTE TO MARIA THERESA, 17 JULY 1772

[The Queen]…wrote me a charming letter. She is drunk with joy and had to share it with a sister who shares her sentiments.

I saw Mercy and, having read your dear letter, spoke to him about it. I will do my best to preserve the alliance. Where would I be if there was a rupture between my two families? I hope that the good Lord will preserve me from this misfortune, and will show me my duty; I have prayed for this sincerely.

There are not a lot of people at Compiegne. The quarrels between the princes and the ministers have kept many away. Thank God, M. le dauphin is very well!

MERCY TO MARIA THERESA, 18 JULY 1772

Mme la dauphine's disposition to hear the truth, her slightly increased experience and her just and natural discernment, which is developing more and more, protect H.R.H. from many of the traps around her.

[However] for some time I have seen that Mme la dauphine's character is contracting the imprint of weakness, which is only because of the examples before her eyes. H.R.H. is accustoming herself to be afraid of everything and to let herself be subjugated by this very fear. Those who are bold enough to dare to fatigue her with their importunities, are almost sure to acquire an influence over Mme la dauphine even though she does not respect them. Although she realizes the injustice of their requests, she often acquiesces, only from fear, while she finds no difficulty in resisting more appropriate requests, if they are put to her in a moderate, discreet and respectful way.

The comtesse de la Marck [Edit: step grandmother of the comte de la Marck whose correspondence with the deputy Mirabeau offers an insight into the Revolution], aided by the comtesse de Noailles [Edit: her sister in law], obtained from Mme la dauphine an allowance of 1000 ecus for a new convert [Edit: a Dutch friend who had adopted the Roman Catholic faith]. I complained about this, as there are ecclesiastic funds for this purpose. Mme l'archiduchesse told me she had been caught unawares and felt that her kindness had been slightly abused.

Recently, the comtesse de la Marck decided to marry Mlle de Nievenhem, who is twenty two years old, to the duc de Lauraguais, who is almost seventy years old. The public thought this ridiculous. However these considerations did not stop the comtesse de la Marck, who, in a bold and indiscreet way, procured a private audience with Mme la dauphine to extort a promise to speak to the King. Mme l'archiduchesse, although shocked, gave in to her importunities and spoke to the King, and when he refused [Edit: his permission for the marriage], she was compromised. The comtesse de la Marck then only redoubled her audacity, and, in a second audience, she asked Mme la dauphine to insist to the King that he give Mlle de Nievenhem an allowance of 10,000 livres…[and other sums].

As soon as I heard of these new demands, I told Mme l'archiduchesse that…[the comtesse de la Marck] risked punishment in daring to abuse her kindness in this way and I told her the consequences which could result, either at present, or on similar occasions in the future. H.R.H. understood what I was saying perfectly; but I saw with regret that this was counteracted by embarrassment and a sort of fear which the comtesse de la Marck's audacious and decisive manner inspired in her. However the comtesse de la Marck wrote and I succeeded in persuading Mme la dauphine to refuse all the points requested.

A little firmness in Mme la dauphine would deflect all dangers of this type, but H.R.H. greatly needs to be encouraged in this; she has expressly forbidden me to tell you of this instance, therefore I must ask you not to appear to know of this. The underlings serving Mme la dauphine, find it equally easy to obtain what they want from her, so long as they dare to importune her, and it is always embarrassment that makes Mme l'archiduchesse yield.[21]

During the stay in Compiegne, I will insist that Mme la dauphine speaks more often to people of note, and that she does not take part in the little jokes that are sometimes played on older people, or those who have some striking faults in their face.

---

[21] This tendency in Marie Antoinette to yield to importunities, led to her granting of many favours to Polignac, her best friend, when Queen, and caused resentment and jealousy amongst the aristocracy.

SECRET LETTER

I have learned from the comtesse de Noailles, the abbe de Vermond and my own observations, that for some weeks now Mme l'archiduchesse has been feeling occasional moments of sadness, which do not last long but seem to indicate that she is troubled at the incomprehensible behaviour of M. le dauphin, and about the uncertainty as to how long his coldness will last, and its possible consequences. I have been afraid for a long time that this would happen and I have used all manner of means to try to delay this moment.

When H.R.H. talks to me, I take care to present to her the most favourable aspect of matters. She told me recently that I saw everything in a very positive light, but that I was unaware of the circumstances which could affect her and pain her. I believe that what Y.M. can say to her to console her and calm her anxieties of this nature, would be necessary and useful, while waiting for heaven to kindly alter circumstances which have no obvious cause.

…[Later, having discussed the situation between the two courts in Vienna and Versailles], I spoke of the position of a dauphine, and of how her situation is critical until she has produced a son.[22]

MERCY TO MARIA THERESA, 14 AUGUST 1772

On the 23 rd, H.R.H. played piquet with M. le comte de Provence. M. le dauphin was present, holding a baguette in his hands, and amused himself by hitting the comte de Provence's arm with it. The prince became impatient and after a few warnings, which did not stop this teasing, M. le comte de Provence jumped on the baguette and tried to tear it away from M. le dauphin. The quarrel heated up; but Mme la dauphine seized the baguette, tore it to bits and ended the dispute.

When H.R.H. told me this, I begged her to complain very firmly to M. le dauphin and make him realize the possible

---

[22] In light of the previous paragraph, this statement seems insensitive, at best.

annoying consequences of such childishness. Mme l'archiduchesse spoke to M. le dauphin about it next day; the prince listened to the lesson quietly and docilely: he promised to abstain from such behaviour and seemed very satisfied with the care Mme la dauphine took to make him realize its drawbacks.

M. le dauphin would be fine if not for his excessively bad education; he shows signs of essential qualities as far as his character is concerned, he is upright, listens when told the truth; it is not even necessary to use circumlocution to do so: indeed that is what Mme l'archiduchesse does daily, and not without success.

This young prince has acquired the habit of talking to me, and this is even more remarkable as he hardly speaks to anyone. I reply very frankly to his questions. A short time ago he asked me if I enjoyed hunting. I told him that I enjoyed it as a form of exercise but I unhesitatingly added the drawbacks it had when it became a passion; I emphasized the dangers of excessive fatigue and the loss of precious time which should be used in instruction for princes, and for which they are accountable to God and to man. Everything I ventured to say, very firmly, on this subject was listened to in silence, but placidly, and M. le dauphin has only treated me better since.

H.R.H. spoke to me about M. le dauphin's honest character, his gentleness, his kindness; Mme l'archiduchesse told me that with regard to all these points she was content. I saw however that she was pained with other reflections, which she could not explain.

[A playlet was staged by the marquise de Durfort, attended only by the royal family, however M. le dauphin]…was kind enough to have me sit beside him; he spoke a lot to me and I was surprised by the ease of his conversation, as he hardly ever speaks, normally, especially when he is out of his rooms.

On the 2nd, I noticed that Mme la dauphine was speaking more attentively and graciously to all the distinguished people who came to pay court.

On the 4th, an incident occurred…[which again showed the weakness of which Mme la dauphine is capable] H.R.H.

wanted to go to the theatre in town. The comtesse de Noailles had suggested the idea; etiquette and usage did not conflict with this. M. le dauphin himself wanted to see it. [However] Mme la dauphine felt she needed Mesdames' permission as well as the King's; she thought of several little indirect means, dictated by fear, to secure this agreement, and she wanted the comtesse de Noailles to charge herself with the task of obtaining it.

When H.R.H. told me of her bother, I forcefully opposed this behaviour. I explained that it was necessary to obtain the King's permission and that of M. le dauphin, but not that of Mesdames, that seeking their advice was merely an attention and not a duty on Mme l'archiduchesse's part, and...[this behaviour] resembled dependency as doubts and fears were mingled with it. Mme l'archiduchesse agreed with me, but she preferred to suspend her project of going to the theatre, rather than risk the disapproval of her aunts.

SECRET LETTER

Mme l'archiduchesse's recent good conduct is due to Y.M.'s secret letter. Mme la dauphine was so struck by it that she has spoken of it to me almost every day since.

MERCY TO MARIA THERESA, 16 SEPTEMBER 1772

Mme l'archiduchesse has grown suddenly and this has made her thinner. She eats healthily and always without excess.

On the 14th, the duc d'Aiguillon told me that...[because Mme la dauphine was receiving the favourite better], the King was encouraging her to present herself more often at Mme l'archiduchesse's, but that they wished my advice. I replied that it would be prudent for the comtesse du Barry to appear rarely, rather than often, as that would only cause agitation in the royal family, embarrassment for Mme la dauphine and no useful purpose for the favourite; that she must be content to be well received two or three times a year, until time had completely calmed the situation, and custom had made people see her differently.

[The abbe de Vermond is pleased with Mme la dauphine's reading]…What is certain is that Mme l'archiduchesse knows the anecdotes and memoirs of previous reigns better than anyone else in the royal family. I often take the liberty of insisting that H.R.H. finds means to engage M. le dauphin to read a few good books; she has made several attempts at this which have not been totally fruitless. M. le dauphin has begun to read the memoirs of Sully. He has a good memory and discernment; a little application could produce marvellous results in this young prince.

Considering M. le dauphin's character and behaviour, it is almost inevitable that Mme la dauphine will one day be called upon to govern France. It would be premature, perhaps even dangerous to present these ideas too often to Mme l'archiduchesse, but I am trying to prepare her gradually.

For a long time, and for the sake of Mme la dauphine, I have been trying to win the good opinion and trust of M. le dauphin. The cold and reserved character of the young prince caused me to meet difficulties which I often felt to be insurmountable, and I must say that, if I have succeeded in removing some, I can only attribute this to the help and kindness of Mme l'archiduchesse, as she has made her husband favourable to me. In the meantime, I will cultivate this fortunate state of affairs.

MARIA THERESA TO MERCY, 2 OCTOBER 1772

I agree with you that it is best not to make my daughter anticipate too much, a future which may place the government of France in her hands.

MARIE ANTOINETTE TO MARIA THERESA, 14 OCTOBER 1772

Please accept my good wishes and respects for Saint Theresa's day; I will certainly ask tomorrow through the intercession of this patron saint for the conservation of your precious health.

135

My sister Marianne has kindly told me that there is a new portrait of Y.M. I would be delighted if you could send me a copy.

The milk treatment is continuing to do me good. I sleep every morning for one or two hours after taking it. People who have not seen me for some time, think I have put on weight.

Although the day here is very full, I read at least a little every day.

My dear mother has often denied herself care, but she must now indulge herself because of the love and anxiety of her children. I especially have great need to be reassured; it would be the greatest consolation I could have.

MERCY TO MARIA THERESA, 16 OCTOBER 1772

H.R.H.'s behaviour in public is improving more and more, the only point she needs to be encouraged in is that of finding less repugnance in speaking to those who pay court. She behaves very well with people in the ministry; but it would be desirable for her to be the same with people who, by birth or rank, have a distinguished position in this country.

I warned Mme la dauphine that M. le dauphin would be inspecting his regiment of infantry soon and that it was necessary that the young prince should appear to be gallant and kind on such an occasion, and that Mme la dauphine, who would be present, should be the same. I gave Mme l'archiduchesse a list of officers[23] who, by their merit, could hope to obtain some distinction; I begged H.R.H. to ensure M. le dauphin behaved in a way which would not displease.

MARIA THERESA TO MERCY, 31 OCTOBER 1772

It is essential for my daughter to accustom herself to being seen by the public or, however pleasant and gracious she

---

[23] As on so many other occasions, one wonders why the Austrian ambassador had to undertake this task, which should surely have been carried out by a French minister.

136

is in private, she will not succeed in gaining the love and esteem of the public, in the long run.

I am pleased that my daughter is friendly to her brother in law but I do not want her to give him too many confidences. He seems deceitful to me, and as he cuts a better figure than the dauphin, and is gallant while the other is a lout, the comparison which my daughter could make between them might not be to the advantage of her husband.

However pleased I would be to be rid of Rohan [Edit: the French ambassador to Austria], I agree with you that it is best to be circumspect, in order not to displease his partisans, who could then try to harm my interests [Edit: Rohan's family was very powerful in France].

MERCY TO MARIA THERESA, 14 NOVEMBER 1772

I talked to H.R.H. about M. le dauphin's review of his regiment. I observed that it was essential for him to appear benevolent. I took the liberty of suggesting [some ideas]…and spoke with frank respect of the bad effects which his taciturnity could produce, and the lack of concern to please, which, until now, has characterized all the actions of the royal family.

Mme la dauphine told me that Mme la comtesse de Provence had given M. le comte de Provence's regiment 50 louis in the previous year, when M. le comte de Provence reviewed them. I said there was no comparison between a dauphine and a comtesse de Provence, and there should also be a difference in their generosity. Mme l'archiduchesse did not seem too pleased with this remark; in general she inclines towards economy, which is a little too strict. However she gives to those who have the boldness to ask and pester her; but, with the exception of some small donations to charities, there is no example of Mme la dauphine being markedly generous of her own free will.

I still have about three quarters of the money Y.M. gave me for H.R.H.'s use, and when I remind her of it, she replies that it is good to keep it in reserve. However, being too severely economical would harm the public's just opinion of Mme l'archiduchesse's kindness and grandeur.

On the 19th…[M. le dauphin reviewed his regiment]. Mme la dauphine had the duchesse d'Aiguillon and the duchesse de Mirepoix in her train [Edit: friends of du Barry], as I had requested. On the arrival of the King, M. le dauphin himself uttered the commands for the regiment. This young prince walked through the ranks and spoke to all the officers; he presented them to Mme la dauphine who, with her own hand, gave each a cockade. She began with M. le dauphin; he took it and put it immediately on his hat. When the King left, M. le dauphin and Mme la dauphine remained for almost an hour in the midst of the officers and showed them much kindness. Everyone was amazed at the conduct of M. le dauphin; it surpassed everything I had hoped for and I had the satisfaction of hearing, that night, that they attributed M. le dauphin's behaviour to Mme la dauphine. The King talked about it a lot next day.

H.R.H. spoke bitterly to me about the duc d'Aiguillon, and also about the favourite who has recently built a pavilion beside her rooms, taking ground from a garden, on the same level as Mesdames' rooms, such that this garden which was previously reserved for the royal family, is now overlooked by this new building. Mme la dauphine found this very impertinent, and in fact she is right. I saw that they had embittered Mme l'archiduchesse and it was not without difficulty that I convinced her it was best to be prudent and moderate.

[I told Mme l'archiduchesse that the comtesse du Barry might come to pay court to her]…H.R.H. seemed disconcerted; but she assured me that all would go well.

On the 27th, I was worried because of the indecision I had noticed on the day before…[in Mme la dauphine, therefore] I went to see her; she was coming back from mass. "I have prayed," she told me. "I said: 'Dear God! If you want me to talk, make me talk; I will act in the way You deign to inspire me!'" I replied to Mme l'archiduchesse that the voice of her august mother was the only one which could interpret the will of God in matters of conduct, and that she was thus already inspired as to how to behave for the best.

138

After dinner the comtesse du Barry came, accompanied by the duchesse d'Aiguillon. Mme la dauphine spoke to the latter and then, looking at the favourite, she spoke of the weather. These words were not directly addressed to the person, and whether because of the tone, or the expression, the reception was not of the best. Fortunately M. le dauphin was present on this occasion and I blamed this for Mme l'archiduchesse's coldness and embarrassment. Finally I succeeded in persuading the comtesse du Barry that her reception had in fact been good.

She told me she thought she had noticed that Mme la dauphine had been favourably inclined to her but that the presence of M. le dauphin had been an obstacle to a more favourable reception and that is much better than what circumstances could have led me to hope.

H.R.H. is not sufficiently considerate to the King; all the advances always come from him, and they are very often received with an expression of respect, but at the same time of coldness, which annoys the King and which is surely not pleasant for him.

H.R.H. spoke to me about M. le dauphin in a more satisfied way, telling me that he was beginning to show more inclination to read and other useful occupations. It is certain that this young prince is continuing to change to his advantage; when he decides to talk, he expresses himself with a lot of good sense and it is easy to see that the roughness of his looks does not extend to his character, which seems rather to incline to moderation and gentleness.

The doctors gave M. le dauphin medicine as a precaution; Mme l'archiduchesse spent the whole day with him; H.R.H. did not even want to go to the play at court, but the young prince insisted she should. Immediately afterwards, Mme l'archiduchesse spent the rest of the evening in M. le dauphin's room.

SECRET LETTER

The King, when with his family, has sometimes spoken of matters in Poland and Sweden [therefore] I felt it would be useful to enlighten Mme la dauphine on these matters, so that she would not be embarrassed by what was said in her presence. I asked H.R.H. if the King seemed bad tempered or personally involved when he spoke of these affairs. Mme l'archiduchesse assured me that on the contrary, the King had once told her jokingly: "We must not talk about Poland in front of you, as your relatives do not think as we do."

On another occasion, the King told her laughingly: "The emperor wants to oppose what is happening in Sweden; it will lead to quarrels, and I will send you back to Vienna," and then he embraced her – this was done with an air of gaiety. This language seems to prove that the King does not take these affairs personally; the distinguished and kind reception he gives me is another proof.

MARIA THERESA TO MERCY, 30 NOVEMBER 1772

Try to ensure that [the situation in Parma]…does not reflect on the dauphine. I must admit that your report disturbed me slightly; my daughter could well be as insincere in the confidences she makes to you, as on those about the hunt which she makes to me. I do not find fault in her doing so, but she persists stubbornly in presenting matters in a different light, and this is insincere, and reveals a character which is not totally honest, and this, added to the diabolical intrigues of the court, could become very dangerous. The only resource I can trust in is your care, for which I am very grateful.

MARIA THERESA TO MERCY,
(SAME DATE, ANOTHER LETTER)

I warn you that, as my daughter wrote only quite briefly to me, I did not want to write a long letter in reply, but here are two passages that I thought I should warn you about: "What you tell me about the dauphin's horse riding does not please me; but there are other rumours here, such as that you also ride with the hunt, and that you had an accident; some say a fall, others a near fall. I do not believe this, as I believe your promises. I will write to Mercy to clarify the matter...I must

140

admit it pains me that you neglect this personal gift, this charm which you have when people are presented to you, which won you all hearts on your way to France; but I would be even more annoyed if you did not feel more liking for your fellow countrymen. German blood runs in your veins, do not be ashamed of it."

I have finished my letter thus: "Be assiduous in paying court to the King and anticipating his wishes. The political crisis demands all your attention; the happiness of our houses and of yours in particular depends on it."

MARIE ANTOINETTE TO MARIA THERESA, 15 DECEMBER 1772

Madame, my very dear mother, the gazettes are not yet right: I do not despair of it happening soon. I believe he is not yet strong enough; certainly the moment it happens, I will not lose a moment in telling you. Mercy will surely also second my eagerness.

I suspect that you have been told more about my riding than is the case. I will, dear mother, tell you the whole truth. The King and M. le dauphin enjoy seeing me on horseback. I only mention this because everyone has noticed it; during the trip to Compiegne, they were especially delighted to see me in riding costume. Although I must admit that I did not find it difficult to conform to their taste, I can nonetheless assure you that I have never let myself be persuaded to follow the hunt, and I hope that, despite my thoughtlessness, I will always let myself be guided by the sensible people who accompany me, and I will never be caught up in the crowd.

I could not believe that what happened to me at Fontainebleau could have been passed off as an accident; now and again there are spots in the forest, covered in pebbles; in one of these spots, climbing up very slowly, my horse missed one of these stones, which was covered with sand, and slipped; I made a movement which checked him and then continued.

Esterhazy danced with us yesterday. I should have spoken to him when he was presented to me: my silence was only embarrassment, not knowing him. They do me a great injustice in believing I am indifferent to my homeland: I have more reason than anyone to appreciate every day the value of the blood which runs in my veins, and it is only from prudence that, on some occasions, I have not shown my feelings on this matter.

All the letters…[you see] will surely mention the new disposition of the princes. M. le prince de Conde wrote to the King in his name, and in that of his son to attest his submission. The letter was quite good, although he did not talk of the parlement in it, but that had been agreed previously. The King allowed him to come the next day, and he and his son have visited us all, and this went quite well on both sides. A few days later, with the King's permission, I invited the duke, the duchesse and Mlle de Bourbon to the ball. As for M. le duc d'Orleans, his son and M. le prince de Conti, they have not yet come back, but it is to be hoped it will not be long before they do.

I neglect nothing when paying court to the King and anticipate his wishes as much as possible. I hope he is pleased with me; it is my duty to please him, my duty and my glory if I can contribute to preserving the union of our two houses.

Mercy must be pleased with the silence I have maintained for a long time on all the complaints about the favourite.

Because I cannot depend on the post, I will give you my wishes for the New Year in advance. From the bottom of my heart I wish for your continuing good health, and to merit the continuation of my very dear mother's kindness and love.

MERCY TO MARIA THERESA, 16 DECEMBER 1772

Mme l'archiduchesse dances with such grace that one could truthfully say that because of her lovely face, she effaces all the young people who appear at her balls. M. le dauphin[24] has not benefited quite so much from the dancing lessons which he took very assiduously; however his expression no longer shows so much embarrassment: he holds himself better

---

[24] At times, Mercy is a master of understatement.

and is no longer so clumsy in his movements, nor in his bearing.

Mme la dauphine has a very frank character, dissimulation is difficult and painful for her; but when serious subjects are being raised, she feels extreme apprehension at the possibility of being compromised, and this fear makes her more circumspect than her age and high spirits would seem to indicate. I can say with certainty that with the exception of M. le dauphin, the abbe de Vermond and I are the only people H.R.H. really trusts.

Mme la dauphine requested a benefice for her almoner, [from cardinal de la Roche-Aymon]…according to custom. The cardinal waited eight months and then gave him a small abbey. Mme la dauphine thanked him, but said that she hoped that she would not have to wait so long next time. Although the cardinal was at fault, he complained to the comtesse de Noailles, his friend, and told her to tell Mme l'archiduchesse that he would not go to her again unless she ordered it. The comtesse de Noailles was stupid enough to tell Mme la dauphine this and Mme l'archiduchesse was understandably piqued and replied that she would go straight to the King next time.

The prelate and the comtesse de Noailles were both in consternation at this firm reply, which they had not expected and they came to me as usually happens when something has to be remedied. I pointed out to the cardinal that he was wrong in his conduct. Then I told Mme l'archiduchesse [about this]…and asked her to be lenient with the cardinal. I found H.R.H. little disposed to pardon him purely and simply. She told me that the cardinal had only to come back, but that, the first time he did so, she would not talk to him. I still insisted on a less severe pardon; but it seems that matters will remain thus.

However I saw with great pleasure that Mme l'archiduchesse on this occasion was beginning to adopt a tone which will make her respected. I have never failed to represent the usefulness of this system, which is even more necessary at this court as the King tolerates arbitrary conduct which is never reprimanded, and this could easily result in licence and disregard of the respect due to the royal family.

I urged Mme la dauphine to tell M. le dauphin this and it appears that he has drawn the necessary inferences. In fact I have noticed over the past five or six months, that people at court are becoming more circumspect and careful in the way they treat Mme la dauphine and M. le dauphin. The ministers, even the favourite, are more guarded now than previously, in their behaviour; it is not the same with regard to Mesdames and I have not failed to point this out to Mme l'archiduchesse who is now as enlightened about them as I always wished.

Mesdames are grieved at the decline in their influence and the despotism they were accustomed to exercise in the family; they show their resentment of this in petty criticism of Mme la dauphine and by affectedly praising Mme la comtesse de Provence.

The only drawback in the liaison between the young princes and princesses is that occasioned by the suspect character of Mme la comtesse de Provence. Since I asked Mme la dauphine to observe her closely, she has noticed several very disagreeable incidents of falsity. If M. le comte de Provence were informed of this, it would certainly add to the indifference and sometimes disgust which he feels for his wife; but Mme l'archiduchesse, because of her kind character, is trying to bring them closer together. She always takes the comtesse de Provence's part, and, while recognising her character for what it is worth, she is reserved in her complaints and occupies herself only in turning unfavourable points into favourable ones.

SECRET LETTER

It is only from Mme la dauphine herself that Y.M. can learn of the exact situation in which she presently finds herself in relation to her husband. The circumspection which I must use in my enquiries on such a delicate matter means I could easily miss something. The dauphin knows I constantly use language which is designed to deflect curiosity and attention from that subject, and I believe this is the reason to which I must largely attribute the singular kindness he shows me.

While he hardly speaks to anyone, he always has something to say to me; he comes to me wherever he sees me and on the 7th of the month, at the ball, when he saw me arrive, he left his place, and crossed the room to converse with me. Unfortunately these conversations are so disconnected in form and substance that it is hard for me to find means to say a few useful words. However this happens sometimes and I see that it is not that M. le dauphin is lacking in desire to discuss serious matters, but rather that he lacks the habit of doing so and the assurance he would gain as a result. Mme la dauphine has won him over to reading and I still flatter myself that this young prince will turn out well.

I would be betraying my most sacred duties in every important matter if I asserted something to Y.M. of which I was not absolutely certain. This princess does not, I believe, wish to conceal matters from me; but if she did intend this, (although her character would not permit it), she would not be able to succeed, because of all the infallible means I have to enlighten me on the truth of matters relative to H.R.H.

MARIA THERESA TO MERCY, 31 DECEMBER 1772

[The letters my daughter sends to me do not show the same love and trust as those to the emperor]…Her letters to him are very good, playful, and show a lot of spirit. This is only for you.

MARIA THERESA TO MARIE ANTOINETTE, 31 DECEMBER 1772

What you say to excuse yourself for having broken your word to me and ridden with the hunt, would have been fine if you had told me, a year or more ago, when you first did so. Your candour and love would have made the broken promise a little less hurtful, but being informed by the gazettes, that I admit hurt me, and will cast a shadow over my trust in you, in the future. To claim it was a lapse of memory cannot serve as an excuse, as it is this lapse I am complaining about. Young people never remain measured in their amusements. I foresee therefore that you will be the same. I have no more to say about the matter as the King and the dauphin approve: you will not hear another word about it from me; but what upsets me is your silence.

Your embarrassment in relation to Esterhazy is another point I cannot let pass. How is it that Antoinette at twelve or thirteen years old knew how to receive people very well, say something polite and gracious to all; this truth, all of Vienna, all the Empire, Lorraine and France have seen and yet the dauphine is embarrassed now with one private individual? Do not grow accustomed to these frivolous excuses: embarrassment, fear, timidity, they are illusions! It is only the unfortunate habit of living life unthinkingly and not bothering oneself about matters, which makes people use these words. You know how your affability won over hearts: you see every day how the opposite works, and yet you let matters drift and neglect this important point!

My sermons will end with the old year; you will do me an injustice if you do not realize they are a sign of my love and of the deep interest I have in your future well-being, a matter which continually occupies me. I expect to see from your behaviour to the favourite on New Year's Day, the effect of my advice.

1773

MARIE ANTOINETTE TO MARIA THERESA, 13 JANUARY 1773

You punish me a great deal for a lapse of memory; above all do not talk of having no trust in me; or I will be inconsolable. I certainly told you the truth about the approval of the King and M. le dauphin; it is true that I lost nothing in agreeing. I would not dare to say that I ride carefully, if I did not have my two equerries to attest to the truth of this, as they never leave me, and are very serious and reasonable people.

I have learned of the Queen's pregnancy [Edit: Marie Caroline of Naples was pregnant again], and what pleased me most, is that they say her pregnancy is totally different to the previous one, which makes me hope for a boy; when will I be able to give you the same news.

The portraits of my little brothers give me great pleasure. I had them mounted into rings and wear them every day. People who saw them at Vienna think the portraits look like them, and people in general find their faces charming.

You will have learned, my dear mother, that the duc d'Orleans and the duc de Chartres have returned. I am pleased for the sake of peace and harmony and for the happiness of the King; but I do not believe that my dear mother, in the King's place, would have accepted the letter which they dared to write and which they will have printed in the foreign gazettes.

Despite the pleasures of carnival time, I am always faithful to my dear harp, and it is believed that I am making progress in it. I also sing every week at my sister Madame's [Edit: the comtesse de Provence] concerts; although there are very few people there, we still enjoy ourselves. I still find time to read a little; I have begun the 'History of England' by M. Hume; it seems quite interesting, although it is necessary to remember that it was written by a protestant.

All the gazettes will mention the cruel fire at the Hotel-Dieu; they have had to move the sick into the cathedral and to the archbishop's house. There are usually 5,000 or 6,000 sick people in the hospital; despite the care taken, they could not prevent part of the building being burnt, and although it is a fortnight since the incident happened, the cellars are still burning. The archbishop has published instructions to organise collections; I sent a thousand ecus. I said nothing about it; nonetheless they are embarrassing me with compliments, but they claim that this is necessary in order to use me as an example. As usual, my dear mother, I am sending you the Almanacs.

I have just reread your letter to see if there is anything I have forgotten: I am overcome at the reproach of lacking in truthfulness; my heart has never deserved that. Will you allow me to send you my love?

MERCY TO MARIA THERESA, 16 JANUARY 1773

At the beginning of December a book entitled 'Provincial Letters' appeared...[I marked passages] and asked Mme la dauphine to give it to M. le dauphin to read; I was not sorry to grasp an opportunity to stir this young prince's mind a little. In fact he was quite struck by these passages. I had mentioned some thoughts to Mme l'archiduchesse so that she could talk to him about them...[I told Mme la dauphine] that it was not enough for M. le dauphin to be an ordinary man, and that it was up to Mme l'archiduchesse to cultivate or awaken ideas in her husband which could stir his mind and give him the prudence and foresight necessary to avoid problems such as those of the present and others in the future.

I noticed that this speech took Mme l'archiduchesse aback. She told me her opinion of M. le dauphin; she felt he had a decided inclination towards justice, order and truth, good sense and astuteness in the way he examined affairs; but she feared the effects of his nonchalance, his languor and, finally, his lack of spirit, without which it is impossible to think or feel deeply enough to impel oneself into effective action. This portrait of M. le dauphin seemed to me to resemble him closely; I am convinced however that he is capable of changing to his advantage, and I am trying to encourage Mme l'archiduchesse to bring her care and attention to bear in this, and also to give him an example of prudent conduct herself.

My representations succeeded in persuading Mme l'archiduchesse to talk to the dauphin and discuss all the most essential matters; she exhorted him to make better use of his time, to be more sociable and polite and she especially insisted on the reasons which necessitated him treating the favourite in a way which would not displease the King and which would stop the complaints and quarrels with which the royal family was incessantly tormented.

This language made such an impression on M. le dauphin that, on New Year's Day, when the favourite presented herself to him, he treated her quite well and spoke some words to her, to the great astonishment of everyone. However, in an unexpected contrast, Mme la dauphine received the comtesse du Barry very badly, and said nothing to anyone, not even to the duchesse d'Aiguillon or the marechale de Mirepoix, who accompanied the favourite. I complained to Mme l'archiduchesse about this behaviour and said that this conduct destroyed my good work and that I would find difficulty in explaining to Y.M. the scant regard Mme la dauphine showed for Y.M.'s repeated warnings. Mme la dauphine seemed quite embarrassed and said that she felt she had done enough for the moment, in persuading M. le dauphin to behave with better grace; that, as for herself, by talking to no one, she had treated each one equally and therefore they could not complain.

The duc d'Aiguillon told me, amongst other cutting remarks, that it seemed that Mme la dauphine planned to mock the King in the way she treated the people he most cared for. I firmly replied that it was as unjust as it was absurd to always complain about Mme la dauphine who had the right not to depart from the example given her by her husband and by the King's own daughters, in what concerned the favourite.

SECRET LETTER

I spoke to Mme la dauphine of your great love for her and she replied effusively: "There is nothing I would not do to show my love for my mother." Then she added: "I love the empress, but I fear her, although she is far away; even when I write, I am never at ease with her." I replied that this shyness seemed uncalled for and inappropriate and that I had not noticed this fear in H.R.H. when her brother had scolded her in my presence, as he often did: "Oh! That was quite different, because the emperor is my brother; I was used to replying to him when he annoyed me, and joking with him."

This accounts for the difference in styles when Mme la dauphine writes to you, and to H.M. the emperor. What is more the abbe de Vermond has never dictated a whole phrase in H.R.H.'s letters, but she sometimes says something to him and if he thinks the expression is not correct, he will warn her.

It is very true that du Tillot has constantly maintained the most respectful language here in reference to the infante and infanta [Edit: Marie Antoinette's sister and brother in law in Parma], blaming their mistakes on the malice of their associates and praising their personal qualities [Edit: a technique also used by Mercy in many of the later letters concerning Marie Antoinette].

MARIA THERESA TO MARIE ANTOINETTE, 31 JANUARY 1773

I am pleased your carnival time is so enjoyable. This year all the talk is of your pretty face and the way you dance: everyone finds a great change and Stormond found you had changed greatly and to your advantage, and was very pleased with the reception you gave him. You would not believe how much a look, a greeting, a word from you can have an effect on these people: that in turn is spread throughout the kingdom. These good people are not accustomed to young people and courtiers only being interested in ridiculing them. I was also delighted by the 1,000 ecus you sent to the Hotel-Dieu. You say quite rightly that you were annoyed they publicized this;

these actions should only be known by God, and I am quite sure you did it with this intention; but the others also have good reasons to have it made public, as you say yourself.

I am not pleased with what happened on New Year's Day; you were too tense, you will have to make up for it on the first available occasion.

While everyone is at the masked ball, (I even sent all my ladies), I am spending some delightful moments with my adored child, and in embracing you tenderly, I am...

MARIA THERESA TO MERCY, 1 FEBRUARY 1773

Despite all the trouble you take to direct my daughter's steps, I see only too well how much it costs her to make an effort to follow your advice and mine. I will still give her some warnings from time to time, so long as you believe them to be useful, and I will write to her making the points you have suggested, and mixing in a little flattery, although I dislike such a style. I am sending you her latest letter, which will give you new proof of her lack of frankness to me. (On this point, I must admit, I am not at ease; I find her too often in the wrong, and she knows how to wriggle out of explanations only too cleverly, and present matters in a different light even if truth suffers as a result, meanwhile carrying on as she wishes, notwithstanding her promises and her repeated admissions of not realising what she was doing)
.

MARIE ANTOINETTE TO MARIA THERESA, 15 FEBRUARY 1773

Last Thursday, M. le dauphin, the comte and comtesse de Provence and I went to the Opera Ball in Paris; we kept this secret. We were all masked; however we were recognised after half an hour. We returned here at seven in the morning, and heard mass before going to bed. Everyone is delighted that M. le dauphin agreed to go, as it was thought that he was averse to such amusements.

If I were seen in private with the King, it would be agreed that I do not seem constrained; in public it is another matter, but then I would be blamed for acting as I do in private. It is believed that the marriage of the comte d'Artois with the sister of the comtesse de Provence has been decided, although not yet made public. We are still living together in harmony. When the courier arrives, Lent will already have begun; I dread its effect on my dear mother's health. Please remember that your children need you, I more than the others.

MERCY TO MARIA THERESA, 17 FEBRUARY 1773

[H.R.H. discussed with me her behaviour with regard to the favourite]…She said: "I admit that when I first came here I made a great mistake, agreeing with what was said to me and the impressions I was given; but the wrong being done, and having adopted a particular path which everyone has noticed, don't you agree that it is very difficult to retract and to act in a totally contradictory way?" I told Mme l'archiduchesse that this was not the case…[Later I told Mme la dauphine] that if this monarch was wrong, it was not up to his children to point it out; that God cursed Noah's son who laughed at his father's drunkenness, and blessed those of his children who covered his nakedness.

M. le comte de Provence is singularly well instructed in all the satires, songs and epigrams which are circulating concerning the favourite and the ministry. He told Mme la dauphine of them and I had reason to worry about the possible use she could make of them; but H.R.H. being kind enough to tell me all of this, I told her that it could be dangerous to seem informed of certain things whose odiosity one shared, by knowing of them. Therefore I asked her to tell the comte de Provence she did not want to hear such talk. Mme l'archiduchesse did so and for the past fortnight, M. le comte de Provence has not mentioned them again.

[When Mme la dauphine sent her gift to the Hotel-Dieu hospital]…there was no precaution she did not take to conceal this. She told no one, not even the abbe de Vermond. It is quite certain that this [gift] was not made by example, as no one else in the royal family thought to help the poor in their desperate situation.

153

H.R.H [had] a little operation to remove a tooth which was beginning to go bad.

SECRET LETTER

I saw Mme l'archiduchesse almost in tears [after reading Y.M.'s letter]...It would have cost her too much to admit that it was from weakness and from fear of reproach from the family that she did not obey Y.M., although she intended to.

The appalling confusion at the heart of this court excuses Mme l'archiduchesse a little in certain instances; but nothing is lost, because her heart, her spirit and her character hold their own and will always do so, because of her unassailable purity.

I saw Mme la dauphine yesterday and thought to shake her from her complacency by talking vaguely of Y.M.'s worries. Mme l'archiduchesse cried in such a disconsolate way that I was astonished.

MARIA THERESA TO MERCY, 3 MARCH 1773

I am surprised that, contrary to custom, they want to bring two sisters into the same family.

I am sending you my daughter's reply to my last letter, which certainly does not seem to have had the great effect which you flattered yourself it had had. It is drier than any of the preceding letters. [Therefore] how can I count on the assertions she makes to you of her love for me, without seeing it proved by the facts. Whatever happens, I will continue to try to be as useful to her as possible, with my advice, and will not reveal anger in my letter. I have enclosed a copy, this one is the most indifferent I have yet written to her. Do not point this out; I am curious to see if she notices or if she is so childish or absent minded not to notice.

I hope that my daughter succeeds more and more in inspiring the dauphin with a taste for study (having no taste for it herself, there is little to hope for); and I am pleased he continues to show you affection.

MARIA THERESA TO MARIE ANTOINETTE,
3 MARCH 1773

Your trip to Paris was well received by the public. What you tell me about the marriage of the comte d'Artois astonishes me: two sisters from the same house; they were talking of a princess from Saxony. I must admit that this great eagerness to marry off the third gives me a lot to think about, and it is not at all pleasant; the dominant party is becoming strong; you have even more reason to be careful and to neglect nothing which could be used against you. My health is good; I was bled, five days ago, as a precaution. I am abstaining from meat [for Lent], but that is always good for me and does not inconvenience me at all.

With all my love.

MARIE ANTOINETTE TO MARIA THERESA,
15 MARCH 1773

You are lucky that meatless meals do not inconvenience you; I am observing Lent, I must admit that meatless meals do not appeal to me, but they do not inconvenience me. I feel obliged to continue, and I hope that I will do so until the end of Lent.

The marriage of the comte d'Artois with the sister of the comtesse de Provence will be announced in public tomorrow. Since talk of this marriage began, I have thought a lot about how close the two sisters are bound to be; with prudence and the support of M. le dauphin's love, I hope that they will not make me uncomfortable. I know very well that the rush to marry the comte d'Artois does not reflect well on my sister and I.

This Lent we have a very good preacher three times a week; he talks of the good moral principles in the Gospels and tells everyone many truths; however I prefer the Masillon series of sermons for Lent, because they are more to my taste.

It was thought in Paris that we would return to the Opera Ball; as a result crowds have turned up and the people at the Opera have greatly benefited. I hope that next year we will not attract so many and that we will be able to go more than once.

MERCY TO MARIA THERESA, MARCH 1773

H.R.H. understands perfectly how important it is to please the King and charm him; at the same time she believes she can only succeed up to a certain point, because she thinks the monarch is indifferent to all around him. Mme l'archiduchesse unfortunately can be only too shrewd in noticing certain things. At the same time she has too much intelligence to be satisfied with poor excuses and it is often difficult to give her sufficient reasons to suffice to efface her impressions which are sometimes well founded.

M. le dauphin is becoming accustomed to read for some moments every day, and he is not too embarrassed to grasp opportunities to make use of the little knowledge which he has gained in his reading. That is what I have noticed in my talks with him during his suppers.

SECRET LETTER

Pregnancy would have a decisive and healthy effect [Edit: on Mme la dauphine's conduct], and would temper her disorderly and thoughtless behaviour, which is only caused by the incredible and dangerous whirlwind of this court.

Mme la dauphine noticed a difference in style in Y.M.'s last letter, but H.R.H. did not see it as being cold and I felt it best to leave things like that, and come back to it at the first opportunity. I believe...[Mme la dauphine will] mention that M. le dauphin saw doctor Lassone.

MARIA THERESA TO MERCY, 3 APRIL 1773

I approve of you entering into detail with my daughter about the political situation, using your usual circumspection. I will make any necessary observations to her about matters, guided by your ideas.

MARIE ANTOINETTE TO MARIA THERESA, 18 APRIL 1773

It was more than time for the courier to come; I was desperately worried for four days. I am relieved that my dear mother is pleased with me.

The wedding of the comte d'Artois is arranged for the 16th of November; part of his household was named the day before yesterday, it will be as numerous and as well composed as that of the comte de Provence; however my brother needs responsible and intelligent people around him because, although he is very pleasant, he is very lively.

It is to be hoped that the congress brings peace; I hope that the Turks and the Russians will grow weary of waging war.

I am delighted that the Queen is better; I hope that she will give us a boy. If I had the happiness of being pregnant, I would hope that my dear mother would help me to raise him by giving me her good advice, and would have the consolation of seeing him married. My brother Ferdinand will be very pleased if his hopes for his wife's pregnancy are confirmed. I no longer hear talk of the infante. I do not know how she [Edit: the infanta] can live without receiving news from the best of mothers. May God preserve me, my dear mother, from such misfortune.

MERCY TO MARIA THERESA, 20 APRIL 1773

Since the duc de la Vauguyon's death, Mme Adelaide has taken over the supervision of M. le comte d'Artois' education. The governors gave an account to her and received orders from her which she considered appropriate. The King seemed to approve of this arrangement therefore Mme Adelaide felt assured she would dispose of the positions when it came to forming the young prince's household; because of this, she had already promised a number of the positions in question; but the comtesse du Barry thought differently and had no great difficulty in overturning all Mme Adelaide's arrangements, appropriating the right to place her friends in the positions.

As a result, Mme Adelaide became bitter. At first she thought of bringing all the royals on to her side, and claimed that Mme la dauphine should complain to the King; this negotiation was made with all the passion and agitation possible; Mme l'archiduchesse seemed uncertain for a moment as to how she should act and she told me of her embarrassment. I let H.R.H. see that it was impossible for her to become involved in this without exposing herself to a great deal of trouble. However Mme Adelaide could not resolve to talk to the King; she showed her temper in her speech, which produced no effect other than that of embittering spirits. I limited myself to making it known that Mme la dauphine had nothing to do with this regrettable dispute.

M. le dauphin is showing curiosity about what is happening in public life; he has the gazettes and some journals read to him, and he sets aside some time for reading other historical works. This new interest in applying himself is without doubt the effect of Mme l'archiduchesse's suggestions, and she is justifiably taking pride in this.

SECRET LETTER

Mme l'archiduchesse showed me H.M. the emperor's last letter. It was quite short and dry. The monarch said he had learned with pleasure that Mme la dauphine had enjoyed carnival time but that she was indulging in too many pleasures and neglecting essential matters. The emperor added that he knew Mme la dauphine joked about his letters which she looked on as curiosity pieces only suitable to be displayed in a cabinet, and drew no lessons from them. Mme l'archiduchesse was not concerned about this letter; but I told her she should be, because if the emperor thought his advice was useless, he would gradually lose interest in Mme la dauphine, which would eventually have regrettable consequences. H.R.H. then became serious; she said she would write to H.M. the emperor in a way which would leave him in no doubt as to how important his letters were to her.

[Mme l'archiduchesse]...has natural judgement and truly astonishing wisdom, and despite the thoughtlessness and liveliness appropriate to her age, her ideas are developing markedly day by day. My only difficulty is in encouraging her to moderate certain impressions which she must not allow to be seen...[For example] she feels an aversion towards the duc d'Aiguillon which passes all bounds, based on her opinion of the malicious character of this minister. Unfortunately this is only too true; but I never stop telling her that it is essential not to let people know she understands their worth.

MARIA THERESA TO MARIE ANTOINETTE, 4 MAY 1773

I am sorry that the late arrival of last month's courier caused you worry; bad news always arrives quickly and you can be assured that, if something happened to a member of the family or to me, we would send a courier; therefore in future do not worry your sweet and loving self about these delays, as they occur very easily but, considering your loving interest in us, you will have your wish, and every week you will receive a letter from one of your brothers or sisters.

Mercy is very pleased with the way you are grasping business matters...[Remember that] when you follow Mercy's advice, you are only following mine, as he justly has my trust. The Queen worries me; she says she is big and heavy at five months, but that should not be; she has had some signs of miscarriage but after being bled they disappeared; however I am still worried. I am not able to have the consolation of seeing you in that situation, my dear daughter. I admit, it is the only thing which could interest me in prolonging my very unhappy days, being always...

MARIA THERESA TO MERCY, 5 MAY 1773

My daughter does in truth have a lot of intelligence and talents; but I still fear her lack of interest in studying, her neglect of anything which might cause her some bother, the

159

bad example of a dissipated court, and the petty schemes of her associates.

MARIE ANTOINETTE TO MARIA THERESA, 17 MAY 1773

We have been plagued by illness but thank God, all are well now. M. le dauphin had a sore throat and a slight fever which only lasted three or four days; he does not have it any more and is to be purged today.

I hope and wish that the good relationship between our two countries is maintained; there is one good thing about this country: it is that even if unpleasant rumours spread quickly, they dissipate just as quickly. [Edit: a reference to the talk in France about the negotiations between Austria, Russia and Prussia]

I am hoping that M. le dauphin and I will make our official entry into Paris next month, which will give me great pleasure. I do not dare talk of it yet, although I have the King's word; it would not be the first time they have made him change his mind.

MERCY TO MARIA THERESA, 18 MAY 1773

Mme la dauphine and Mme la comtesse de Provence went to visit Mme Victoire. Coming out of her rooms, Mme l'archiduchesse and her sister in law stopped in a little court to examine a great sundial which was built into the wall. At that moment, a bucket of water was thrown from the second floor, from a window in the comtesse du Barry's flat, and some of it fell on the two princesses. This incident, which was only caused by the thoughtlessness of some domestic, caused Mme la dauphine to be annoyed, with reason; she immediately went to the King and told him: "Look papa, what happens when people walk below your windows! You should make them be more careful."

The King, slightly taken aback, questioned her about the circumstances. In order to cover his embarrassment, he was very loving to Mme l'archiduchesse, telling her that he would punish those who had been so careless. After her initial irritation, Mme la dauphine was prudent enough to turn the incident into a joke therefore neither complaints nor bitterness resulted, although many people tried to turn the incident into a reason for quarrelling.

Lately the conversation of the royal family has centred on discussions about possible changes which could occur at court. Mme la comtesse de Provence, although very keen to be attentive to the comtesse du Barry, is however the first to predict that the favourite will soon be dismissed, and this usually leads to imprudent talk which it would be best to avoid...[I told Mme la dauphine this]

I added that if the comtesse du Barry were dismissed, and a new favourite appeared, to scandalize everyone, Mme la dauphine would reproach herself eternally, as it depended on her to foresee and avert this by attracting to herself the trust and affection of the King and by occupying herself with finding means to supply the King with pleasure and sweetness in the midst of his family which he had never before found there, and which he had thus been led to find in such an annoying and illicit way. I begged Mme l'archiduchesse to speak of this to her husband, but as if it was her own thoughts.

Mme la dauphine assured me I would never risk anything in being cited to M. le dauphin, because she knew he was kind to me and trusted me, and he sometimes asked Mme la dauphine what my advice would be on specific matters. However I insisted. Mme l'archiduchesse told me that she felt she could direct M. le dauphin in his intentions, but that it would not be as easy to determine him in matters of action and of words, because both were difficult for him because of his timid and slow character.

SECRET LETTER

Mme la dauphine, because of her grace, has won over public opinion, although the public has never seen her. I suggested to Mme l'archiduchesse to seize an appropriate moment to suggest to the King that she was curious to see the capital, and consequently he would be reminded about the

161

public entry. H.R.H., from timidity, could not at first resolve to do this; however then she decided and the King, without hesitating, told her she could arrange a time to carry out this ceremony.

MARIA THERESA TO MERCY, 2 JUNE 1773

I have every reason to be pleased with the conduct of my daughter, the Queen of Naples. She surpasses my expectations in many ways; but, without wishing to oppose myself to the idea of having her take part in matters of state, especially if she gives birth to a boy, I love her too much, just like the dauphine, to wish to see them engaged in such a painful career, where they would naturally be the focus of their subjects' discontent about the unhappy state of affairs, and where they would be exposed to the intrigues of so many factions. (Knowing this delicate and thankless career, I would not like them to embark on it.)

ANOTHER LETTER, (SAME DATE)

No one could wish more than me for the King to live a long life, without seeing my daughter having to take part in the governing of France.

MARIE ANTOINETTE TO MARIA THERESA, 14 JUNE 1773

My very dear mother, your kindness puts me to shame. The day before yesterday Mercy gave me your precious letter, and yesterday I received a second; that was a lovely way to spend my name day. Last Tuesday I had another celebration which I will never forget for the rest of my life; we made our official entry into Paris. As for honours, we received everything imaginable; all that, although wonderful, was not what touched me most, rather it was the love and eagerness of the poor people who, despite the taxes which burden them, were overcome with joy to see us.

When we were walking in the Tuileries, there was such a great crowd that for three quarters of an hour we were unable to move backwards or forwards. M. le dauphin and I several times asked the guards not to strike anyone, and this was very effective. Everything was so well ordered that day that, despite the enormous crowd which followed us everywhere, no one was hurt.

When we came back from the walk, we went up to an open terrace and stayed there for half an hour. I cannot describe, dear mother, the transports of joy, and the affection which was shown to us at that moment. Before leaving, we waved to the people, and this greatly pleased them. How lucky we are in our position to be able to win the affection of a whole people in such a simple way! Nothing can be so precious; I felt it deeply and will never forget it.

Something else which gave me great pleasure that beautiful day, was M. le dauphin's conduct. He replied very well to all the speeches, noticed everything which was done for him, and responded especially to the joy and eagerness of the people, to whom he was very kind. We are going tomorrow to the Opera at Paris; this is very much wished for, and I even believe that we will be going on other days to both the Comedie Francaise and the Comedie Italienne. I appreciate more and more every day what my dear mother did for me in marrying me here. I was the youngest daughter, yet I was treated as the oldest; how can I not feel overwhelmed with gratitude?

The King has been kind enough to free three hundred and twenty prisoners. They had debts to the wetnurses who had fed their children: this amnesty took place two days after our entry.

I am overjoyed at Y.M.'s hopes for the maintenance of peace; while the intriguers in this country are busy destroying one another, they cannot bother their friends or neighbours. Neither of us will go to the processions for the Fete-Dieu, as we are both taking asses' milk, to prevent us overheating.

My dear mother praises me too much for my love and attachment; I could never repay even half of what I owe you; I love you with all my heart.

MERCY TO MARIA THERESA, 16 JUNE 1773

The King's initial taste for the favourite has deadened with time, and as this woman has very little intelligence and a nondescript character, the King only finds mediocre distraction in her presence, mingled with all the drawbacks his relationship with her entails...[For example] her continual importunity to obtain favours which are often unjust, almost always for people who do not deserve them and have no worth except that given to them by intrigue. All that is repugnant to the King who, although apparently indifferent and inexplicably weak, nonetheless evaluates the people around him very well. This boredom of the King with his private circle seems to alarm those who compose it...[therefore because] H.R.H. markedly pleases the King…[they wish to include her on more of the King's trips].

The public was very enthusiastic about Mme la dauphine… [on her official entry into Paris]. They said "that her beauty and her kind appearance showed her to be the daughter of the august Maria Theresa." Wherever Mme la dauphine went, she smiled at the people; she greeted people of distinction. After lunch, she walked in the gardens of the Tuileries,[25] where without exaggeration there were more than 50,000 people. Some people had even climbed the trees, and H.R.H. ordered the guards not to push the people away, and to let them come as close as they wished. Mme la dauphine's attendants were cut off from her by the crowd several times, and all that could be heard was clapping and exclamations being repeated everywhere: "How beautiful she is! How charming she is!"

After walking about, when she was just about to leave, H.R.H. again went on to the great balcony at the front of the chateau and waved to the people both on the left and on the right, who called out with joy and pleasure. M. le dauphin, who for his part, had behaved very well, was looked on merely as an

---

[25] Where she would endure the last months of her reign, under very different circumstances.

accessory[26] at this ceremony. Everyone spoke only of Mme la dauphine's entrance and the rector of the University of Paris, when he published the speech he had made on the occasion, which I enclose, only gave an incidental mention to M. le dauphin.

No one can recall an entry which caused such a sensation and which had such popular success. What was even better was that M. le dauphin's kind expression, his polite words and the attention he showed everyone were attributed, with reason, to Mme l'archiduchesse's advice. [Edit: Mercy had of course given Marie Antoinette extensive advice before the entry] The King complimented her and seemed enchanted by the excellent success of the ceremony. It is still the subject of conversation in Paris, as much as on the first day.

SECRET LETTER

The day Mme Victoire's illness [measles] was diagnosed, the King was ready to go to Saint-Hubert and Mme la dauphine said to him: "I know papa, you will not go to Saint-Hubert because of my aunt's condition." The King having replied that the princess was not ill enough to prevent his trip, Mme l'archiduchesse replied: "I do not think that is quite right." H.R.H. was shocked by the conduct of the King. She felt it indicated a lack of sensitivity which disturbed her, and seemed to distress her beautiful soul. I had a lot of trouble effacing this impression, and it is not the first time I have encountered this.

Mme la dauphine shows evidence in all essential matters of a kind and compassionate heart and anyone who does not appear to think in a similar way appals her. I have experienced times when, for similar reasons, her opinion of the King has taken a direction which has frightened me. However up till now, I have always succeeded in bringing Mme l'archiduchesse back to a more appropriate way of thinking, and this is very important, as, with her sincerity and the frankness natural to her, she would have difficulty in

---

[26] Shades of Charles and Di.

concealing her thoughts and showing the King the respect she owes him, if she were to believe that the King's personality did not deserve this.

MARIA THERESA TO MERCY, JULY 1773

The success of my daughter's entry into Paris filled me with joy.

MERCY TO MARIA THERESA, 17 JULY 1773

M. le dauphin and Mme la dauphine have recently come every week to Paris to see there successively, plays at the Opera, the Comedie Francaise and the Comedie Italienne. The King wanted Their Royal Highnesses on these initial visits to be accompanied by all the ceremony which would be observed if the monarch himself were present. Consequently, on each trip they fired cannon from the Hotel des Invalides and from the Bastille. Two companies, one from the Gardes Francaises and the other from the Gardes Suisses, were on parade at the theatres, with their flags, when Their Royal Highnesses arrived.

All that pomp, while inspiring respect, could have spoiled the public's joy, but it did not do so and it would be impossible to add to the demonstrations of contentment, goodwill and enthusiasm which this same public showed with its usual vivacity. These displays were always directed at Mme la dauphine, and I could write volumes on all the moving words heard about Mme l'archiduchesse's face, her grace and her expression of affability and kindness. It is true that H.R.H. did not once fail to show these qualities, and the people were infinitely touched at her oft repeated orders not to push away anyone in her path.

This universal homage to the charming qualities of Mme la dauphine and the public's attraction to her have had the double effect of both pleasing the King and embarrassing the cabal at Versailles. M. le dauphin and Mme la dauphine have thus acquired standing based on public opinion and that is what had always made me wish for their entry into Paris.

[The comtesse de Narbonne, in order to acquire favours from the duc d' Aiguillon, is trying to encourage the royal family to be more favourable to him]...Acting on the advice of the comtesse de Narbonne, Mme Adelaide contrived a conversation with M. le dauphin and Mme la dauphine, in which she tried to suggest to them several reflections which were very close to the views the duc d'Aiguillon appears to have. Mme la dauphine listened without saying what she thought. M. le dauphin, in a frank but slightly brusque tone, replied: "Aunt, I advise you not to become involved in M. d'Aiguillon's intrigues, as he is an unpleasant person." The forceful way he expressed himself silenced Mme Adelaide and I very much doubt if after all that she will again try to act as a mouthpiece for her dame d'atours.

Until the departure from Versailles of l'archiduchesse, her serious occupations have been neither interrupted nor neglected.

SECRET LETTER

Although the union between M. le dauphin and Mme la dauphine is perfect, sometimes however H.R.H. has reasons for displeasure, which she is good enough to confide in me.

All her ascendancy over M. le dauphin has not yet been able to deter this young prince from his extraordinary taste for building work such as masonry, carpentry and others of the like.[27] He always has something new to work on in his private rooms; he himself works with the labourers to move the materials, the beams and the paving stones, and because he devotes himself to this exhausting exercise for hours at a time, he sometimes comes back more exhausted than workmen obliged to do this kind of work. Mme la dauphine recently was excessively annoyed and pained by this behaviour; I can judge

---

[27] During the Revolution, Louis XVl constructed a secret cupboard in his rooms, containing his correspondence, with a Jacobin workman. This workman informed the revolutionaries of this cupboard – the correspondence was seized – and as a result, advisors to Louis were guillotined.

this by the intensity of the complaints she makes to me, and by the inferences she draws about the effects such excessive exercise could have on the well-being of her husband.[28]

I tried to pacify Mme l'archiduchesse in this respect, telling her of the only means she could use to gradually withdraw M. le dauphin from these sorts of occupations. It would be dangerous to openly forbid him; it is only the lure of other more pleasant and appropriate amusements which will dissuade him from this. I begged H.R.H. to be neither too sharp nor sour in her remonstrances about the matters which displeased her; sweet and consistent persuasion would be much more effective.

All the new manoeuvres of the duc d'Aiguillon have one cause: he has quarrelled with the relatives of the favourite and she has become very cold to him. If the duc d'Aiguillon were to fall from grace, then the prince de Soubise and the Rohans would acquire a very decided credit, and I believe that it would be best to be careful with them, at least until the present crisis has developed further.

MARIE ANTOINETTE TO MARIA THERESA, 17 JULY 1773

Your satisfaction is all I need to add to the joy I will feel all my life at my reception in Paris. I will admit to my dear mother that in leaving for Compiegne I felt regret to be moving away from that good city; it is quite true that I was moved to tears, especially at the Comedie Italienne when the people in the stalls joined in one voice with the actors and cried out: "Long live the King!" Clerval, one of the actors, added: "and his dear children!" and he was enthusiastically applauded.

I can only compare that wonderful day to the one when my dear mother went to the play after the birth of my nephew in Florence. [Edit: Maria Theresa's first grandson] Although I was still just a child, I realized that everyone was moved by the presence of my dear mother. M. le dauphin has been wonderful

---

[28] It is thought that Louis was trying to build up his physique, in order to aid his performance in the marital bed!

each time he has been to Paris, and if I may say so, the look of closeness between us has made the people even more fond of him; perhaps that is why they say he kissed me in public, although that is not true; but my dear mother is very wrong in thinking he has not done so since my arrival; on the contrary for a long time everybody has noticed his eagerness to be with me.

MARIA THERESA TO MERCY, JULY 1773

Prince Kaunitz sees your letters to me, except the private ones; no one has seen them except Pichler and sometimes Starhemberg. The emperor knows you write to me but not having wanted to see them from the very beginning, even finding it unfortunate that I kept up this correspondence for my consolation, I no longer insist. He has never asked me since, if I continue to write or not, wanting to make me believe, because it is not the case, that the moment a member of the family leaves, he no longer thinks of them and only wants to read their news in the gazettes; I never say a word to him about the family unless he starts the conversation himself.

You can imagine that this gives me no pleasure, but that is my sorry position with my son, even though he is very kind and talented. I alone find no consolation in him and am often thwarted by him. Burn this note. You often sustain my saddest days with your letters, but even more with your advice and prudent conduct in political matters. Save me from this wretched Rohan. Yours affectionately.

MARIA THERESA TO MERCY, 2 AUGUST 1773

Considering the present state of affairs, I feel it is in our interest rather than contrary to it that the duc d'Aiguillon remains in his post, at least until there is peace between Russia and the Turks, and until the Poland affair is concluded. Gifted with little genius and talents, without credit and harassed ceaselessly by factions, he is not in a position to thwart us. Our situation would be much more difficult if the duc de Choiseul, well intentioned as he was, were still in post, and it could be the same if Broglie were to replace d'Aiguillon.

MARIE ANTOINETTE TO MARIA THERESA, 13 AUGUST 1773

I am being painted at present; it is quite true that the artists have not yet painted a good resemblance of me: I would happily give all I own to anyone who could express through my portrait the joy I would have in seeing my dear mother again; it is very hard not to be able to hug her, except in a letter.

My husband is touched at your kindness; I hope he will continue to deserve it.

MERCY TO MARIA THERESA, 14 AUGUST 1773

Mme Adelaide was persuaded by the comtesse de Narbonne to write to the King. She wrote that...[she wished to know his thoughts about his family] The King replied that he noticed with distress that M. le dauphin had no taste for society and "that he showed decided aversion towards the fair sex:" that he, the King, wished that Mme Adelaide would try to encourage more sociable conduct in M. le dauphin.

This caused a lot of trouble. M. le dauphin was in a bad temper. Finally all the family...[told Mme Adelaide that they disapproved of her conduct]

On the 20th, Mme la dauphine was to go to the hunt; but was prevented as, during the previous night, M. le dauphin had had indigestion. This indisposition had been very slight; however the young prince kept to his bed, even against the doctors' advice, and they complained greatly about the apprehension and dejection to which M. le dauphin is subject at the slightest signs of being indisposed. Mme l'archiduchesse did not leave him all day.

On the 6th, Mme la dauphine was into the sixth day of a critical time. Despite that she wanted to ride on her horse; her doctor opposed this, but she did not listen to him. However

Mme l'archiduchesse was sufficiently cautious only to ride slowly and for a short time.

[Next day I]…spoke to doctor Lassone, reproaching him for his weakness in letting H.R.H. go on her horse.

SECRET LETTER

It is quite certain that H.M. the emperor is not serious when he speaks indifferently of the members of his august family who are absent. Until the very moment he left on his trip, the monarch has never stopped writing letters to Mme la dauphine, full of very wise advice and warnings, sometimes a little dry, but which show the very real interest which H.M. takes in Mme l'archiduchesse.

There is one matter about which I cannot stop insisting, and which seems to me to merit all Y.M.'s attention: Mme la dauphine understands affairs of state extremely easily, but she fears them excessively; she will not allow herself to think that she may one day have power and authority; as a result her character inclines to passivity and dependency; as a consequence she has a habit of being timid and fearful on the slightest occasion.

H.R.H. is afraid to talk to the King; she is afraid of the ministers; even the people in her service can be imposing to her. Nonetheless it is of the utmost importance that Mme l'archiduchesse learns to better understand and appreciate her strengths. I would answer with my life that if she were to take advantage of her ascendancy over the King, there would be no favourite nor even a minister who could resist the power, influence and credit which Mme la dauphine would procure from that moment; besides M. le dauphin, although he is sensible and has some good qualities, will probably never have sufficient determination nor willpower to reign by himself. If Mme l'archiduchesse does not govern him, others will.

MARIA THERESA TO MARIE ANTOINETTE, 29 AUGUST 1773

I have never heard of a happier delivery than the Queen's; she is enchanted with her little Louise; she thinks she is beautiful and more like our family than the older one. She is much more reasonable than both of us in this matter; but what bothers me even more is that she will probably have a third daughter. As for you my dear children, nothing is lost; you are only beginning, you can afford to wait; but I am coming to the end of my life and that is the difference, and the fact there is no change in your situation no longer suffices.

As for Rohan, it is because of the influence this wicked bishop could have on you that I still conceal my feelings about him.

MARIA THERESA TO MERCY, 31 AUGUST 1773

I tell you frankly that I do not wish my daughter to gain a decided influence in matters of state. I have learned only too well, from my own experience, how the government of a huge kingdom is an overwhelming burden. Besides I know the youth and thoughtlessness of my daughter, and that she has little taste for study (in fact she knows nothing), which would make me even more fearful for the success of the government, as the monarchy in France is so near collapse; and if my daughter could not re establish it on a firm footing, and if the state of this kingdom were to deteriorate further, I would prefer that some minister was blamed rather than my daughter (and that the other was at fault). Therefore I cannot bring myself to talk politics and affairs of state to her, unless you think it appropriate and you tell me EXACTLY what I have to say.

There were instances here of how she is so accommodating and lets herself be drawn into misplaced recommendations because of the importunities of her people, and I occasionally had arguments about this with her in the last months before she left here.

MARIE ANTOINETTE TO MARIA THERESA,
14 SEPTEMBER 1773

I have never disparaged my sister Provence's conduct; but my dear mother will allow me to tell her confidentially of a few little differences between us: 1.Being Italian gives her resources I do not have [Edit: that is, she was deceitful (unlike Marie Antoinette's dear friend Lamballe, who was also Italian)]; 2. When she arrived here the comte de Provence was mixed up in intrigues, and wished his wife to act as he did; as for me, on the contrary, I am quite sure that M. le dauphin would not have liked me to do so.

When we came back from Compiegne I very much wanted to return to Paris, with good reason, as we were very well received; I intend returning there to see the paintings; I loaned that of my dear mother, and people are eager to see it.

MERCY TO MARIA THERESA, 16 SEPTEMBER 1773

[The abbe de Vermond informed Mercy that he wished to resign because he displeased M. le dauphin, who had never spoken to him; and because Mme la dauphine did not act on his advice]…M. le dauphin's actions are not as a result of ill will or prejudice, but due to embarrassment and timidity towards a man who is accepted, with reason, as having intelligence and knowledge and therefore overawes the young prince.

I prevailed on the abbe de Vermond not to resign.

[Having spoken to Mme l'archiduchesse about this affair, Mercy found her worried]…She spoke to me of him in a way which let me see that she appreciated the zeal and honesty of that faithful servant. She added that she would not let him retire. Her main worry was fear of Y.M.'s anxiety.

Mme la dauphine spoke to M. le dauphin about the abbe de Vermond; the young prince explained himself in a most satisfying manner about this priest and he is therefore happy, and continuing his service.

MARIE ANTOINETTE TO MARIA THERESA, 21 SEPTEMBER 1773

It is impossible for me to tell you how much I appreciate your kindness. [Edit: Maria Theresa had sent Marie Antoinette a carnation set in diamonds] When Neny arrived, the ambassadress of Sardinia and all the diplomatic corps were having an audience with me. What joy and pride I felt in showing them such a charming sign of maternal love! M. le dauphin added to my joy by showing Neny the respect he felt for my dear mother.

MARIA THERESA TO MERCY, 3 OCTOBER 1773

I am pleased that the abbe de Vermond has decided not to retire. I know how much my daughter likes to follow her own inclinations. She has not even tried to conceal this aspect of her character from you, telling you lately (for the second time) that "when one has adopted a system of conduct, it is difficult to change." I am relieved to see the abbe de Vermond staying in his position, in order to have at least one dependable man near her, capable of informing you of everything.

MARIA THERESA TO MARIE ANTOINETTE, 3 OCTOBER 1773

[Your present]…arrived at the right time to serve as a demonstration to the diplomatic corps of my love for you. Indeed I would like all Europe to know how much I love you and that my happiness depends on that of my children.

I am pleased you still enjoy your trips to Paris; the Queen never went, nor did the late dauphine, nor your aunts, yet the King is willing to agree to all that, because it pleases his little dauphine; you owe him so much.

I was very pleased with the care and attention you showed your aunt, when she was unwell; that is as it should be and shows your kind heart.

MERCY TO MARIA THERESA, 17 OCTOBER 1773

Paris is enchanted with Mme l'archiduchesse. The ill will of different parties has not succeeded in making the King take umbrage at the striking successes of Mme la dauphine and he even seems to view them with great pleasure. However Mesdames and the young princes and princesses regard this differently. They are jealous and this is encouraged by intriguers.

When M le comte and Mme la comtesse de Provence made their entry, the King was asked that they be granted the same ceremonial as that accorded to M. le dauphin and Mme la dauphine. This parity was observed in all respects. Mesdames have often come to Paris to the walks, to the shops; but this has had no effect on the public; the whole family is continually and totally eclipsed by Mme la dauphine: people only talk of her and only want to see her and attribute any pleasant aspect of M. le dauphin to her. I tried to persuade Mme l'archiduchesse that it was just as easy to please the whole court, especially the King's circle; but when I mentioned them, because of the favourite, I always have to combat a dislike which I cannot completely overcome.

The jealousy of the rest of the royal family has had no impression on Mme la dauphine; her frank and kind character has not allowed her to notice such weaknesses, and she would have pardoned them if she had noticed it.

SECRET LETTER

Although Mme l'archiduchesse's intimacy with M. le dauphin continues, there is however still no sign of pregnancy; but as one can with reason flatter oneself that such a desirable event may occur any day, I never stop asking Mme la dauphine, and even urging her, to be careful to ride moderately.

MARIA THERESA TO MERCY, 6 NOVEMBER 1773

Neny has given me a detailed report about my daughter and I have every reason to be pleased. I am equally pleased about what he told me of your situation, that you are as well thought of at court, as by the public and that justice is rendered to your merit.

Once the comte d'Artois' wife arrives, the Piedmontese party will increase, and having two princesses of Savoy at its head, the cabal could become stronger. I would be grateful to receive precise information about the character, intelligence and looks of this princess, how she behaves in relation to my daughter, and how she is received by the family and the public.

SAME DATE, ANOTHER LETTER

I have just this evening received the pleasant news that my daughter in law in Milan has given birth to a daughter. That makes three grandchildren this year and I am expecting a fourth in December. May God be praised! But the dauphine is not among them, and I must admit that I am tortured now with the desire to see her pregnant, as I am not persuaded that she is lacking, but that it is the dauphin; it has dragged on too long for me to dare to hope for a change.

MERCY TO MARIA THERESA, 12 NOVEMBER 1773

On the 16th of October, at the hunt, the stag, closely pursued by the dogs, jumped into an enclosed field which the worker[29] was busy cultivating and struck him twice with his antlers. The wife of the unfortunate man, seeing what had happened, was overcome with despair and ran towards a group of hunters whom she saw in the distance; it was the King and his suite. She called for help, told of the disaster which had happened to her husband, and then fell down in a faint.

The King ordered that she be taken care of, was kind and compassionate and then left; then Mme la dauphine who had just arrived, stepped down from her barouche, ran towards the woman, and held perfume to her face, thus bringing her round. Mme l'archiduchesse gave her all the money she had

---

[29] Because of the connotations of 'paysan/peasant' I have given the translation – worker.

with her, but what was even more admirable was H.R.H.'s words of kindness and consolation to the poor creature. Indeed Mme l'archiduchesse, who was moved and upset, began to cry and this caused more than one hundred spectators to do so too. These people were clustered round her, unable to move because they were struck with admiration at such a unique and poignant scene. Then, having sent for her barouche, Mme la dauphine ordered them to put the woman and her two friends in it and take them back to their cottages. H.R.H. enquired about the help given to the injured man, and it seemed at first that he would not recover.

I cannot tell Y.M. how widespread and heartfelt was the sensation caused by this event, not only amongst the people at court, but even more amongst the people of Fontainebleau and the surrounding area who for several days have gathered in the places where they are likely to see Mme la dauphine pass by. The Parisians, learning of all this, have seemed very moved, and there is but one voice of joy and admiration when the talk is of Mme l'archiduchesse.

Since the accident on the 16th, H.R.H. has not forgotten the injured man and has often enquired after him. At first it was thought there was no hope, but now it seems he may survive, due to the care the royal surgeons have been ordered to give him.

I told H.R.H about how relations between the ministers stood. I suggested some useful ideas to mention to M. le dauphin in moments of closeness. Mme l'archiduchesse told me that M. le dauphin sometimes spoke to her of the present intrigues and that he never expressed himself very clearly. I observed that, in the extraordinary circumstances of the present, the royal family, and especially M. le dauphin and Mme la dauphine, could have no other conduct than that of observing all in silence, taking no one's part, being neutral to all parties, and treating equally all those at court, according to their rank, without favouritism or dislike.

I have no doubt that Mme la dauphine will explain herself to Y.M. regarding her hopes of pregnancy, but it appears that this happy event is not yet as probable as would be desired.

In my last audience with Mme la dauphine, she deigned to confide in me a very interesting conversation she had had with M. le dauphin. They had been talking about how Mme la comtesse d'Artois would soon arrive and of the sensation at court and with the public if that princess became pregnant before Mme l'archiduchesse. M. le dauphin was the first to talk of this, and hugging Mme la dauphine he said: "Do you really love me?" H.R.H. replied "Yes and you cannot doubt it; I love you sincerely and esteem you even more." The young prince was very touched at this; he embraced Mme l'archiduchesse lovingly and told her that when they returned to Versailles, he would again follow his regime and that he "hoped that all would be well."

MARIA THERESA TO MERCY, 1 DECEMBER 1773

I see from my daughter's persistent refusal to stop horse riding how self-willed she is. (In the circumstances I cannot oppose this exercise, which is innocent and can spoil nothing)

I have just learned that the prince de Rohan could leave here for Paris in a few days, with the intention of being exonerated of all charges against him, and will then return here to be recalled in a way which will protect his reputation. As his relatives in France are numerous and quite powerful, there are those who fear that they will revenge themselves on my daughter[30] for the wrongs they claim he has suffered because of me. [Edit: Rohan was the French ambassador to Vienna and

---

[30] Rohan was later involved in the so-called 'Affair of the Diamond Necklace,' which greatly damaged Marie Antoinette's standing in the eyes of the public, just before the Revolution (Marie Antoinette was accused of secretly borrowing money to buy more diamond jewellery).

Maria Theresa wished him recalled because of his dissolute behaviour]

MERCY TO MARIA THERESA, 18 DECEMBER 1773

Mme la comtesse d'Artois [has arrived]...M. le comte d'Artois seemed satisfied at the appearance of his wife. However that does not seem to be this young princess' most advantageous aspect; she is quite small, has a mediocre figure with no shocking defects; her colouring is quite pale, her face thin, nose long and badly rounded off, she has a slight cast in her eyes, a big mouth, in sum an irregular face which is not very pleasant and what is more, looks quite common.[31] However her demeanour, her timidity, and her embarrassed air are even more irritating; she cannot speak a word, despite the attempts of her lady of honour to suggest appropriate phrases.

My immediate impression of Mme la comtesse d'Artois was very unfavourable and all the public have immediately formed a similar opinion of her. Although none of this can have escaped Mme la dauphine, she spoke kindly and indulgently to me of the young princess. Mme la comtesse de Provence up till now has not seemed very interested in her sister. Apparently, as children, they were not very close and instead, a motive of rivalry has entered into their relationship since the marriage of Mme la comtesse de Provence, and increased their mutual indifference.

H.R.H.'s immense advantages are increasing more and more due to her personal qualities, which eclipse all at this court. I can see quite clearly that people are trying to win the protection and favour of Mme l'archiduchesse, in preference to anyone else. Even the favourite has clearly adopted this system. When it was time to nominate the ladies for Mme la comtesse d'Artois' household, Mme la dauphine insisted that the marquise de Trans be given a position and two days later, the marquise de Trans was given the position in question. The controleur general in his department, is no less eager to agree to what Mme l'archiduchesse tells him she wishes, and many

---

[31] What more can be added to this description!

179

financial favours have been granted because it was H.R.H.'s wish.

Although the other ministers, because of the nature of their departments, do not have such frequent opportunities to obey Mme l'archiduchesse, they are no less eager to find means to please her, and this is quite remarkable in contrast to the position of the other princes and princesses of the royal family. With the exception of M. le dauphin, who has never requested anything from the ministers, his brothers and even more so Mesdames, whether because they themselves wish, or because they are urged by their associates, daily make the most unreasonable requests, which are constantly refused and which only succeed in establishing the total lack of credit of these princes and princesses.

[Recently at cards]…Mme la dauphine won more than twelve hundred louis; she seemed both embarrassed and irritated at this, and tried everything possible to lose them again, without however succeeding. Next day, she herself decided to send fifty louis for the poor to each of the two parishes in Versailles; she deigned to consult me later about how to distribute the rest of the sum, which she did not want to keep. I proposed to her to use it to give bonuses to her staff in proportion to their merit and their indigence, as they are owed eighteen months salary; H.R.H. adopted this plan. Until now Mme l'archiduchesse has only rarely shown signs of being inclined to generosity, and amongst the people at court this has led to talk and doubts which I intended informing Y.M. of in the future.

The King has always had a decided liking for the house of Savoy, to which he is so closely related; but he finds the two Piedmontese princesses unattractive in face or figure, and he is agreeably struck by the difference with Mme la dauphine.

Mme la comtesse d'Artois does not seem to be very intelligent. People in general are displeased by the taciturn and ungracious way in which she receives everyone; she has failed with the public, but is very attentive to Mme la dauphine.

SECRET LETTER

Such a long delay in becoming pregnant is even more afflicting as it is the one and only element lacking to affirm the favourable and even brilliant position of Mme l'archiduchesse. Due to inconceivable misfortune, any hopes in this respect, instead of increasing, seem to be diminishing.

H.M. the emperor has deigned to mention to me his plan to come to France.[32]

MARIA THERESA TO MERCY, 20 DECEMBER 1773

Judge of my situation; it is such that it cannot continue, and that is my hope. [Edit: Kaunitz wanted to resign as it was difficult working with both Maria Theresa and Joseph, as joint heads of state, so Maria Theresa asked Mercy to join her council]...I must admit that my poor daughter's situation concerns me, but the good of the state must take precedence.

---

[32] Joseph intended to go to France to enquire personally into the marital state of his brother in law and sister. However circumstances delayed his visit by a few years – with disastrous consequences for Marie Antoinette.

1774

MARIA THERESA TO MERCY, 3 JANUARY 1774

The coldness of the dauphin, a young husband only twenty years old, in relation to a pretty woman, is inconceivable to me. Despite the assertions of the doctors, my suspicions with regard to the physical constitution of this prince are increasing, and I have almost no other hope than that of the emperor's intervention, as he will perhaps, on arrival at Versailles, find means of engaging this lazy husband to better acquit himself of his duty.[33]

MERCY TO MARIA THERESA, 9 JANUARY 1774

Y.M.'s very gracious letter has left me overwhelmed with gratitude…[However I must refuse the offer]

I must admit that my pain in leaving Mme la dauphine would be inexpressible. I have been here since this princess arrived and she has honoured me with her confidence, which she has continued, as she knows my uprightness, my honest zeal and my respectful attachment to her. M. le dauphin, for the same reasons, shows me a kindness which few people have experienced from him. The King, contrary to his custom, is in the habit of speaking to me informally and if an urgent matter arose, I could address myself directly to him. My successor would take a long time to reach this point.

---

[33] Maria Theresa later berated Marie Antoinette for her lack of respect for her husband, but she shared her daughter's sentiments, as revealed in this letter.

The comte d'Artois, now freed from the constraints imposed upon him by his governors,[34] shows increasing signs of a passionate, haughty and inconsiderate character. He has already drawn severe reprimands from M. le dauphin for having sometimes forgotten the respect he owes him. When this happens, Mme la dauphine always intervenes to reconcile the two brothers and she has adopted the best possible stratagem with regard to M. le comte d'Artois in that she teases the young prince when he says or does something which is unreasonable. This mortifies him and imposes on him much more than a more serious reprimand would, thus he only fears Mme l'archiduchesse, and apart from her he pays attention to no one else; he is not even careful with regard to the favourite and all the dominant party.

He has demanded that his wife should speak neither to the comtesse du Barry nor to any of the ladies who form her circle. He says openly that they have composed his household with a collection of fools from whom he will free himself whenever the opportunity arises. These words, which were quickly reported to the King, have irritated him and as a result the young prince is treated coldly.

Mme la dauphine shows her [Edit: the comtesse d'Artois] much kindness and would like to draw her out of her state of apathy but unless something unforeseen happens, Mme la comtesse d'Artois' role will always be negligible.

Mme l'archiduchesse holds an unfavourable opinion of the ministers and without treating them badly, her frankness and sincerity prevent her from being kind to them. Perhaps Y.M. could mention this to Mme la dauphine.

Mme la dauphine's balls have started again on Mondays and all who are admitted to pay court are enchanted with Mme l'archiduchesse's grace and kindness.

Even with these distractions, H.R.H. regularly reads each day for one hour and a half or two hours, and has useful

---

[34] Being of an age to marry, he was no longer deemed to need education.

talks with the abbe de Vermond. She also devotes about the same time to music and dance.

SECRET LETTER

With reference to the important and delicate matter, Mme l'archiduchesse's tranquility, her prudence, and conduct are beyond praise and are what one would expect from her truly virtuous soul and noble spirit.[35]

MERCY TO MARIA THERESA, 19 FEBRUARY 1774

Mme la dauphine does not seem to have the same taste for the amusements of carnival, as before. She likes a ball more for seeing people now, than for dancing. On the 30th of January, the three princes and the princesses went to the masked ball at the Opera House in Paris: they remained there for a long time without being recognised, due to well chosen measures. M. le dauphin behaved marvellously; he circulated round the ballroom, speaking indistinctly to all these he knew as he walked round. The public was delighted with M. le dauphin's behaviour; it caused a great sensation in Paris and people have not failed to attribute to Mme la dauphine the improvement which they have noticed in the way her husband behaves.

SECRET LETTER

[The King has recently been reflecting on]…his age, state of health and on the frightening account which he will one day have to render God of the way he has lived his life. These reflections, occasioned by the death of some people of the King's age, some almost before his very eyes, have greatly alarmed the people who maintain this monarch in his present

---

[35] In January, Marie Antoinette encountered Fersen at a masked ball in Paris. The attraction between the two, was noticed by courtiers. Perhaps Mercy is alluding to her resistance to temptation, in his description of her "truly virtuous soul."

errors. Foreseeing that the King, becoming again pious, could put himself in the hands of his confessor, and knowing that the person who occupies that position was too virtuous to incline towards intrigue, they tried to have him dismissed in order to substitute someone who could be more easily manipulated.

As soon as I was instructed of this matter, I did not hesitate to tell Mme la dauphine about it. I proposed to Mme l'archiduchesse to tell the King of the esteem and trust which she felt for her present confessor [Edit: who was also the King's confessor].

Mme la dauphine followed this advice and spoke to the King just in time, as they had involved Mme Louise, the Carmellite nun, but the King declared that he would never remove Mme la dauphine's confessor from her.

MARIA THERESA TO MERCY, 8 MARCH 1774

I pardon my daughter for not being so interested in dancing. (Her enjoyment has been lost too soon; I hope that serious reflection comes to her as late as possible)

The intrigue hatched against the confessor of the King and my daughter, fills me with horror. How I pity that good prince, subjugated by the cabals of his unworthy favourites! All that remains to him is trust in the mercy of God, who, from pity for the noble (but weak) feelings of this unfortunate sovereign, will perhaps at the end open his eyes to the danger he risks of becoming irredeemably lost.

MERCY TO MARIA THERESA, 22 MARCH 1774

Mme l'archiduchesse counts amongst her ladies, a comtesse de Mailly. This woman had an only son and on losing him she was deeply distressed. Mme l'archiduchesse, touched at her misfortune, wanted to visit the comtesse de Mailly but Mesdames told Mme l'archiduchesse that it was not the custom for princes and princesses to go visiting individuals. Mme la dauphine... [then asked the King for his permission, which he readily granted]. This kind act had all the success it deserved with the public in Paris, who are unaccustomed to kindliness from the princes and princesses in the royal family.

SECRET LETTER

Although Mme la dauphine has always showered Mme la comtesse d'Artois with kindness and consideration, nevertheless this princess, whose character seems to be as unpleasant as her face,[36] instead of responding with sensitivity and gratitude to Mme l'archiduchesse's actions, seemed to feel only indifference, which I attributed at first to a lack of intelligence; but other circumstances have combined to show that ill will is involved.

On the other hand, Mme la comtesse de Provence, despite her appearance of kindness and friendship, tries to act a part when with Mme la dauphine, who is easily deceived in this way as her candour, frankness and excellent character do not permit her to be suspicious of others.

Mme la dauphine had a great desire to go to the masked ball at the Opera House; but, knowing that M. le dauphin does not like these sorts of balls, and fearing to stretch his obligingness too far, she asked Mme la comtesse de Provence to talk to M. le dauphin, say she wanted to go to the ball, and not let the young prince know that Mme l'archiduchesse had anything to do with the request. Mme de Provence promised to do this; she then reported that M. le dauphin had not wanted to agree to this proposal, and that she would have to abandon all thought of persuading him.

Several days later, M. le dauphin and Mme la dauphine were having a friendly and loving talk and the question of the ball arose. M. le dauphin told Mme l'archiduchesse that when Mme la comtesse de Provence had spoken to him about the ball, she had told him to keep it a secret but that Mme la dauphine had asked her to approach him; that she, the comtesse de Provence, did not enjoy these types of amusements, and that she would be happy not to go, and that she only went from

---

[36] It seems a safe bet that Mercy disliked the comtesse d'Artois.

obligingness to Mme l'archiduchesse, who only seemed to find pleasure in these frivolous amusements.

The venom of such thoughtless spitefulness had greatly shocked M. le dauphin, and he told Mme l'archiduchesse in a kindly way that, in order not to expose herself in the future to such duplicity, he was telling her once and for all that he would always approve of her carrying out the arrangements necessary for her amusements.

MARIA THERESA TO MARIE ANTOINETTE, 3 APRIL 1774

M. d'Esterhazy behaved badly in every way. He is married but he kept another man's wife. I know you have been kind to him, that is characteristic of your good heart; but unfortunately, being a sovereign, one cannot allow oneself to follow one's inclination; most of the time it is necessary to act against it. That is my distressing and disagreeable situation and eventually it makes our position intolerable and even dangerous.

I have learned from the gazettes of your visit to Mme de Mailly. That has caused a very different sensation; but all hearts must approve. M. d'Aiguillon in his new position as minister of war has begun by wanting to win your good graces; that is right, and you must also be kind to him as he deserves it. I do not wish you to be base, but simply non partisan.

Your situation is too brilliant not to make people envious; they will not neglect any opportunity to trouble you, it is necessary therefore to be circumspect. I am only occupied with your happiness my dear daughter, and I would procure it for you at the expense of my own life.

MERCY TO MARIA THERESA, 19 APRIL 1774

I told you of Mesdames' jealousy. I limited myself to begging Mme l'archiduchesse to appear not to notice such pettiness. Daily I see the good effects of this in that Mesdames are beginning to abstain from all misplaced criticism and they are beginning to act reasonably.

It is not the same with regard to M le comte and Mme la comtesse d'Artois who are turning out to be so disagreeable that the whole court is repelled. The young prince treats ministers badly, announcing his orders to them in a harsh and peremptory tone; he cares for no one. Until now she [Edit: Marie Antoinette] controlled him by joking in a playful way; but it seems that this has lost its power with the young prince and it will be even more difficult to control him as the King does not exercise his authority with him or with any of his children. Mme la comtesse d'Artois, for her part, has no qualities to compensate for her husband's failings.

[ON THE 28TH OF APRIL, THE KING BECAME ILL. ON THE 30TH, HIS ILLNESS WAS DIAGNOSED AS SMALLPOX]

MERCY TO MARIA THERESA, 1 MAY 1774

Sacred Majesty, in those first grave and critical moments, the main question was whether Mme l'archiduchesse should ask to remain with the King, or whether it was preferable for her to stay with M. le dauphin. I proposed that M. le dauphin should make the decision; at the moment of writing, I do not yet know what has been decided. In the meantime, it will be recorded that Mme l'archiduchesse offered to shut herself up with the King and she will at least have the merit of this act of kindness.

I anticipated a possible situation in which the favourite, in her dilemma, could decide to address M. le dauphin and Mme la dauphine to know their intentions, that is, whether she should stay at court or leave. I persuaded Mme la dauphine to make no reply, but to limit herself to saying that neither she nor the prince her husband had anything to say about what the King's associates should do. This circumspection seemed necessary to me, because if the King confesses, it is up to the priests to send away the favourite, and if the monarch recovers, it could be very dangerous if M. le dauphin could be accused of having thought of sending the comtesse du Barry away.

I am moving to Versailles tonight. Mme l'archiduchesse behaved in a very touching manner when she first heard.

MERCY TO MARIA THERESA, 8 MAY 1774

As H.R.H. is writing to Y.M. about the present condition of the King, his receiving of the sacraments, the speech by the grand almoner on that occasion, and the dismissal of the favourite, I will limit myself to brief comments about these matters, in the short time I have.

The King's illness has followed the normal pattern, and what constitutes the greatest danger, is the enormous quantity of little pustules with which the King is covered.

It seems certain that it was the King himself who unexpectedly asked for his confessor at half past two this morning. The princes timed this and the confessor was alone with the King for sixteen minutes, and from this moment until the sacraments were received, the King called him back three times.

After the confession, at five o'clock in the morning, the King sent for the duc d'Aiguillon and spoke to him in a low voice. It was said that it was orders to send away the comtesse du Barry; but at the end, one could see that the King clung to this favourite much more than one could have imagined, and if the monarch comes through this illness, it is to be presumed and even more to be feared, that this woman will be recalled to court.

At this critical and delicate time, Mme la dauphine is behaving like an angel and I cannot express my admiration for her piety, prudence and reason. The public is delighted with Mme la dauphine and justly so. H.R.H. has kept herself perfectly secluded even from the people in her service, and apart from the royal family, she has only seen the abbe de Vermond and I. I told Mme l'archiduchesse everything I could think of, whether about the present circumstances, or about possible future circumstances. I believe Mme la dauphine is well prepared and forewarned of anything that may happen.

If the King loses his life, it would be very useful to the good of the service, if Y.M. would deign to write to Mme la dauphine and ask her "kindly to listen to me with regard to the important matters which could influence the union and the system of the two courts." This advice from Y.M. would give all the necessary weight to what I have to say and would moreover fix Mme l'archiduchesse's attention as she has always kept herself aloof from serious matters. However it is necessary that, to ensure her happiness, she begins to seize the power which M. le dauphin will never exercise except in a precarious fashion, and considering the type of people who compose this court, and the spirit which animates and guides them, it would be dangerous for the state and for the system in general if someone other than Mme la dauphine controls M. le dauphin.

I have just heard the news from Versailles. The night was spent quite well, but at five o'clock this morning the King was being sick and is totally delirious; the doctors fear that there is infection in the head, in which case there is little hope. In any case the King is in imminent danger.

MERCY TO MARIA THERESA, 10 MAY 1774

The King was in the throes of death since yesterday. He received Extreme Unction in the evening and died this afternoon between three and four. He was always aware and until the last moment showed signs of penitence and truly Christian piety.

Everything here is in extreme confusion. The royal family is going to Choisy. Mesdames will be in a separate house there. I have taken the Queen's orders. She is very well, but her distress and the fact it is impossible to leave her husband the King for a moment, prevent her from writing to Y.M. at this time. It was a further pain for her and she has asked me to tell you so.

Yesterday, when the calamity was already certain, I had a long audience with the Queen. I told her everything useful I could think of in these circumstances. H.M. understood me and I dare to flatter myself that I persuaded her.

We will soon see whether the Queen will be consulted by the King and to what extent. It would be dangerous for her to seem to want to meddle in matters without first being asked.

If the Queen is consulted, I have advised her to encourage the King not to change anything in the ministry until he has had time to think and knows what he is doing.

I have also advised that measures be taken so that in forty eight hours time the price of bread will fall in Paris, as the people have been saying openly that they expect this favour from the Queen, who is adored.

The prompt expediting of this express obliges me to reserve all detail for the next courier; but I dare assure Y.M. that she can be tranquil about everything concerning the Queen.

MARIE ANTOINETTE TO MARIA THERESA,
14 MAY 1774

My very dear mother, Mercy will have told you about our misfortune; happily that cruel illness left the King aware until the last moment, and his death was very edifying. The new King appears to be loved by his people; two days before the death of his grandfather he had two hundred thousand francs given to the poor, and this made a very good impression. Since the death, he has not stopped working and replying by hand to the ministers, whom he cannot yet see,[37] and to many other letters. What is certain, is that he has a taste for economy and the greatest desire to see his people happy. In every area he has as much desire to be instructed as need, and I hope that God will bless his good intentions.

The public expected lots of immediate changes; the King limited himself to sending the creature away to a convent and expelling from court all who bear that scandalous name. The King owed that example to the people of Versailles, who, even as the King was dying, showered abuse on Mme de Mazarin, one of the favourite's humblest servants.

---

[37] The ministers had been in contact with the late King, and might therefore infect Louis XV1.

I am repeatedly asked to beg clemency from the King for a number of corrupt souls, who have caused much harm over the past few years. I am very inclined to do so; but, in the midst of all this, I cannot stop thinking of Esterhazy's fate.[38] I believe they have turned Y.M. against Esterhazy with reports which are false in some respects and exaggerated in others. It is true that he has had many faults; but nonetheless it is agreed that he is honourable and has integrity, and there is every reason to hope that, removed from the temptations of this dangerous country and living in the bosom of his family, he will become a good subject. On the other hand, I fear that, if he were treated with all the severity he deserved, he would not be strong enough to resist committing some new imprudence. I hope that my dear mother will not think me sufficiently thoughtless to wish to give her advice. I realize that, having the responsibility of governing, she is obliged to be just; I only wish that she does not turn totally against Esterhazy.

They have just come to forbid me going to my aunt Adelaide's, as she has a fever and backache: we are afraid it may be smallpox. I tremble at this thought and do not dare think of the possible consequences; it is ghastly that she is paying the price of her sacrifice so quickly. I am delighted that Lacy was pleased with me. I must tell my dear mother that I was quite upset when he took leave of me, thinking how rarely I see people from my own country, especially those who are lucky enough to be near you.

The King has given me total freedom to choose people for the new positions in my household, as Queen. Although God had me born into this rank I cannot stop admiring the will of Providence, which chose me, the youngest of your daughters, as Queen of the most beautiful kingdom in Europe. I realize more than ever what I owe to the love of my august mother, who gave herself so much care and effort to procure me this beautiful establishment. I have never wanted to be able to throw myself at her feet as much as now, embrace her, show her how much I love her and let her see how I am suffused with respect, love and gratitude.

---

[38] See Maria Theresa to Marie Antoinette, 3rd of April, 1774.

P.S. The abbe throws himself at your feet; he feels as much respect and gratitude for your kindness, as attachment to me.

[Edit: in the King's writing]: I am very pleased dear mother, to find an opportunity to prove my love and affection for you. I would very much like to have your advice at this awkward time. I would be delighted to be able to please you and to show you all my affection and gratitude for giving me your daughter, with whom I am pleased and could not be more so.

[Edit: the Queen again]: The King would not let me send my letter without writing a few words. I know that it would not have been too much for him to write a separate letter; I beg my dear mother to excuse him, because of the great number of matters which are occupying him very much just now, and also his shyness and natural awkwardness. You will see, my dear mother, at the end of his note that, although he loves me a lot, he does not spoil me with empty compliments.

MERCY TO MARIA THERESA, 17 MAY 1774

[Edit: written before Louis XV's illness]

Mme la dauphine's taste for plays has made M. le dauphin decide to have these sorts of amusements presented from time to time. He is attentive to the point of gallantry and is seriously concerned to please and amuse his august wife. His confidence in her increases from day to day and he is always the first to admire Mme l'archiduchesse and to boast of everything she says which is useful and appropriate.

[Edit: written after Louis XV's illness was diagnosed]

I went to Versailles. I found Mme la dauphine so overcome by the upset of the preceding days that I was worried for her health. The feelings of her beautiful soul were displayed on her face; she had edified the whole court with her expressions, her words, her care for the young royal family [Edit: Louis XVI's young sisters], and with the frank and evident way she demonstrated her filial piety and her feelings for the King.

H.R.H. ordered me to tell her everything which I thought could be appropriate and useful for her conduct in such a delicate situation. I replied that she should persuade M. le dauphin to neither see nor speak to any of the King's ministers, and to leave him alone as little as possible with the people in his service, or anyone at all; to keep the young family together and, as much as possible, always with M. le dauphin and Mme la dauphine, in order to prevent intriguers gaining access; to eat together, see no one, not even at the usual times, and to send away without reply any request whatsoever that people would make to try to ascertain their dispositions, whatever they may be, whether in relation to the King, or concerning some matter at court, as, with regard to the King, Mesdames had undertaken to look after his needs and, as regards any other matter, it would be dangerous for M. le dauphin and Mme la dauphine to take it upon themselves to issue orders, whatever they might be.

The fermentation at Versailles determined me to give this advice. Mme l'archiduchesse agreed, and it was followed to the letter, M. le dauphin having unhesitatingly concurred.

The duc d'Aiguillon came to ask for orders from M. le dauphin and Mme la dauphine. M. le dauphin said that the royal family was seeing no one.

On Tuesday, Mme la dauphine had a slight migraine occasioned by the worries of the preceding days. The King was better however; he was the same even on the morning of the following day, at which time some symptoms became more alarming. It had however been decided the previous day that the King should be informed of the nature of his illness, which he had been unaware of until then. The favourite's departure was also decided upon. The duchesse d'Aiguillon took her in her carriage to a country house belonging to the duc d'Aiguillon. Immediately after the favourite left, the confessor went into the King's room to begin to carry out his spiritual functions; then the fermentation became stronger than ever in the interior of the chateau. I went to see Mme la dauphine; I found her quite worried. I begged her to be more reserved than ever before about whatever was happening.

From Thursday the 5th until Tuesday the 10th, the day of the King's death, his condition deteriorated. From moment to moment there were little crises and glimmers of hope, but they vanished almost immediately. I learned the facts of the situation every day from Mme la dauphine's principal doctor, M. Lassone. The rumours, manoeuvres and intrigues increased everywhere; the different parties looked for means of reaching the confessor, who still remained inaccessible. They tried to gain access to the young royal family, while, on my part, I was constantly watchful, in order to at least prevent them making suggestions to Mme la dauphine. The abbe de Vermond and I tried to ensure that nothing escaped our vigilance.

On Monday the 9th, a day of great distress, M. le dauphin asked the director of finances to send two hundred thousand livres immediately, to be distributed to the poor in Paris, meaning to withdraw that sum from the allowances given to the dauphin and Mme la dauphine. This produced a great sensation with the public. It would be impossible to imagine better or more moving behaviour than that of M. le dauphin and Mme la dauphine.

SECRET LETTER

Sacred Majesty, Y.M.'s attention could only be disagreeably occupied by the details of the grim days I spent at Versailles between the 1st and the 10th of this month. The manoeuvres and intrigues have now failed and only merit complete disregard.

This is a crucial time for the Queen's happiness. She has never had, nor ever will have as much need of advice from her august mother; but Y.M. will know the appropriate form to give to that advice. There are some who would perhaps only need a tone of kindliness and friendship; others are susceptible to the tone of maternal authority. Up till now the Queen has feared being scolded (that was her expression) about the trivial matters of her occupations and her amusements. Y.M. can judge whether now a tone of indulgence and gentleness might not be better used on these occasions. As for those matters where more positive and forceful advice seems necessary to me, here are the points which seem to be most important.

1. The Queen knows Mesdames her aunts however, to my great distress, at the very last moment, Mesdames succeeded in persuading the Queen to let them go to Choisy after the death of the late King, although, after my representations, it had firstly been decided that Mesdames would go to Trianon and remain separated from the King and Queen for some time. Consequently, what I had foreseen occurred; the first act of Mesdames was to interfere in matters of government, give advice, propose that the comte de Maurepas be sent for, and the Queen, adding indulgence to indulgence, was herself the instrument which brought Mesdames' ideas to the King, or as I should say, those of the intriguers who influence them.

If, from the beginning, the King lets himself be governed, and the public realizes that Mesdames enjoy that advantage, then the Queen's credit will receive a mortal blow. I have begged her to be very careful when meddling in politics; but she must not allow any other member of the family to interfere in these matters. This applies to M. and Mme de Provence, M. and Mme d'Artois as much as Mesdames and is the main point on which I believe it is very necessary for Y.M. to deign to give a forceful warning.[39]

2. The role of a French prime minister has always been to block and destroy the credit of the Queen. History is full of striking examples of this; the Queen knows this; and if she wants to take the necessary measures, it will be very easy for her to oppose the idea of having a prime minister, who would eventually become too inconvenient.

3. The King, who I believe has some sterling qualities, has very few likeable ones. He looks rough; politics could even sometimes make him bad tempered. The Queen must learn to tolerate this: her happiness depends upon it. She is loved by her

---

[39] The wisdom of excluding Provence from the King's council is questionable, as he may perhaps have encouraged the King to be decisive, especially in the Revolution. However Mercy always demanded that the Queen did not trust Provence, and Louis XVI also adopted this policy.

husband; with moderation, kindness and affection, she will acquire absolute power over the King; but she must govern him without appearing to wish to do so.

4. Of the utmost importance is that the Queen takes measures to ensure that she never sleeps apart from the King. I believe it is essential for Y.M. to deign to mention this in your letters, and to declare that you would be worried if you learned that this was not the case.

I have mentioned in my ministerial dispatch the serious reasons which oblige me, in these early stages, to keep away from court. This precaution is necessary in order not to alarm people and in order to avoid dangerous impressions. The Queen is agreed that this conduct is indispensable; besides I hear from the abbe de Vermond about everything that is happening. I can use him to tell the Queen everything I believe is useful to her, and in five or six days, when people are less agitated, and they have decided that I am not trying to gain too much influence, I will then reappear in a strong position.

MARIA THERESA TO MERCY, 18 MAY 1774

Yesterday at 9 o'clock in the evening the courier brought us news of the cruel death of our King and friend. I am very upset and what concerns me even more is the future of my daughter, which can only be very great or very unfortunate. The King's character, the ministers, even the state itself have nothing about them to tranquillize me; she is young, has never wanted to apply herself and never will, or only with difficulty. I feel her happy days are over. Here is the letter I wrote to her; I wanted to write to the King but I thought that that would annoy him: she can show him my letter to her.

I thought I should put something about poor du Barry; she wrote an impassioned letter to me on the 7th in which she referred to her as "creature." That unfortunate woman is to be pitied more than all of us; she has lost everything and has neither consolation nor resource in religion, which, on these sorts of occasions, is the only effective relief.

I will not recommend my daughter to you; I have too much confidence in your attachment and the services which you have given and give continually; everything depends on those in whom they confide, and you gave them good advice not to change anything, I hope they will take it.

I am always, although overcome with sadness, yours affectionately.

MARIA THERESA TO MARIE ANTOINETTE, 18 MAY 1774

I will regret this prince and friend, your good and loving grandfather, for the rest of my life. At the same time I am full of awe at God's grace in giving the King time to have recourse to His divine mercy, and the words of the grand almoner, pronounced on behalf of the King, cannot be read without dissolving into tears and hoping for his salvation. We immediately banned plays here and declared that we would see no one before the 24th when we will go into mourning clothes, and I will wear them for the rest of my days.

I will not congratulate you on your new rank, which has been bought at a great price, but the price will be even greater if you cannot continue to live the quiet and innocent life you have lived for the past three years due to the goodness and kindness of this good father. It has brought you the approval and love of your people: a great advantage in your present situation, but you must learn how to conserve it and use it for the good of the King and the state. You are both so young, the burden is great; it worries me – very much so. Without your adorable father, when a similar thing happened to me, to sustain me, I would not have been able to prevail, and I was older than both of you.[40]

All that I can say and wish is that you both rush nothing: use your own eyes, change nothing, let everything continue as before, otherwise chaos and intrigues could become insurmountable, and you, my dear children, would be so troubled that you would not be able to extricate yourselves.

I am speaking to you from experience; what other reason could I have to advise you to listen to Mercy's advice

---

[40] Maria Theresa became empress in her early twenties.

especially? He knows the court and the town; he is prudent and very attached to you. At this moment, look on him as being as much your minister as mine, indeed the combination is a good one. The interests of our two states demand that we remain closely linked from interest as well as for family reasons. Your glory and your well-being mean as much to me as ours. These unfortunate times of jealousy no longer exist between our states and our interests; but our blessed religion and the good of our states demand that we remain intimately linked through our hearts and our interests, and that people are convinced of the solidity of this bond. I myself will neglect nothing, and my old age will have a smooth course if you two, my dear children, are happy. I pray for this and will pray constantly on this subject; my blessing to you both.

P.S. I hope there will be no more talk of poor du Barry, to whom I was never inclined except inasmuch as was required by your respect for your father and sovereign. I hope I will never again hear her name, except to learn that the King treated her generously, confining her and her husband far from court, and mitigating, as much as possible and as demanded by humanity, her sad fate.

MARIA THERESA TO MERCY, 25 MAY 1774

I am sending you a courier and I will send one every fortnight in these first critical days of the new reign.

It is said that on his deathbed the late dauphin confided secret instructions to M. de Maurepas, with the order to give it to his son, the present King, only when he came to the throne. I would be grateful to be informed of the details of the King's death. Some claim that, when he made his confession, (finished in only sixteen minutes), and when he had the known declaration published via his almoner (of which he cannot have known the details), his head was confused. I would also like to know if, as they claim, they found in his treasure chest 40 million livres or florins.

Rohan is helping to circulate once again the rumour which circulated in the past that Choiseul had the late dauphin and his wife poisoned. Choiseul will be recalled I hope, without becoming a minister again; I admit, I fear him. I am only writing to my daughter about general points, at the same time telling her how much her silence hurt me and advising her always to listen to you, follow your advice and be careful not to become involved in politics; to be the confidante and friend of the King. Her situation is very delicate and she is only 19 years old! My only hope lies in you. I must not forget the abbe de Vermond. They have already tried to blacken him here and ascribe to him much bad advice given to my daughter; this is also only for your information.

(I would like to have a portrait of my daughter in mourning, dressed as she is, they say even without powder. Even if the portrait does not resemble her, I would like to see her dress and the background as soon as possible. They say here that the King avoided all the formalities and had his grandfather buried without the usual ceremonies.)

MARIA THERESA TO MARIE ANTOINETTE, 30 MAY 1774

You will have realized how worried we were, when we sent you a courier on the 26th, having had no news since the ghastly day of the 10th. It is important for me to know what is happening as the alarming rumours often cause me unbearable worry.

They said that the King was ill and Mesdames Adelaide and Sophie were suffering from the same illness. Nothing could be more natural for these two princesses as they were with the King; but nothing would be more frightening than to know that the King had smallpox. God preserve us from that! He is the consolation and hope of his people, his allies and his family. I cannot tell you how touched I was by the lines the King wrote at the end of your letter; I prefer that cordiality to everything, and his attention in saying he was pleased with my daughter and that he thought of me in the very first moments of his tragic situation, moved me to tears. He even says he would like to have my advice; how appropriate that is, as he is so young.

My advice is to change nothing; to let it be seen that he only wishes the public good and to be the father of his people and that those who suggest means to achieve this will be listened to and recompensed and that he wishes to learn. If he has no confidence in those in charge of the various departments, after due consideration, he can appoint those whom he considers most skilful, who are Christians with high moral standards.

Do not appoint people who are fiery, hot headed and ambitious; do not have a prime minister as he would cause disputes with his peers, and make the people suffer. The King should be his own prime minister and carefully chose his ministers for the different departments, listen to them and then draw his own conclusions. Fortunately we are at peace, so there is no urgency; France has immense resources. There are many abuses; but they can be abolished and thus are a source to draw down on the King the blessing of his people. The future therefore looks wonderful.

With the grace of God, and by following the path of virtue, by distinguishing those who have good moral standards and dismissing those who do not, I flatter myself that the reign of Louis Auguste will be happy and glorious. Clemency and generosity are two qualities which, if used appropriately, will surmount all; but everything must have its limits: to use them indiscriminately would entirely remove their merit.

I have elaborated on these points rather too much, encouraged by the King's request, and wishing because of my love, to see you both happy and glorious. I am speaking to the friend and confidante of the King, who must devote herself only to his happiness, and must deserve his total trust. I hope that, at such a glorious time as this, those who are exiled will be pardoned and that Choiseul and his sister will be included. Fortunately our interests, in matters of the heart, as well as affairs of state, are so closely linked that in order to do good, we must do so together, as the late King wished. From my dear children, I would hope for as much; a diminution in our alliance would kill me. Our two kingdoms only need peace to put our affairs in order. If we act in unison, no one will be able to trouble us, and Europe will find happiness and tranquility.

All the letters and gazettes which are read to me, relating to France, are only full of praise for the King's kind acts.

I am only surprised at the choice of Maurepas, but then that is attributed to Mesdames. I cannot tell you how astonished I am that they were allowed to go to Choisy without the slightest precautions being taken: if they develop smallpox I fervently hope that you will leave immediately. My God! How frightening that would be!

Esterhazy will have to submit. I cannot prevent myself drawing your attention to your protection of this young man and your harshness towards the family or friends of that unfortunate woman [Edit: du Barry]; that is the last time we will discuss these two subjects, and I only mention it in passing.[41]

MARIA THERESA TO MERCY, 1 JUNE 1774

I realize the delicacy of your present position; but, having so many proofs of your adroitness, I am convinced that you will render to my daughter and to me, in these critical times, services as essential as these you have rendered to me since you first went to the court of France.

---

[41] At the end of May, with Marie Antoinette now Queen, Fersen quit France, and did not return for four years. The Swedish ambassador wrote to Gustavus, praising Fersen, "It is not possible to be more honourable than he has been." [Klinckowstrom (1877, p. IX)] It is beyond belief that Mercy, and therefore Maria Theresa, did not know of the attraction between the two, given Mercy's extensive network of spies, and the fact that Versailles was at any time, a hotbed of gossip and tittle tattle. However Maria Theresa did on rare occasions write additional letters to Mercy, and on these occasions she would ask Mercy to burn the additional letter – it is likely that Mercy would have burnt his copy of any letter to Maria Theresa, informing her of his concerns, either on this occasion, or at a later date. Joseph himself, in a private letter to his brother Leopold, on 9 June 1777, whilst visiting Marie Antoinette in France, wrote, "She is a pleasant and upright woman." [Vol I, p. LXXIII of Arneth & Geffroy (1875)] He even repeated this description, as if emphasizing the point to his brother, as if indeed, they had been concerned about the matter.
Mercy for his part, throughout these letters, praises Marie Antoinette's virtuous and even austere character, as regards the issue of morality.

I would very much like to be informed of the King's last actions and any details of what occurred in the last moments of the King's life.

I enclose my daughter's last letter, which although affectionate, says nothing important, but I was very touched at the King's attention in adding some words to his wife's letter. I have replied in the same way to him in my letter to my daughter. Apart from that, I do not think it appropriate to suddenly adopt a less strict tone with her, so as not to create any suspicion that I wish to exact favours from her.

Have the Queen give you back my private letter, in case it becomes mislaid.

MERCY TO MARIA THERESA, 7 JUNE 1774

After my audience with the Queen on the 13th, I spent five or six days in the country. This step had a much better effect than I had hoped for and when I returned, I found people talking of my alleged negligence and idleness at a time when people expected to see me play an important role, and this idea had disturbed and annoyed many people.

The King is confident, eager to state his ideas, his plans and his worries to the Queen. I saw that, for her part, this princess had been very careful to follow her plan of circumspection in her replies and that she showed no desire to know of affairs unless the King found pleasure in talking to her about them.

Except when the King works alone in his office, or with his ministers, he is with the Queen almost all the time. The royal family eats together in the Queen's apartments and the King acts in a simple, friendly and easy way with his brothers and his sisters in law; he ordered them not to address him as Your Majesty, when they talk to him.

The abbe de Vermond did not leave the court, as I begged the Queen to order.

For a long time, the Queen has wanted her own country house. The comte and comtesse de Noailles suggested the Petit Trianon; the comte de Noailles wanted to negotiate this with the King. I told H.M. that there must be no intermediary between herself and the King, and I asked her to ask the King herself. The King eagerly replied that he was delighted to give the country house to her.

The Queen treated those coming to pay court with grace and goodness, except for the duc and duchesse d'Aiguillon who were received coldly.

Many people who did not always behave in an appropriate way towards Madame, the former dauphine, and who feared her resentment, have only experienced generosity and clemency from the Queen. She has forgotten everything which could have displeased her, with the exception of the duc and duchesse d'Aiguillon.

SECRET LETTER

It was the Queen who proposed to the King to write a few lines in her letter to Y.M. and it was also the Queen who dictated them. It is only the last lines which are in the style of the King. Afterwards he said to his august wife that he had wished for a long time to write to Y.M. and he had thought about it, especially when Neny was here but did not, due to embarrassment. I think that from time to time some direct marks of affection given to this prince in a letter, would have an excellent effect.

The King confided to the Queen that all the letters which came in the post to her while the late King was alive, had been opened, but that he had just given orders to the sieur d'Ogny, who was responsible for this department, not to open any letter or parcel addressed to the Queen in future.

Until now, court etiquette has always forbidden Queens and princesses from eating with men. This has resulted in many problems; for example it led to the establishment of hunting parties which contributed so much to plunging the late King into the disorder in which he lived.

The present King loves hunting; he will certainly want to dine sometimes with those who follow the hunt. I did not hesitate to propose to the Queen to try to abolish an etiquette which only succeeded in separating her from the King, and knowing this country thoroughly, I think this is a very important matter. If the Queen is present at all the King's suppers, she will also be present on all the little trips. Madame [Edit: a new title for the comtesse de Provence, on her brother in law's accession to the throne, just as the comte de Provence was now termed Monsieur] and Mme d'Artois could also go from time to time; but not always, as only the Queen should enjoy this advantage; her presence would prevent any licentious company and all the dangers which follow it. I have been assured that Mesdames will oppose this; but during their illness the Queen can profit from their absence.

This absence of Mesdames is very fortunate. It is incredible that, in the very first moments, Mme Adelaide wanted to interfere in everything and adopt an absolute tone. I told the Queen everything it was possible to say about this; but I cannot hide from Y.M. that some weakness and fear on the part of the Queen makes it difficult for me to persuade her even in matters which she herself knows to be useful and necessary.

The Queen, because of her personality, is only too inclined not to involve herself in serious matters and I feel it would be better if Y.M. were to deign not to recommend her to abstain too much. The Queen is inclined to be totally uninterested in politics and that extreme position would be deplorable. No one knows the Queen better than the worthy and virtuous ecclesiastic who is her reader. This man lives to serve her glory and I asked him to write down his thoughts about her.

From the moment the late King asked for his confessor, it is certain that this prince showed many signs of repentance and of tranquility. His confession was made on several occasions; the first lasted sixteen minutes, but there were three others, of differing periods. The King had a clear head almost all the time and certainly when the grand almoner pronounced his confession. In his last moments, he neither took food nor medicine except when asked to by his confessor; the King showed him absolute deference, he called him "good friend" and that priest did not leave him for a moment.

[What the King left]…is not as considerable as the public thought.

Everyone here knows that it was in concert with the late duc de la Vauguyon that the comtesse de Marsan, because of her implacable hatred, spread the rumour that the duc de Choiseul had poisoned the late dauphin. The public was indignant at such an atrocious lie; it was known in any case that since his smallpox, the late dauphin never had a moment's good health, that his chest had been weakened and that his wife caught the same illness and died of it.

It is true that the late King was buried without the usual ceremonies. The reason is that, at the moment of death, his body was so putrefied that there was no possibility of performing the usual autopsy. A workman who soldered the coffin with lead, died within twenty four hours and even at Saint-Denis, it was necessary to wall in the coffin, because, despite all the precautions taken, it gave off a stench which no one could bear. Besides, after forty days, the funeral service will be held, according to custom, with all due pomp.

THE ABBE DE VERMOND TO MERCY, 7 JUNE 1774

The Queen seemed to me to be upset about the fears of the emperor and empress on the dangers of meddling in politics and the drawbacks of making requests and recommendations. The Queen examined herself and decided she was not at fault.

The abuse of recommendations has up till now led to many inconveniences. Is it necessary to forbid the use of protections and recommendations? That is impossible in France, without reforming the system of the monarchy, perhaps even the national character. Y.E. knows better than I that from time immemorial, three quarters of the positions, the honours and pensions have been granted, not for services, but from grace and favour. That favour is usually founded on one's birth, friendship and fortune; it nearly always has no other source than that of patronage and intrigue. This process is so well established that it is respected as a sort of justice even by those who suffer most as a result.

The Queen, from principle and character, feels aversion and embarrassment in recommending; if she has sometimes importuned, the occasions have been rare and unimportant.

[I sometimes advise the Queen to make recommendations, but only after due care]…If the Queen refused to make recommendations, her family would not ignore this, and her court would be reduced as people would go to other members of the royal family, and the positions would not be any better filled.

With regard to involvement in politics, I would prefer, although it is not likely, that the Queen would listen and occupy herself sufficiently with politics to maintain and increase her husband's confidence. Since he has mounted the throne, the King has been truly preoccupied with it all; and it would be impossible for him to have great confidence in the Queen without talking to her of business, but he will not continue to do so, unless she accustoms herself to understand and reason. The Queen herself told me that she would be ill if ever there was a dispute between the two courts. "How can I prevent this," she said to me, "if I can never become involved in business?" I know that it would be quite dangerous for her to want to influence matters on a daily basis; but, for that to happen, it would be necessary to change her from head to toe.

MERCY TO MARIA THERESA, 15 JUNE 1774

[People]…have been admitted to pay court. All were enchanted with the Queen. When H.M. goes out for her walk, many Parisians come to see her and there are always acclamations of joy which prove their extreme eagerness to honour the Queen.

SECRET LETTER

Y.M.'s letter to the King had a good effect on the spirit and heart of the young monarch.

MARIA THERESA TO MERCY, 16 JUNE 1774

The emperor has made known his desire to see the letters which you write to me, since the King's death, therefore I have shown him the ostensible ones, and will keep the private ones for myself. I find nothing extraordinary in the sending of more frequent couriers, at least as long as the present critical circumstances persist. It is necessary for me to be informed promptly and exactly of what is happening in France at this decisive time and to send word in the same way of what suits my interests. [Edit: Mercy was anxious that these couriers would cause people to conclude that Maria Theresa wished to influence matters]

However pleased I am with the feelings the King has demonstrated until now to my daughter, I do not feel I yet know his character enough to understand it.

Bitterness suits no one and even less sovereigns. But as for the d'Aiguillons they have only themselves to thank for their cold reception. I am glad the King no longer sleeps apart from the Queen; but I would be surprised to see a positive result from this, having already waited for four years.

[I hear rumours]…that one of the Mesdames had a child, or even several. What do you think and which of the Mesdames was it? If this story is true, I will have compassion for the weakness of human nature; but if not, I will be pleased to silence the insolent calumniators.

MARIA THERESA TO MARIE ANTOINETTE,
16 JUNE 1774

I cannot tell you how much you console me and give me joy because of all I hear from France; everyone is ecstatic. The reason is: a King of twenty and a Queen of nineteen,[42] whose actions are all dictated by humanity, generosity, prudence and great judgement. At the same time, religion is not forgotten nor are the high moral standards which are so necessary to attract the blessing of God and to keep the people content, therefore I am overjoyed and pray God that he will keep you thus for the good of your people, the universe, your family and for your old mother, whom you have revived.

I will say nothing to you about the choice of ministers, which everyone finds suitable. I am very pleased that

---

[42] In fact, the Queen was 18, Louis 19.

d'Aiguillon and de Vrilliere were dismissed without lettres de cachet, as that is a harsh method only common in France at present and I want, my dear children, to see you always loved and esteemed and full of kindness. How fulfilling it is to make one's people happy, even if only momentarily! How I love the French at the moment! What resources you have in this nation which experiences everything so vividly! I would only wish for them some constancy and less frivolity; when they rectify their morals, that will change also.

People have great expectations from the millions which were found in the King's chest, all that will ease the generous intentions of the King. Refusing the don gratuit and the ceinture de la Reine [Edit: taxes paid to new monarchs on their accession] was an act worthy of you both, and your witticism, that people no longer wear belts, pleased me. The recovery of your aunts is of interest to all, but do not let them approach the King until after ten weeks.

Treat me not only as your loving mother, but your close friend. If I have too often recommended to you not to meddle in recommendations, it was because I thought it could be dangerous, due to your kind heart, and as you say yourself, you let yourself be led into taking decisions, either from nonchalance or laziness. Now that the choices have been made and the King has a council, I am no longer worried and you would be wrong and act contrary to our intentions if you stopped making recommendations entirely.

MARIE ANTOINETTE TO MARIA THERESA, 27 JUNE 1774

My dear mother's letter overjoyed me; I can only be happy if she is pleased with me. The late King's chest had less money in it than was thought; there was scarcely 50,000 francs. I told the King of your kind remarks; he is touched and grateful.

MERCY TO MARIA THERESA, 28 JUNE 1774

The council of state which is held on weekdays, was interrupted on Sunday. The King did not want to give up his work, but the Queen insisted, on the request of the doctors.

SECRET LETTER

Amongst the great number of papers of the late King, the present King found letters from the comte and comtesse de Provence discussing matters with the King, and saying things which were totally different to what they were saying in the family about people in their service, which proves the falsity of M. and Mme de Provence, who did not foresee that this would be discovered. The King was taken aback at this, as was the Queen; I used this incident to impress on the Queen the necessity for circumspection but she is so frank, good and easy going that she does not always maintain this behaviour. The King is more resolute, steady and logical in his opinions, and his bad feeling towards the prince his brother was shown in the following incident. Recently, amongst themselves, the princes and princesses decided to act out several scenes from the comedy 'Tartuffe.' M. le comtc dc Provence played this role. Afterwards the King said he was very natural in it.

The Queen permits too much familiarity and freedom to her brothers in law. This is not serious but it is important to have dignity in the supreme rank of Queen.

As for the King's trust in the Queen, her opportunities to decide what she wants, suggest ideas and have them adopted by the King, there is nothing left to be desired in these important matters. The Queen is progressing steadfastly in her credit and she will be able to use it successfully whenever she wishes. The ministers are beginning to notice this, especially the comte de Maurepas, and I notice they are all eager to be liked by the Queen.

It is only too true that at one time it was said that the late dauphin and Mme Adelaide shared a more than fraternal love and then it was said that the princess had a liking for the bishop of Senlis, that Mme Victoire had had a child and they dared to name the late King as capable of this incest. I would never have dared to mention these wicked rumours if Y.M. had not ordered me to say what I thought...[There is constant calumny here]. People are inundated with anonymous letters but it has no effect, what is said one day, is forgotten the next.

MARIA THERESA TO MERCY, 30 JUNE 1774

I cannot yet decide on the character of the young King, and I fear that he is inclined to dissimulation (and irritability). Some traits in his behaviour also make me wonder if he will be as compliant and amenable as you think, and let himself be governed: time will reveal more about him and his new minister the comte de Vergennes.

I feel that Rohan is much less dangerous than the comtesse de Marsan [Edit: his aunt], and the way the King demonstrates such trust and kindness to this woman, formerly his governess, whom he calls his dear mother, could well have consequences more curious than mere gratitude. (I must admit, I do not trust the King's character)

I am pleased with the news you gave me of what happened in the late King's last moments.

MERCY TO MARIA THERESA, 2 JULY 1774

Mesdames' return to court has not had any great effect up till now. They are keeping quiet and Mme Adelaide seems to have greatly moderated her desire to meddle in everything. The Queen received Mesdames in a kind and friendly way, but in a manner designed to show them that their domination is over. The Queen is now totally occupied with an English garden which she wants to have made at Trianon. This amusement would be very innocent if it left time for serious matters.

The Queen could be assured of her influence over the young monarch's spirit if she chose to...[discuss matters with him], as he is often embarrassed at what he has to do and comes eagerly to find support in his august wife's intelligence and judgement. However if this is lacking, eventually he will go elsewhere, and the Queen will lose all her influence. This is what I told H.M. in my usual frank and zealous way. She deigned to assure me that she would correct herself.

MERCY TO MARIA THERESA, 15 JULY 1774

H.M. is on her guard in relation to intrigues, she is circumspect and prudent; but she thinks that by avoiding any mention whatever of politics, and even refusing to listen to gain information, she will avoid any trouble which could result, in the present or the future. This system was fine for a dauphine, but is not suitable for a Queen, especially in this country and during this reign.

Mesdames are eager to be deferential in every way to the Queen. The two princes and their wives are the same; but I am far from believing in this impressive demeanour; on the contrary I am waiting to see what suspicious behaviour this conceals. I am always warning the Queen about this.[43]

The friendship of the Queen for the princesse de Lamballe had given rise to the rumour that the latter would be made superintendent in the Queen's household. This suspicion immediately alarmed the comtesse de Noailles; when she spoke to me about it I reassured her, having firstly checked that the Queen had no such thoughts.

SECRET LETTER

When, two days after the death of the late King, I went to Choisy, I told the Queen that it was important for the state not to rush any changes in the ministry, that it was necessary to take time to think, and in particular that it was to the advantage of the present system, and especially to Y.M., that the duc d'Aiguillon be left in his position, as there was a risk of making

---

[43] It is hardly surprising that, with such constant advice from Mercy, and as their reign progressed, the king and queen trusted fewer and fewer people, so that by the time of the Revolution, they trusted only about four people, two of whom were Mercy and Fersen, as Fersen confided in a letter to his father.

a rash choice for the position of minister of foreign affairs. This motive should have been very important to the Queen; I thought I had convinced her, and I was under this erroneous impression until recently, when I discovered that, as she was unable to control her resentment, the Queen alone was responsible for the dismissal of the duc d'Aiguillon, as he would otherwise still be in his post. The King had decided to keep this minister in place for a long time yet; it was only the pressing and daily entreaties of the Queen which led to his dismissal. This is proof of the Queen's great credit, but I was grieved at the use she made of it in this instance.

When, in accordance with the instructions which came to me from the ministry of foreign affairs in Vienna, I told the Queen of the importance of the choice of a minister for foreign affairs, and spoke to her about cardinal de Bernis, I found her cold, indifferent; it sufficed that the decision had been taken to dismiss the duc d'Aiguillon, as far as she was concerned. She would have preferred the baron de Breteuil in the ministry, but this predilection and the advantage to the Queen in creating a minister herself, were not sufficiently powerful motives to make her act, unlike the motives of hatred and bitterness. In fact the Queen was barely informed before M. de Vergennes was nominated, and she was less bothered by this than anyone else.

Different motives, which are often useless and sometimes harmful, impel her into action, then she uses her power and influence and she succeeds, while more important and truly worthwhile matters do not in any way receive attention.

The recall of the duc de Choiseul...[is another proof of the Queen's credit]. The King was very reluctant to give him his liberty, he resisted the Queen and even asked if the recall could take place in two months' time; the Queen was so firm that she replied that she "demanded" that indulgence from the King and that she wanted it immediately, at which the King gave in.

It is certain, as Y.M. deigns to note, that it is not possible to judge and know this King within two months as, until he mounted the throne, he was impenetrable to even the most intent observation. This could be as a result of dissimulation or of excessive timidity and I believe the latter is more likely than the former. Everything about the King seems to point to a weak character. His rough appearance only applies to him physically and not morally. If the Queen does not dominate him in his early reign, it could be more difficult later, if someone else is influencing him.

The King no longer calls the comtesse de Marsan "his dear mother" and treated her coldly recently.

MARIA THERESA TO MERCY, 16 JULY 1774

I think we should be content if the Queen keeps enough credit to influence the choice of ministers and to prevent the princes and princesses gaining ascendancy over the King.

MARIA THERESA TO MARIE ANTOINETTE, 16 JULY 1774

I promised to tell you or warn you of anything I heard from abroad concerning the happy reign which they are predicting from Louis XVI and his little Queen. Here it is, it remains to be seen whether it is all true. Everyone is ecstatic, and crazy about you both; they are forecasting the greatest possible happiness for everyone, and you are reviving a nation which was in the abyss, and which was sustained only by its attachment to its princes. That must be said in praise of the nation, but it is changeable and the more it needs and hopes for everything from the King, the more difficult it will be to content it; to accomplish that there is only one means, to decide on principles and not to deviate from them. It is better to be exact and economic, just and religious, as it is believed Louis XVI will be; than to believe that he will be incapable of preventing himself from being led into being kind or even worse, being weak, and not sustaining the first impression that the public formed, and from which you have seen marvellous effects, even abroad.

The payment of 500,000 livres to d'Aiguillon, [Edit: Maurepas was d'Aiguillon's uncle and this was supposed to be recompense for his expenses as a minister], Monteynard's pension, and other payments have caused a great sensation, not because the public admire the generosity of the King, but they are talking about who could have influenced him, and the conclusion has been drawn that he will not be firm, and will have favourites who will influence him.

There is also talk of millions to be spent on buildings; at this time, when the cost of the horses has been cut, expenses which could be ten times worse were not expected.

It is said that the Queen cannot be distinguished from the other princes, that their familiarity is extreme. God preserve me from wanting to encourage you to make them aware of your superiority, God having put you there, but you have already been compromised often both by the aunts and by the comte and comtesse de Provence. They say that the comte d'Artois is excessively bold; you should not tolerate this as in the long run you could be harmed; it is necessary to remain in one's position and to know how to behave in that role; in that way both you and everyone else will be at ease. Be kind and attentive to all but do not be over familiar, or too friendly and you will thus avoid being harassed into making recommendations.

At this time the important point is your pleasure seeking, which until now was all, and even a necessary consequence of change. I fear this for you more than other points; you absolutely must occupy yourself with serious matters, as this can be useful, if the King asks your advice or speaks to you as a friend.

Do not lead him into exceptional expense; this first charming present from the King [Edit: Trianon] must not lead to great expense[44] and even less, extravagance; everything depends on this happy beginning, which has surpassed belief, being maintained, and thus making you both happy, by making your people the same, as they depend on you for their happiness.

---

[44] Unfortunately the empress was correct – Trianon did lead to great expense, and the Queen was even interrogated about this particular expenditure, at her trial. See volume II.

This monarch will become respected by friends and enemies if he proves he has an upright character, which is also kind and economical when appropriate. I myself blushed that after thirty three years reign I have not done what this dear prince has done in thirty three days. The King must have honest people around him and chase away intriguers. He must have friends who can tell him the simple truth without embellishment. I do not know if the Cologne Gazette is right when it quotes the King's response: "that he wished to be informed of his faults in order to rectify them," but the response was admirable and drew tears from me. With the help of God and these admirable intentions, all will go well.

MARIE ANTOINETTE TO MARIA THERESA, 30 JULY 1774

Your last two letters gave me great satisfaction because of the kindness with which my dear mother thinks of everything which concerns me and by her good advice, which is more a result of love and friendship than a mother's rights; if I do not profit from it as much as I should for my own good, at least I will reply to my loving mother sincerely and trustingly.

It is true that praise and admiration for the King have been heard everywhere. He deserves it because of the uprightness of his soul and his desire to do good, but I worry about this French enthusiasm for the future. The little I hear of politics lets me see that it can be very difficult and awkward.

It is agreed that the late King left matters in a very bad state; people are divided and it will be impossible to please everyone, in a country where they are eager for everything to be done immediately. My dear mother is quite right when she says it is necessary to decide on one's principles and not deviate from them. The King will not be as weak as his grandfather. I also hope he will not have a favourite, but I fear that he is too gentle and easy going, as when M. de Maurepas had him give 500,000 francs to M. d'Aiguillon. The pension to M. de Monteynard is altogether different. He was only given what is always given to retired ministers; he behaved honestly, and his only fault was to displease these unpleasant people who were in power.

My dear mother can be reassured that I will not lead the King into great expense; on the contrary I myself refuse the requests they ask me to make to him for money. The King is not thinking of spending millions on buildings, that is an exaggeration, as are many others including that of my familiarity, which could only be seen by a few people. It is not up to me to judge, but it seems to me that between us there is only the close friendship and gaiety appropriate to our age. It is true that the comte d'Artois is quite lively and thoughtless, but I know how to put him in his place. As for my aunts, it can no longer be said that they dominate me; and as for Monsieur and Madame, not by a long way do I trust them entirely.

I must admit to my flightiness and laziness in applying myself. I wish and hope to correct myself gradually, and without ever becoming involved in intrigues, be in a position to merit the King's trust, as he continues to be a very good friend to me. What the Cologne Gazette said is what he feels, but I do not think he said it.

The King has sacked M. de Boynes, minister for the navy; this was not because of his liaison with and servility to du Barry, but for his incapacity, which was recognised by everyone; his successor has the reputation of being a very honest man [Edit: Turgot]. I am annoyed at the disgrace of the ducs d'Orleans and de Chartres because I did not want any more quarrels. I hope that this one will not last: they have not been exiled anywhere; only forbidden to come to court. The King could not ignore the fact that they refused to go to the service for his grandfather.

MERCY TO MARIA THERESA, 30 JULY 1774

The Queen is much occupied with the English garden which is being constructed at Trianon. The King is very eager to cooperate in every way in whatever amuses his august wife.

The King is displeased with M. le comte d'Artois and he proposes to let him know this. This young prince is very thoughtless in his speech; he is neither measured nor dignified in his conduct; he is disdainful, imperious, and even bad tempered.

The King, Queen, young princes and princesses came to walk in Paris. On that occasion the people showed their joy and goodwill, much more however for the Queen than for the King, because of the exile of the duc d'Orleans and the duc de Chartres, not that the public take a great deal of interest in these princes of the blood, but because they believe that their disgrace is due to their attachment to the former parlement, to which the people are more attached than ever.

SECRET LETTER

A few days ago the Queen told the King that he was so busy every day that she did not have the opportunity to talk to him. The King replied that that was true, that however he had many matters to confide to the Queen and on which he wanted her advice and that they would have to set aside half a day to talk together at their ease. I have not yet been informed as to whether this conversation has taken place.

I beg Y.M. to give no credit to rumours about the Queen. The exuberance and liveliness of the Parisians often give rise to rumours of incredible absurdity; these rumours go round one day, and are contradicted the next. It is not possible for anyone to have the means I have to be precisely informed of everything...[therefore rest assured] that Y.M. will always know the slightest detail. [Edit: this could refer to Maria Theresa's point in a previous letter, that rumour was ascribing responsibility for the King's inoculation against smallpox to her daughter, who in fact was not even consulted about this decision by the King]

MARIA THERESA TO MERCY, 31 JULY 1774

I was struck by the way my daughter acted in the affair with d'Aiguillon and with that of Choiseul, and especially at her vengeful behaviour towards the former. Sometimes I fear her lack of warmth and feel that she is not entirely sincere.

I am pleased that the reserved character of the King is due to excessive timidity rather than dissimulation.

MERCY TO MARIA THERESA, 15 AUGUST 1774

MM. the comtes de Provence and d'Artois and their wives have refused to pay court daily to the King and Queen in the morning, at the time when people are normally present, as was the custom with the late King. I found the Queen taken aback at this refusal and disposed to involve herself in a heated argument. I told H.M. that a question of this nature neither could nor should be decided by anyone except the King.

Although it is not clear what has caused this, it seems and is indeed almost certain that Mme Adelaide's insinuations gave rise to this dispute, this princess and also her sisters having immediately made known that they supported their nephews' case. Since Mme Adelaide returned to court, she has constantly been showing signs of annoyance that she has not been able to gain influence and ascendancy over the King. The comte de Provence, for his part, flattered himself he would enter the council of state and play a great part, and has become impatient on seeing his hopes destroyed or at least delayed. It was thought that the Queen was the obstacle to such projects and that suspicion has caused the jealousy.[45]

The Queen, who noticed this, has not been able to avoid showing her impatience sometimes, and although, because of her character, she is not inclined to bitterness, she has often permitted herself remarks on the superiority of her rank, and made slightly mortifying comparisons with the other princes and princesses.

It must be said in this respect that the King is at fault. The sort of equality which he established between himself and his brothers from the beginning has led them to abuse it. On public occasions when the royal family is together, a stranger would not be able to distinguish the King; the comte d'Artois is

---

[45] Mesdames continued to encourage talk disparaging the Queen, at least until the Revolution. Provence was more subtle in his opposition to his sister-in-law.

the one who would seem to be King. At court he will pass in front of the King many times, pushing him and almost treading on his toes without being at all bothered, and [behaving] in a truly shocking manner.

In relation to Y.M.'s opinion of the Queen's character, I will say that there are occasions when that august princess holds strongly to her own opinions and ignores the counter reasons that can be proposed. I must say however that these cases are quite rare and have only occurred because of rancour or pleasure seeking. However apart from these occasions, I have never noticed a lack of sincerity in the Queen; she has almost always warned me in good faith when she was not disposed to listen to my representations; it was only in relation to the duc d'Aiguillon that the Queen deviated from her normal openness, and afterwards she even agreed with me. It is noticeable that even when the Queen resists my ideas, she ends up however agreeing partly or in total with the well founded reasons I give her.

SECRET LETTER

The King showed a lot of indecision and weakness in the dispute with his brothers; but despite that I saw clearly that if the Queen had wanted to insist, she would almost certainly have persuaded the King to pronounce against the princes. But I begged her not to use her ascendancy on this occasion, as it would have been obvious she had done so, and this would have caused bitterness and ill will in the princes which it is best to avoid.

H.M. told me that in her last letter to Y.M., she had sincerely acknowledged to Y.M. that she was not very good at applying herself, but that she now felt it was time to change. In fact, recently, not only has the Queen listened very carefully to everything the King wanted to say to her, but she even gave him very wise advice which impressed the King.

Since they first arrived at Compiegne, the King has spent the nights with the Queen.

H.M. understands very well how useful the abbe de Vermond is to her, and she consults him about everything, but sometimes she tells him frankly, as she sometimes tells me, that she is not prepared to take his advice.

After the death of the late King, it seemed that the young monarch was prepared to moderate his taste for hunting, but instead he has taken it up again even more than before, without however abandoning his work. The King works for three or four hours in the morning, and in the evening, when he comes back from hunting, he spends some time in his study or talking to ministers.

MARIA THERESA TO MERCY, 28 AUGUST 1774

You will see from the accompanying letters what has just happened here, and I cannot deny that I did not think that the inveterate hatred against the Austrians, against my person and the poor innocent Queen were still so deeply rooted in the hearts of the French.[46] This then is what all that lavish praise comes to! This is their love for my daughter! Never has anything so atrocious appeared, and it has placed in my heart the most bitter contempt for that nation, which has no religion, morals nor feelings.

[Edit: Beaumarchais had notified the Austrian court of a scandalous book which had been published, about Marie Antoinette, and had presented himself to Maria Theresa and read it to her. Next day, he was arrested, as Kaunitz suspected he was the author. This was to be amongst the first of many scandalous books about the Queen]

I am saying nothing about this to my daughter, and I would like her to be unaware for ever of the kind of people with whom she has been entrusted, surrounded as she is by traitors and scoundrels, without hope of succession.

I will let you decide whether to talk to my daughter or Vermond about this distasteful business, but she will not hear of it from me; I do not want to contribute to poisoning her days even more than they already are, and will be still more.[47]

---

[46] The Austrians and French were long standing enemies.
[47] A very prescient statement by Maria Theresa.

MARIA THERESA TO MERCY, 31 AUGUST 1774

I fear more and more the irksome disposition of Mesdames. You are right to make my daughter realize the drawbacks of the hasty words which escape from her now and again; but you will agree that at her age it is difficult to repress them, especially in her circumstances when she has more than enough reasons to be irritated and even outraged.

MARIE ANTOINETTE TO MARIA THERESA, 7 SEPTEMBER 1774

I have already told my dear mother that M. Turgot is a very honest man and that is essential in the department of finance. M. de Sartine has the naval department; he made himself adored by the people when he was lieutenant of police; I do not know however if he is appropriate for the navy, perhaps later his position will be changed; however it is still very fortunate that such a decent man is working with the King; I am delighted.

Coming back from Compiegne, I felt slightly indisposed; I had left immediately after eating, and that, in conjunction with the great heat and the movement of the carriage, made me unwell and I was sick, which pleased the public, but unfortunately as my dear mother knows, I am far from being pregnant. My dear mother does not mention her health; I hope it is good, but I would dearly love to be reassured about the one person in the world who is most dear to me.

MERCY TO MARIA THERESA, 11 SEPTEMBER, 1774

The deplorable dissoluteness of the late King during the last four years of his life has totally eclipsed his reign. The state was at the mercy of a vile creature whose relatives and associates formed a collection of contemptible and despicable people, under the yoke of whom France found itself enslaved. Honest people kept away and thus made way for scoundrels of all kinds who inundated the court; from that moment there was nothing but disorder, scandal, injustice, all was overturned; there was no moral standard, no principles, and everything happened by chance. The government had no jurisdiction; the opprobrium with which the nation saw itself covered, caused shame and inexpressible despair. Scoundrels alone remained at the scene, and amongst them a spirit of intrigue and of cabal developed whose ferocity was without example. From that time, even the most sacred of duties were forgotten; nothing was respected or safe from the worst possible horrors.

Y.M. will recall that at times I have often cited in my very humble reports, especially in that of the 28th of June, examples of that sad truth. Then I avoided entering into details which would be too distressing and useless besides, and limited myself to indicating the problem, only with a view to alerting Y.M. to try to spare her the pain which she would be caused by the slanderous and unspeakable rumours with which we were inundated here and which I realized could one day be drawn to Y.M.'s attention; unfortunately I was not at all wrong and I have just received the proof.

I have just indicated the origin of the appalling events which infected this country; I believe I have proved that they had their source in the upheaval of the last years of the previous reign. I will add that, as the evil has formed such deep roots, its effects will be felt for a long time, no matter what care the new government takes, or means it uses to remedy the situation.

Now two questions must be examined. The first consists in determining the degree of attention generally merited by the aforementioned amorality, through a consideration of the effects which it could produce here. The second question is whether this amorality could influence the Queen's situation in any way what-soever. The first question is answered if Y.M. deigns to observe, that one cannot confuse the French people in general with a small number of people who only form the dregs, and who are disowned and abhorred by this very nation, which, although indiscreet and thoughtless, is not at all naturally wicked, and is the first to become indignant at the ghastly slurs presented to it.

As for the second question, whether these horrors, whatever they are, can harm the Queen, I can reply with the greatest confidence that these same horrors cannot have the slightest prejudicial effect on this august Princess.

Up until now, on the question of morality, there has never been the slightest nuance in the Queen's conduct of anything which has not borne the imprint of a most virtuous, upright and strict soul, which adheres to principles conforming to the honesty of her character; my reports are teeming with proofs of this. No one is more firmly convinced of this truth than the King, and that is also proven by daily events.

The great and truly rare qualities of the Queen are no less known by the public, she is adored with an enthusiasm which has never failed; a striking proof of this has occurred just recently. When the people, to show their hatred against [ex] chancellor Maupeou, decided to burn his effigy in a public place, the worst accusation this same people could think of against the chancellor was to say: "Let's revenge our charming Queen, against whom this wretch dared to speak ill and write libels!"

I have mentioned at other times that the people of Paris, when demonstrating their love and attachment for the Queen, always add that she is the daughter of the august Maria Theresa, and thus show their very real and profound respect for the sacred person of Y.M. Consequently, if the loathsome libel in question today were known in Paris and its author were equally known, I would aver that no power could protect this monster from being torn apart by the people.

This Beaumarchais, who is generally known for his extravagant and fantastic stories, has never until now shown himself capable of criminal action. I cannot prevent myself being suspicious of other people, as I will explain in my dispatch. [Edit: in his dispatch, Mercy explains that he believes d'Aiguillon may be responsible for these libels]

These horrors, whatever they are, merit only the greatest scorn, like their authors, and such means will never succeed in besmirching the Queen.

I may talk to the Queen of what has occurred. It could be important, even at the expense of causing her some distress, to try to fix her attention on serious and striking matters.

MERCY TO MARIA THERESA, 28 SEPTEMBER 1774
SECRET LETTER

The Queen is naturally good and well meaning, but she felt the duc d'Aiguillon hurt her too much, and in his case alone she cannot prevent herself feeling some hatred and desire for revenge because of the offensive and imprudent actions of this wicked man while the late King was alive…[Also] there is a suspicion that the duc d'Aiguillon is involved in the anonymous writings against the government, which are especially trying to harm the Queen.[48]

Each day the comte de Maurepas becomes more indignant at the overwhelming credit which the Queen can procure, and if he is not careful it is certain that she will take as decided an aversion to this ambitious old man as that she has taken to the duc d'Aiguillon. I am trying to prevent this and would succeed were it not for the people who try to cause trouble in the hope of gaining some personal advantage.

The Queen sent for me and told me that the day before the King had come to her and told her in an affectionate way of what had happened in Vienna with regard to Beaumarchais. The King had spoken in a way which showed his gratitude at Y.M.'s friendship, and, in speaking of the libel, implied that he had not read it, as he had joked about Beaumarchais' thoughtlessness and imprudence. The King had added that his only regret was the worry that such an incident would have given Y.M.[49]

---

[48] D'Aiguillon and other disgruntled aristocrats, were amongst those who continued, throughout Louis XVI's reign, to produce malicious writings against the Queen.

[49] Throughout his reign, Louis XVl dismissed such libellous writings as unimportant, but they influenced the public's attitude to the Queen, much as the worst excesses of tabloid journalism still do nowadays, to the extent that, at her trial, people were prepared to believe that the Queen had committed incest with her son.

226

At this point the Queen told me that her worry was greater and that she wanted me to tell her everything about this strange incident. I firstly told the Queen that it was only from solicitude for her that Y.M. had not told her anything about this. I told the Queen that in her position it was not enough simply for her to avoid doing wrong, but that she must positively accomplish all the good she could, as all of France was watching her. The Queen told me she was afraid that some samples of the libel might escape destruction and then another edition could be brought out. I told her that such libellous remarks could only hurt their despicable authors.

Later the King came up to me and told me laughingly and in a quiet voice, that Beaumarchais "was imprudent and a fool."

The finance director [Edit: Turgot], both in his character and in his talents, is visibly superior to his colleagues and is very keen to be on favourable terms with the Queen. He is the abbe de Vermond's close friend. [Edit: Mercy wrote to Neny about Turgot's task: "The minister seems slightly apprehensive at the enormity of his task."]

MERCY TO MARIA THERESA, 7 OCTOBER, 1774

There is not a day passes when M. d'Artois does not cause the greatest scandal and the Queen tolerates it. I told H.M. that this tolerance was weakness. The Queen replied that the fault was the King's, as he was too indulgent towards his brother, but I begged H.M. to realize that, if the King is too indulgent, it was even more necessary for her to counter the licence which could result, and that this was the only way to bring the King to behave in a dignified way.

MARIA THERESA TO MERCY, 13 OCTOBER 1774

My daughter's last letter was, as usual, uninteresting and my reply will be the same.

There is a rumour going around here that the King had an operation and that good results are expected; I do not believe it as you have said nothing about it.

MARIE ANTOINETTE TO MARIA THERESA, 18 OCTOBER 1774

Before coming here [Edit: to Fontainebleau], we spent five days at Choisy; the King was marvellous there, courteous to everyone, especially the ladies, towards whom he was much more attentive than would have been expected from his upbringing. We had supper every night with people from Choisy and equally with those invited from Paris; that was greatly approved of and I believe that nothing is more appropriate to help the King develop confidence and make him loved. I would like him to agree to do the same here. As for the hunt, it is true that sometimes it is a quite strenuous form of exercise; I am very annoyed at it, but however I must admit that he has moderated this exercise since becoming King, and he has greatly decreased the number of hunts he attends.

MERCY TO MARIA THERESA, 20 OCTOBER 1774

During the trip to Choisy, the King invited a number of women from Paris, each day, to come and spend the day at court, and while dignity and decency were not forgotten, there was no splendour, nor embarrassment, nor ceremony. The King and Queen in a sense did the honours of the table, with all possible grace; it was remarked with surprise, that the King was deliberately striving to be attentive and polite to everyone, making polite conversation on trivial matters in a cheerful and charming way. This behaviour had the best possible effect, and the Queen reaped almost all the benefit.

I took the opportunity, in an audience which the Queen granted me, to insist forcefully on the establishing of society suppers.

MARIA THERESA TO MERCY, 11 NOVEMBER 1774

It is incomprehensible that the King or his ministers should have destroyed the work of Maupeou. [Edit: The King had re-established the parlements, which his grandfather had had dismissed because of their constant opposition to him]

MARIE ANTOINETTE TO MARIA THERESA, 16 NOVEMBER 1774

The critical business with the parlements is now resolved; everyone says the King was marvellous. Although I did not want to be involved or even put questions about these matters, I was grateful that the King trusted me. My dear mother will judge this from the paper I am sending her; it was written by the King, who gave it to me the day before the lit de justice. Everything happened as he wished, and the princes of the blood came to see us the next day. I am delighted that there is no one still in exile or unhappy; when they suppressed the parlements, half of the princes and peers were opposed; today everything has succeeded and yet it seems to me that if the King maintains his work his authority will be greater and more solid than in the past [Edit: in Louis XV's time].

I would have regretted this chancellor [Edit: Maupeou] as defender of the King's rights; but, apart from the fact he often acted in bad faith, it is claimed that he deliberately engineered the crises in order to control matters and arrange them to suit his interests.

I am very pleased I persuaded the King to invite ladies and gentlemen to supper with us once a week. I fccl it is the best way to prevent him being led into bad company as was his grandfather. It is also good, as it will diminish the familiarity which he might have developed with his valets.

MERCY TO MARIA THERESA, 17 NOVEMBER 1774

The King has decided to abolish the etiquette excluding men from sitting at table with princesses from the royal family. It is known that this plan was initiated by the Queen and it has been generally applauded. It could have led to jealousy but the King prevented this by saying there would be no etiquette at them and also that each person would have a turn.

At Fontainebleau, the court was crowded with eager, select people. The comtesse de Maurepas has been treated slightly coldly up till now, but had every reason to be pleased with the Queen's kindness. The various courts of Madame,

Mme la comtesse d'Artois and Mesdames were almost deserted. If this caused some jealousy, at least they were prudent enough not to let it show. Although Mesdames have openly declared against these suppers, since they arrived at Fontainebleau, it is apparent they hope to be invited to these suppers from time to time.

Several times in their private conversations, the Queen has told the King that it is necessary to have consistency and strength of character, and to avoid behaving in an indecisive way. She has prevented the King giving in to some misplaced requests and to agreeing to claims for certain expenses for the day to day running of the court.

SECRET LETTER

The Queen first thought of the idea of social suppers herself, a year ago...[When I reminded her of this], I found her uncertain and embarrassed...[however she spoke] to the King who firstly seemed to approve. Later the young monarch said they would have to wait as he wished to write to Mme Victoire about the matter. This was said with a gentle and embarrassed expression.

At first the Queen was only surprised by this. I was in consternation because if the King consulted Mesdames rather than the Queen, her influence would be publicly compromised and Mesdames would abuse their power, therefore I persuaded H.M. to tell the King that he would be publicly debased if he flaunted such misplaced subjection to Mesdames, and it would create dissension in the family in future, because the Queen would not agree to share this weakness and would in future put strict limits on her obligingness, and keep Mesdames firmly in their place.

I explored every possible argument and eventuality with the Queen, so that it would all be clear in her memory. I also pointed out to her the slight trace of duplicity and weakness in the King in saying he would write to Mme Victoire, when it was evident that it was Mme Adelaide he was going to consult. Finally I succeeded in arousing the Queen and the abbe de Vermond seconded me.

The Queen had her argument with the King. She was very lively, even better than we had suggested. The King defended himself a little at first, but in an extremely gentle way. He then gave in and was instantly resolved and made the decision public.

As soon as the public heard of this, the universal sentiment was approval.

It is only too true that the Queen's character is slightly irresolute, and in spite of that, often wilful. It is often difficult to persuade her to do something if she has decided against it, and only Y.M. can do this.

MARIA THERESA TO MARIE ANTOINETTE, 30 NOVEMBER 1774

I am sending you back that precious paper by the King; it was a great day and I hope that the future will confirm the justness of the enterprise. I approve totally, my dear and prudent daughter, that you did not become involved in this more than delicate matter, and that you did not even ask questions: it honours you and is discreet for your nineteen years; but the King's confidence in you, shown by he himself telling you all, before undertaking it, totally flatters and consoles me.

I will not mention politics to you, Mercy can tell you: matters are very disagreeable whether in Poland or Moldavia, and quite contrary to my way of thinking, but I could not separate myself from the two other powers without exposing myself to a war which I was not then in a position to wage. I will finish by embracing you tenderly, assuring you that you will make me live ten years longer, because of how much you console me.

MARIA THERESA TO MERCY, 1 DECEMBER 1774

All I wish is to see my daughter resolve to profit from the talents with which she is abundantly furnished, and from the advice you give her, so that she can help the King. It is only this fatal matter relating to the marriage which bothers me.

MARIE ANTOINETTE TO MARIA THERESA, 17 DECEMBER 1774

I am delighted to have been able to give you some satisfaction. You will not be so pleased to learn that it is believed that the comtesse d'Artois is pregnant; she has passed the 14th for the second time; she is not at all unwell. I must admit to my dear mother that I am sorry that she will be a mother before I am, but I do not believe I am thus less obliged than anyone else to be attentive to her. A week ago the King had a long conversation with my doctor; I am very pleased with the result and I have great hopes of soon following my sister's example.

The business with the parlement continues to go well, however there has already been an assembly of peers; my brothers went to it, nothing was decided, and they settled for the advice of the prince de Conti, which was to postpone the deliberation until the 30th of this month; that seems fine to me as it leaves time to take any necessary measures.

I only saw Mercy for a moment on the day he gave me the letters; I am expecting him on Tuesday so that he can talk to me about Poland and Moldavia; these disagreeable matters afflict me for a thousand reasons, but especially because of how they torment my dear mother.

MERCY TO MARIA THERESA, 18 DECEMBER 1774

For some days while the snow lay on the ground, H.M. profited from it to go out on her sleigh.

The period of mourning is now over and the King has given the Queen the responsibility of making any arrangements necessary to make the court entertaining and sparkling this winter. Consequently the Queen has decided that there will be three plays each week and two balls. I found H.M. very inclined to avoid all useless or superfluous expense which could be caused by these sorts of amusements. Their Majesties will go to Paris to see the Opera play, which cannot be transported to Versailles except at great expense.

The public is satisfied that at a time when economy has become so necessary, the sovereigns are submitting to it in the matter of the expenses for their pleasures. I take great care to make people aware that it is the Queen who is responsible for this wise and moderate system. In this respect H.M. is very restrained, and she would never hesitate to renounce the amusements which she believed could become too expensive and awkward.

Since Mme la comtesse d'Artois was believed to be pregnant, the Queen has been more attentive and kind to her; this is one of these occasions when the Queen's character and soul reveal themselves most fully and advantageously, and the public is infinitely touched.

SECRET LETTER

I have tried to inspire the members of the parlement of Paris with the desire to attach themselves to the Queen. I told the Queen of my ideas about this and she treated the deputation from the parlement with kindness and grace which produced the best possible impression on them.

The Queen, struck by the comtesse d'Artois' pregnancy and reflecting on her own condition, finds it, with reason, a very serious matter, which pains her, and I regret to note that H.M. is deeply upset. Because of the kindness and trust which she deigns to accord the abbe de Vermond and I, we are the only people to whom the Queen can confide about this disastrous occurrence, and she even wants Y.M. to be unaware of her feelings, as she herself says, so that her august mother will not be upset too.

1775

MARIA THERESA TO MERCY, 3 JANUARY 1775

[My daughter's]…distaste for reading, which, I must admit, is common to almost all my children, seems to require time to be corrected, because of her youth.

I approve totally of the way my daughter treats the comtesse d'Artois in her presumed condition. This behaviour honours her.

MERCY TO MARIA THERESA, 15 JANUARY 1775

The Queen's balls continue to take place on Mondays; they are becoming busier and more brilliant. The King has not yet danced at these balls. He usually comes about nine o'clock, walks about, talks to everyone and does not stay in one place. The Queen daily becomes more perfect in the way she holds court, and everyone is delighted.

The 1st of January was a noteworthy day because of the huge crowd eager to see the Queen. H.M. counted more than two hundred women who were presented to pay court. On that day, I was present at the Queen's toilette. I saw the King's ministers and those with important offices who have the grandes entrees, arriving in succession. The Queen spoke to each and treated the comte de Maurepas and those of the ministers who merit most attention particularly well. The latter are increasing in respect and deference for the Queen; their conduct is regulated by the degree of influence and credit the Queen enjoys.

The Queen went to the Opera. On the way the people showed in their acclamations exceptional and most heartfelt proof of their love for the Queen. In the Theatre, an actor, moving forward towards the stalls and boxes said:

"Let's sing, in celebration of our Queen.

Hymen has you chained and under its dominion,

But will make us live happily ever after."
This was seized on by the public with incredible enthusiasm; only cheers and clapping could be heard; and the audience had this chorus repeated, which is something which has never happened before at the Opera, and mingled acclamations of "Long live the Queen!" with it, which suspended the performance for about ten minutes.

The Queen was so moved that tears came to her eyes. H.M. was accompanied by Monsieur, Madame and M. le comte d'Artois, the King having remained at Versailles. It was noticed that they were first to clap their hands. Entering and leaving, the Queen acknowledged the public with such grace and kindness, that the cries of joy were redoubled.

MERCY TO MARIA THERESA, 19 JANUARY 1775 SECRET LETTER

A young man found a note in the ballroom at one of the Queen's balls: it was a declaration from a woman to her lover. The young man was imprudent enough, it is claimed, to have this note read out to other young people and this led to suspicion about several women and lots of talk. The Queen heard, imposed silence and forbade the marquis de Douvetot from returning to the balls at court.

MARIA THERESA TO MERCY, 4 FEBRUARY 1775

I do not mind her taking part in all these entertainments, which are appropriate at her age and are the custom, but I would prefer the King to share them with her always, and that he would dance at the balls himself and that my daughter were with him as much as possible at the parties of pleasure. For that reason the events at the Opera would have pleased me more if the King had been there. I must admit that my daughter's progress surpasses my expectations; I see it as your work.

MERCY TO MARIA THERESA, 20 FEBRUARY 1775
SECRET LETTER

Y.M. will surely deign to realize how impatient I am for this carnival to end, as with the excessive pleasure seeking it occasions in the Queen.

On the 21st of last month I went to see the Queen about eleven in the morning. She was not yet up. The King was in informal dress at the Queen's bedside. I was able to see the unaffected friendship between the King and Queen during their private conversations. However later I observed to the Queen that it was essential not to disrupt the King's normal routine too much.

MARIA THERESA TO MERCY, 4 MARCH 1775

I cannot disapprove of how my daughter is behaving during carnival time.

I am persuaded that, far from wanting to derange the King's normal routine, my daughter would rather comply with it exactly.

SAME DATE, ANOTHER LETTER

What upsets me most is that the emperor sets the tone in these conversations, at the expense of Breteuil [Edit: the new French ambassador to Vienna]. Once on seeing him, the emperor made a mocking[50] sign to the abbe Georgel [Edit: Rohan's associate], which was seen by Kaunitz also. This was perhaps noticed by others besides me.

MARIA THERESA TO MARIE ANTOINETTE,
5 MARCH 1775

Thank God, this eternal carnival is over! You will think this exclamation shows my age, but I would claim that these late nights caused too much tiredness; I trembled for your

---

[50] Marie Antoinette and her brother Joseph, both had a tendency to mock.

health and for the normal routine of court life, which it is essential to adhere to. When you are young, you do not think; as you grow old you learn, but then other weaknesses take over.

Also I cannot prevent myself mentioning to you a point which the gazettes often repeat: that is your hairstyle. They say it is thirty six inches high, and that feathers and ribbons make it even higher! I who love my little Queen and follow her every step, cannot prevent myself warning her about this little frivolity, although, as regards everything else, I have so many reasons to be satisfied and even glory in everything you do.

MARIE ANTOINETTE TO MARIA THERESA, 17 MARCH 1775

It is true that I spend a little time on my hairstyle, and as for feathers, everyone wears them, and I would look strange if I did not do so. Since the end of the balls, the height of the hairstyles has decreased.

MERCY TO MARIA THERESA, 18 MARCH 1775

I told the Queen that the most important factor necessary to secure her happiness was to act in conformity with the principal traits in the King's character, that this prince loved order, was methodical, quite serious, very contemplative and quiet, and that by abandoning herself to noisy and continual pleasure seeking, she was acting in a way totally contrary to her husband's lifestyle. I repeated forcefully that by unceasingly presenting to the King an image of unlimited pleasure seeking, she would only succeed in making him more serious, and imperceptibly his soul would close in upon itself, his trust in her would also decrease, he would no longer be so kind, and by that stage everything would be lost.

I must tell Y.M. that the scene I presented to the Queen was blacker and more critical than circumstances warranted, but such is the harm accomplished in the Queen's soul by constant pleasure seeking, that only disagreeable and forceful reflections can make her more thoughtful. I saw that the Queen was upset by my remonstrances; she seemed sad and thoughtful; however she proved she had taken my lecture to heart by entering into details about the matters which pained her in her circumstances, and added that it was necessary to be distracted and that she could only be so in amusing herself. [Edit: Marie Antoinette was upset at her childless state]

SECRET LETTER

M. le comte d'Artois has decided to establish horse races this spring and to hold these sorts of tournaments in a park near Paris called the Bois de Boulogne. During carnival time the continual quadrilles gave the young people only too much access to the Queen, and although the purity of her soul certainly places her outwith danger, there still remains the problem of familiarity, to which the French are more subject than any other nation. This matter is so important that I would consider it very useful if it were to please Y.M. to give the Queen whatever warning you consider suitable in this respect, claiming that Y.M. heard that the Queen was surrounded by young people, whose presence usually deterred people who were more reasonable and had a certain importance. Besides [these amusements]...can only displease the King and nourish the pernicious dissipation which the Queen loves so much.

Lately H.M. wanted to come to see a horse race which took place near Paris. The Queen came with Monsieur, Madame and M. le comte d'Artois. Although there is nothing wrong with this type of amusement, it was regarded as a consequence of an insatiable desire for amusement.

A huge crowd attended this spectacle and the Queen was not received with the same applause and demonstrations of joy which are usual. The reason is that the public had formed great hopes based on the Queen's influence in useful matters, and in their idea she would use her credit for the good of all. Now, the public sees with displeasure that the Queen is concerned only to amuse herself and neglects every opportunity to play the role to which she was destined, in the opinion of the public.

The comtesse de Marsan is making great efforts to become friends with the comtesse de Maurepas, whom I observe very carefully as she dominates her husband, and I very much suspect her of bad will towards the Queen. [Edit: the comtesse de Maurepas was the sister of the duc de la Vrilliere and the aunt of the duc d'Aiguillon]

MARIA THERESA TO MERCY, 1 APRIL 1775

You have reason to fear the bad effects of my daughter's pleasure seeking.

I am not sorry that she was not greeted with the usual acclamations at the horse races; she should conclude that unless she is supported by consistent credit she cannot count on the continuation of public approval, especially among such a fickle people as the French.

MERCY TO MARIA THERESA, 20 APRIL 1775

Lately the Queen has been more affected than usual by the talk of the public on the court's movements. I was not sorry to see the Queen like this because it is the most proper means of making her attentive to what influences her credit and glory.

The Queen was informed that people in Paris were talking with too much licence, therefore the Queen summoned the lieutenant of police and asked him to take all necessary measures to repress this licence of speech in the cafes and other places where the idle gather to discuss matters of government and the hearsay actions of the royal family. The Queen intended going to Paris to see an opera, but changed her mind, as she was afraid the public would not give her as good a reception as usual. I took the liberty of making some observations on the just value of public demonstrations.

In the main, the public's affection for the Queen has not altered. Some secret schemes have been developed to attack the Queen's reputation, but they have not succeeded.

SECRET LETTER

After meticulous observation and investigation, I have daily acquired more evidence that the duc d'Aiguillon is the principal instigator of all the little schemes which are being plotted against the Queen. The ex-minister in question has gained ascendancy over his aunt, the comtesse de Maurepas, and that woman, who dominates her husband, has never stopped inciting his jealousy at the Queen's influence.

I told the Queen of my discoveries, and suggested means which seemed most appropriate to me to thwart such cabals, who are not sufficiently dangerous to warrant a great fuss;[51] but this was only partially carried out.

The Queen had a talk with the King and told him of her problems with the duc d'Aiguillon and demanded that the duke be sent to his country estate with an order not to return to Paris or to court for a certain time. The King agreed, although he was quite embarrassed at this request. Next day however he told the Queen that as the duc d'Aiguillon was about to be involved in a lawsuit with the comte de Guines, it would not be fair to oblige him to leave Paris. The Queen said nothing and the matter was closed. I believe it was the comte de Maurepas who suggested this to the King. However this has had a good effect in that they will be aware of the danger of being opposed by the Queen. Since then, the Maurepas party has considerably changed its tone.

It is known that H.M. has pressed the King to retire the duc de la Vrilliere and to give his department to M. Sartine. Sooner or later this will take effect, if the Queen persists in her resolution, and the project is good and useful in itself. The duc de la Vrilliere is generally despised and the only thing in his favour is the support of his sister the comtesse de Maurepas.

---

[51] In this respect, Mercy, despite his wisdom, greatly underestimated the cumulative effect of the dangerous cabals around Marie Antoinette.

MARIA THERESA TO MERCY, 4 MAY 1775

It is inconceivable that, although gifted with so much talent, intelligence and such high moral standards, the emperor lets himself be entertained by all these appalling rascals, and protects them, and [yet] he distrusts people who deserve respect and ridicules them. Eventually he will find himself surrounded by these flatterers. One day he will find them inconvenient and inadequate and then I fear the other extremity, that he will become a misanthropist. He seeks out wit, flattery and especially novelty. That is what makes both myself and the monarchy wretched, and as there is no remedy, it is even more distressing.

[I would like to retire]…I have devoted thirty years to the public and would like some peace for the time that is left to me. I am so demoralised, that I do more harm than good.

MERCY TO MARIA THERESA, 18 MAY 1775

[Riots had taken place in Paris and Versailles and other places because of the price of bread]…The Queen was upset and embarrassed to tell Y.M. what had happened. I agreed it was disagreeable, but I said it gave the Queen an opportunity to behave in a way which could be very useful to herself and therefore very welcome to Y.M. I said it was necessary to repress the disturbances with firmness, but not too much rigour, and that it was essential to suspend or at least moderate amusements, as the people felt they were suffering.

This remark was necessary as for the past three weeks the Queen has been abandoning herself to entertainments which have disturbed Paris. M. le comte d'Artois, who cares only for trivialities, has decided to come to the Bois de Boulogne often, to hunt bucks. The Queen could not resist M. le comte d'Artois' pressing invitations to attend these hunts. Paris has noted with regret that the Queen associates herself with M. le comte d'Artois' pleasures, and this latter, because of his frivolity, is suffering more and more in public opinion.

Two days ago there was another hunt in the Bois de Boulogne; M. le comte d'Artois drove the Queen there in an open carriage. There has been talk in Paris about this. The King is displeased at all of this. He does not blame the Queen, but his annoyance is directed at the comte d'Artois who is the instigator of it all.

SECRET LETTER

The Queen had a cold. It should have gone in three or four days, but lasted for a fortnight as no measures were taken; the Queen was coughing at night so she asked the King not to sleep with her until her cold was over. I then insisted the Queen recall the King to her room and I saw she was not eager to do so. The abbe de Vermond and I found it difficult to convince the Queen that her worst possible failing would be to let the King become accustomed to sleeping apart from her, or even to let him think that she was indifferent about this. I told the Queen of what could happen to her credit and how she could be harmed in the opinion of the public, by this.

[Therefore I would be glad]…if you would deign to mention that all Paris is aware that the King and Queen slept separately for several weeks, and would ask her to go and find the King often during the day by means of the communicating corridor to be built between the two rooms, [Edit: Mercy had insisted that this communicating corridor should be built between their rooms to allow them to visit each other without being seen by the courtiers who were always around], knowing that the King will be delighted, and that she must talk to the King about politics every day, showing pleasure in this and a wish to be useful to the King and to be his best friend.

I am still so distressed by the contents of Y.M.'s very gracious letter, that it pains and upsets me to return to this very important matter. If Y.M. were to abandon the reins of government, the prospect of all the fatal consequences which could result, appals me, but Y. M. imposes silence on me, I must obey.

MARIA THERESA TO MERCY, 2 JUNE 1775

I have told the Queen of the birth of a son to the Queen of Naples, and told her how I wished she could imitate her sister's example, but I think she, like her husband, is too feeble and indolent to think seriously about a matter which so much concerns the felicity of both of our houses and the well-being of our people.

Thank you for your remarks about my situation, but sometimes there are ills which eclipse possible remedies.

MARIA THERESA TO MARIE ANTOINETTE, 2 JUNE 1775

I was delighted at what you told me about the King's behaviour, and the orders to the parlement in that unfortunate riot. Like you, I believe that there is something behind it all. The same language which you mentioned to me also influenced our people in Bohemia, although yours were concerned about the high price of bread, and ours were concerned about the corvees [Edit: unpaid labour required of countryfolk by the local aristocrat][52] In general this spirit of mutiny is beginning to become familiar everywhere: it is the result of our enlightened century. I often complain about it, but the depravation in morals, indifference to all matters related to our holy religion, and continual pleasure seeking are the reasons for all these ills.

I must admit that I have been distressed to read in the printed sheets that you are abandoning yourself more than ever to all sorts of excursions in the Bois de Boulogne, near Paris, with the comte d'Artois, and without the King. You must know better than I, that this prince is not at all esteemed, and that you will therefore share his reputation. He is so young, [Edit: two years younger than Marie Antoinette], so thoughtless: his behaviour is just acceptable for a prince; but these faults are

---

[52] Alternative translation – feudal dues extracted from peasants by their lord. The issue of corvees was one of the contentious matters dealt with in the revolutionary National Assembly of 1789.

much worse in an older Queen who had a totally different reputation.

I am even sadder about another point: all the letters from Paris say that you sleep separately from the King, and that he does not trust you very much. I must admit that that strikes me even more as in the daytime you are amusing yourself without the King, and therefore this friendship, and custom of being together will end soon, and I can only foresee unhappiness and pain for you in your brilliant position, although Rosenberg assured me that the King loved and esteemed you, and therefore you could easily maintain your position.

Your sole task must be to spend the whole day with him as much as possible, to keep him company, be his best friend and confidante, and to try to know what is happening in order to be able to talk to him and support him; then he will never find more pleasure and comfort elsewhere than in your company. We are not here to amuse ourselves, but to become worthy of heaven. Forgive these sermons, but I tell you, this sleeping apart, and these trips with the comte d'Artois have pained me greatly, as I realize the consequences, and cannot present them to you too dramatically, as I wish to save you from the abyss towards which you are racing. My love requires me to warn you of these matters, do not dismiss my words too hastily.

MARIE ANTOINETTE TO MARIA THERESA, 22 JUNE 1775

The coronation was perfect in every way; it seems that everyone was very pleased with the King; he in turn must be so with all his subjects. They all showed the greatest interest in him; the ceremonies in the church were interrupted at the moment of coronation by the most touching acclamations. I could not restrain myself, I wept despite myself, and the people were pleased. I did my best during the whole trip to respond to the people's acclamations, and although it was hot and there were lots of people, I do not regret my tiredness, which in any case did not affect my health.

It is both astonishing and fortunate to have been so well received two months after the riots, and despite the high price of bread, which unfortunately continues the same. It is fascinating how the French let themselves be misled by loathsome ideas, and then quickly reject them. It is certain that seeing the people treated us so well, even though they are unhappy, we are even more obliged to work towards ensuring their happiness. The King seemed to me to be wholly convinced of this truth; as for me, I know that I will never forget the day of the coronation for the rest of my life, even if I live to be one hundred years old. My dear mother, who is so kind, would have shared our happiness.

The cold I have had for a while has entirely cleared, due to the use of milk. It is true that while it lasted the King slept in his room; but my dear mother must not worry about this matter, as he came back a long time ago. I am sorry that my dear mother bases her judgement of my trips to the Bois de Boulogne on the public newsheets; they are often wrong, and always exaggerate. On the days I accompanied the comte d'Artois, the King was hunting and it was absolutely impossible for me to go. Besides the King always knew I was going on these outings, and there were always lots of men and women from court.

I have just suffered a great loss because Mme de Cosse, my dame d 'atours, is leaving; I could not refuse because of the grave condition of her son. He is only four years old, she fed him herself, six months ago he was inoculated and after that unfortunate inoculation, his health deteriorated. In her grief, Mme de Cosse can think of no other expedient than to take her son to the waters at Savoy, and spend the winter in the south. I will miss her greatly because she is a woman of merit, and one of the most honourable that I could ever find.

Mme de Marsan seems decided to leave court at last. That will mean one less source of intrigue and spitefulness. We have already gained something in this respect, in the advice the King gave M. d'Aiguillon not to go to the coronation, and to retire to his estate at Aiguillon: he has avoided actual exile, which is barbaric, although he himself used it.

246

Mme la comtesse d' Artois is progressing well in her pregnancy; she is lucky enough not to fear the birth. It is true that she is such a child that she is overjoyed because she has been promised that she will not have to take any black medicine.

MERCY TO MARIA THERESA, 23 JUNE 1775

The comte de Guines' lawsuit is over [Edit: his name was cleared], and the duc d'Aiguillon has been sent back to his estate.

On the 8th of June, H.M. left Compiegne at eight in the evening, and arrived at Rheims at one in the morning. A crowd of people had waited in the moonlight to see her arrive; she was received with great acclamation.

As the King was crowned, the Queen was so moved she began to cry; she was obliged to retire and when she reappeared a few moments later the whole cathedral resounded with cries, clapping and acclamations. Everyone was in tears; it was noted that the King, on raising his head, looked at the Queen, and there was written on the face of the monarch a look of contentment, about which one could not be mistaken.

The Queen's sensitivity made such an impression on the King that for the rest of the day, he looked at his wife with an expression of adoration, which cannot be described. He spoke constantly to his courtiers about the Queen's tears, showing satisfaction and gaiety which have rarely been seen in him until now.

Towards seven in the evening, the King, in informal dress, took the Queen by the arm and they walked along the great gallery. Their Majesties had no guards; only a few soldiers followed them. The people outside were only separated from them by a simple balustrade. The cries of "Long live the King and Queen!" resounded about them. They walked about for almost an hour and the public was drunk with emotion, especially with the Queen's expression of kindness and affability. H.M. had suggested this walk and this was known.

Next day...[I took] the liberty of repeating to the Queen what I had often said to her of her friendship with [the comte d'Artois]...and on the possible drawbacks which could result. The Queen listened attentively and, while agreeing to this truth, told me that she had always hoped to bring M. le comte d'Artois round to more reasonable conduct, and that if he were left to himself, he could end up with greater failings. Whilst agreeing with this, I observed however that great precautions were necessary and that, if the Queen neglected them, she would fail in her objective of correcting the prince, and would expose herself rather to sharing his failings.

SECRET LETTER

Your letter made a great impression on the Queen. She exclaimed in surprise that matters were being exaggerated to Y.M. I took the liberty of entering into details which tended to prove the contrary and the Queen could not deny them.

At the moment the Queen is surrounded by all the duc de Choiseul's partisans, who are behaving selfishly and not thinking of the Queen's glory. They are inciting in her feelings of hatred and vengeance which are not in the character of this young princess. She capitulates however to those who pester her, and that is what led to the comte de Guines' lawsuit, the dismissal of the duc d'Aiguillon, and the present intrigues to bring the duc de Choiseul back into the ministry, if it were possible to overcome the King's excessive repugnance towards him.

With regard to bringing Choiseul back into the ministry, I have restrained the Queen until now; while at Rheims she granted an audience of three quarters of an hour to the duc de Choiseul; she told me this herself.

MARIE ANTOINETTE TO MARIA THERESA, 14 JULY 1775

My very dear mother, your love and kindness touch me greatly, but at this moment they only underline my sorrow: for four days I have been suffocated by Monsieur and Madame's happiness. [Edit: they were going to visit Madame's family] It is not that I do not find it natural; I approve of it so much, that I hid my tears in order not to detract from their joy. How wretched I am that I cannot hope for the same happiness!

We live in harmony with Monsieur and Madame. Madame is Italian in body and soul; Monsieur's character is similar. We have settled into our roles, we will always live together without discord or trust, and I believe that the King agrees with me on this matter.

At any moment now we are awaiting the comtesse d'Artois' delivery.

We will have very few fetes. Money will be saved, but what is even more essential, is to give a good example to the people, who have suffered greatly because of the high cost of bread. Luckily hope is reviving, as the corn looks very good and it seems that the price of bread will decrease after the harvest.

Will my dear mother accept a watch which contains the King's hair and mine? I have tried to have petrified wood imitated in it; we would be very happy if our hair reminded our very dear mother of us.

MERCY TO MARIA THERESA, 17 JULY 1775

The comte de Maurepas was well treated at an audience he requested with the Queen.

In spite of everything, the comte de Maurepas, M. de Malesherbes and the director general, are all resolved to omit nothing to win over the Queen. They told me this and asked me to help them; therefore I can simultaneously serve both Y.M. and the Queen.

Although the King is very annoyed with the comte d'Artois, he only shows it by cold silence, and puts no obstacle in the way of his irregular life.

The Queen does not use the passage between her rooms and those of the King, as often as would be desirable, and unfortunately it is not serious occupations which prevent this.

SECRET LETTER

Although the duc de Choiseul greatly wished to talk to the Queen, I know that he did not ask for an audience, but asked the baron de Besenval to suggest this to the Queen. H.M. did not conceal this from the King and told him two days before, in a very natural way, that she would like to chat to the duc de Choiseul, but did not know when to do so as, while they were at Rheims, they would hardly have a spare moment. Despite the King's aversion towards the duke, he himself suggested to the Queen the best time for this. In the audience, the duc de Choiseul began by praising the Queen for the firmness with which she had protected the comte de Guines.

The duc de Choiseul made no formal request for himself, but he recalled the wrongs done to him. He jokingly said everything unfavourable that he could think of about the present ministry. In sum, the duke's requests and advice were the result of intrigue, rather than originating from zeal for the Queen.

During this critical time, the comtesse de Brionne did not leave Versailles, and played a most active and dangerous role. She suggested to the Queen the tone to adopt with Maurepas. What mostly hindered the ongoing schemes, was fear of the representations which both myself and the abbe de Vermond might make; nothing was omitted to try to keep us away. We have never been in such a difficult position, as the Queen was so overwrought that we ran the risk of offending her with our remonstrances, which would have compromised our zeal for a long time. The abbe was so worried and discouraged that he wanted to leave, at least for a while and it was not without difficulty that I kept him in a position to be able to act in concert with me.

I know that the duc de Choiseul, whether himself or through his friends, has given the Queen to understand that she has to chose between two options, influencing the King through kindness, or dominating him through intimidation. It is obvious that the Queen inclines to the latter course; this could succeed because of the King's natural timidity, but it has great drawbacks and I will endeavour to indicate them to the Queen.

[Edit: Mercy wrote to Neny, on the 16th of August: M. de Malesherbes is just, which disconcerts the courtiers, and humane,[53] which enchants the common people. The similarity between his views and those of M. Turgot will produce a great reform of abuses, if they are allowed to do so, which is doubtful. They are truly rare because of their virtue and impartiality. The French ministers all seem very worthy; there is little intrigue amongst them, but in contrast, there is a great deal amongst the courtiers.]

MARIA THERESA TO MERCY, 31 JULY 1775

I am not pleased at the way my daughter is behaving. You will recall that, even in the midst of the praise which has been lavished on her, I have always fretted at the way she lets her behaviour be determined by her high spirits and thoughtlessness, at her lack of application and her inclination to be headstrong, while at the same time she ignores remonstrances. Here is a copy of her last letter, which is full of fine words, but tells me nothing. Therefore I think I will reply to her in the same tone, telling her of my satisfaction at her present, although it could have been made with the intention of distracting me.

The emperor will not act in the same way; displeased as he is with the conduct of his sister, he has resolved to make her feel her fecklessness by using the strongest of terms. He is shocked by the style of her letter to Rosenberg where she talks of having spoken to Choiseul without having asked permission, and of having inveigled "the poor man," that is to say the King, into proposing her conversation with Choiseul himself. I note with regret that if she continues thus, my daughter cannot fail to hasten her fall. I am greatly distressed at this thought, and I can only console myself with the thought that it will perhaps be the only way to assure her redemption.

---

[53] Malesherbes' qualities were revealed in his memoirs, in which he described the last days of Louis XVI, as he had represented him before the Revolutionary Tribunal. See volume II.

I have just seen the letter to Rosenberg, which I had only heard of when I mentioned it to you, above. I enclose a copy. My trust in you is absolute, otherwise I would not have sent you this. I must admit it has shaken me to the core. What a style, what a way of thinking! It serves only to confirm my worries; she is rushing headlong to her ruin, and it will be fortunate indeed if in doing so, she preserves the virtues of her rank. If Choiseul enters the ministry, she is lost. The emperor wanted to send this [letter in reply]...but he changed it when I begged him, making it less harsh and shortening it.

Burn these letters and do not mention them. The more assiduous you are with my daughter, the better, and do not ever let the Queen think that you have given in to her for fear of offending her. I foresee Vermond's departure one of these days; that will mean the downfall of my daughter, who prefers to make herself feared rather than loved by the King. I tell you, my worries for these past two years have not been for nothing or too much; I am resigned to many setbacks. Yours affectionately.

MARIE ANTOINETTE TO ROSENBERG, 17 APRIL 1775

My tastes are not the same as those of the King, who is only interested in hunting and physical labour. You will agree that I would look silly beside a forge; I could not be a Vulcan, and the role of Venus might displease him more than my other tastes.

Our present life bears no resemblance to carnival time. Just think how unfortunate I am, for the devotions in holy week gave me a worse cold than all the balls [Edit: during carnival time]. Every Monday I hold a concert in my rooms, and they are charming. All etiquette is ignored. I sing, as do other well-chosen ladies. There are some likeable men present, but they are not too young. It lasts from six till nine in the evening and does not seem too long to anyone.

MARIE ANTOINETTE TO ROSENBERG, 13 JULY 1775

I was not at ease monsieur, when I wrote my last letter, as it went by post. I have to go back to the time of M. d'Aiguillon's departure to give you a full account of my conduct. His departure was entirely due to me. I was not prepared to tolerate anything further; that wicked man was engaged in all sorts of spying, and spreading of gossip.[54] He had tried to brave me more than once in the Guines' affair; immediately the judgement was reached, I asked the King to send him away. It is true that I did not use a lettre de cachet; but nothing was lost in doing so, instead of staying in Touraine, as he wished, he was asked to continue to Aiguillon.

You will perhaps have learned of the audience I gave the duc de Choiseul at Rheims. It has been talked about so much that I would be surprised if old Maurepas had not been afraid to relax, even at home. You will of course realize that I did not see him without first mentioning it to the King, but you will not guess how skilful I was in arranging all this, without seeming to ask for permission. I told him that I wished to see M. de Choiseul and that the only problem was deciding on a day. I did it so well that the poor man himself arranged the best time for me to see him. I believe I used my feminine wiles cleverly on that occasion.

We are finally going to be rid of M. de la Vrilliere. Although he is hard of hearing, nonetheless he heard that it was time to leave, for fear the door would be shut in his face. M de Malesherbes will replace him.

Monsieur and Madame are going to Chambery to see the King and Queen of Sardinia. They are overjoyed, and I am heartbroken not to be able to do the same. I cried for a long time when I heard their news; but I have not let them see my heartbreak so as not to disturb their happiness. In the name of God therefore try to persuade my brother to make up his mind

---

[54] In fact Marie Antoinette was absolutely correct in her assessment of d'Aiguillon.

to come here: I am depending on it and I will die if he does not.[55]

I have yet another plan. The marechale de Mouchy is going to leave, so they say. I do not know whom I will take in her place; but I have asked the King to take advantage of this change to make Mme de Lamballe my superintendent. Just imagine how happy I will be; I will make my best friend happy, and myself even more so. It is still a secret, I have not mentioned it yet to the empress. Only the emperor knows; warn him not to mention it, you know why. [Edit: Maria Theresa would disapprove]

JOSEPH TO MARIE ANTOINETTE

[Edit: this letter was not sent, at Maria Theresa's request]

My very dear sister, the courier has just given me your precious letter. I was pleased that you are longing to see me. You cannot doubt how much I share this feeling. However allow me to speak to you, dear sister, with all the frankness which friendship and interest authorises.

How can you expect me to come to see you knowing your circumstances? As far as I know you become involved in many matters which do not concern you and about which you know nothing. The cabals and associates who pander to you and who know how to arouse your self esteem or your desire to be the centre of attention, or even foster a feeling of hatred and vindictiveness cause you to take one step after another which will eventually destroy your peace of mind, and which must necessarily bring in their wake pressing problems. These problems, while decreasing the King's friendship for you and his esteem, will also cause you to lose the approval of the public, which you have kept, astonishingly enough, until now.

Why, my dear sister, do you become involved in sacking ministers, in having a minister exiled to his country estate, in choosing to award a ministry to this person or to that

---

[55] Marie Antoinette, like her mother, had the greatest confidence that her brother would be able to resolve her marital problem – as he did – eventually.

254

one. Have you ever asked yourself what right you have to interfere in the government of France? What studies have you completed? What knowledge have you acquired to dare imagine that your advice or opinion is useful, especially in matters which require a breadth of knowledge? You are a pleasant young person who thinks only of her amusements all day long, but never reads nor listens to reason for even one quarter of an hour in a month.

Could anything more imprudent, unreasonable and foolish be written than your remarks to the comte de Rosenberg concerning the way in which you arranged to have a conversation at Rheims with the duc de Choiseul? If ever a letter like that were to go missing, or if ever similar words and phrases were to escape from you when talking to your close friends, as I have no doubt they do, I can only foresee great unhappiness for you, and I must admit that, because of my love for you, that troubles me greatly. Those who encourage such behaviour are your enemies; they want to destroy all the influence which you could have by pushing you to these steps. Believe me, listen to the voice of a friend, of a man whom you know loves you; distinguish him from those who praise you; and believe that no one can or will tell you the truth like I.

Therefore do not involve yourself at all in politics; dismiss and even repulse all those who try to encourage this for their own gain. Decide to earn the friendship and trust of the King, it is your state duty and the only interest which you could or should have. Discover his tastes, conform to them; try to be with him often, however do not irritate him, and earn his confidence by your discretion and reliability. Do not discuss politics with ministers, and never make recommendations. If solicited, only say you will talk to the King. In a nutshell, read, keep busy and find resources in yourself in case the public's great approval of you suddenly deserts you, and this cannot but happen.

MARIE ANTOINETTE TO MARIA THERESA, 12 AUGUST 1775

The comtesse d'Artois gave birth on the 6th, and it was an easy delivery. She only had three bad pains and was only in labour for two hours. I was with her all through her labour: there is no need for me to tell my dear mother how much I suffered in seeing an heir who is not mine; however I succeeded in showing every attention to the mother and child. [Edit: Maria Theresa's letter to Marie Antoinette scolding her about the letter to Rosenberg is not included in the French collection and her reply to her mother about this matter is cut from the above letter] Respectfully your loving daughter.

EXTRACT FROM MME. CAMPAN 'MEMOIRS' [56]

While the Queen, neglected as she was, could not even hope for the happiness of being a mother, she had the mortification of seeing the comtesse d'Artois give birth to the duc d'Angouleme.

Custom required that the royal family and the whole court should be present at the accouchement of the princesses; the Queen was therefore obliged to stay a whole day in her sister in law's chamber. The moment the comtesse d'Artois was informed a prince was born, she put her hand to her forehead and exclaimed with energy, "My God, how happy I am!" The Queen felt very differently at this involuntary and natural exclamation. Nevertheless, her behaviour was perfect. She bestowed all possible marks of tenderness upon the young mother, and would not leave her until she was again put into bed.

She afterwards passed along the staircase, and through the hall of the guards, with a calm demeanour, in the midst of an immense crowd. The poissardes, who had assumed a right of speaking to sovereigns in their own vulgar language, followed her to the very doors of her apartments, calling out to her with gross expressions, that she ought to produce heirs. The

---

[56] Extract from Campan, vol I, p.174

Queen reached her inner room, hurried and agitated; she shut herself up to weep with me alone, not from jealousy of her sister in law's happiness – of that she was incapable – but from sorrow at her own situation.[57]

MERCY TO MARIA THERESA, 16 AUGUST 1775

[Edit: Mercy, in his dispatch of the 16th of August, said that the nomination of Malesherbes was contrary to the wishes of the Queen; that she received him quite coldly when he was presented, but that she quickly changed her mind and at the first opportunity afterwards, she received him warmly. She was cold to Turgot as he had suppressed a post for which she wanted to nominate someone, but Turgot declared to his friends that he was quite happy with his reception. The Queen wanted Vergennes to recall a secretary from the embassy in London, as his deposition in the Guines' case was not sufficiently favourable. To Vergennes' objections, the Queen had replied: "I persist and I will demand this." Vergennes did not dare reply, but instead went to Mercy who spoke to the Queen]

Since the end of last month, the Queen has regularly accompanied the King once or twice a week to the hunt at Saint-Hubert. They spend the evening there and do not return until after supper. These hunting parties will take place all through the summer and will usefully replace other outings which the Queen usually takes without the King.

---

[57] Every armchair psychiatrist can deduce that the birth of children to d'Artois' wife, hugely inflates the despair of Marie Antoinette, shown in 1775 by her dismissive talk of her husband, and in 1776, by her dismissal of the ministers Malesherbes and Turgot, on a whim. Torn every which way by her mother's exhortations to show only patience and kindness to her incompetent husband, while at the same time Maria Theresa announced every new birth in the family to her daughter, accompanied by a scold; by the whisperings and mocking of the public, and by the repeated pleas from her husband, that an operation was not necessary, that a little more exercise would strengthen his physique, Marie Antoinette not surprisingly exploded into thoughtless behaviour, at times.

If unfortunately the King does not have a child within the next few years, it will be difficult to keep Monsieur, as heir presumptive, excluded for long from the King's council. Having a brother of the King in the council would be too much like having a prime minister and in order to prevent this difficulty, it would be advantageous if the Queen had a prime minister, that is, if the Queen were assured of the devotion of two or three principle ministers of the King through the protection which she accorded them, however I have not yet persuaded the Queen of this.

This month the Queen was received with acclamations of respect, joy and affection by the public when she went to the theatre. In this respect, there have been moments of coolness, which have now passed.

[Edit: on the 23rd of August, 1775, Horace Walpole wrote about the Queen to friends in England: "Everyone had eyes only for her. Standing or sitting, she is the personification of beauty. She was dancing out of step, but the step was at fault."]

When Mme la comtesse d'Artois was in labour, it would have been impossible for the Queen to have shown more grace and kindness than she did. On all delicate occasions, the Queen's kindness of heart and character is always admirable and in this instance in particular, everyone was moved.

SECRET LETTER

I am sorry this letter [Edit: from Marie Antoinette to Rosenberg] upset you so much; however I beg you to deign to allow me to observe that the purport and general effect of this letter originate only from the Queen's petty vanity in wanting to appear to be in a position to dominate the King, and that in fact the Queen did not intend using these terms in a pejorative way. Y.M. will see this if you deign to look at my report of the 17th of July, when I mention how the King himself suggested an appropriate time to have an audience with the duc de Choiseul. When the Queen told me this, she spoke of it as a chance event, and one in which she had neither used subterfuge nor had any particular plan. It was not therefore until afterwards that H.M. decided to make a joke of it, although it had happened quite naturally.

I have always maintained that at first sight the Queen is sometimes slightly lacking in attention and respect for the King; but in the essentials it is certain that she esteems her august husband, that she is even protective of his glory and that only minor actions originating from high spirits and thoughtlessness sometimes mask this manner of thinking and feeling. However, although in the fundamental principles of her morals and conduct, the Queen is without reproach, she is not absolutely so in the forms, appearances and in the prudent conduct which is necessary to establish the consistency and credit of H.M.

I remarked to the Queen that her letter to Y.M. was dry and was not a suitable reply to Y.M.'s truly loving and maternal effusiveness. She replied that she was too upset to write a longer one, and that she thought to give Y.M. a mark of submission and respect on this occasion by not entering into any detail.

The letter from H.M. the emperor only made the Queen vexed.

MARIA THERESA TO MERCY, 31 AUGUST 1775

The terseness in my daughter's last letter, as you observed, is without doubt due to the agitation she felt in writing to me. If it is thought appropriate to operate on the King, it would be better to do so quickly, rather than to postpone it for too long; but it is a point about which, anxious as I am, I must trust in Providence and wait submissively for a fortunate outcome. I am very pleased by my daughter's attentiveness towards the comtesse d'Artois during her delivery.

MARIA THERESA TO MARIE ANTOINETTE, 31 AUGUST 1775

I must admit, that easy delivery of your sister in law moved me a little because of the very reason you mentioned to me; however it is still preferable to wish for an heir from yourself. It has been a long time since I heard anything about this important matter, which is so fundamental to your happiness; it seems to me that you are not so bothered by it, and do not sufficiently occupy yourself with the matter. I was pleased with your care and attention for the mother and child; in that I recognise my dear child, and it has earned you approval and love, justly so; only kindness earns this for us.

MARIE ANTOINETTE TO MARIA THERESA, 15 SEPTEMBER 1775

The comtesse d'Artois is still very well; she was at chapel last Sunday [Edit: to be churched], as five weeks have passed. The King gave her a thousand louis after her delivery, her husband, diamond bracelets enclosed in a diamond case and a portrait of her son.

The comtesse de Noailles has resigned [Edit: to be with her husband]; the King has granted me Mme de Lamballe as superintendent.

MERCY TO MARIA THERESA, 18 SEPTEMBER 1775

This month there have again been several intrigues to persuade the Queen to make misplaced requests in favour of some individuals. Fortunately H.M resisted these indiscreet solicitations on this occasion.

The Queen came to Paris to the theatre, and also saw an exhibition of paintings in the Louvre.

Every time the Queen came to town, she was received with acclamations, despite the price of bread and the poverty, which makes the people ill tempered.

SECRET LETTER

The Queen was worried about the letters she had received, but even more so about how she had replied to them; she talked very movingly about this and in a way which showed her love and great respect for Y.M. "My mother sees things from a distance, she does not evaluate them from my point of view and she judges me too harshly, but she is my mother, she loves me greatly, and when she speaks I can only hang my head."

I told her that everything was going badly for her, that she reflected about nothing, acted on impulse and according to the wishes of her associates, and that she only occupied herself with useless or dangerous amusements and therefore risked losing the trust, veneration and love of the public, and also her influence over the King which could be dangerous.

Y.M. will deign to note that I painted everything in a much worse light than is the case as, to be exact, there is little to be displeased with at present, except for all lack of commendable actions. I believe I succeeded in disturbing her, but I am uncertain as to how long the impression will remain with her.

MARIA THERESA TO MERCY, 5 OCTOBER 1775

The confidence the Queen made to the baron de Besenval about the King's personal matter is a new proof of her lack of reflection. You were right not to mention this in your dispatch as the emperor would have found out and he likes to mock anecdotes of this nature too much. In any case, the King would be better not to postpone the operation in question.

MARIE ANTOINETTE TO MARIA THERESA, 17 OCTOBER 1775

The death of marechal du Muy is ghastly, especially for his wife, who is loved by everyone for her gentleness and integrity. My dear mother would be moved by the frightful state she is in. She only discovered that they were operating on her husband when she heard his cries; on entering the room she collapsed at the doorway, and remained there for the whole of the operation, which lasted for thirty five minutes. He suffered incredible pain and died within forty eight hours.

It is feared that the marechale will not survive him for long; that is what she wants. The King gave her 10,000 francs of an allowance on her marriage, he has just given her another 30,000; it is unparalleled treatment for the widow of a minister who had the position for such a short time; she deserves this exceptional treatment, and they will never be able to be as good to her as I would wish.

I have nothing to reproach myself with regarding the choice of a new minister for war; I can only praise Maurepas' attentiveness and consideration as he confided his ideas in me, before coming to any conclusion, and then informed me of the choice he had proposed to the King.

MERCY TO MARIA THERESA, 19 OCTOBER 1775

When the Queen determined to establish the princesse de Lamballe as superintendent of her household, I insisted that firstly she clarify the nature, rights and prerogatives of this position. The Queen approved of this, and the ministry was even more pleased…[when it discovered that the Queen was prepared] to prevent abuses and curtail expenses. However, just as this was agreed, the princesse de Lamballe, while employing sweetness and tears, told the Queen that the duc de Penthievre was opposed to his daughter in law accepting a position which had been stripped of its former prerogatives, and therefore she could not accept the position.

[As a result]…H.M. gave in to her feelings for the princesse de Lamballe.

The princesse de Lamballe…[is claiming the same enormous salary as the previous superintendent], and this is causing difficulty at a time when the government is trying to economise; however the comte de Maurepas has seized on this to try to gain the Queen's good graces by persuading the King to agree to this. H.M. is also pleased with M. de Malesherbes but is still cold to Turgot.

The Queen went to Paris to lay a stone. The people showed little eagerness and satisfaction on seeing her, but this is not because of ill will towards the Queen, but because of the continuing high price of bread in the capital. The Queen went to a horse race near the Bois de Boulogne with M. le comte d'Artois.

262

Y.M. will deign to see that the Queen resisted the appeals of her associates with regard to nominations for a new minister of war.

SECRET LETTER

The Queen [told me]...that she thought it was possible she was pregnant. It is about a year since she last said this to me. The Queen is becoming fond of the princesse de Guemenee who has succeeded to her aunt's position as governess of the royal children. [Edit: The princesse de Guemenee did not have a pure reputation, as she lived apart from her husband, and her liaison with the duc de Coigny was well known.] This princess is as much the enemy of comtesse de Marsan [Edit: her aunt], as the friend of the duc de Choiseul; she gathers round her lively young people. The Queen intends spending evenings with this princesse de Guemenee often.

Mme de Polignac [Edit: the Queen's close friend, like the princesse de Lamballe] has little intelligence and is dominated by her very dangerous associates, especially the comtesse d'Andlau, her aunt, a well known intriguer, who was sent away from court and from the service of Mme Adelaide twenty years ago, for having procured obscene books for this princess. The Queen is aware of this. However the comtesse d'Andlau no longer appears at court.

MARIE ANTOINETTE TO MARIA THERESA, 12 NOVEMBER 1775

The King's friendship for and trust in me increase all the time, and there is nothing lacking in these respects. As for the important matter which worries my dear mother, I am very sorry I cannot tell her anything new; the apathy is certainly not from my side. My dear mother must realize that my situation is difficult and that I can hardly use means other than patience and sweetness.

MERCY TO MARIA THERESA, 15 NOVEMBER 1775

The baron de Besenval tried to wrest the secret of…[the name of the person in the position of minister of war] from the Queen. She resisted, but I wish she had been more imposing and dignified.

However this is not the only time I have realized that the Queen is capable of keeping a secret, but if she is convinced that a matter is not important, she will give in more easily.

The princesse de Lamballe is supported by M. le comte d'Artois, the duc de Chartres [Edit: later known as the duc d'Orleans, who scandalized people in the Revolution, by voting for the King's death] who is her relative, and by all who frequent the Palais-Royal [Edit: the duc de Chartres' palace], whose intrigues I dread. The comtesse de Polignac, for her part, is championed by the baron de Besenval, several young people at court, an aunt with quite a bad reputation, and associates who are equally dangerous.

The duc de Chartres and those who frequent the Palais-Royal gather at the princesse de Lamballe's. The comtesse de Polignac, the baron de Besenval and numerous other young people go to the princesse de Guemenee's. I believe that the baron de Besenval acts according to the duc de Choiseul's suggestions.

MARIE ANTOINETTE TO MARIA THERESA, 15 DECEMBER 1775

I am convinced that if I had to choose a husband from the three [brothers], I would still prefer the one heaven gave me: his character is steadfast and although he is awkward, he is as attentive and as kind as possible to me.

We are experiencing an epidemic of satirical songs. No one at court has been spared, men or women, and the French thoughtlessness has even extended to the King. As for me, I was not spared. Although wicked writings normally please the people here, these are so unimaginative and in such bad taste that they had no success, either with the public or in company.

MERCY TO MARIA THERESA, 17 DECEMBER 1775

The princesse de Lamballe has given herself a lot of trouble to [obtain a favour for a friend]...I proved to the Queen that the princesse de Lamballe cost the state annually more than one hundred thousand ecus, including the allowance her brother had obtained, and numerous expenses occasioned by the restoration of the position of superintendent, that these useless expenses had occurred only to satisfy the Queen's affection for her, and that this person should therefore be only too circumspect and not abuse the Queen's kindness.

SECRET LETTER

Mme la comtesse d'Artois is almost certainly pregnant again and this occasions many disagreeable reflections. I am truly worried about the long term effects on the Queen's spirit. However brilliant her position is at the moment, it will only have a solid foundation once she has presented an heir to the state. Until that longed-for epoch, even her advantages entail drawbacks; her influence and power sometimes worry a nation which is petulant and thoughtless and fears to be governed by a princess who is not a mother and therefore cannot be regarded as French. This is very important and I never stop telling the Queen how necessary it is for her to be prudent and moderate in the exercise of her credit. Similarly this constrains my position in relation to the Queen.

1776

MARIA THERESA TO MERCY, 4 JANUARY 1776

I can only approve of the reserve you used in talking to the Queen about the operation in question. I scarcely count on it any more (except that the emperor will come once) and I will leave all to Providence. Moreover I realize perfectly well how my daughter will feel about the comtesse d'Artois' pregnancy.

MARIE ANTOINETTE TO MARIA THERESA, 14 JANUARY 1776

When I left Vienna, I was still a child; my heart was torn at separating from my dear mother, but my head and my soul were far from realising that I would never again find that love nor such useful advice.

My dear mother has every reason to attack the French thoughtlessness, but I am truly upset that as a result you have conceived an aversion for the nation. Their character is quite inconsistent but it is not wicked; pens and tongues say lots of things which do not penetrate to the heart. The proof that they do not feel hatred is that on the slightest occasion they say pleasant things about people and praise them much more than is merited. I have recently experienced this. There was a frightening fire at the Palais, where lawsuits are heard in Paris. That very day I was to go to the Opera; I did not go and I sent 200 louis for pressing needs. From that moment, the same people who had repeated the words and songs against me, praised me to the skies.

I am scarcely more happy than my dear mother at the doctor's words. [Edit: the doctor had said that the operation was not necessary, but the King had promised to have it if there was no change in his circumstances.]

Although the changes occurring in this country can only be regarded as the work of the present ministry, nonetheless these changes, which are leading to considerable alterations in the fortune of many individuals, are causing them to be bad tempered with the court in general, and as a result these embittered people are becoming more critical and spiteful, and the annoying consequences can be seen daily in certain songs which are doing the rounds in public.

The Queen has been sufficiently prudent not to interfere at all in the present reforms, and while leaving the ministers free to act, the Queen has limited herself to saying at every opportunity that she was sorry to see the good of the state requiring irritating sacrifices from many and that she sincerely pitied them. This language had a very good effect on the people who thought they had a right to complain.

Although, in the course of last year, the King on different occasions gave more than one hundred thousand ecus in diamonds to the Queen, and H.M. already has a prodigious quantity of them, nevertheless she had a great desire to purchase earrings which were shown to her and for which the jeweller wanted 600,000 francs. I was careful to tell the Queen that, in the present circumstances, it would be prudent to delay such expenditure; but the temptation was too strong, and the Queen could not resist. In truth the Queen was quite careful about this. She kept her desire for the diamonds a secret from the King, wanting to pay for them from her allowance at the rate of 460,000 francs. The jeweller having agreed to keep two big diamonds which formed drops for a pair of earrings which the Queen did not like, H.M. will pay off this purchase within four years, in order not to dip into her allowance too much, so as to leave sufficient funds for gifts, charity and other such uses.

SECRET LETTER

M. de Malesherbes spoke to me about how to try to discover the source of the insolent stories about the King and the Queen.

Although the Queen is well aware of M. le comte d'Artois' bad qualities, nonetheless the lure of entertainments draws her back unceasingly to this very harmful liaison. He has recently abandoned himself to gambling for high stakes and has already made considerable losses. The public is turning against him and as he is always in the Queen's retinue, when she comes to Paris, this has a bad effect.

MARIE ANTOINETTE TO MARIA THERESA, 27 FEBRUARY 1776

The nominations for the cordons bleus gave me a lot of pleasure. The baron [Edit: de Breteuil] has reason to be pleased; although he deserves it, it was a great favour to have obtained one in the first set of nominations which the King has made; but he owes this attention to my dear mother. The King granted my request with good grace, as also with the duc de Civrac, previously the marquis de Durfort, who is also quite happy to have been in Vienna.

The King has proclaimed new edicts which will perhaps occasion new quarrels with parlement. I hope they will not go as far as they did under the previous reign and that the King will maintain his authority.

MERCY TO MARIA THERESA, 28 FEBRUARY 1776

The Queen holds balls on Wednesdays, the princesse de Guemenee on Saturdays; the latter are more lively, but too boisterous because of the card games for high stakes, established to please M. le comte d'Artois. The Queen has never played and the King, who always arrives at these balls around ten o'clock, brings back order. They are careful quarter of an hour beforehand to clear the tables and the cards away; these balls finish around eleven o'clock.

SECRET LETTER

The Queen took a convenient moment to talk to the King and said that she felt that for some time he had begun to love her less. The King, very moved at these words, protested to the contrary. This all arose because Y.M. said in one of your letters that you distrusted the accuracy and the good faith of the doctors and surgeons at Versailles and the Queen became very preoccupied after this.

The Queen went to a ball held by the duc d'Orleans, contrary to custom; however this was with the King's consent, but the monarch did not go. Madame, who had promised to accompany the Queen, pretended to be indisposed just before leaving, so H.M. only had her two brothers in law in her suite. M. le comte d'Artois, the duc de Chartres and some young people have brought horse races back into fashion; they take place near Paris and the Queen goes there regularly.

The Queen was at an Opera ball until five in the morning, came back to Versailles at half past six and left at ten to watch a horse race near the Bois de Boulogne. This continual amusement merry-go-round is causing criticism of the Queen, but it is useless to complain, because the King is the first to encourage the Queen to amuse herself.

Recently the Queen was at an Opera ball accompanied by Monsieur and by M. le comte d'Artois. H.M. went walking round the ballroom between Monsieur and a lady in her service. A masked man bumped into Monsieur who pushed him back with a punch. The masked man complained to a sergeant in the guards, who, not recognising Monsieur, was about to arrest him until an officer from the bodyguard told him it was the prince, and the sergeant retired. This led to all sorts of ridiculous stories. The Queen walked about for a few moments with the duc de Choiseul at the ball; this led to more stories about the important matters the Queen was discussing with the duke.

MARIA THERESA TO MERCY, 31 MARCH 1776

I wish the Queen would go less to these noisy and public entertainments, especially when the King does not go and shows proof of his solid character on every occasion. If he does not oppose the Queen's inclinations, it is because of his kindness bolstered by the probable decision to excuse these amusements in the hope that the Queen will not become attached to others which are less suitable.

I find it indecent that at the princesse de Guemenee's balls, they dared to play cards for high stakes, and were not discouraged by the presence of the Queen, before the King's arrival. As for Monsieur's adventure at the Opera ball, it is rumoured that at the above ball, the Queen was left alone for two or three hours by Monsieur, and then talked without distinction to different masked men who each in turn took her arm.[58]

The emperor and other individuals here have obtained newssheets written in Paris, filled with conflicting news, especially about my daughter. I know these articles are open to question, but for several reasons it is best to be informed about them [therefore have]... them sent here.

MARIE ANTOINETTE TO MARIA THERESA, 10 APRIL 1776

It is quite true that I was at the evening ball and Madame was not there, but that is because her health, which for a long time has not been good, prevents her staying up late.

I will send my dear mother drawings of my different hairstyles with the next courier; you may find them ridiculous, but here people are so used to them that they are no longer noticed, because everyone has similar hairstyles.

---

[58] The newssheets took a nugget of truth and embellished them with fantasies. However because the people did not know what was truth and what was lies, many began to believe all they read.

MERCY TO MARIA THERESA, 13 APRIL 1776

Each week M. le comte d'Artois and the duc de Chartres have organised several horse races, and the Queen, who has acquired an extraordinary taste for this, has missed none. There is always a crowd of badly chosen people present. These races usually take place on Tuesdays; therefore the Queen does not receive the ambassadors or foreign ministers, who have been deprived now for three weeks of the honour of paying court to H.M.

This august princess has too much intelligence and judgement not to appreciate the intrinsic value of the people around her, but she is not sufficiently guarded with them. She condones everything from those who amuse her and it is almost always this motive which determines the more or less favourable reception she gives people. However there are exceptions; the abbe de Vermond and I.

SECRET LETTER

I discovered and then pointed out to the Queen, that the comtesse de Polignac has obviously been won over by the comte de Maurepas and is being directed by him. This was borne out by the comtesse de Polignac's seemingly casual suggestion that it would be in the Queen's interest to encourage the King to nominate the comte de Maurepas as prime minister.

Pregnancy would be the remedy for all the little problems involving the Queen, because of the advantageous changes in her behaviour which would result.

With regard to Monsieur's adventure at the Opera ball, nothing happened apart from what I told Y.M.

The present crisis in the ministry is causing me a great deal of concern because of the various possible courses the Queen could take, dependent on which cabal's advice she will accept. Despite her invariable trust in me, I sometimes cannot surmount the obstacles created by her associates, which distresses me.

MARIE ANTOINETTE TO MARIA THERESA, 15 MAY 1776

I need to be reassured...[about your health]. However if your indisposition continues, I know of a remedy which is successful with the British, that is to come to France.

M de Malesherbes left the ministry the day before yesterday. M Turgot was dismissed the same day. I am not sorry at these dismissals, but I was not involved [Edit: Pichler, Maria Theresa's secretary, wrote to Mercy on the 31st of May, that Maria Theresa found her letter as sterile as usual, and written in such a rush that the Queen forgot to add the last period and sign her name.]

MERCY TO MARIA THERESA, 16 MAY 1776

The Queen is bored at Versailles, which she finds sad and deserted; I observed to her that this was mostly because of her arrangements, because her continual trips, which occupy whole days, make people uncertain of when they can pay court. There is hardly ever [etiquette prescribed] card play at the Queen's in the evenings. As a result less people come to Versailles every day.

Madame is always well treated but Monsieur is sometimes received in a markedly cold manner. He does not complain nor does he become disheartened and it is precisely this careful politicking which offends the Queen and encourages her aloofness.

Although H.M. is not going quite so often to the princesse de Guemenee's, she is still however going too often. It is there that dissipation and intrigue is encouraged, and traps are set for the Queen which she does not avoid.

SECRET LETTER

I cannot and must not conceal from Y.M. that for some weeks, things have taken a turn contrary to the Queen's interest. Y.M. can see the effect of the Queen's credit, which may one day bring just reproaches from the King and even from the nation [Edit: Fouquier-Tinville's eventual indictment of the Queen, made mention of some of the issues raised here by Mercy].[59]

In the Guines' affair, the King has acted in an inconsistent manner. In letters he wrote to the comte de Vergennes and to the comte de Guines, letters which are mutually exclusive, he has compromised himself and all his ministers. The public is aware of all the circumstances. Furthermore, the people know that this happened because of the Queen, exercising a sort of domination she has acquired over the King.

[Edit: The comte de Creutz, Swedish ambassador, wrote to King Gustav on the 12th of May 1776, "The grace the King showed M. de Guines in making him a duke is the work of the Queen; this princess conducted herself in this affair with a secrecy and skill beyond her age; she has never uttered a word in public to M. de Guines all this time; it was believed she had abandoned him, when suddenly we saw the most striking example of her credit. Her power over the King is no longer doubted."]

The finance minister, aware of the hatred the Queen bears him, decided to retire, largely for that reason; the Queen's plan was to demand of the King that M. Turgot be dismissed and even sent to the Bastille on the same day that Guines was to be created a duke, and the strongest and most insistent endeavours were needed to arrest the effects of the Queen's anger, which had no other origin than the steps which Turgot had thought he should make to recall the comte de Guines. As this same finance minister enjoys a great reputation for honesty and is loved by the people, it is regrettable that his retiral is partly the work of the Queen.

H.M. also wants to dismiss the comte de Vergennes, because of the comte de Guines, and I do not yet know if it will be possible to persuade the Queen not to do so. Y.M. will no doubt be surprised that this comte de Guines, for whom the Queen has not and cannot have any personal affection, is however the reason for such great upheavals; but the answer

---

[59] See volume II

lies in the associates of the Queen, who are all united in their support of the comte de Guines. H.M. was as if in agony, she had to relieve the burning pain; they succeeded in piquing her self esteem, in tormenting her, in blackening those who resisted her will for the good of all; this occurred during races or other entertainments, in evening conversations at the princesse de Guemenee's; finally they succeeded so well in making the Queen beside herself, in intoxicating her with a frenzy of dissipation that, together with the extreme condescension of the King, there was no way to bring her back to reasonable conduct.

[Edit: the weakness of the King prevented him from arresting all the schemes which ended the wise reforms promised at the start of his reign. Turgot and Malesherbes, men who could perhaps have changed the destiny of France, with their great plans for the future, fell because they did not know how to defend themselves against these intrigues]

I must believe that this is only a storm which will dissipate, because the Queen's basic good character and intelligence have not changed, these qualities are merely in suspense, but while that is the case, the abbe de Vermond and I feel we must be prudent. Last week, when she was going to carry out her plans, she skilfully prevented me from talking to her in private. [60]

The Queen goes to the King from time to time in the mornings, but only when she wants to persuade or compel him to act in ways which are repugnant to the young monarch.

MARIA THERESA TO MARIE ANTOINETTE, 30 MAY 1776

The remedy for my indisposition which you propose to me so sweetly could well encourage me to give in to this unpleasant inconvenience and not struggle against it. I beg you

---

[60] During the Revolution, Mercy wrote to La Marck, about Marie Antoinette and her husband, describing them as "those…who cannot see nor sufficiently understand matters if they are not looked after and enlightened." (14 Jan 1791)

to tell me how middle aged women dress; this is not a criticism, but I cannot believe that reasonable people dress as they say they do here.

I am glad you had no part in the dismissal of the two ministers, who have a good reputation with the public and only failed because they took on too much at once. You say you are not sorry: you must have good reasons; but for some time the public has not been praising you so much and attribute to you all kinds of petty scheming which is not appropriate in your position. For more than a year, there has been neither reading nor music and I only hear about horse rides and hunts with badly chosen young people, and always without the King, which worries me greatly as I love you so much. Your sisters in law are different.

MARIA THERESA TO MERCY, 31 MAY 1776

I see with regret that the events only justify my apprehensions too much.

Perhaps if she experiences some inconvenience from her misjudgements, so long as they are not on fundamental issues, she will become more circumspect and attentive to your advice.

The fecundity of the comtesse d'Artois will win her the affection of the nation, despite the fact she is a nonentity.

MARIE ANTOINETTE TO MARIA THERESA, 13 JUNE 1776

The hairstyles of middle aged women are like all the articles of dress and finery, except for rouge, which old people here still use, and sometimes even slightly more than young people.

It distresses me that my dear mother believes to my disadvantage, reports which are often false and almost always exaggerated. I cannot guess what is meant by petty scheming inappropriate to my position: I let the ministers be nominated without becoming involved in any way; I told my dear mother

276

quite frankly that I was not sorry that these ministers had left; this was because they displeased almost everyone.

I am attentive to old people, when they come to pay court. I agree there are not many amongst my particular friends; but must they say to my dear mother that they are mostly badly chosen young people, when they are in fact people of good birth, who almost all occupy positions at court, and are 35 to 40 years old and older.

The comtesse d'Artois has a great advantage, that of having children; but it is perhaps the only thing which makes her noticeable, and it is not my fault if I do not have that merit.

MERCY TO MARIA THERESA, 15 JUNE 1776

Everything at Versailles is very quiet, at least in relation to the Queen, so there is little for me to tell Y.M. The Queen has resolved to perform the pious duties necessary for her to gain the jubilee. H.M. has almost daily completed the five Stations of the Cross [61] in the main churches of Versailles, and in the meantime she has stopped going to plays, the usual trips to Paris and every type of amusement which is too public, such as horse races and hunting in the Bois de Boulogne. The Queen is limiting herself to horse riding, some musical recitals in her rooms, and painting.

The little trips to Saint-Hubert have taken place alternatively once or twice a week. The Queen has not missed one of these trips, and this seems to have given the King great pleasure. The King and Queen host card games after supper and go back to Versailles towards midnight or one o'clock.

SECRET LETTER

The Queen was scarcely bothered at M. le comte d' Artois' illness, which seemed dangerous at first, and it was easy to see that, apart from sharing his amusements, the Queen has little interest in her brother in law, as I suspected.

---

[61] Despite Marie Antoinette's denials, the rebuke from Maria Theresa had hit home.

MARIA THERESA TO MERCY, 30 JUNE 1776

Although my daughter says that she does not wish to see Choiseul come back into the ministry, I very much doubt the sincerity of her words. You are anyhow, I believe, persuaded that a minister with Choiseul's character would not suit us in the present circumstances!

EXTRACT FROM LA MARCK'S CORRESPONDENCE WITH MIRABEAU [62]

After the death of Louis XV, the court in Vienna ardently desired to see the duc de Choiseul enter the new King's ministry. It cannot be doubted that she spoke of this to the King, but Louis XVI had a pronounced feeling of aversion towards M de Choiseul, therefore the Queen refused to mention this matter again.

The abbe de Vermond, who was familiar with the Queen's dispositions, warned M de Mercy that it would not be possible to persuade the Queen to change her resolution, and the ambassador eventually prevailed upon the court at Vienna to abandon any idea of bringing M de Choiseul into the ministry.

MARIA THERESA TO MARIE ANTOINETTE, 30 JUNE 1776

My heart is always with you and I only believe any adverse reports about you very reluctantly; but I believe I must inform you as a mother and a friend of what is being said, to keep you on your guard in the midst of such a thoughtless and fawning court. You need, my dear daughter, a friend such as I.

---

[62] Extract from M. Ad de Bacourt 'Correspondance entre le Comte de Mirabeau et le Comte de La Marck' (1851), vol 1, p.46, La Marck (the Queen's adviser) talking.

MARIE ANTOINETTE TO MARIA THERESA,
14 JULY 1776

Mme Chabrillant, M. d'Aiguillon's daughter, died at Aiguillon where she had gone to visit her father. As soon as I knew she was in danger, I realized that if M. d'Aiguillon lost his daughter, it would be inhuman to oblige him to stay in the place where his daughter had died. I asked the King to give him the freedom to go wherever he wanted, except court; the King granted me this.

MERCY TO MARIA THERESA, 16 JULY 1776

With regard to the revocation of the duc d'Aiguillon's exile, I have discovered that the comtesse de Polignac and the duc de Guines persuaded the Queen to take this step, and on talking to the Queen...[I discovered that] the deciding factor had been that the Queen had been convinced that perhaps without her knowledge, the duc d'Aiguillon, because of his daughter's death, would be given total freedom; that consequently it was good politics for the Queen to secure this favour for the duc d'Aiguillon herself. I found the Queen convinced of the skill and wisdom of this advice; she was greatly surprised when I showed her that dishonesty and bad faith had dictated this counsel, that is, the comtesse de Polignac leads the Queen into error and in a way betrays her every time she wishes to use her favour to make herself esteemed by the comte de Maurepas.

I mentioned to the Queen how unperturbed she was at M. le comte d'Artois' illness and she replied quite naturally that she had no interest in her brother in law, that they were together only for amusements and that apart from that, there was no bond as the prince had no quality which was worthy of her affection. I begged the Queen to keep quiet about this, as when Monsieur was ill she had said too openly that she did not care. The King, for his part, did not show the least sign of affection for his brothers.

SECRET LETTER

[Starhemberg (on a visit to France) and I discussed]…the Queen's taste for independence, her dislike of being governed, her knowledge of her superiority over the King, and her certainty that no authority exists which can oppose her wishes.

The Queen's desire for jewellery is still not satisfied; H.M. recently bought some diamond bracelets. In exchange, the Queen gave some gems for which the jewellers paid a small amount; it was necessary to put down a considerable deposit towards the balance. This purchase was decided on due to the temptation of her associates.

The Queen had to work out the state of her finances and then she became uneasy. We discovered that, apart from the old debt of 100,000 ecus for the earrings, H.M. owed a further 100,000 francs, and nothing was left of her allowance for current expenses. Because of this, the Queen, albeit with extreme reluctance, decided to ask the King for 2000 louis. The King listened to this request with his usual kindness; he only allowed himself to say gently that he was not surprised that the Queen had no money, considering her liking for diamonds.

I believe that this recent discomfiture will make more impression on the Queen as she is naturally more inclined to economise than to squander money, and it is only inadvertently that she recently deviated from her usual reserve in expenditure.

MARIA THERESA TO MERCY, 31 JULY 1776

Although my daughter was very young when she left here, I saw in her character thoughtlessness, lack of application, obstinacy and skill in evading remonstrance. It remains to be seen if age and reflection will correct these failings.

That apart, I will be relieved to be able to dispense with discussing my daughter's conduct with her in the future. I only lent myself to it from time to time because of your entreaties. Henceforth I will not meddle unless you propose so yourself,

280

giving me the details with which to fill my letters, which would otherwise only concern the weather, as my daughter gives me no other information in her correspondence. Therefore should I write to her about the new diamonds she has bought, telling her that the public knows about this, and about the King's generosity? In confidence I admit that I do not think there is anything I can contribute.

My happy days are over; all that remains is for me to endure this sadness. Courage is necessary; I must admit that it is lacking often.[63]

MERCY TO MARIA THERESA, 17 AUGUST 1776

No one in the royal family showed more interest in and friendship for Mme la comtesse d'Artois, when she was being delivered, than the Queen. M. le comte d'Artois was very caring towards his wife, but it is known that the Queen's advice contributed quite a lot to his behaviour, and therefore H.M. has also been praised.

Despite all my attempts to try to dissuade the Queen from carrying out a plan which I believe to be very prejudicial to her service, H.M. has persisted with this plan, which consists in giving her first equerry, the comte de Tesse, a survivancier in the person of the comte de Polignac, husband of the Queen's favourite. [Edit: a survivancier was the person who 'inherited' a position, after the retiral of the incumbent. The custom was to hand the position down to a relative.] The comte de Maurepas has been one of the principal agents in this matter, which proves distinctly that the comtesse de Polignac is closely allied to this minister, and that it is through her that he is always so well informed of all the Queen is thinking and planning.

It is the custom here not to give a survivancier except at the request of the individual with the position; acting contrary

---

[63] Maria Theresa broke off all contact with her daughter in Parma because of her thoughtless and irresponsible behaviour, but she did not do so with Marie Antoinette, or even threaten to do so. Was it because she feared her daughter's reaction, and because, for reasons of state, it was necessary to maintain France as an ally? Or was it, on the other hand, because of her great pity for her daughter?

to the wishes of the holder, can lead to unpleasantness. The comte de Tesse did not deserve this. Being married to a Noailles, he therefore belongs to that powerful family. None of these considerations could restrain the Queen's partiality for her favourite, and her resulting kindness.

The Queen, to maintain an appearance of even handedness in her granting of favours, had the governorship of Poitou given to the duc de Chartres, at the request of the princesse de Lamballe.

Sometime ago the Queen was passing through a village near Versailles and saw a good old peasant woman surrounded by several little orphan children. Their attractive faces interested the Queen. She gave the grandmother money for them, and deigned to ask if she would give one to H.M. The smallest, a boy of three, was given. He is lively, cheerful and amuses the Queen. He stays in her rooms, but is neither unruly nor annoying.

SECRET LETTER

I feel that advice given to the Queen must be exact, as before the news arrives at Vienna and the letters then return, some incident almost always occurs in the intervening period which casts a different light on the Queen's actions and she then cleverly seizes on those nuances which suit her. The Queen can almost never be reproached for something done of her own volition, which was not suggested by a favourite, or at least by someone who was a favourite at the time.

With the next courier, I will give Y.M. all the facts [relative to the Queen's purchase of jewellery]...which will leave her unable to dispute your information.

I was upset by the last lines in Y.M.'s letter. Y.M.'s happy days cannot be over, because your great soul enjoys and always will enjoy the contentment your faithful subjects experience, living under an adored and blessed monarch, whom God in His Grace has granted us.

MARIA THERESA TO MERCY, 31 AUGUST 1776

I will write to her about her expenditure in the [general] way you have suggested.

MARIA THERESA TO MARIE ANTOINETTE, 2 SEPTEMBER 1776

All I hear from Paris is that you have bought bracelets worth 250,000 livres and it is supposed in consequence that you will lead the King into much needless expenditure which has in any case been on the increase again, and is leading the state into financial distress. I believe these articles are exaggerated, but I felt it was necessary to inform you of the rumours which are going around, as I love you so much. These sorts of rumours cause me anguish and make me afraid for the future.[64]

My son [Edit: Leopold] and his wife are here for a fortnight longer. She is pregnant again, with her eleventh child. I cannot prevent myself wishing you had two of their six sons. The Queen of Naples' son was not very well, and she herself has not been well since her last delivery, and is in despair at not being pregnant: I wish a couple of sons for her because one is too alarming. My son Ferdinand has lost his son; he is inconsolable as a result and I am very sorry for him. His wife is quite advanced in her pregnancy; hopefully their loss will soon be made up; but his heart will always feel it. With all my love, my dear daughter.

MARIE ANTOINETTE TO MARIA THERESA, 14 SEPTEMBER 1776

My fever has been over for the past eight days. I was in a lot of pain. I took quinine afterwards. They were obliged to purge me.

---

[64] Even in her most despairing moments, Maria Theresa did not envisage the agonising future of her daughter.

I was struck by Ferdinand's misfortune: even if I had, like him, the hope of having many children, I would be inconsolable to lose my first son.

I have nothing to say about the bracelets; I did not believe that they would try to worry my dear mother with such trifles.

MERCY TO MARIA THERESA, 17 SEPEMBER 1776

While the Queen was unwell, she saw quite a few people but this was decided by the Queen's inclinations and not by the right of different people to pay[65] court...[This aroused jealousy in the ladies of the palace], especially as the comtesse de Polignac spent almost every day with the Queen. People are convinced that by means of the favourite, the operations of the director general, which are universally displeasing, will be supported by the credit and protection of the Queen, and this idea suffices to draw onto H.M. the public's dislike whenever the people feel they have a right to complain. All these reflections have been put to the Queen but her fondness for the comtesse de Polignac prevents this making an impression.

Throughout her illness, the Queen suffered from a nervous ailment termed the vapours. At the start of the attacks I often saw her shed lots of tears which were simply a physical effect, for which there was not the slightest reason.[66] However this was accompanied by an inclination towards impatience and sadness which did not permit serious topics of conversation.

SECRET LETTER

The comtesse de Polignac flaunts her lover, or at least appears to do so without regard for what the public thinks. Her conduct in matters of dogma is no less equivocal and the principal doctor Lassone, who knows her, told the abbe de Vermond one day that he feared their friendship would

---

[65] Even when unwell, etiquette required that a Queen be visited by those with a right to do so, not by those whom she wished to see.

[66] The previous month, d'Artois' wife had had a second child.

eventually undermine the Queen's piety. I could never allow myself to suspect that this fear could be realized, at least in essential matters, but a disinclination to fulfil her pious duties and the using of a certain language in important matters, are the drawbacks resulting from close contact with people whose minds have been corrupted by the errors of the century.

In the comte de Tesse affair, the abbe de Vermond and I tried to suggest our ideas to the Queen, but she always replied "that she would have to take advice" and her advisers, who were the comtesse de Polignac and her friends, were not slow to thwart us in every way. The abbe de Vermond was so demoralised that he has asked leave to resign. The Queen thinks she will be able to dissuade him with a show of kindness, as she has already done three times.

Although I did not take your letters to Versailles, I nonetheless heard of how they were received. The Queen, reading Y.M.'s letter, said to the abbe de Vermond: "News of my bracelets has reached Vienna." When the abbe asked if Y.M. seemed annoyed at this purchase, the Queen replied: "So, so."

[Edit: the whole conversation was as follows. In a note from the abbe dc Vermond to Mercy of the 2nd of September, Vermond writes: "In reading the letter the Queen, in a light tone, told me: 'News of my bracelets has reached Vienna! I bet that news came from my sister Marie.' 'Why?' I asked, – 'Jealousy, that's the way she is.' I asked if the empress was annoyed: 'So so, you'll see;' and she gave me the letter."

[In another note from Vermond to Mercy, there is a record of a conversation between Vermond and the Queen. "You are indulgent of the morals and reputation of your friends. I could prove that at your age, this indulgence, especially in women, has a bad effect, that you make of {a woman} your friend, your society, simply because she is kind, but misconduct of every kind, bad morals, lost and corrupt reputations are the key for admittance to your society, that is what is infinitely wrong. For some time you have not even had the prudence to maintain a friendship with some women who have a reputation for reason and good conduct." Vermond added: "The Queen listened with a smile and a sort of clapping

285

of acknowledgement to this entire sermon. She only picked out the last remark, citing the good reputation of Mme de Lamballe."]

Amongst the rumours circulating, which are detrimental to the glory and reputation of a Queen of France is one...[in which] they are complaining publicly that the Queen occasions considerable expense.

The public was pleased at first when the King gave Trianon to the Queen, but it is now beginning to be alarmed and worried at H.M.'s expenditure there. On the Queen's orders, the gardens are being dug up to make a garden in the English style. The Queen has had a theatre built at Trianon, but has only had one play performed there so far. The Queen's expenses have increased considerably. The discontented reproach the Queen for the expenses incurred by the balls and the suppers in the King's rooms, and her apologists keep quiet because of so many other matters which cannot be justified.

These expenses have resulted in many others being attributed to her, although she was only involved in them indirectly.

A pension has been awarded to Mme d'Andlau, one time under-governess to Mme Adelaide, who was dismissed and exiled because she loaned a loathsome [Edit: pornographic] book to that princess. People are furious to see that woman rewarded in this way. Perhaps the Queen had nothing to do with this allowance, but how is it possible to convince people of this. It was granted on Mme de Polignac's request; she is the niece and intimate friend of Mme d'Andlau and the Queen's favourite.

The Queen's credit is such that most ministers simply obey her, without making comments. The Queen makes her requests as often from embarrassment at refusing, as from her own inclination. She will gain to her advantage, when she acquires sufficient resolution to refuse requests which appear unreasonable and which do not interest her.

The Queen's income has more than doubled, however her donations to charities have not.

People know about the Queen's debts. Her card play has become very expensive; she no longer plays the usual [Edit:

etiquette] games, in which losses are necessarily limited. Lansquenet has become her usual game and sometimes pharaon, when her card play is not totally public. Her ladies and other courtiers are afraid of and distressed at the possible losses they may incur when paying court to the Queen. Besides it is true that expensive card play displeases the King, and the fact it goes on is hidden from him as much as possible.

MARIA THERESA TO MERCY, 1 OCTOBER 1776

I am distressed that my judgement of my daughter's character has been only too justified by the events. I have studied her carefully since her early childhood. It is very important to keep the abbe de Vermond in his position, as he is an honest and zealous servant to my daughter.

I thought this note for Vermond would not be too much; I pity him a great deal, but I pity my daughter even more.

The emperor seems to me to be preparing for a trip to Paris. Remember that he has never seen our secret correspondence. [Edit: Maria Theresa to Vermond: I am touched by your services and attachment, which are without example; but I am also touched by my daughter's situation, as she is racing to her downfall, being surrounded by low flatterers who urge her to act only for their own advantage. In these circumstances my daughter needs your support. Mercy and I hope that you will not refuse our request to try to delay your departure until after winter; if matters have not changed by then, I will not demand new sacrifices from you. I will always esteem you and be grateful to you.]

MARIA THERESA TO MARIE ANTOINETTE,
1 OCTOBER 1776

I am reassured about the health of the Queen of Naples, and especially about her son. If I was even able to hope for one for you I do not know what I would do; I pray to God about this every day.

You pass over the bracelets very lightly, but it is not as you would like to think. A sovereign demeans herself by bedecking herself in that way, and it is even worse if she uses considerable sums to do so, especially at this time. Do not lose through these frivolities the credit which you acquired at the beginning; the King is known to be very moderate, so you alone will bear the blame. I do not wish to survive such a change. I am all yours.

MERCY TO MARIA THERESA, 18 OCTOBER 1776
SECRET LETTER

I fear that this monarch's [Edit: the emperor] perceptiveness will reveal to him too many shortcomings in this nation, especially in its present government, and that will only result in contempt, the consequences of which cannot be foreseen.

SAME DATE, ANOTHER SECRET LETTER

I must protest at the feet of Y.M. that, independently of what I owe my august sovereign, I am so respectfully and totally attached to the Queen, that all that concerns her affects me as much as what concerns me myself. I owe this zeal to the Queen for many reasons; sometimes she saddens me, but she [normally] treats me with so much grace and kindness that I am overcome.

MARIE ANTOINETTE TO MARIA THERESA,
OCTOBER 1776

My dear mother, I am ashamed that I am obliged to make excuses to my dear mother because I was late in sending you my respects and good wishes for Saint-Theresa's day; the trip from Choisy followed by the departure for Fontainebleau disorientated me a little, and besides I was hoping that the courier would have come sooner.

[Edit: Pichler corresponded with Mercy about this letter thus: I enclose a copy of the Queen's last letter. Y.E. will doubtless notice the coldness which is increasing between the

288

mother and daughter; all Y.E.'s insight and zeal is needed to arrest this.]

MARIA THERESA TO MERCY, 31 OCTOBER 1776

As the King of Prussia believes my daughter enjoys ascendancy over the King and consequently has influence in politics to the extent that ministers dare not make a move which would displease my daughter and bring France and Prussia closer, it is good politics to do whatever is necessary to encourage the King of Prussia in this opinion, and for this reason, you will not decrease your diligence to my daughter, at least in appearance, even if the effect does not correspond to your care to be useful to her.

I will pass lightly over my daughter's forgetfulness in relation to my name day [Edit: Mercy had suggested that Maria Theresa should scold Marie Antoinette about this]; I would even prefer not to make fresh remonstrances at this moment (believing them to be totally useless). However I will do so, when you think it necessary.

I do not greatly fear that the emperor will make very strong reproaches to my daughter. [Edit: this was Mercy's fear;] He likes to please and to shine; besides he will probably not be immune to my daughter's protestations of friendship, which are complemented by her attractiveness.[67]

THE ABBE DE VERMOND TO MARIA THERESA, 17 OCTOBER 1776

The Queen's associates monopolise her and nullify anything I say, but I cannot stop hoping to become useful again to her. She has more perception and judgement than those who obsess her; her youth and her taste for trying everything without delving too deeply is the source of all her faults: she will grow out of this. For more than a year she has not listened to me very much, but she still trusts me, tells me her ideas and

---

[67] Maria Theresa was right; Joseph was won over by his sister's charm, just as Mercy and Vermond had been.

shows me her feelings. I even believe that there are still some matters she only discusses with me. I can keep myself within reach in order to be useful to her again when time and events bring her to herself.

I am consumed by thought of the sorrows which the Queen may be storing up for herself; but if she suffered in this way, I would again be the man in whom she could most easily confide. My heart and my soul belong to the Queen; I will be at her feet whenever I can be useful. M. le comte de Mercy can never tell you of all the consideration, devotion and respect with which I am, Madame, the very humble and obedient servant of Your Sacred Majesty.[68]

MARIA THERESA TO MARIE ANTOINETTE,
31 OCTOBER 1776

Your excuses for forgetting my name day are accepted without bitterness; but my dear daughter, I do not want you to think of me once a year, but every day, week and month, I want you to remember my love, advice and example.

I must admit that this continually dissipated life is upsetting me. That is the point which hurts most, that you do all this without the King. I am sure and know your heart, that the thought of the pain this irresponsibility causes me would restrain you. It will end of itself, but perhaps too late for your happiness and glory.

---

[68] La Marck wrote of Vermond in the previously cited book, vol I, p.40: "The Queen had so much trust in the abbe de Vermond, that he wrote most of her letters and she limited herself to merely copying them out. He was attached to the Queen, indeed even passionately so, and although he was a chatterbox, and spoke incessantly of his relationship with the Queen, no indiscretion ever escaped from his lips. Moreover, Marie Antoinette considered him to be quite ordinary, as regards his intellect, and depended more on his devotion than on his insight. She was only attentive when he was transmitting a message from the comte de Mercy, and even then she only took from these messages what she considered appropriate."

MARIE ANTOINETTE TO MARIA THERESA,
12 NOVEMBER 1776

My dear mother's kindness on my birthday and her extreme indulgence for my forgetfulness were a very loving reproach. How could I forget for one moment all that my dear mother has done for me? I will always take pride in her example, and I would be only too happy if I could emulate it, although imperfectly.

MERCY TO MARIA THERESA, 15 NOVEMBER 1776

The suppers in the Queen's rooms with the King, to which were invited those with the entrees to the bedroom, have not taken place this year, and I regret them as these were the occasions when the King was kind enough to talk to me.

As for the suppers in the private rooms, they still take place, but the choice of people admitted to them has deteriorated, and is confined to favourites, while middle aged people are almost excluded, even when their rank should have secured them that honour.

The Queen has been hunting two or three times a week, sometimes with the King. However there have often been other hunts with M. le comte d'Artois. They are different because of the number of young people there and because of their ease in approaching the Queen, closer than is proper. H.M. goes to these hunts on horseback and the young people try to entertain her in foolish ways. For example a young Englishman decided to make his horse jump over a reasonably high fence. This amused the Queen and they decided...[he should] make his horse jump over another horse; the Queen wanted to stop this...[but the Englishman went ahead and] he was lucky to escape with bruises.

The Queen regards the princesse de Guemenee as dangerous in every way; but this does not stop her going there to be entertained.

The Queen goes less frequently to the princesse de Guemenee than to the princesse de Lamballe, but at the latter's there is just as much intrigue, the only difference is that the intriguers are better known. The duc de Chartres goes to the superintendent's and sometimes Monsieur and Madame. The comte d'Artois is always there.

SECRET LETTER

The Queen has finally decided to talk to the abbe de Vermond about his plans to leave, and with the greatest kindness told him that she would never agree to such a project, as he was necessary to her.

The King's attitude is that of the most attentive courtier, to the extent that he is the first to treat those of the Queen's associates whom she most favours with marked distinction, although it is well known that the King does not like them at…[I spoke to the Queen, but] H.M. often ended up joking, saying that she would become reasonable sometime but that it was necessary to be amused for now.

The Queen wanted to play pharaon; she asked the King for his permission to have the bankers sent from Paris. The King observed that as it was forbidden to play games of chance, even for princes of the blood, it would be a bad example to permit them at court; but the King, with his usual gentleness added that it would be of no consequence if the game were just for one night...[However the game went on over three days] and one of the late nights took place on the eve of a holy day. This led to talk amongst the public. The Queen extricated herself by joking, telling the King that he had permitted a card game but had not specified how long it should last, and that therefore they had a right to prolong it over thirty six hours. The King began to laugh and replied gaily: "Oh go away, you are all worthless!"

The horse races were almost improper because of the circumstances. The comte d'Artois was running about, laying bets, overjoyed when he won, desolate when he lost. He presented to the Queen the winners of the races. I was distressed to see this and even more to see the irritated faces of Monsieur and Madame, and Mme d'Artois.

In the evenings the Queen walks about the ante-chambers, which are full of people, with only the comtesse de Polignac on her arm and no suite except for a valet and two guards. During card play there are always some thoughtless people flitting around the Queen's table, and the Queen talks constantly to them, while more considerate courtiers stand respectfully aside and are hardly ever addressed.

The King, despite his dislike of games of chance, seeing the Queen liked them, he himself suggested having the bankers come back from Paris to the princesse de Lamballe's, and this is what happened. This is really distressing because it precludes the possibility of dissuading the Queen from participation in events which cause her harm.

I will always maintain the necessary demeanour to convince the King of Prussia of the Queen's influence in politics, and I will even take great care to ensure that the baron de Goltz is informed of the frequent access I have to the Queen in her rooms whenever I present myself. [Edit: Goltz was the Prussian ambassador to France]

SAME DATE, ANOTHER SECRET LETTER

The Queen deigned to let me read part of H.M. the emperor's letter. I remember part of it which was roughly as follows: "You know, dear sister, of my earnest wish to see you again; my presence here is quite useless, I am the fifth wheel on the chariot; however I am charged with several details which concern the service of my sovereign, I cannot dispose of myself with the certainty of carrying out the projects I wish to undertake."

The Queen is sometimes torn between her desire to see her august brother whom she truly loves, and fear of what he will see and will find fault with in the Queen's conduct, and one day she admitted as much to me.

MARIA THERESA TO MERCY, 30 NOVEMBER 1776

The emperor's phrase to my daughter, that here he is only the fifth wheel on the chariot is not new to me: it is what he usually says in the company he frequents; but unfortunately I find myself only too often in a position where I am unable to do as I wish and moreover what I do is done in a way which is repugnant to my principles and feelings.

While the emperor is in France, write official letters only, as will I, and do not let the emperor know about the secret ones. It is a nuisance to use these sorts of precautions, but I could never depend on the use the emperor would make of my confidences.

MARIA THERESA TO MARIE ANTOINETTE, 30 NOVEMBER 1776

If you were even in the company of the King, I would be silent, but you are always without him and with all the youngest and most disreputable people in Paris, so that the Queen, this charming Queen, is almost the oldest in the company. These gazettes and newssheets which charmed me and which mentioned the good deeds and the very generous traits of my daughter, have changed; now there are only reports of horse races, games of chance and late nights such that I no longer want to see them. I often avoid being in company, in order not to hear upsetting stories.

MARIE ANTOINETTE TO MARIA THERESA, 16 DECEMBER 1776

Truly I could feel miserable because of the different stories which circulate about me. While you are persuaded that I am only found with people as young as I, for a year, the very young people here have believed themselves badly treated and isolated from me, and only a fortnight ago there was talk of a little intrigue amongst them not to come to my balls. However they all came.

My dear mother can well imagine the pleasure I will have in seeing the emperor; I have been longing for it for so long, that I dare not count on it yet. Apart from my satisfaction, my greatest pleasure will be that he will be able to disabuse my dear mother of the prejudices people are trying to give her against me.

MERCY TO MARIA THERESA, 18 DECEMBER 1776

[Since arriving back at Versailles]...H.M. has come to a play every week in Paris; she has not been received with the usual acclamations, but these slight variations in the public's reception are only caused by fleeting ill humour.

The balls have begun again at Versailles. The first of these balls was very quiet and consisted of ten to twelve women dancing. Gradually the Parisian women are losing the habit of going to Versailles.

1777

MARIA THERESA TO MARIE ANTOINETTE, 2 JANUARY 1777

In a month's time you will see the emperor. I hope the King will be pleased with him, and that, once the initial awkwardness is over, they will become friends and trust each other. Remember your mother when you are together.

MARIA THERESA TO MERCY, 3 JANUARY 1777

I am not hopeful of a good outcome from this journey. If I am not wrong, either my daughter will win over the emperor with her kindness and attractiveness, or he will irritate her by wishing to indoctrinate her. The first seems to me most likely.

MARIE ANTOINETTE TO MARIA THERESA, 16 JANUARY 1777

I am overwhelmed with the hope of seeing my brother soon. I know his discretion and will talk to him in confidence. After the initial meeting, which will perhaps be slightly awkward, the King will be pleased to see him and talk to him: the consequences can only be favourable, both in matters of politics and for me personally.

MERCY TO MARIA THERESA, 17 JANUARY 1777

When the emperor comes, I will take him to the Queen by backstairs corridors so that no one will see them at their first meeting. The King will come in a few moments later.

SECRET LETTER

Shortly after the last courier left, I found the Queen worried and embarrassed at the amount of her debts, not even knowing what the total was. I added them up and found the total was 20,303 louis. The Queen was quite surprised at this and decided, although reluctantly, to sound out the King to ascertain whether he would take on at least some of her debts. As soon as the Queen began talking about this, the King, without hesitation and with the best grace possible, immediately agreed to pay the whole amount. He only asked for a few months delay, as he wanted the debt to be paid off from his own allowance, without the intervention of any minister.

The King's behaviour is even more remarkable as he is naturally very economical and I saw that the Queen was amazed at his prompt and easy compliance, which she had not expected. I observed that, although he made no demands on the Queen and seemed to renounce his own likes in preference to those of his august wife, it would nonetheless be dangerous to make use of the King's condescension without ever making a return.

The Queen has been slightly reassured by H.M. the emperor's last letter, in which he said "that he was not coming to observe and criticise, and even less to give lessons; that his sole aim was to enjoy the pleasure of seeing his august sister, and that he wanted nothing to spoil this."

MARIA THERESA TO MERCY, 31 JANUARY 1777

I would be inconsolable if, depending on the King's generosity for the future, my daughter does not put her finances in order.

Rohan seems more and more dangerous to me, and I fear that one day his position as grand almoner will give him influence and even access to my daughter. The emperor despises him, but he still enjoys his company: he even wrote to him (as Goltz noted in his correspondence) [Edit: the Austrian court intercepted the correspondence between Goltz and the

298

Prussian court] Moreover you will find in Goltz's correspondence quite striking references to my daughter's frivolity, and the emperor's character, which furnish material for reflection.

MARIA THERESA TO MARIE ANTOINETTE, 3 FEBRUARY 1777

The emperor and the King are so young and both being so good hearted, my hopes, which I believe to be well founded, are that they will acknowledge and consolidate mutual trust, which will be so necessary and useful to them in political matters, and which will make them happy and render their states and even all of Europe, the same. These reflections of a good old mother and sovereign have made me decide to send new instructions to Mercy, telling him to give you more information and concert with you how to behave in relation to your ministers.

Our wicked neighbour [Edit: Maria Theresa is referring to the King of Prussia. She had succeeded to the throne as a young woman in her early twenties and immediately the King of Prussia had invaded her territory, winning part of Silesia] spreads every possible calumny, especially in France. The King of Prussia's joy when the emperor cancelled his trip to you [Edit: it was only postponed] is a sure sign of how important it is to him and must bind us closer together, such that neither he nor anyone else will dare to trouble us.

[Edit: on the 13th of July, 1776, Louis XVI wrote to (his minister) Vergennes: "I believe that this trip will make the King of Prussia mad with jealousy."] I cannot conceal from you that your private life interests the King of Prussia, and I have mentioned to Mercy some aspects which have upset me for a long time, such as your pleasure seeking, card playing, horse rides: being unfriendly to the King, sleeping separately, remaining all night at cards, which the King did not want you to do: that you were worried about the emperor's arrival and did not want him to come. All these ideas are sent from Berlin to Saxony, Poland etc. and I admit have caused me great sorrow for some months.

My only consolation was that these were calumnies against you, just as they spread calumnies against the emperor and me; but my dear child, the gazettes only confirm these different amusements which my dear Queen enjoys without her sisters in law or the King, and have caused me a lot of sadness. Loving you so much, I can see ahead to your future and I ask you to do so too.

MERCY TO MARIA THERESA, 15 FEBRUARY 1777

Versailles has not been as deserted as it has been this winter, for a long time, and it could become worse, if the reasons for the ill humour and jealousy which have caused this, are allowed to continue. The Queen seems seriously preoccupied by this matter.

Although H.M. treats everyone with kindness and grace when they are before her, it is nonetheless true that the few people the Queen calls "her society" alienate most of the courtiers and lessen their opportunities of paying court. As a result, the benefits and pleasures which people hope to obtain in approaching their sovereign, disappear when the latter adopts a kind of private life which is incompatible with the running of a great court, where all subjects of a certain rank have the right to claim treatment determined by their position, their age, their personal merit and their services.

The quietness of the season at Versailles determined the Queen to go to masked balls at the Opera. Sometimes at the balls, the Queen deigns to dance with some men, although always well known men of distinction. H.M. has also granted this honour to some foreigners and this has led to misplaced and unfair talk. The Queen agreed with me that while attending innumerable entertainments, she had however been little amused. I told her that this was always the case with such entertainments, which only left emptiness afterwards.

MARIE ANTOINETTE TO MARIA THERESA, 17 FEBRUARY 1777

Yesterday I saw Mercy and he spoke to me as you had instructed. I am more outraged than astonished at the spitefulness and villainy of our wicked neighbour. His ambassador has been known for a long time as a man with few scruples.

The grand almoner is dying; prince Louis [Edit: de Rohan] will take his place. I am very annoyed about it, and the King will only appoint him reluctantly; but two years ago, he let himself be surprised by M. de Soubise and Mme de Marsan [Edit: Rohan's aunt] into making a half promise, which they converted into a full promise when thanking him, and now they are exploiting this. If he behaves as he did in the past, there will be many intrigues here.

MERCY TO MARIA THERESA, 19 FEBRUARY 1777 SECRET LETTER

The Rohan family is a source of intrigue at present and the comtesse de Marsan directs them...[Some time ago] the Queen was given the King's "word of honour" that the coadjutor of Strasbourg [Edit: Rohan] would not become the grand almoner of France. This was instigated by the duc de Choiseul, his mortal enemy, and unfortunately the Queen told the duke of the King's agreement.

Recently the comtesse de Marsan decided to assure herself that this promise, agreed to by the late King, and confirmed by the present King, would be executed; but the aforementioned countess was astonished to find obstacles and blamed the Queen; the Rohans busied themselves and succeeded in winning over the comte de Maurepas. The duc de Choiseul, for his part, intrigued to maintain the blow against his enemy and this led to relentless war. The prince de Soubise had the princesse de Guemenee write to the Queen. H.M. was embarrassed and replied vaguely but in a way which showed she was not opposed. The comtesse de Marsan had an audience with the King and spoke in such a way that the King was intimidated and wished to capitulate. Finally the King said the coadjutor could have the position if he agreed in writing to resign at the end of a year. The comtesse de Marsan was too skilful not to agree to this, as she realized it was an illusion. The King told the Queen immediately and they were convinced that he had perfectly accomplished their views and assured the coadjutor's departure.

I predicted to the Queen that the coadjutor, once in place, would use all sorts of tricks to stay there and he would be aided in this by the Queen's associates, who were all in league to mislead her and procure the comte de Maurepas' cooperation, at the expense of the Queen. H.M. cannot suffer this coadjutor, and treats him badly, without intimidating him, and he will be even more poisonous in his new position because of the machinations of which he is capable. The comtesse de Marsan's cabal is one of the most dangerous at court; anything goes when it comes to achieving their aims and they have the people for this, for example the abbe Georgel, who, I know, writes forged letters and spreads rumours among the public.

Because the Queen is not at the stage where I can prudently tell her that the letters [Edit: from Prussia] were intercepted, I only told her that zealous men serving Y.M. had found means to discover that the King of Prussia was busy trying to put obstacles in the way of the Queen's success at court; and that they had obtained a letter from the King of Prussia to his ambassador Goltz, and having sworn the Queen to secrecy, I read to her the Prussian dispatch of 16th of February. The Queen was extraordinarily struck by it. I warned her especially that it was important that ambassador Goltz should notice nothing in her expression or in her speech to show that the Queen had suspicions about him or his court, and H.M. understood.

MARIE ANTOINETTE TO MARIA THERESA, 4 MARCH 1777

The King has had the flu and has not left his room for a week; I have been his constant companion during that time. I hope it will soon be over.

MERCY TO MARIA THERESA, 18 MARCH 1777

Mesdames de France are no longer seen outside their rooms, and in my ambassadorial dispatch, I have mentioned the very serious quarrel which has arisen between Mme Louise, the Carmellite nun, and the King. [Edit: In this dispatch, Mercy explained that Mme Louise claimed an allowance of 200,000 livres, just like that given to the other aunts. However Louis XVI found this very strange, as Mme Louise had taken a vow of poverty; he did not reply to her, and stopped visiting her, as he had been in the habit of doing, previously]

Mme Adelaide does not like the Queen at all, and Mme Sophie likes her even less; Mme Victoire maintains friendly relations with the Queen.

During the King's indisposition, the Queen showed him all possible care and attention, and this seemed to touch the King.

SECRET LETTER

One of the most regrettable current issues, both because of the unfortunate effect it has on the public and because of the very grave consequences it may entail, is the Queen's immoderate taste for games of chance. These games, although prohibited in public edicts, have begun again in Paris, since the court set the example by flaunting the law; last winter, these games gave rise to such considerable losses, and to so much fraud and ugly incidents, that the government has had to renew the prohibition, and make the penalties more severe. The Queen showed the King that this annoyed her and he, because of his instinctive kindness and gentleness, has hardly dared to tell her that he has been obliged to renew the prohibitions; so the Queen is simply ignoring them and they are playing pharaon in her rooms almost every day.

The Queen is losing a considerable amount [Edit: at card play] almost every day. Besides the money the King intended to pay off the Queen's debts, and which he gives her each week, is swallowed up, at least in part, by the daily losses, and if this continues the Queen will find herself doubly embarrassed at having increased her debts, and at having in a way, abused the King's benevolence.

MARIA THERESA TO MERCY, 31 MARCH 1777

You may well believe that one of the most important points to be clarified is whether there is any hope of succession, and you will investigate this with the emperor.

MARIA THERESA TO MERCY, 11 APRIL 1777

Breteuil arrived the day before yesterday. He excuses all the Queen's frivolity and even hopes for a change in her state of marriage with the arrival of the emperor. I wish this too, but am not very hopeful.

MERCY TO MARIA THERESA, 16 APRIL 1777

A woman called Cahuet de Villers, wife of a treasurer in the King's household, was imprisoned on my request[69] for using the Queen's name to borrow money from different people; to effect this, she fabricated and produced letters supposedly from the Queen; she falsely boasted of having frequent audiences with the Queen, although in fact she has never been near this august princess, and finally she also procured a register with the arms of the Queen on its cover and showed this alleged register of accounts to the dupes to whom she addressed herself, to disconcert them.

---

[69] Again, as on so many other occasions, one has to wonder why the Austrian ambassador has to undertake such duties.

The ease with which it is possible in this country to make people believe in the most absurd situations served de Villers so well that, through her stratagems, she procured for herself 100,000 ecus from sire Berenger, treasurer of the duc d'Orleans, and a sum of 100,000 livres from a banker called Lafosse. In the investigation into all this woman's schemes, many other intrigues were discovered in which a number of quite well known people would be compromised, if the final judgement on this criminal were made by the ordinary tribunals. I proposed to H.M. to have an open trial; but the King's ministers were reluctant to do so, especially the comte de Maurepas, and it could be that he feared that his nephew, the duc d'Aiguillon, could be implicated in the machinations of this de Villers, who had a large part in the rise of the comtesse du Barry. It is to be presumed that this incident, which has led to a lot of talk in Paris, will be mentioned in the gazettes which are sent abroad.

I know that, in the depraved vortex of this court, there are contemptible people who secretly contemplate plans to induce the King into debauchery; they even dared to mention to him an actress in the Comedie Francaise. These loathsome attempts had no effect and I am quite certain they never will; however the Queen will have to be vigilant, and I have informed her of this matter.

SECRET LETTER

H.M....[has been to the theatre recently] and was received with acclamations each time; I was agreeably surprised.

MERCY TO MARIA THERESA, 7 MAY 1777

Only this monarch [Edit: Joseph] will be able to tell Y.M. all that his presence here has accomplished. Although I expected favourable results in this respect, I dare say that these I have seen have exceeded my hopes.

It is not yet possible to judge what effect H.M. the emperor's presence has had on the King. The character of this prince does not incline him to react promptly and energetically to matters, however striking they may be. However it is not to be doubted that H.M. the emperor's conversations and his good example in every area, will develop some ideas in the King which eventually will bear fruit.

MARIE ANTOINETTE TO MARIA THERESA, 14 JUNE 1777

It is true that the emperor's departure has left a void which I cannot fill; I was so happy during the short time he was here that it all seems like a dream to me now. But what will never be just a dream, is all the good advice and guidance which he gave me and which are forever engraved on my heart.

I will admit to my dear mother that he gave me something which I requested and which gives me the greatest pleasure: that is, written advice. It is my main reading at present and if ever, (which I doubt), I could forget what he told me, I would nonetheless always have his words with me to recall me to my duty.

The King was truly affected at the departure. As he does not find the conventions easy it is hard for him to show his feelings; but everything I saw convinces me that he is truly attached to my brother and feels very friendly towards him. At the moment of departure, when I was most in despair, the King was so attentive and loving to me that I will never forget it all my life, and it would make me care for him, if I did not already do so.

It would be impossible for my brother not to be pleased with this country.

I have just this minute received a letter in the post from my dear mother. What kindness to think of my name day when you have so much to occupy you! It overwhelms me. You sent wishes for my happiness: my greatest wish is to know that you are pleased with me, to merit your kindness always, and to be able to persuade you that no one in the world loves you more tenderly and respectfully than I.

MERCY TO MARIA THERESA, 15 JUNE 1777

On the 19th, the emperor arrived at Versailles at half past nine. The abbe de Vermond was waiting for the carriage; he led the emperor, alone, via a secret stairway to the Queen's rooms, without going through the antechambers, which were full of people.

The first moments between the emperor and the Queen were most touching; they embraced and remained silent for a long time as they were both full of emotion. They went into a back room and remained there for nearly two hours, alone.

There they opened up to each other; the Queen was very moved and became even more so because of two remarks the emperor made which showed his great pleasure in seeing her again. He said that, if she were not his sister and if he could marry her, he would not hesitate to do so in order to acquire such a charming companion. Then he told her that if she became a widow and did not have children, he would like her to come back and live with Y.M. and himself. These words moved the Queen to the extent that, from that moment, she felt able to open up to the emperor and talk openly to him of the most essential factors of her position. She spoke firstly of the circumstances relative to her matrimonial intimacy and Y.M. will learn from H.M. the emperor, that this matter was clarified as much as possible, with a satisfactory result. Then the Queen spoke of her way of life.

The Queen took him to the King and the two monarchs embraced; the King said a few words which showed his desire to appear warm and courteous; the emperor noticed this and was pleased; with his intelligence and charm, he was able from the first moment to put the King at ease.

On the 21st, the emperor talked to the King and Queen for more than two hours; they spoke about different matters, even about matters of state. The emperor found that the King was not absolutely devoid of knowledge, that he appeared to hold to his ideas more from obstinacy than through reason, and that he seemed inclined to wish for good. The emperor paid some more visits, amongst others, one to the comtesse de

Maurepas. Then H.M. returned to the Queen's rooms, and after the concert, both went to sup with Madame.

The supper was more than merry, that is to say on the part of the King and his brothers. They were so much at ease that, on rising from the table, they amused themselves childishly, running around the room, throwing themselves on the sofas, to the point where the Queen and the princesses were embarrassed because of the emperor's presence. He, without appearing to notice this unseemliness, continued his conversations with the princesses. Madame, in an outburst of impatience, called to her husband and said she had never seen him acting so childishly. It all ended happily however, without the emperor showing the surprise which he had felt at such a strange sight.

On the 22nd, the Queen sent the abbe de Vermond to me. He told me of her misgivings that in leaving the emperor alone with the King, the emperor might discuss her too harshly with the King and establish maxims which would tend to curtail her influence in the areas of recommendations, protections and politics. I told the abbe to make the Queen see how badly she misjudged the emperor's intentions, as, in his private conversations with the King, he would be concerned to establish her credit even more solidly than is the situation at present. Wherever the emperor appears, he is received with lively acclamations.

On the 26th, the emperor went to a horse race organized by M. le comte d'Artois, which the Queen and the princesses attended. H.M. was very displeased with the disorder and the familiarity which reigned there.

On the 27th, I went to see the emperor and told him how the King glories in the Queen's charms and qualities, that he loves her as much as he is capable,[70] but that he fears her at least as much as he loves her. I observed that the Queen neglected him too much and intimidated him often. I remarked

---

[70] It need hardly be said that Mercy did not have a high opinion of Louis XVI. La Marck shared this low opinion of Louis XVI. In a letter to Mercy of 28 Sept 1791, he wrote, "The King is incapable of reigning…'

on the Queen's inclination to distrust,[71] which is often soothed only by the lure of amusements.

HM went to Versailles, where he wished to observe the court's routine on a Sunday. [Edit: Joseph described this visit to Leopold, on the 29th April: "Yesterday I observed what occurs at Versailles on a Sunday; the lever, mass, eating in public; I mingled with the people, watching all. I must admit that it was amusing, and that, as I act out this little comedy so often myself, it is fascinating to watch others do the same."]

As H.M. [Edit: Joseph] receives neither visits, nor petitions, nor tributes in any material form whatsoever, everyone comes to me all day and I have no time to reply to the hundreds of letters which come from all over.

On the 28th, H.M. told me that the day before, to please the Queen, he had accompanied her to the princesse de Guemenee's in the evening and that he had been shocked by the bad tone of the gathering and at the atmosphere of licence there. H.M. saw pharaon being played; he even heard reproaches made in the presence of the Queen to Mme de Guemenee about her suspect manner of playing. The emperor was indignant at this impropriety; he told the Queen quite plainly that this house was a real gambling den; the Queen tried to make excuses, she even returned after midnight on the pretext that she had promised to do so; the emperor was vexed at this and concluded that the Queen was dishearteningly obstinate.

H.M.was quite pleased with the King; he did not feel the same way about Monsieur [Edit: Provence wrote thus to Gustavus about Joseph: "The emperor is very persuasive and enjoys making protestations and oaths of friendship, but if you examine them closely, his protestations and apparent openness mask his desire to dissimulate his real feelings. Far from being seen through by him, he is easily seen through. His knowledge is very superficial." Joseph wrote to Leopold (his brother): "Monsieur is indefinable, better than the King, but he is

---

[71] As mentioned before, neither Marie Antoinette nor Louis XVI trusted those around them. During the Revolution, this lack of trust led to their increasing isolation.

mortally cold. Madame is ugly and coarse. M. le comte d'Artois' wife can only make babies and is an absolute imbecile."]

Mesdames have been very pleased with the emperor's attentions. One day when he was at Mme Adelaide's, under the pretext of letting him see some portraits, she took him into a private room and being alone there, she kissed the emperor, telling him that this mark of friendship could be allowed to an old aunt [Edit: the emperor and Mme Adelaide were close together in age, both being around forty, although Mme Adelaide was slightly older]

On the 2nd, the emperor went to see the Salpetriere general hospital.

On the 3rd, the emperor visited the Gobelins factory and the King's natural history room in the botanical gardens.

The emperor told me he was surprised to find the Queen full of intelligence and wisdom.

On the 8th, the emperor went to see the royal printing works, the Savonnerie factory and the King's physic's study at Passy. [Edit: Joseph in a letter to Leopold on the 11th of May wrote: "Each minister is absolute master in his own department, but has a continual fear of being, not directed by the sovereign, but dismissed. As a result each is only concerned to keep his position and any good he does is done only if it does not conflict with this aim. The King has absolute power only in passing from one form of slavery to another."]

H.M. had an enamelled box and gold medal presented to the abbe de l'Epee who teaches the deaf and dumb. H.M. had seen the school two days before and had been very impressed by the zealous and virtuous man who runs it free of charge. The public heard of this and was pleased. [Edit: until Joseph's visit, the school had not attracted interest; afterwards everyone wanted to see it]

On the 9th and the preceding day, the emperor had private conversations with the King. He also had some with the Queen when he gave her some advice, but a little too forcibly, so that it led to arguments.

On the 12th [the emperor went]…to the veterinary school. He deigned to tell me that he had had an affectionate

310

and loving conversation with the Queen, and that the emperor's friendly and cheerful tone had reestablished the Queen's trust and goodwill, and that she herself had asked him to write down some points to serve as rules for her future conduct.

On the 14th, the emperor went to see the villa at Louveciennes. The comtesse du Barry, who had remained in possession of this house, was there: the emperor met her in the gardens and spoke to her for a few moments; H.M. found the countess just as I had described her. On returning to Versailles, the emperor had a private talk with the King, who made new confidences to him about his marriage state: but only the emperor can give Y.M. an account of this matter. In a visit to the comte de Maurepas, the old minister seemed to want H.M. to protect him from the Queen.

On the 15th, H.M. heard a case being pled in the parlement. [Edit: Campan, in her memoirs,[72] wrote: He (Joseph) disguised none of his prejudices against the etiquette and customs of the court of France; and even in the presence of the King made them the subject of his sarcasms. The King smiled, but never made any answer: the Queen appeared pained. The emperor frequently terminated his observations upon the objects in Paris which he had admired by reproaching the King for suffering himself to remain in ignorance of them. He also reproached him for not having visited the Hotel des Invalides nor the Ecole Militaire: and even went so far as to tell him before us that he ought not only to know what Paris contained, but to travel in France, and reside a few days in each of his large towns. The emperor loudly censured the existing practice of allowing shopkeepers to erect shops near the outward walls of all the palaces, and even to establish something like a fair in the galleries of Versailles and even upon the staircases.]

On the 18th, the King again spoke of his marriage state and made new confidences to the emperor about it.

On the 22nd, H.M. saw some artists and told me to send the comte d'Angivillers [the director of buildings for the King] a box ornamented with diamonds and decorated with H.M.'s

---

[72] Extract from Campan, vol 1, p.224

portrait. [Edit: Joseph also gave gifts at the Sevres factory and at the Gobelins and Savonnerie factories] He also performed many acts of charity in the hospitals and wherever his kindliness found the opportunity.

On the 27th, I went…[to see] the emperor. The principal doctor Lassone had been with H.M. for an hour.

The emperor deigned to tell me that he had spoken to the King for nearly two hours the day before and was astonished to hear ideas and reasoning that he had thought beyond the grasp of the King. [Edit: Joseph wrote thus to Leopold on the 9th of June: "This man is quite weak but not stupid; he has ideas, judgement, but is apathetic in body and mind. He can hold a reasonable conversation but has neither desire to learn nor curiosity."]

The King also spoke of his great desire to have children. He spoke tenderly about the Queen. This conversation was so frank and cordial that the emperor told me: "If I had been so inclined, the King would have shown me his papers and told me everything I wanted to know about political matters."

The Queen told me that the King had told her of his regret at being separated from the emperor just when they were starting to know each other and become close, and that the King had said to the Queen: "We have been together more often and for longer periods while the emperor has been here, and I am obliged to him as a result." Between eleven o'clock and midnight, the emperor said his farewells; the Queen was very moved but strained to disguise her heartbreak, at least partially. The emperor, embracing the King, said in a voice filled with emotion that he earnestly recommended his sister to him as he loved her so tenderly "that he would never be happy unless he knew her to be happy." The King replied that this was his dearest wish and the object of all his care. The emperor returned to his rooms and I saw that he was very affected.

The Queen, who had tried too hard to preserve a calm countenance, that same evening had violent convulsions; but next day I found her calm and in good health, although greatly saddened. She wanted to be alone, so she went to Petit Trianon accompanied by the princesse de Lamballe and the comtesse

312

Jules de Polignac. That very day a courier brought a letter from Y.M. for her. The contents of this letter soothed her.

We cannot presume that the King has a sufficiently developed and decided character to make him capable of conceiving profound esteem or strong friendship for anyone; these sentiments require more sensitivity, willpower and reflection, qualities which cannot be attributed to the King; but to judge from appearances, he felt as affectionate towards the emperor as he is capable of feeling and one cannot expect more.

SECRET LETTER

The emperor noted in the King all the shortcomings caused by his upbringing; but I believe he judged him too harshly in relation to his intelligence and abilities. It seemed to me that the emperor thinks the King is more limited than he is.

The 9th. Until now the emperor had maintained very cordial and measured language when talking to the Queen; on this day he changed his tone and adopted one which could have led to serious quarrels. The question arose of a plan to encourage the King to travel about his kingdom, and especially to go to Brest; this idea had first been suggested by the emperor, the Queen had adopted it and suggested it to the King. The emperor decided afterwards that in the case of such visits, the Queen should not accompany the King, "because she was not good for him." This phrase was followed by a few reproaches for "her offhand manner when with her husband," "her language which was not sufficiently respectful" and "her lack of submission." These terms had greatly upset the Queen; she was no less upset when the emperor, in front of the duc de Coigny and the comtesse de Polignac, had told her dryly to go and find the King in his rooms.

In addition to this, after the supper at Mesdames, the Queen had suggested taking the air on a terrace, the King and Monsieur had immediately prepared to do so, whereupon the emperor teased them for their obligingness, adding that, as for him, he would not go out. All these little grievances combined to put the Queen in a bad mood.

The 14th. The emperor had a very interesting conversation at Versailles with the King, who confided to H.M. his pain at not having children; he entered into the most detailed aspects about his physical state, and asked the emperor's advice. This very important matter can only be explained to Y.M. by the emperor in person, and Y.M. will then be able to draw your own conclusions.

On the 23rd, the emperor tried to encourage the comtesse de Polignac to speak about important matters concerning the Queen; the said countess did not do this well, and the emperor drew the obvious conclusion.

On the 27th there was another little dispute when the emperor told the Queen that if he were her husband, he would know how to direct her wishes and make them develop in the way he could wish.

The 28th. [I had advised H. M. to keep the rules short]…the emperor agreed at first and then changed his mind.

[JOSEPH'S ADVICE TO MARIE ANTOINETTE

Do you make yourself necessary to the King? Does he see that your affection is centred solely on him? Do you encourage your desire for glory at his expense? Are you totally discreet about his defects and weaknesses? Are you sociable and loving when you are with him? Your sole object must be to earn the friendship and trust of the King.

As Queen you have a very clear role. Is your manner not slightly too offhand, and have you not adopted the behaviour which was prevalent when you came here. Have you thought of the effects of your relationships and friendships, if they are not centred on people who are totally irreproachable? Have you thought of the frightening consequences of games of chance? Think for a moment if you will of the difficulties which you have already encountered at the Opera balls and of the incidents which you have yourself recounted to me which occurred at them…]

However what I had foreseen, happened. The Queen, on receiving them, immediately said that she wanted to reply to

314

all the points and prove that her conduct had almost always been reasonable and directed by just motives. Nonetheless, from that moment she decided to gradually stop going to the princesse de Guemenee's, to abstain from card play for high stakes, to occupy herself every day for a few hours in her rooms, and finally and most importantly, to be more attentive to the King than in the past.

JOSEPH TO LEOPOLD, 9 JUNE 1777

I left Paris without regret, although I was treated marvellously there. Leaving Versailles cost me more, as I have become very fond of my sister, and I saw her grief at our separation, which increased mine. She is a pleasant and honourable woman, slightly immature, thoughtless, but truly honourable and virtuous and living a respectable life. In addition she is intelligent and has such insight that I was often astonished.[73] Her first impulse is always correct. The situation between the King and Queen is peculiar…

MARIE ANTOINETTE TO MARIA THERESA, 16 JUNE 1777

My brother's departure made me ill: I suffered as much as is possible, and my only consolation is that he shared my pain: all the family here were touched and upset by it. My brother behaved so perfectly with everyone that he was admired by all, and is regretted by all; he will never be forgotten.

[Edit: Joseph wrote thus to his brother Leopold on 11 July, about his reception in France: "You are worth more than me. I am more of a charlatan, and in this country, it is necessary to be such. I have been overdoing it a little, appearing simple, natural, thoughtful – even excessively so. That is what has caused this great enthusiasm which is really embarrassing. During my tour of the provinces, I went to no

---

[73] This was the true assessment of Marie Antoinette by her brother – a very favourable one.

play, no entertainment; I tried to conceal myself rather than let myself be seen. I spoke to the most learned people in each place, for hours, but only three or four in each place; they repeated what I had said, everyone wanted to hear me speak, and not being able to do so, I was seen as an oracle without being so. Tomorrow I am leaving for Geneva and I will leave this country quite happily and without regret, because I have had enough of my role. I have seen much that is interesting and I have encountered a willingness in people to speak to me of the most secret things, which has astonished me, but I will take care to protect their confidences."]

As for me, I would be very unjust if my grief and the emptiness I feel only left me with regrets. I cannot repay him for the happiness I felt and the friendship which he showed me. I was quite sure that he only wanted my happiness and all his advice proves that to be the case; I will never forget his guidance. All he lacked was the time necessary to become better acquainted with the people with whom I live.

It is believed that the comtesse d'Artois is again pregnant. That is quite a disagreeable thought for me after more than seven years of marriage; however it would be unfair to show temper as a result. I am not without hope; my brother will tell my dear mother what the situation is. The King spoke to him sincerely and trustingly about this matter.

MARIA THERESA TO MARIE ANTOINETTE, 29 JUNE 1777

I foresaw the effect of the parting on you, and this thought upset me: they say in fact that your nerves were affected by it. I hope that there will be no after effects. I find it very flattering and comforting that my dear son attracted such general approval, but what pleases me above all is what you tell me of the friendship and mutual trust between the two brothers in law. God grant that these feelings will persist throughout their reigns, both for the good of their states and for our families, which I have regarded for a long time as the same! You can contribute most to this auspicious beginning, by following your brother's advice. [I am glad]…you seem so

316

contented with and convinced by this advice; and everything you tell me about it and about the papers he left you moved me to tears.

The emperor was touched by you, he liked you very much; he thought your conversation and friendship were very sweet. I am not being disloyal to him in quoting his actual words, which I could never render so well: "I left Versailles with sorrow, as I was truly fond of my sister; I found a sort of sweetness of life which I had renounced,[74] but for which I see I still retain a liking. She is pleasant and charming; I spent hours and hours with her, without noticing time passing. Her emotion at our parting was great, her expression brave; I needed all my strength to tear myself away."

You can imagine how much this account consoled and touched a mother who greatly loves her children. I am expecting positive consequences from the visit and I have also been led to believe that there is reason to be hopeful about your marriage state: but everything is delayed until he returns, when he will be able to talk to me. I must admit, it angers me[75] slightly because having children means everything to you, and I sympathise with your feelings about your sister in law's pregnancy.

Please excuse my persistent requests for a large portrait of you. I would like to see your figure and court dress, even if it does not much resemble you in the face. In order not to be too much of a nuisance to you I will be content with your figure and bearing, which I am not familiar with, but with which everyone is so pleased. Having known my dear daughter as an infant and a young child, this desire to know how you have matured must serve as the excuse for my importunity, coming, as it does, from my maternal love.

MERCY TO MARIA THERESA, 1 JULY 1777

In the last month, the Queen has only been to Paris once to attend three plays; she has accompanied the King to several

---

[74] Joseph's two wives had both died, not long after marriage.
[75] See Mercy's subsequent letter of 12 September 1777, for an explanation.

hunts. The princesse de Guemenee is neglected more and more each day and she has as a result become resentful and is trying to inspire her relatives with this same emotion. The Queen spends an hour and more almost every day alone in her rooms, where she reads. The Queen is more dignified and kind than previously, especially to people who are older and hold positions at court.

MERCY TO MARIA THERESA, 15 JULY 1777

The Queen sees the King more often, and nearly every day after midday they spend an hour or two alone together in their rooms. The Queen seems to be growing to like her chateau at Trianon more, and when she goes to spend the afternoon there, she is only accompanied by two or three of her ladies. Nor has she deviated from her wise resolution not to play outside her own rooms, but as for this latter point, there is only a partial improvement because the pharaon, which is played each night at the Queen's, is too high.

MARIA THERESA TO MERCY, 31 JULY 1777

I can see that the emperor's advice has not led to the sudden complete change in her lifestyle that I wished for. I thought that would be the case.

I would have been happier if the emperor had decided not to see that despicable du Barry, and I am delighted that in passing through Geneva, he avoided visiting that wretched Voltaire.

MERCY TO MARIA THERESA, 15 AUGUST 1777

H.M. is losing enough money to be constrained in the rest of her expenses. The debts contracted in buying the diamonds are not being regularly paid; there is no more money for gifts of charity and worst of all is the bad example, the regret this causes the King, and the displeased reaction of the public.

MARIE ANTOINETTE TO MARIA THERESA,
19 AUGUST 1777

The cardinal de la Roche-Aymon is dying and prince Louis [Edit: de Rohan] will take his place. I will not conceal from my dear mother that this bothers me, and the King himself is not happy about it; he was dreadfully misled in that matter. That is what comes from the misfortune of being young and having no one dependable to guide him.[76]

MARIA THERESA TO MARIE ANTOINETTE,
30 AUGUST 1777

The emperor is back and I notice he has lost weight. He is very pleased with the King and even more so with his dear and beautiful Queen: if he found another like you, he would immediately marry, for the third time.

MARIE ANTOINETTE TO MARIA THERESA,
10 SEPTEMBER 1777

The birth of a son to the Queen of Naples gave me such joy that I cannot put it into words. I must admit that this new birth has pleased me even more because I hope I will soon have the same happiness.

MERCY TO MARIA THERESA, 12 SEPTEMBER 1777

According to what the Queen deigned to tell me, she grasped the opportunity to tell Y.M. very interesting facts relating to her conjugal state, when a French courier left recently. The secrecy which the King demanded on this matter prevented me from learning of it for ten days.[77]

---

[76] Marie Antoinette had herself been instrumental in having men of honour – Turgot and Malesherbes – dismissed.

[77] This seems to imply that Louis XVI finally had the remedial operation he had required since his marriage, to permit him to ejaculate, which is alluded to throughout the later letters.

A new type of amusement has recently become established here which is not very suitable, but hopefully it will cease with the arrival of winter. For a month the bands of the French and Swiss guards have been established towards ten in the evening on the great terrace of the gardens at Versailles. A crowd of people, even the people from Versailles, gathered there and the royal family walked in the midst of this crowd, without suite and almost indistinguishable from everyone else. Sometimes the Queen and princesses were together; sometimes they walked separately, taking the arm of one of their ladies. The King came once or twice, alone, to these promenades; he seemed to enjoy them, and that has encouraged them even more. However, such walks could lead to problems, especially for the Queen; in this country, where the young people are so thoughtless and inconsiderate, one cannot be too much on guard against occasions when one is not recognized

[Recently, because of M. le comte d'Artois]... gambling has again become popular at Versailles, and, despite all I said and even the fact that the Queen listened and agreed to what I said, she has let herself be persuaded to attend, although with a sort of reluctance which is not however sufficient to dissuade her. However there is still an advantage in that this august princess continues to read and takes time to think.

SECRET LETTER

I found the Queen absorbed with her joy at the thought of being pregnant [Edit: Marie Antoinette had reason to believe she was pregnant, for a short time]...I told her that the time had finally come when she would find herself necessarily obliged to forget frivolity and adopt behaviour more appropriate to that of a wife and mother. The Queen agreed.

MARIA THERESA TO MERCY, 1 OCTOBER 1777

The change in my daughter's conjugal state is something which I find absorbing. If my daughter ever becomes pregnant, I must tell you that I would fear for both the mother and the child, before and after the birth. The most

320

atrocious crimes count as nothing in a country where irreligion is extreme. I would be reassured if I were able to place a faithful person with my daughter and more especially with the child, in the event of a pregnancy; but as this will probably be unacceptable, I will have to trust in Providence to pacify my anxieties about the appalling examples of horrors of this type, revealed by the history of France.

MERCY TO MARIA THERESA, 17 OCTOBER 1777

The court's preparations for travel have been postponed for the past month, as the King has declared he will not leave Versailles if there is the slightest possibility the Queen may be pregnant; but on the first of this month it became obvious that there was no possibility of pregnancy for another month, so the court left for Choisy. As the Queen felt she had to give up horse riding, she has decided to compensate herself for this self-denial by playing more games of chance.

For the past two months, H.M. has made many demands from the ministers, especially those in the finance and war departments: she has had a number of positions in the farming of taxes allocated, and this has led to complaints from people who claim to have been unjustly treated because of the Queen's wishes. I inform H.M. of all that is said about these matters. My words are always received with kindness and grace; but for some time, I have had little success, and there is not even an opportunity to reiterate my comments about the most important matter, that of card play, because the Queen shows by her expression or her silence that it is useless to talk to her on this matter.

SECRET LETTER

I am amazed at the short duration of the impressions made by H.M. the emperor on the Queen. Everything...[has returned] to a state which is actually worse than before the emperor's trip here. I have reason to believe that H.M.'s rules of conduct have been discarded and burned. The Queen knows that I am totally devoted to her, and in that she is only rendering me justice, but at the same time she believes that my attachment to her is such that I could never take it upon myself to tell Y.M. of this august princess' behaviour, and this idea, in which the Queen fortunately persists, sustains my credit with her, but means however that I can tell her the truth but cannot persuade her to follow my advice. I am always obliged to return to hopes of a pregnancy, and the change which that will effect on the Queen.

The comtesse de Polignac's favour and that of the duc de Coigny have ever more disturbing effects every day; these two people extort graces from the Queen which occasion continual complaints from the public. No minister dares resist the Queen's will, and they blame H.M. when people address complaints and reproaches to them.

I always insist on the necessity of never sleeping apart from the King. The Queen realizes the importance of this and would lend herself to this if her late nights, caused by card play, did not present an obstacle.

Y.M. can be perfectly reassured with regard to the atrocities which occurred previously in France, and which could be feared from treacherous villains. I must admit to Y.M. that for some time, I have been preoccupied with this matter and I have scrupulously examined both the individuals and the locale of Versailles. The court certainly abounds in unpleasant characters; but at this moment they are not of the type to commit atrocities of this nature.

MARIE ANTOINETTE TO MARIA THERESA, OCTOBER 1777

We have been at Fontainebleau for a week; the King has had a cold since we arrived. I have used this opportunity to take baths over the past eight to ten days as I badly needed them, being overheated. As for late nights, I hardly have them any more, and all summer I hardly left my rooms. I read, I embroider, I have two music teachers, one for voice and the other for the harp; I have taken up drawing again. As for card play, already for more than two months I have only played in my own rooms, where it is absolutely necessary to do so once or twice a week, and if my dear mother could observe the situation herself, she would see that it could not be otherwise.

I am delighted that the emperor has finally come back from all his trips in good health. He wrote to me: it seems that he is not too pleased with the French people we sent him this year, but that is the misfortune of every country: it is never pleasant or intelligent people who travel about.

MARIA THERESA TO MERCY, 3 NOVEMBER 1777

My daughter is very skilled in excusing her behaviour therefore I do not see the point in reiterating my comments.

I hear that M de Saint-Priest [may become ambassador here]…It would be impossible to have Mme de Saint-Priest presented at court, amongst the aristocracy, as is usual, because of her obscure birth. M. de Saint-Priest would therefore have to decide to leave his wife in France.

MARIA THERESA TO MARIE ANTOINETTE,
5 NOVEMBER 1777

I was delighted with your last letter. Nothing I hear from you bores me. I am pleased you are continuing your music, embroidery and especially your reading, as the King does not like all these boisterous entertainments. If not because I know the problems they bring, why would I want to deprive you of them. Gambling is surely one of the worst.

MARIE ANTOINETTE TO MARIA THERESA,
18 NOVEMBER 1777

Pharaon was very inconvenient at Fontainebleau because of the crowds: but at Versailles matters will be different, and I will arrange matters such that there will be no complaints about card play at court.

MERCY TO MARIA THERESA, 19 NOVEMBER 1777

I told the Queen that the King, because of his character and because of a historical tendency in his family, would become a man of habit, naturally virtuous and placid, and that he would not become prone to passionate affairs if he found in his marriage the peace and contentment he craved, but that if this did not happen, the King could abandon himself to affairs, as had his forefathers, and then perverse intriguers would be quick to use this opportunity and the Queen would only be left with regrets.

At the Queen's card play, everyone was free to choose whether to sit or stand, as a result there was no semblance of a court, but only improper confusion. I told the Queen that it would involve very little privation for H.M. to allow card play to continue at court in the old manner, that besides the government having recognised the danger of games of chance and tried to stop them being established, it was unbelievable and scandalous that these very games were established at the Queen's precisely when the time should be devoted to etiquette card play. The only reply I received to this remark was that she was "afraid to be bored."

[Edit: Joseph wrote to Mercy about this gambling on the 2nd of November, thus: "I am really sorry that our arguments had so little effect on the Queen because in her heart my sister does not even like gambling."]

Despite this uninterrupted pleasure seeking, the Queen is not at all contented and she has deigned to admit this to me. She is losing so consistently every day in her card play, that she is totally revolted.

SECRET LETTER

I told the Queen it was necessary to be with the King as much as possible, but the Queen has formed a very poor idea of the character and mental faculties of her husband. She believes him too apathetic and timid to believe that he could ever indulge in such out-of-the-ordinary activities as conducting an affair. The Queen is so convinced of this that she has even said

324

to some of her associates that she would neither be grieved nor sorry if the King took some momentary and passing fancy, provided he could thus acquire more ardour and dynamism.

The Queen believes that, having taken a decided ascendancy over her husband, she will always have the means to master him, and that, as the King is not very sensitive to attentions, she would only disturb herself needlessly in behaving thus and that, being able to govern him through fear, that method is as sure, quicker and more convenient than is that of using care and respect.[78]

By the 25th of October, H.M. had lost all her money; next day she ordered her treasurer to bring her November's money, which was swallowed up a few days later.

The Queen hides nothing from the comtesse de Polignac. I suspect she has seen at least some of Y.M.'s letters, and that she is consulted on the responses to make.

As the Queen is putting little effort into politics, the ministers are becoming accustomed to fear the Queen less, and are persuaded that, so long as they are careful of the favourites, they have nothing to fear from the Queen. I told her this and also told her that consequently the public was permitting itself more ribald talk about and criticism of the Queen than it had ever allowed itself before, and that could have dangerous consequences, as the French needed to be restrained by a little fear, without which they would sometimes forget the respect they owed to their sovereigns.

I notice that the Queen's letter from Fontainebleau [October], is lacking in the honesty and frankness which I have always found in the character of this august princess. It is really deplorable that the Queen puts so little attention into such an important matter [Edit: sleeping with the King], and what makes things worse is that the King, from obligingness and weakness, although against the grain,

---

[78] By the time the Revolution broke out in 1789, Marie Antoinette had reverted to being respectful towards her husband, and refused to question his decisions – with disastrous results both for her family and for the country.

seems to approve of all the Queen's amusements, and is almost the first to suggest them.

MARIA THERESA TO MARIE ANTOINETTE,
5 DECEMBER 1777

Do not be under any illusions; gambling always brings bad company and conduct in its train. That is well known. No one can advise you better than I, because I was the same. If I get nowhere with you, one day I will go to the King[79] himself, to save you from even greater peril. You are losing esteem in the eyes of the public,[80] especially abroad, and this greatly upsets me, as I love you so dearly.

MERCY TO MARIA THERESA, 22 DECEMBER 1777

The Queen has deigned to tell me that balls and plays alike are indifferent to her, and that she is often at a loss to find means to protect herself from boredom.

The Queen was embarrassed by the point in your letter where you announced that you might address yourself to the King to stop the games of chance.

---

[79] Unfortunately the political crisis in Austria, which occurred almost immediately, prevented Maria Theresa from carrying out this threat. However it has to be wondered whether Louis XVI would have insisted that Marie Antoinette change her ways – when he had not done so previously.

[80] Marie Antoinette's reputation in the eyes of the public, was now on an inexorable downward path.

1778

MARIA THERESA TO MERCY, 4 JANUARY 1778

The elector of Bavaria has just died: this is a disastrous event and one I had hoped not to outlive. The King of Prussia will certainly oppose our plans for expansion and will try to turn France against us. I would be inconsolable if our system with France collapsed because of differences of opinion over the succession in Bavaria.

[Edit: the elector of Bavaria died on 30th of December, 1777. Austria signed an agreement about the lands with elector palatin Charles Theodore on 3rd of January 1778, having been secretly negotiating it till then and immediately Austrian troops took possession of the lands. The emperor only saw a "rounding off for the monarchy of an invaluable prize" and flattered himself that "this could succeed without the need for war," (letters to Leopold on the 5th and 12th of January). Maria Theresa however doubted their right to do this and wanted to at least avoid violence, fearing above all a new war with Prussia and rupture of the alliance with France.]

MARIA THERESA TO MARIE ANTOINETTE, 5 JANUARY 1778

The very thought that a courier could bring me news of a pregnancy, brings me some consolation; at sixty years of age I do not have a lot of time. Your balls are fine and other people's balls, as you must entertain yourself, but the Opera balls are not suitable for you.

We have just learned of the death of the elector of Bavaria; I am very sorry about it; Mercy is informed of the details and will tell you about them, and I would like you to listen attentively. This matter may have repercussions for the peace of Europe.

Mercy has [described to me the painting which you want copied]…I will try to send it to you within the next eight years, which is how long I have been eagerly awaiting your portrait; but I will not let it go before receiving your long awaited portrait. I know I am vindictive, but peace will easily be made when I see your face. With love.

MERCY TO MARIA THERESA, 17 JANUARY 1778

Versailles has never been so deserted: even on New Year's Day, there was not even half the people one is accustomed to see.

The Queen is behaving very well in relation to the King, who for his part lives with his wife in the fullest sense of the expression.

SECRET LETTER

The death of the elector of Bavaria…[and the fact that Austrian troops moved into the territory immediately] at first drew a general call for war. Although this is ridiculous and absurd, the Queen was struck by it, and, to relieve her anxiety, she wrote to the comtesse de Polignac that she was afraid that her brother, the emperor, "was up to his usual tricks." These were the words which were reported to me. I wrote to the Queen that if these words were known by the French ministers, they would soon conclude that the Queen, far from sharing the views of her august house and supporting them, on the contrary feared them and disapproved of them.

[Edit: Joseph wrote to Mercy: "The death of the elector gives us much to do; it is one of these occasions which only occur once in an age and which we must not miss. This will not greatly please the country you live in."] When the courier came, I wrote to the Queen asking her to kindly maintain the language I had suggested whether with regard to the King, or his ministers, if this subject was mentioned in her presence.

The measures taken by Y.M. in the present circumstances are not seen here in a very kindly light; however

329

France has many reasons to be prudent and wise therefore she can do very little.

MARIA THERESA TO MERCY, 31 JANUARY 1778

The death of the elector of Bavaria is leading to a crisis, therefore it is more than ever necessary that my daughter exercises her ascendancy over the King.

MARIA THERESA TO MARIE ANTOINETTE,
1 FEBRUARY 1778

Mercy's illness is very awkward for me: at this moment I need him to be active and all your sentiments for me, your house, and native land, and I count entirely on the facts he may perhaps have to tell you about several major matters, on the insinuations which will be made from all sides about our dangerous views, especially by the King of Prussia, who is not delicate about his assertions as he has been hoping to draw closer to France for a long time, knowing very well that we two [Edit: Prussia and Austria] cannot co-exist; if they drew closer that would change our alliance, which would kill me, loving you as I do. The King of Prussia fears only you and, I admit, that gives me great pleasure both for you and for us.

All my love my dear daughter; I hope I will soon be able to say: my dear mother-to-be! Everyone here is praying for you.

MARIE ANTOINETTE TO MARIA THERESA,
13 FEBRUARY 1778

The King of Prussia has certainly not changed; he has already sent five couriers in a month.

Matters between France and Britain are deteriorating; they have attacked several of our vessels and finally it is felt that we should no longer try to hide the dispositions being made here to avenge their insults; ships are being armed and we have just marched some troops and artillery into Brittany.

Perhaps our preparations will make them wiser: it is not yet sure that we will have a war.

MERCY TO MARIA THERESA, 18 FEBRUARY 1778

The Queen, who until now has always been averse to thinking of affairs of state, is preoccupied with this matter and takes an interest in proportion to the fear I have always noticed in her, when she feels an issue could diminish the friendship and harmony which exist between her august house and France. I have carefully informed the Queen of the reasons which support Y.M.'s rights in Bavaria, so that the Queen could give the details to the King and thus prove her capacity to know and reason about serious affairs.

Since the start of the month, the balls at court have become more popular; Parisian women are attending in greater numbers and the Queen's kindnesses to them have encouraged them to be a little more eager to find opportunities to pay court.

SECRET LETTER

The Queen is truly incensed with the King of Prussia and his minister at this court. She speaks passionately about him to the King. The Queen must not forget to point out the immense advantage which France enjoys at present in the situation with Britain, because of its union with the august house of Austria, as it only has to think of deploying its maritime forces and need have no worry about a land war. [Edit: France had decided to take the part of the British colonies in America.]

The Queen having spoken quite clearly to her husband about Bavaria, the King replied: "It is your relatives' ambition which could overturn everything: they began with Poland, now Bavaria is next: I regret it on your behalf." – "But," continued the Queen, "you cannot deny Monsieur that you were informed about this matter and were in accord with us." – "I am so little in accord with you," replied the King, "that orders have just been given to the French ambassadors to make it known in the courts where they are our representatives, that this dismemberment of Bavaria is happening against our wishes, and that we disapprove."

Until recently I have never noticed the present French ministers behaving in a suspicious manner: but they are acting as if they are stunned by this event, and especially by the swiftness of the measures taken in Bavaria. I have recent proof of the vivid impression produced on the Queen by Y.M.'s [letters, as for example]…by the passage in Y.M.'s letter where, talking of the King of Prussia, you expressed yourself thus: "We two cannot coexist, that would destroy our alliance, which would kill me." I saw the Queen grow pale as she read that to me, and it is this shock which has motivated her to act and caused her so much worry. Because of her trust in the abbe de Vermond, she told him this.

MARIA THERESA TO MARIE ANTOINETTE, 19 FEBRUARY 1778

Just imagine how upset I am, the emperor, your brother [Edit: Maximilian] and prince Albert will be directing events: even the idea of it makes me despair, and if I do not die, living will be worse than death. With love.

MARIA THERESA TO MERCY, 3 MARCH 1778

You know how much it cost me to go into Bavaria entirely against my wishes.

What concerns me most in this crisis is my daughter's situation. I am convinced of her attachment to her family and her desire to prove it as much as her irresponsibility allows her to reflect, but she must act carefully and skilfully in order not to make herself troublesome and even suspect to the King,

The way the King spoke to my daughter about our ambitious intentions has given me matter for thought and I recommend to you my daughter's situation more than our affairs.

[Edit: Pichler wrote to Mercy that Maria Theresa was very upset at Prussia's preparations for war. He wrote: "I have never seen her so distressed in thirty four years."]

MARIA THERESA TO MARIE ANTOINETTE, 6 MARCH 1778

Your letter of the 13th consoled me because of the kind and loving points you made about our affairs in Bavaria.

I have inflammation in my gums and my face, even up to my eyes. As for the portrait of me which you wish, I would pity the artist who had to apply himself to painting something as ugly as a woman of sixty.

MARIE ANTOINETTE TO MARIA THERESA, 18 MARCH 1778

I would be very worried if my dear mother had not been kind enough to tell me you had no fever. I am very pleased with the King: he sincerely wants to maintain the alliance. He had M. de Goltz told that he wanted nothing to do with his master's affairs. The King had the King of England told that he has concluded a treaty with the Americans. May it please God that all these moves do not lead to a land war.

MERCY TO MARIA THERESA, 20 MARCH 1778 SECRET LETTER

Sacred Majesty, I must not conceal from Y.M. the fact that, despite my insistent and almost daily talks with the Queen, I have not been able to persuade her to take the sufficiently precise and consistent steps necessitated by the present circumstances. Although the ministers fear the Queen, they realize that her lack of single mindedness and consistency provide them with means to resist her will.

The arrival of the poet Voltaire occasioned much extravagance in the form of tributes which people wished to accord to this dangerous person. It was suggested that he be summoned to Versailles and then granted a distinguished reception. The Queen was entreated to do this: but H.M. refused quite plainly and declared she did not wish to receive a man whose morals had occasioned so much trouble.

MARIE ANTOINETTE TO MARIA THERESA, 19 APRIL 1778

My first thought, a week ago, which I am sorry I did not follow through, was to write of my hopes to my dear mother. I hesitated, due to my fear of causing too much pain if my hopes were unfounded; I am not yet entirely sure as I cannot count on them until the beginning of next month. That will be the second month. I am very well, my appetite and the number of hours I sleep, have both increased. My dear mother may be sure that I will be very moderate and careful in everything I do.

After talking to Mercy about how grave the situation has become, I sent for MM. de Maurepas and de Vergennes. I spoke to them quite forcefully and I believe I made an impression, especially on the latter. I was not too pleased with these gentlemen's quibbling.

MERCY TO MARIA THERESA, 20 APRIL 1778

The abbe de Vermond and I can only praise the Queen for the wise regime she has adopted. The King is delighted. Monsieur and Madame are behaving reasonably. It would be useless to try to fathom how sincere they are, but the joy in Paris and the good wishes of the people are not at all equivocal.

H.M. has given up playing billiards: her amusements are confined to music and having long and frequent conversations with the people around her. Games of chance take place rarely.

SECRET LETTER

I am consumed by a mixture of joy, hope and worry.

The Queen is trying to bring the King round to her point of view, and in a manner of speaking, set him in opposition to his ministers. I feel it would be very useful if Y.M. could tell the Queen that Y.M. is pleased with her: this will encourage the Queen and will make it easier for me to persuade her to act as necessitated by circumstances, in the future.

The Queen deigns to show me most of H.M. the emperor's letters. The last made an excellent impression. Amongst others there was this phrase: "As you do not wish to prevent the war, we will fight bravely, and whatever the circumstances, my dear sister, you will not be required to blush for a brother who will always deserve your esteem." The Queen was moved to tears by this letter.

MARIA THERESA TO MARIE ANTOINETTE, 2 MAY 1778

My dear daughter, the courier brought me consoling news which I sorely need in the present circumstances. May God be praised, and may my very dear Antoinette be confirmed in her outstanding position, by presenting heirs to France! You must be careful for thirteen weeks, especially in a first pregnancy, in order to be sure. I believe that when you are more advanced in your pregnancy, and feel your child, you should not remain seated or lying too long on a chaise longue, unless there is an accident. May God preserve us from that! In that case you would follow Lassone's advice totally, as he has acquired my trust and justly so. I hope he will choose the midwife, and that this person will be an expert and a Christian.

I do not experience joy very often and I have been accustomed to much sorrow over the past thirty six years; it has become second nature; therefore a moment of joy is good for me. But what can I say my dear daughter, about what you tell me, and even more the faithful Mercy, of how you used all your skill and charm! The ministers in Bavaria and Ratisbonne are already talking differently and I dare contend that if things had not been spoilt at the beginning, they would never have come to this point, the war would not have happened and we would not have jeopardised the alliance: our aim was and always will be to secure our position, and not expansion. Imagine how much all this upheaval worries me, especially because of the dangerous position of my dear son the emperor, as he will not only be more exposed than the others, but,

335

because of the weight of work and the strain, he will have no rest and must succumb in the end.

I have always believed there was no ill will in your country, but rather weakness and prejudice about our plans because of our former rivalry. Our army has never been so strong, is lacking in nothing, strongly motivated and burning with desire to pit itself against the Prussians.

I beg you not to worry so much; that is easier to advise than to do, but you must try to be more calm. Everyone is concerned for you, everyone is praying; but if our hopes come to nothing, do not worry. At least it is possible and God will bless this wise and virtuous King, my dear son-in-law. With all my love.

The Queen of Naples will be overjoyed; I bet she will cry when she hears.

MARIA THERESA TO MERCY, 2 MAY 1778

Flattering as is the news of my daughter's pregnancy, I must admit that I am almost tempted to doubt it until she has actually given birth, as my hopes have been frustrated for so long.

MERCY TO MARIA THERESA, 5 MAY 1778

The Queen finds it difficult to interpret the ministers' language, they use fine phrases to aid their evasiveness and she does not realize how worthless these words are. As a result the Queen is lacking in confidence and is hesitant, especially in her opinion of her own potential influence.

Just when I was least expecting it, the abbe de Vermond wrote to the Queen last week. He said that, as he was not well enough known by the King and his ministers, he could be suspect to them in the present circumstances, as his respectful and decided attachment to the Imperial Court was well known, therefore the abbe de Vermond felt he ought to absent himself for some time. I found him distressed that the King never spoke to him, although he saw him constantly at the Queen's. The abbe concluded from this that the sight of him revolted the

King…[Finally, after representations from the Queen], he came back.

MARIE ANTOINETTE TO MARIA THERESA, 5 MAY 1778

My dear mother, I was outraged at that dishonest dispatch they concealed from Mercy. The King showed me the [new] dispatch sent a week ago. I do not understand politics well enough to form a judgement about it; but Mercy, who did not seem to me to be too pleased with the substance, seemed happier with its style and phrasing.

MARIE ANTOINETTE TO MARIA THERESA, 16 MAY 1778

I am still very well, apart from some breathlessness, which is inevitable. I am already beginning to visibly put on weight, especially around my hips. For such a long time I did not ever dare to hope I would experience the happiness of being pregnant, so now I am enjoying it even more, and there are still moments when I feel it is all a dream; but the dream has not ended, and I believe there can no longer be any doubt.

I forgot to tell my dear mother that I asked the King for 500 louis which I thought I should send to Paris for the poor who are in debtor's prison for money owed to their wetnurses, and 4,000 francs here in Versailles, also for the poor. This was a way of being charitable at the same time as informing the people of my condition. I know my dear mother well enough to know that she will approve of these actions.

The King is behaving perfectly towards me, because of my condition, and is very attentive. I must tell my dear mother that I was upset to think you could suspect him for a moment of being responsible for what has happened: rather it was the loathsome weakness of his ministers, and his huge lack of confidence in himself which created all the trouble, and I am sure that, if he would only trust his own instincts, you would see his decency, dependability and discernment.

337

MARIA THERESA TO MARIE ANTOINETTE,
17 MAY 1778

I cannot sufficiently thank God for having granted me the grace of seeing you, my dear daughter, securely positioned for the future. All my wishes for my family have come true; I can now close my eyes in peace. I must admit, your position upset me more than I said, as I love you so much, and the pleasure you have given me came just at the right time to give me strength in my cruel situation.

MARIE ANTOINETTE TO MARIA THERESA,
29 MAY 1778

I am becoming astonishingly big as I do not use binding, except for what is necessary to give me some support.

Oh God! How I wish I could give you my health to make you happy, so that you could enjoy the contentment and peace which you so much deserve. But I am becoming upset and cannot continue. May I send my dear mother my love?

MERCY TO MARIA THERESA, 29 MAY 1778

Because of the custom at this court, the governess of the children of France, because of the rights attached to her position, will be charged with the early education of the Queen's children. The princesse de Guemenee has that position, and there is a lot I could say about that woman. [81]She also has the right to choose the assistant governesses and all the domestic staff; but I see that the Queen has decided to become involved in the choice and to reserve to herself the right to decide whether to accept or reject these nominated for the positions, as need be.

The Queen has the King's word that the choice of a governor, in the case of the birth of a dauphin, will not be

---

[81]But unfortunately he did not do so!

decided for five years. I suggested this. [Edit: the princesse de Guemenee was the daughter of the marechal de Soubise. Her husband's sumptuous prodigality was to lead to his bankruptcy, which was one of the scandals preceding the Revolution]

Monsieur is behaving as usual, however he is basically feeble and apathetic. [Edit: Provence to Gustav (King of Sweden), 5th of October 1778: "You will have heard of the change in my luck. I very quickly mastered my outward appearance and I maintain the same conduct as before, without however, seeming joyful, which would have appeared feigned, and would indeed have been so, because to be frank, as you may well believe, I do not feel this at all – nor do I feel sad, which could only be attributed to feeble-mindedness. It is more difficult to master my emotions; they still sometimes make themselves felt."]

MARIA THERESA TO MARIE ANTOINETTE, 1 JUNE 1778

May God keep you and your dear child, and give you a son, or if not a daughter who will resemble you in every way and will give you the same consolations which you give me!

Too much fussing can do a lot of harm. In the case of infants, especially in the first year, everything depends on the care taken of them: I mean reasonable and natural care, such as not swaddling them too tightly, not keeping them too warm, not overfeeding them with mashed up food, and especially take care to find a good healthy wetnurse. This is not easily done in Paris; and the country folk are just about as bad, considering the prevalence of immorality nowadays.

The weakness and ill will of the ministers and most of the nation, [82]which has been very obvious, will be disregarded and even forgotten by us. We depend entirely on the King's good heart and that of his lovely Queen.

---

[82]Marie Antoinette's perceived position in opposition to the King and his ministers, was another factor resulting in her dislike by many of the French.

MARIE ANTOINETTE TO MARIA THERESA, 12 JUNE 1778

I am becoming very big; I was childish enough to measure myself, and I have already put on four and a half inches. My dear mother is very kind to bother herself about my future child; I dare assure you that I will take the greatest care. They are fussed over less nowadays; they are not bundled up, they are always in a cot or in someone's arms, and from the moment they can be in the open air, they are gradually accustomed to it until they end up being outside almost always. I believe that is the best and healthiest way to bring them up.[83]

MERCY TO MARIA THERESA, 17 JUNE 1778

The trip to Marly was regrettable in that this august princess was very kind to a small number of favourites, almost to the exclusion of other people, and this aroused the jealousy

---

[83] In the summer of 1778, Fersen returned to France. Marie Antoinette was pregnant. He wrote to his father at that time, that "the queen is the sweetest and most beautiful person I know." He later wrote how "she wanted to see me in uniform…in her private rooms." [Klinckowstrom, (1877, p. XXXIII)]

What woman can resist a handsome man in uniform! However it is unlikely they became lovers at this time, as Fersen would certainly not have written to his disapproving and suspicious father about the queen, if they were lovers. It is more likely they became lovers in the late '80s, if at all. There seems no conclusive proof for either standpoint.

Nonetheless La Fayette, commander of the National Guard in Paris, threatened Marie Antoinette in November 1790, telling her that she would be forcibly separated from the king, and obliged to divorce him, if ever she were found with a lover. It would seem likely that with his extensive system of spies in the Tuileries palace, where the royal family then lived, and his privileged position as a member of the aristocracy who had known Marie Antoinette for many years, La Fayette would not have made such a statement without some justification.

What is certain, is that Fersen and Marie Antoinette loved and trusted each other for many years, as is shown in their correspondence, and that Louis XVI himself trusted Fersen, even asking him in 1791 to be his intermediary with the procrastinating powers. See volume two of these letters.

and dislike of the courtiers, and prevented the townspeople from appearing before their sovereign. A private group of friends is not something a great princess can allow herself, as she must attract the love and esteem of the people.

MARIE ANTOINETTE TO MARIA THERESA, 7 JULY 1778

I have been very well. I was bled a fortnight ago and that was very good for me.

MARIA THERESA TO MERCY, 7 JULY 1778

We are now at war and what a war, as there is nothing to win and everything to lose! I do not dare to be too insistent with the Queen, fearing to compromise or distress her. See if you think this [accompanying] letter is suitable, if so, give it to her; I cannot find it in me to fear for her as much as for her sister Marie, my son and my son-in-law.[84]

MARIA THERESA TO MERCY, UNDATED

Our situation is critical and demands a prompt response. If we fall back, as I fear we shall, because of our small army, it is as important to France as to us that we are not exposed to raids, or even losses. Just imagine how I feel; I do not know how I keep going; only my religion gives me strength, but in the end I will perish.

MARIE ANTOINETTE TO MARIA THERESA, 15 JULY 1778

My dear mother, it is impossible for me to tell you how upset and worried I am at present because of this misfortune. I am heartbroken; however I am hopeful! No, God will not permit such a wicked person to triumph! This morning there was a very touching scene with the King. He came into my

---

[84] At times, when Maria Theresa is upset, she seems very heartless.

room and found me so upset and alarmed that he was moved to tears. I must admit that this pleased me as it proves how much he loves me, and I hope he will at last decide for himself to behave as a good and faithful ally should.

MERCY TO MARIA THERESA, 17 JULY 1778

[Since the Queen was bled]…for the first time, she has no longer felt the heaviness in her head and the slight dizziness, which were caused by too much blood.

SECRET LETTER

[The King]…has allowed himself to be so subjugated by the comte de Maurepas that he has neither the willpower nor the firmness to tell this minister his own opinion.

I sent the letter you enclosed with the letter of the 7th, to the Queen. Later I saw her for almost two hours.

[Edit: Mercy, in his dispatch, told how he found the Queen in tears. The King had come into her room in tears, telling her he could not bear to see her so upset, that he would do anything to ease her grief, and that he had always been so inclined, but his ministers had restrained him, as the good of his kingdom prevented him doing more than he had done. In the same dispatch, Mercy described a talk the Queen had with Maurepas. "This gentleman once again had recourse to his usual subterfuges, so the Queen, raising her voice, told him: 'Monsieur, this is the fourth or fifth time I have spoken to you of this matter, and you have never made any other reply to me; until now I have been patient, but the situation is too serious and I will no longer tolerate such lack of response from you.' Maurepas, surprised to hear the Queen talking knowledgeably and passionately, had recourse to excuses and protestations of devotion." When the Queen told him of this conversation, Mercy asked her to behave more circumspectly with Maurepas, in case she would embitter him, but she was disinclined to follow this advice, replying that she "felt it was despicable to be kind to someone who displeased her."]

That very day the Queen intended having a performance put on at Trianon for the King. She deigned to tell me that she had cancelled this, as she could not bear to be amused while tormented by Y.M.'s worries and anxieties. The Queen burst into tears as she said this.

I told H.M. that her desire to cancel the performance at Trianon, seemed reasonable to me, but that her pregnancy necessitated her having some enjoyment. I was obliged to insist before I could prevail on her to moderate her resolution.

The Queen told me that she did not like to tell Y.M. how the King had let himself be subjugated by his prime minister, and that it upset her to talk of her august husband's weakness.

MARIA THERESA TO MERCY, 31 JULY 1778

I am in truth accustomed to being always contradicted and to the fact that nothing I propose is ever approved. I would have thrown myself at the King's feet to achieve peace [Edit: King of Prussia].

Do you think we should try mediation to achieve peace, and can we count on France for this?

[Edit: Maria Theresa, despairing of the success of the war, had decided to begin negotiations with Frederic. Foreseeing that her son would be against this, the empress did not tell him until the negotiations had begun. Joseph felt absolute despair at this step. The King of Prussia rejected the empress' suggestions and proposed others, which were not accepted, so negotiations were broken off.]

MARIA THERESA TO MARIE ANTOINETTE,
3 AUGUST 1778

We can be sad, but never despondent. Our cruel enemy would enjoy that too much. Your pregnancy, which has consoled me so much, requires you not to brood on sad matters, and I beseech you to take my advice on this matter as otherwise you may eventually become depressed, especially in

343

your condition. We should put our faith in God, and ask him not to abandon us but to save us from this perilous state.

MARIA THERESA TO MARIE ANTOINETTE, 6 AUGUST 1778

Mercy is charged with informing you of my cruel situation both as a sovereign and as a mother. As I want to save my states from the cruellest devastation, I must, at whatever the cost, try to stop this war. As a mother, I have three sons who not only run the greatest dangers, but will die from exhaustion as they are not accustomed to that type of life. In making peace now, I will bring down upon myself not only the charge of timidity, but I will increase the King's [Edit: of Prussia] standing, so it is best if it all happens quickly. I admit my head is spinning; my heart has been broken for a long time. But do not worry about my health, it is good and I will keep it so out of love for you.

I will never ask the King to do anything which could draw him into this unfortunate war, but only to make a show of strength, by naming and assembling some regiments and generals to come to our aid in case the Hanoverians and others join with our enemies. It is not right that France should let us be subjugated by our cruel enemy. She will never find a friend and ally more sincerely attached to her than us. I beg you to be careful, to take heart and not become despondent. The good Lord will take pity on us.

MARIE ANTOINETTE TO MARIA THERESA, 14 AUGUST 1778

I decided yesterday to ask the King to mediate. I think I succeeded in having them send someone other than M. Odune, as Mercy said he was not suitable.

My child moved for the first time on Friday the 31st of July at half past ten in the evening; since then he has moved very often, to my great joy. I need not tell my dear mother how much each movement increases my happiness.

MERCY TO MARIA THERESA, 17 AUGUST 1778

[As the comtesse de Polignac was away from court]...when the Queen heard of the enemy's entry into Bohemia, and this caused her much grief and pain, the King wrote to the comtesse de Polignac, asking her to come back to court.

The duc de Guines [has been granted several favours by the Queen]...H.M. would like it to be thought that she had nothing to do with this; but the public was not fooled.

SECRET LETTER

I cannot express the grief and alarm I felt when I received your letter. From the start of this unfortunate matter of the succession in Bavaria, I have never been able to believe it would end favourably.

In accordance with Y.M.'s intentions, I suggested to the Queen to broach the idea of mediation, as if she had thought of the idea herself.

MARIA THERESA TO MARIE ANTOINETTE, 23 AUGUST 1778

You are fortunate you can at least cry, as that is what has always given me relief in my disastrous life. There was some bad feeling between us [Edit: Joseph] because of the negotiations, but I hope that will soon dissipate. I am all yours.

MARIE ANTOINETTE TO MARIA THERESA, 3 SEPTEMBER 1778

My health continues to be very good; I will be bled the day after tomorrow. It is not surprising that my brother, with his character, felt impelled to act as he did in this matter, even though he was wrong, but my dear mother is so kind she understands and attributes it to circumstances.

MARIA THERESA TO MARIE ANTOINETTE,
9 SEPTEMBER 1778

Try, my dear daughter, to end this unfortunate affair as soon as possible; you will thus save your mother, who is at her wit's end, and two brothers who will eventually die, your homeland and a whole country which loves you.[85]

MARIE ANTOINETTE TO MARIA THERESA,
17 SEPTEMBER 1778

I was bled a week ago; they could only fill two very small saucers of blood because of the narrowness of my veins, so I may have to be bled again in a month's time.

MERCY TO MARIA THERESA, 19 SEPTEMBER 1778

[Recently]…the King played pharaon for the first time; it was one of the greatest compliments he could pay to his august wife and it is not to be feared that it will become a habit.

MARIE ANTOINETTE TO MARIA THERESA,
17 OCTOBER 1778

I am grieved at the comte de Maurepas' weakness and vacillation. I have spoken firmly to him several times, but I felt I should restrain myself and not break with him totally, in order not to place the King in an awkward position between his minister and his wife.

EXTRACT FROM LA MARCK'S CORRESPONDENCE
WITH MIRABEAU [86]

At this time, the Queen was pregnant for the first time. The comte de Maurepas used this circumstance quite cleverly, and having

---

[85] That's fine then. That just about covers everyone.
[86] Extract from Bacourt (1851), vol 1, p.42

explained to the Queen the reasons against France taking part in a war which was not in accord with its interests, nor even perhaps with justice, he added: That the interests of France must be even more important than ever before to the Queen, if that was possible, because of her circumstances, in that she was carrying an heir to the throne.

The Queen immediately replied to M de Maurepas that he rendered justice to her feelings for France, and that after the conversation she had just had with him, she would not interfere in the matter again. She kept her word.

EXTRACT FROM ROCHETERIE 'THE LIFE OF MARIE ANTOINETTE' [87]

The Prussian minister to Paris, the count von Goltz, on sending an account of a conversation he had had with the prime minister of France, wrote:

"He, Maurepas, wished to do justice to the princess, the Queen, that she listened to reason; that he had found this to be the case particularly in the affair of Bavaria; that then he, the minister, had said to her that the child she was bearing did not cease to cry to her that she was the Queen of France before everything; that he had added that, being on the verge of the grave, he would not be able to serve her offspring in the time to come, and that, therefore, he would render it the most essential service in pleading its cause before the Queen-mother; that this princess, much moved, had thanked him for thus reminding her of her true duty, and that, in fact, during the whole course of the affair, the Queen had not again appeared." [88]

---

[87] Extract from M de la Rocheterie 'The Life of Marie Antoinette' (1893), vol 1, p.226
[88] It is worth noting that the Austrian court routinely intercepted the Prussian ambassador's dispatches from Paris to Prussia. See Maria Theresa's letter to Mercy, 31 January 1777.

MERCY TO MARIA THERESA, 19 OCTOBER 1778

When the Queen speaks to the King on any matter whatsoever, once she is convinced that her husband and the ministers seem to agree with her she believes that it is unnecessary to return to the matter, and that all will happen as was agreed. As a result, the ministers persuade themselves that the Queen forgets on one day what happened the day before and do not alter their arrangements. I have pointed this out to the Queen.

MARIA THERESA TO MARIE ANTOINETTE, 25 NOVEMBER 1778

I hope that between the 8th and the 15th, God will grant us the consolation of a birth. Everything else is unimportant; sons will follow daughters. They say you intend feeding your baby yourself; that is up to the King and your doctor; I must admit that in their place I would not let you, although it is very good of you to offer.

I have added some lines for the King, not being able to make myself write all that claptrap of political phrases…[in a separate letter] with my own hand.

MARIA THERESA TO MERCY, 9 DECEMBER 1778

Write to me with all the details: how the Queen behaves, how she spends her time, what she is given to eat, the people she sees.

Could you celebrate the birth by releasing some unfortunates from prison or by giving dowries to young girls? May God deliver us soon from this waiting, and keep my dear Queen safe!

MERCY TO MARIA THERESA, 18 DECEMBER 1778

For the past fortnight, the principal doctor and the midwife have been staying near the Queen's rooms. According to custom at this court, four wetnurses have been retained for the royal baby; but it will not be decided until the last moment who will feed the child: the three others will be kept in reserve in case of possible accidents.

The people are very interested in the Queen's delivery. More than two hundred people of quality, who normally live in Paris, have moved to Versailles, where no more accommodation is available, and the price of food has tripled.

EXTRACT FROM MME. CAMPAN 'MEMOIRS' [89]

A few days before the Queen's confinement a whole volume of manuscript songs, concerning her and all the ladies about her remarkable for rank or station, was thrown down in the oeil-de-boeuf [Edit: a room in Versailles]. The King was highly incensed and said it was a capital crime to have made such songs against the Queen herself; and that he wished the author of the infamous libels to be discovered and punished. A fortnight afterwards it was known publicly that the verses were by M. Champeenetz de Riqueboufg, who was not even reprimanded.

MERCY TO MARIA THERESA, 20 DECEMBER 1778

The Queen gave birth to a girl at half past eleven this morning. The pains began at half past midnight; they were very slight at first, with long intervals in between, and time for rest and moments of sleep. The protracted pains did not begin until eight o'clock, and the waters broke at the same time. The Queen bore the pain with great courage; I saw this august princess in the last minutes before her delivery and again a few moments after. Her struggle not to cry out caused a slight convulsion due to the strain on her nerves: it was thought best to bleed her and the incident passed off. The Queen is as well as can be expected in her condition, and her august child, who is big and strong, is doing very well.

The Queen does not yet know the sex of the royal child.[90]

---

[89] Extract from Campan, (1904), vol I, p. 243
[90] Only a man could make such a statement. Campan (following) has another explanation.

The King is showing great joy and happiness because of his satisfaction at this safe delivery.

MERCY TO MARIA THERESA, 24 DECEMBER 1778

The ambassadors and all the court went to see the royal infant on the 20th. Her little face bears regular and charming features, big eyes, a pleasant mouth and a healthy complexion. I asked for, and obtained, permission to see this august child every day, and I will watch over those who look after her and ensure this is carried out carefully.

The Queen will again see the little princess today; the King is totally absorbed in her and it is impossible to imagine greater love and attention than he shows to the Queen.

SECRET LETTER

Although I have slightly recovered from the shock which I experienced a few days ago, I dare to speak of it so that it will serve as excuse to Y.M. for the lack of precision which could be found in my very humble reports. Due to the unusual custom at this court, I was summoned and obliged to be present at the Queen's delivery. I was thus witness to the seizure which she experienced a moment afterwards, which stunned me beyond belief; it is only now that I realize how shocked I was by this. I must add that the Queen is not aware of having been momentarily in danger, and it will be concealed from her, to avoid ideas recurring to her in subsequent confinements.[91]

The Queen's convulsion had several causes; firstly there was the activity of the large number of people present; secondly the efforts the Queen made not to cry out; thirdly she was confused by the fact that, in the first moment, her child did not cry, and she thought it dead; fourthly, when the child cried, her feelings changed from pain to joy. The King and almost

---

[91] Again Campan's account does not agree with Mercy's. The reader can judge which account seems most likely.

everyone followed the child, who was taken into a neighbouring room, and the monarch was not witness to this incident which, because of the midwife's great presence of mind, was over in four minutes because of the five palettes of blood taken from her foot. My worried zeal brought me back by another door into the Queen's bedroom; after that shock, everything has turned out for the best.

Next day, the Queen told me that as soon as she was able to sit on a chaise longue, she would have herself painted with her royal baby in her arms, in order to send it to you. I insisted that, for the first few days, the Queen should see no one, beginning with me. I had this message conveyed to the King, and it was agreed that the Queen's bedroom should be closed to everyone apart from [a few people]... Despite the protests of the ladies of the palace and others, this order has been strictly observed, and doctor Lassone has told me that it was to this arrangement that he attributed in part the Queen's tranquility when her milk came in.

During the Queen's labour, when, in accordance with custom, the Blessed Sacrament is shown in Paris, the people crowded into the churches and showed signs of true affection for the Queen. This affection was obvious even although there was a general feeling of regret that the Queen had not had a dauphin.

The Queen is lovingly preoccupied with her daughter and I do not see any regret at not having had a son.

All the princes and princesses of the royal family have behaved very well.

EXTRACT FROM MME. CAMPAN 'MEMOIRS'[92]

The etiquette of allowing all persons indiscriminately to enter at the moment of delivery of a Queen was observed with such exaggeration that when the accoucheur said aloud, "La Reine va s'accoucher," the persons who poured into the chamber were so numerous that the rush nearly destroyed the Queen. During the night the King had taken the precaution to

---

[92] Extract from Campan, (1904), vol 1. p.245

have the enormous tapestry screens which surrounded Her Majesty's bed secured with cords; but for this they certainly would have been thrown down upon her. It was impossible to move about the chamber, which was filled with so motley a crowd that one might have fancied oneself in some place of public amusement. Two Savoyards got upon the furniture for a better sight of the Queen, who was placed opposite the fireplace.[93]

The noise and the sex of the infant, with which the Queen was made acquainted by a signal previously agreed upon, as it is said, with the Princesse de Lamballe, or some error of the accoucheur, brought on symptoms which threatened fatal consequences; the accoucheur exclaimed, "Give her air – warm water – she must be bled in the foot!"

The windows were stopped up; the King opened them with a strength which his affection for the Queen gave him at the moment [Edit: Mercy places the King outside the room at this moment]. They were of great height, and pasted over with strips of paper all round. The basin of hot water not being brought quickly enough, the accoucheur desired the chief surgeon to use his lancet without waiting for it. He did so; the blood streamed out freely, and the Queen opened her eyes. The

---

[93] Some have imagined that Marie Antoinette, in giving birth publicly, somehow gave birth in such a way that everyone present witnessed the child actually being born, however this seems unlikely in the extreme! It is much more likely that Marie Antoinette's lower body was concealed under a sheet, which was suspended over a frame, and that the midwife would duck under this sheet, to check the progress of the delivery, and to assist in the birth. This, after all, according to Campan, was a woman who was so modest that she bathed in a negligee. Contemporary illustrations of royal childbirth seem to bear out this interpretation.

The purpose of giving birth in a room with many people present, was to ensure there was no skulduggery on the part of the midwife or attendants, either towards the mother, or towards the child. Attempts on the lives of a queen, or her son, at such moments of vulnerability, had been made previously in France. Moreover there was always the possibility of substituting another child – a live child for a stillborn one – even a child from a rival family. Maria Theresa had dreaded Marie Antoinette's labour, as she later mentions in a letter to Mercy (of June 1780), precisely because of such fears. But then, Maria Theresa, with her rather anxious personality, at times saw potential problems around every corner.

valets de chambre and pages dragged out by the collar such inconsiderate persons as would not leave the room. The Queen was snatched from the very jaws of death [Edit: that is, she came round from her faint!]; she was not conscious of having been bled, and on being replaced in bed asked why she had a linen bandage upon her foot.

The delight which succeeded the moment of fear was equally lively and sincere. We were all embracing each other and shedding tears of joy.

A great number of attendants watched near the Queen during the first nights of her confinement. This custom distressed her; she knew how to feel for others, and ordered large armchairs for her women, the backs of which were capable of being let down by springs, and which served perfectly well instead of beds.

M. de Lassone, the chief physician, the chief surgeon, the chief apothecary, the principal officers of the buttery, etc., were likewise nine nights without going to bed. The royal children were watched for a long time, and one of the women on duty remained, nightly, up and dressed, during the first three years from their birth.

1779

MARIA THERESA TO MERCY, 13 JANUARY 1779

The midwife Vermond's behaviour [Edit: Marie Antoinette's midwife had been the abbe de Vermond's brother] on the occasion of the crisis in my daughter's delivery, makes me greatly indebted to him.[94]

MERCY TO MARIA THERESA, 25 JANUARY 1779

The King, for whom habitual exercise has become necessary in order to conserve his health, did not want to leave the chateau even to take a walk, in the first week after the delivery. When the Queen awoke he was first at her bedside, spent part of the morning with her and came back on different occasions in the afternoon, stayed there all evening and spent his time between the Queen and his august child, to whom he shows the most touching love.

The abbe de Vermond is one of the first to go in to see the Queen in the morning...[and has been very zealous]. The King has been so pleased with him that he has finally decided to talk to him and to show him all manner of kindnesses, which has never happened before now.

The Queen is thinking of good works to mark her safe delivery. The King has given her one hundred thousand francs to use at her discretion. Because of what Y.M. wrote to me, I believe some of the sum will be used to marry poor girls and give them a dowry. They will be chosen by the priests of the parishes in Paris; the rest of the money will be used to free

---

[94] Even nowadays midwifery tends to be a woman's profession, and it seems strange to think that two hundred years ago, Marie Antoinette's child was delivered by a man. (She discusses this point in June 1772, in a letter to her mother) Female midwives were possibly for the poor!

some prisoners detained for debt, and some will be given to the hospitals as alms.

I have insisted that it is important the Queen appears at Paris for the first time after her confinement at an event which will please and edify the public.

[I have just heard]…that the King and Queen will come in ceremony to Notre Dame on the 8th of February. On that morning, the archbishop of Paris will bless one hundred marriages, with each girl given five hundred francs by the Queen, and the wedding outfits for each couple bought for them. They will all be at Notre Dame cathedral when the King and Queen come. The Queen has added to this act of charity that of paying for the wetnurses for all the first children who are born of these marriages, observing that, if the mothers breastfeed their children, they will receive fifteen livres a month, and if the same children are put to wetnurses, they will receive ten livres a month.[95]

Sire Necker, by order of the King, has given the Queen a thousand louis for charities in Versailles. The Queen has given six thousand francs to each of the two parish priests in Versailles, to distribute amongst their poor.

The Queen was churched on the 18th by her grand almoner, in the vestry of the chapel at Versailles.[96]

SECRET LETTER

The Queen, after her delivery, was given 102,000 livres by the King. This sum will be very useful to the Queen as her finances are in a deplorable state; H.M. owes more than 3,000 louis. As the Queen makes a note of her gains and losses at cards, I suggested drawing up a balance sheet. The abbe de Vermond did this and it was discovered that the Queen had lost

---

[95] For some reason the use of wetnurses was widespread, even amongst the poor, and not just amongst the aristocracy, as witnessed by the practice of the French court of releasing from prison on celebratory occasions, debtors who still owed money to their wetnurses.

[96]'Churching' was a ceremony which indicated that a woman had been ritually 'cleansed' after giving birth, and was now ready to resume marital relations with her husband.

7,556 louis in 1778 [Edit: a considerable sum, given that she had only been given a thousand louis for charities in Versailles]. The Queen was astonished at this; she assured the abbe and I that she had decided to moderate her expenditure. [Edit: the louis was worth twenty four francs]

The Queen, lately, has become even fonder of the King and more respectful towards him; she has been touched by the love, gentleness and care which the King shows her. She seems to better realize the necessity of gaining his trust.

The Queen's delivery has created a great impression in general on all the orders here, and has been very advantageous to the Queen. When they thought her in danger, the people showed real attachment to her. The sniping of the public stopped and all were united in their wish for her safety.

Despite the contents of the last letter Y.M. received from the Queen, it is however a fact that this august princess was a little disgusted by her delivery and her first thought was not to become pregnant for several months, but it is quite certain that she now wants to be pregnant as soon as possible.

The household of the young princess is considerable, and comes to almost eighty people serving the princess.

MERCY TO MARIA THERESA, 16 FEBRUARY 1779

On the 8th of this month, the King and Queen went to Paris. The public was gathered in crowds along the way and showed its affection and joy; the people noticed with satisfaction the Queen's kindly expression. The one hundred couples who had been married in the morning, and who were lined up when the King and Queen arrived, made a very touching sight which moved the spectators. The Queen's munificence was further demonstrated in the freeing of several prisoners, and alms made as indicated by the parish priests in Paris.

The Queen decided very wisely to prove that her presence in the capital was due only to pious reasons and not to entertain herself; consequently, after the service, held at Notre Dame cathedral, the court went to La Muette to dine, and returned to Versailles in the evening, without H.M. attending

357

different performances in Paris, as she has been accustomed to do in other years. This privation was compensated for by some balls at Versailles. The King and all the royal family gathered at these events; the Queen danced very little at them, and the balls did not continue later than one in the morning.

SECRET LETTER

I cannot conceal from Y.M. that, when the King and Queen came to Paris, the public reception was not what could have been expected. There were cries of "Long live the King and Queen" in certain parts of the city; in others there was great silence, and in general, it was noticeable that the eagerness of the people derived more from curiosity than affection. This halfheartedness had some fortuitous causes, amongst which was the increase in the price of provisions.[97]   Although the Queen has nothing to do with this, nonetheless the ill temper of the public makes it more disposed to criticism.

The thought of her pleasure seeking, the expenses she occasions, and even the impression she gives of an immoderate wish to amuse herself at a time of disaster and war, all combine to alienate people, and require some thought.

In my recent audiences with the Queen, I told her everything I thought necessary, about this. I almost dare to flatter myself that I made some impression on H.M., and that this contributed to her renunciation of all obvious amusements, which she had intended to enjoy, in the last days of the carnival. This sacrifice did not extend to complete renunciation of the Opera balls. The Queen wanted to go on Sunday, and the King agreed to accompany her. This was executed with astonishing secrecy and at this moment, no one yet knows here of this, indeed if the Queen had not told me, I would doubt it had happened.

The Queen has authorized me to see the newborn princess often to ascertain whether she is being well served.

---

[97] This was a standard excuse used by Mercy to soften bad news to Maria Theresa, but there is no doubt she saw it for what it was, although she herself also tries to find an excuse.

This child is becoming for the Queen more and more an object of her care and reflection.

MARIA THERESA TO MERCY, 28 FEBRUARY 1779

I would not be at all pleased if the King, once again able to be a husband, after the churching of my daughter, were to announce to us another delay of eight years before there was a second pregnancy.

The lukewarm enthusiasm of the public at the entry of the King and Queen into Paris could also be due perhaps to the lack of impression that the appearance of sovereigns produces when, contrary to custom, the subjects become used to seeing them more often and without pomp.

MERCY TO MARIA THERESA, 17 MARCH 1779

The Queen had gone to the Opera ball on a Sunday [Edit: as mentioned in the previous letter] with just the King; Their Majesties had remained until six in the morning without being recognized, which seemed to have amused the King. This encouraged the Queen to suggest to him that they should go again on the following Tuesday. This suggestion was accepted at first; but the King then changed his mind and agreed that the Queen should go alone, accompanied by one of her ladies, and take every precaution to ensure this would remain a secret.

Consequently, the Queen left without guards; at Paris she changed carriages at an equerry's house, substituting one which would not be recognised. Unfortunately this carriage was so old and in such bad repair that it broke down in a street at a distance from the theatre. The Queen was obliged to leave the carriage, as was the princesse d'Henin who was accompanying her, and as it was impossible to remain on the street, they had to go into the nearest house, which was that of a merchant who sold silk fabrics. The Queen did not remove her mask; it was found impossible to repair the carriage and it was too late to be able to find a suitable coach, so the first carriage for hire which went past, was stopped, and the Queen arrived at the ball in that vehicle. There she found several people from her suite who had arrived separately, and who did not leave H.M. all the time she was at the ball.

The Queen was not recognized, and left next morning. This incident only made the King laugh and joke about the necessity of travelling in a hired carriage. In Paris reaction was more varied, but however only ridiculous details[98] were recounted, and there was no criticism. I noticed however that the Queen was annoyed at this incident and she deigned to speak of it to me and let me say what I thought.

Since the beginning of Lent, everything at court has again become quiet and measured. The Queen has the happy task of going, at different hours of the day, to see her august child, who is gaining in strength and enjoys good health. The King shares this precious duty with a concern and love which demonstrates his similar feelings for the Queen...[Hopefully] the results of this will be shown in another pregnancy, which the whole nation wants. I have remonstrated with the Queen on this matter and would like Y.M. to use your authority to emphasize this.

MARIA THERESA TO MARIE ANTOINETTE, 1 APRIL 1779

What you tell me about your dear daughter gives me great pleasure, and especially what you say about the King's love. But I admit, I am insatiable; she needs a companion and she needs him soon.

MERCY TO MARIA THERESA, 15 APRIL 1779

[The Queen had had measles and was now moving from Versailles to Trianon to recuperate]...The Queen deigned to tell me of her gratitude for the King's affection and love and that he [Edit: the King] would have continued to see her throughout her illness, if she had not expressly forbidden him

---

[98] The newssheets were full of fanciful stories of secret assignations with lovers etc.

not to do so. She added that the milk treatment to which she had adhered while at Marly, had placed obstacles in the way of resuming a conjugal life in the hope of achieving another pregnancy. Madame and M. le comte d'Artois had enclosed themselves with the Queen while she had had the measles, and had shown her affection and care for which H.M. was very grateful. Finally the Queen asked me to tell Y.M. that Madame and M. le comte d'Artois, who were remaining in Versailles, would spend some time with her every day.

Last Sunday the King had the Queen told he wanted very much to see her and this princess suggested he should meet her at an internal courtyard. The King did so. They spoke together for a quarter of an hour in private and the Queen was pleased with his friendly and loving words.

The Queen's suite at Trianon is very numerous, because all H.M.'s household are established there. There are also some others, namely the duc de Coigny, the duc de Guines, the comte d'Esterhazy and the baron de Besenval; these four people had permission to remain with the Queen while she had measles. The King suggested this and agreed to these four people remaining with his august wife.

Immediately the King suggested this, they took over the Queen's bedroom, and from seven in the morning until eleven at night they only went out for meals. Madame, M. le comte d'Artois and the princesse de Lamballe also remained with the Queen almost all the time. The Queen's ladies were not admitted nor were those with positions in the household; this led to talk and verbal attacks on the four gentlemen who were admitted. The Queen's favourite, the comtesse Jules de Polignac, also had measles at the same time and the Queen was annoyed to be deprived of her company.

SECRET LETTER

What I have superficially described in my very humble ostensible report requires more elaboration.

It is quite true that the King, accustomed to refuse nothing which pleases his august wife, approved of...[the four gentlemen] remaining with the Queen; but this consent was engineered by the Queen who did not at first realize the consequences. The result was all sorts of annoying talk and bad jokes, even at court, where people wondered which four women would be chosen to look after the King if he fell ill.

Scarcely were these four people installed in their posts when they were making requests to look after the Queen at night. I vehemently opposed this ridiculous idea; I insisted doctor Lassone intervene, but he, always weak and afraid, does not dare oppose anything which his position entitles him to oppose. Finally I caused so much fuss, as did the abbe de Vermond, that it was decided that these gentlemen should leave the Queen's room at eleven in the evening, and not return until morning. Apart from the harmful effect of this, I was even more distressed at the thought of all the harmful ideas these gentlemen would suggest to the Queen.

She had insisted, from consideration for the King, that he could not visit her. The aforementioned group dared to criticise the King's acquiescence and she then became angry with him. I trembled at the thought of the consequences such discord could lead to and on the tenth day of her illness, in concert with the abbe de Vermond, I encouraged the Queen to write a few friendly lines to the King. This proposition was at first rejected with extreme bitterness; I must grant the abbe de Vermond the justice of being the one who convinced the Queen to agree.

She wrote: "that she had suffered a lot, but that what had upset her most was to be deprived of embracing the King for a few more days." This note had the desired effect; the King was enchanted and replied in a loving manner within the hour.

This correspondence has continued almost daily; it also caused a great sensation in Versailles, and from that moment, the talk subsided. The presence of Madame modified the talk slightly; but she was not always present. M. le comte d'Artois contributed to the disorderliness. Although these four people have followed the Queen to Trianon, as H.M. is there with all her court, there is not the same danger from private conversations.

362

MARIE ANTOINETTE TO MARIA THERESA, APRIL 1779

My dear mother, the measles I have just had was more painful than is normal in this country; I was just about to be purged, which was something I badly needed, and besides I still had some milk. However it passed off quite well, my eyes were not affected and my chest is fine. I have only been purged once so far; I am moving to Trianon for a change of air for three weeks, and after that period I hope to see the King. We write to each other every day: I saw him yesterday from a balcony in the open air. Will my dear mother let me send my love? I am not strong enough to write more.

MARIA THERESA TO MARIE ANTOINETTE, 1 MAY 1779

My dear daughter, I cannot yet announce that peace has been signed, but it has been agreed and this has relieved me greatly and I would like you to thank the King for his good offices. I also owe thanks to you, my dear daughter, because of his love for you and because of the interest you showed in the matter. In future try to ensure that on both great and minor occasions, we agree from the outset.

MARIE ANTOINETTE TO MARIA THERESA, 15 MAY 1779

Without doubt my greatest task will henceforth be to maintain the union between my two countries (if I may express myself thus). I realize how necessary this is, and the worry and upset I experienced in the past year cannot be expressed.

I still suffer from pains in my stomach, but they are not so severe.

My daughter is very well: she is beginning to know the people she sees most often.

MERCY TO MARIA THERESA, 17 MAY 1779

The stay at Trianon passed more quietly than would have been presumed from the number of people staying there. The Queen began by taking asses' milk, and adhered to a very strict regime. Her first meeting with the King [after her convalescence] was very loving and on the 27th, the court went to Marly. Walks in the park and supper were followed by pharaon, when the stakes sometimes became more considerable than they should have been.

H. M. several times experienced stomach pains which decided the principal doctor Lassone to stop the asses' milk and substitute cows' milk mixed with barley water; this drink was more successful. After a third purgation, the Queen took and is still taking both morning and night, every day, a pill containing a grain of ipecacuanha without the resin. The Queen has never had a better complexion; she is again reasonably plump and her natural cheerfulness has returned.

SECRET LETTER

The twenty one days of convalescence had been over for two days before the Queen came back to Versailles; Monsieur had been to dine with the Queen; the King had not, and this, in addition to some words from the monarch stating his indifference to what happened at Trianon, gave the court and the town much to think about.

The Queen told me she was vexed at this; I tried to calm her, and, begging her not to show any signs of petulance, I suggested the behaviour which seemed to me most likely to dispel this little upset. The Queen deigned to take my advice and on her return was very pleasant, and, from the next day, her relationship with the King was as usual, and he was even more gentle and anxious to please than ever. Moreover, I am convinced that, since the separation, they have been trying to work on the King's mind; however the lack of effect of these manoeuvres is reassuring, but the Queen must take the care which her interests demand.

Last Thursday, the Queen confided in me that they were busy persuading the King to speak as little as possible about serious matters with his august wife, and that the King, constrained by this advice, only made half confidences to the Queen. M. de Maurepas was the originator of this idea.

I observed to the Queen that neither resentment nor reproaches could remedy such problems, that the only means of remedying them was to form a fair idea of matters, to occupy herself with knowledge of the facts, and then to reason on them with the King. If the King did not talk to her, it was in the belief that the Queen, only liking to be entertained, could neither know about serious matters, nor speak of them in an interesting and useful way. The Queen deigned to repeat to me her thoughts about these same people who gather round her, whom she so much seems to favour, and for whom she actually feels very mediocre esteem, their influence being founded only on their ability to entertain her.

MERCY TO MARIA THERESA, 17 JUNE 1779

Matrimonial life has resumed between the Queen and her august husband and a desirable result from this can be expected from week to week.

The Queen is very lovingly preoccupied with her august daughter, whose features indicate beauty, she is lively, cheerful and in the best of health; the Queen sees her several times a day and the King is very loving to her.

Some time ago the Queen acquired the habit of spending some evenings at the comtesse Jules de Polignac, and on these occasions the King very often accompanies her...[this] has led to an increase in respect for the comtesse Jules.

Because of her great credit, the comtesse Jules de Polignac is just about to obtain a favour which will lead to talk at Versailles. The duc de Villeroy, unable to discharge his duties due to ill health, has asked for the duc de Lorges to be given his position. This duc de Lorges deserves the position because of his good reputation and conduct...[however] the comtesse de Gramont, whose son is going to marry the comtesse Jules de Polignac's daughter, thought to procure the position for her son. The comtesse Jules was afraid at first to ask for this, however the Queen very quickly agreed to her favourite's request.

SECRET LETTER

While the Queen was at Trianon, I noticed that they had tried to tempt the King into beginning an affair. In these circumstances, I proposed to H.M. to be with the King as much as possible, to draw him into the Queen's circle of friends, and arrange matters so that he would find his amusement in this. She has drawn the King to the comtesse Jules de Polignac and, although this last point could easily create minor problems, it seemed to me that it was more important to keep the King with the Queen as much as possible.

My second suggestion was to discover which unworthy people had dared to try to corrupt the King and to make a striking example of them. She herself proposed that, inasmuch as it depended upon her, she would not let a week pass without having a conjugal relationship with her husband. In a conversation with this monarch [recently]...the King told her he loved her with all his heart and that he could promise he had never felt attracted to nor aroused by any other woman, apart from herself. The Queen felt that this indicated that the King suspected she knew of the plans to give him a mistress.

MERCY TO MARIA THERESA, 14 JULY 1779

I had hoped to be able to confirm the good news I had announced in two previous letters to Pichler, but unfortunately our hopes for the Queen's pregnancy have not been sustained.

H.M. is more engrossed than ever with her august daughter and the plans for the future education of this young princess. The Queen is convinced that the personal qualities of the princesse de Guemenee are not at all appropriate for the position of trust she will occupy. This could lead to problems because of the extraordinary prerogatives accorded in France to the governesses of the royal children. By a sort of law, or rather from custom, it is understood here that the person filling this

366

post cannot have it removed from her against her will, without firstly instituting legal proceedings against her. However strange this custom is, it is not easy to abolish it, especially in this country where the aristocracy all unite to make common cause when the abuses useful to them are threatened...[However this problem will not occur]…until the young Princesse Royale is two years old.

SECRET LETTER

It is my duty to dare to tell Y.M. that in general the public and the French ministry have total faith in the principles, views and feelings of Y.M., and I can tell you that you are loved, admired and respected in a truly touching and satisfying way; unfortunately people are sufficiently unfair not to have the same trust in H.M. the emperor's way of thinking. His great talent is admired but feared, as it is supposed that he feels estranged from this nation. These absurdities will doubtless disappear; but they demand careful thought in order to ensure the duration of the alliance.

MARIA THERESA TO MERCY, 31 JULY 1779

I am upset, as you may well imagine, to see my hopes of a second pregnancy for my daughter, disappear.

If ever the despicable people who tried to draw the King into an affair are found, it would be just to chastise them; but I cannot conceal from you the fact that I do not want my daughter to be involved in this matter. According to my way of thinking the wife can do nothing other than patiently endure her husband's straying, and has no right to take offence at it.

MARIA THERESA TO MARIE ANTOINETTE,
1 AUGUST 1779

My dear daughter, your letter of the 16th upset me greatly, as all our beautiful hopes have vanished. However nothing is lost: you are both so young, in good health and love each other tenderly, so the situation can be remedied. You must follow Lassone's advice, and although I am opposed to separations, in this case, if the doctor insists, I would be happy for you to comply, provided the King agrees, but not if he does not; but I must admit, I remember that in the past you have been only too inclined to this, and I would not like this to become re established.

I must admit that I am agonising over your fleet, and notwithstanding your great superiority, I am not reassured.

MARIE ANTOINETTE TO MARIA THERESA, 16 AUGUST 1779

My dear mother, everything depends on this moment; our fleets, both the French and Spanish, are together, therefore we have considerable superiority.

At the moment they are in the English Channel, and I cannot think of how, from one moment to the next, the future will be decided, without apprehension. I am also worried as it will soon be September, when the sea routes are no longer practicable; it is to my dear mother that I confide all my anxieties. God willing they will come to nothing.

You may be reassured about my conduct, as I realize too well the necessity of having children to neglect anything relating to that matter. If I was wrong before, it was because of my youth and immaturity, but now I see more clearly, and you can be sure that I am aware of my duties in that respect. Moreover I owe it to the King because of his love, and I dare say, his trust in me.

I am taking the liberty of sending my dear mother my daughter's portrait; it looks very like her. My dear little one is beginning to walk quite well in her frame. A few days ago she said papa; her teeth are not through yet, but they can all be felt. I am pleased she has begun to say papa, as this will attach him to her even more. He still goes to see her very conscientiously, but as for me, I need no prompting to love her more. I know my dear mother will excuse this prattle about my little one, but you are so kind, sometimes I take advantage of you. May I send you all my love?

MERCY TO MARIA THERESA, 18 AUGUST 1779

The associates of the sovereigns are absent at present. Those with positions at court are in the army; most of the Parisian nobility are at their country estates. The comtesse Jules de Polignac is still taking the waters at Spa. The Queen regrets this favourite's absence, as it leaves an emptiness she cannot fill.

It is true that the King is becoming plump; but this is not disproportionate to his height; he is becoming stronger every day.

SECRET LETTER

The Queen's liking for her new confidant has reached such a point that it will be difficult to stop it. The duc de Guines is intelligent, skilful and an intriguer; he has already meddled in political matters by giving the Queen memoranda in which he has combined several good and useful ideas with many traps, whose purpose is to further his ambitious plans. While suggesting that the Queen should treat the present ministers in a kindly fashion, he ruins them in her estimation at the same time, and the Queen's natural frankness does not let her conceal her opinion of them. I would lose all the Queen's trust if Y.M. mentioned the duc de Guines' memoranda, but after consulting the abbe de Vermond, we have devised a plan which could have a positive effect, if Y.M. deigns to agree.

The Queen would be shocked to think that it was believed that she was acting under someone's influence, and this idea in itself would suffice to prevent her doing some things to which she would be inclined even of her own volition. She sincerely believes that people are unaware of the duc de Guines' ascendancy over her. If she were enlightened about this point, it is quite certain that the Queen would be more reserved, and nothing would achieve this more effectively than if Y.M. were to write that everyone is talking about how the Queen is so much under the duc de Guines' influence that she can decide nothing without consulting him.

MARIA THERESA TO MARIE ANTOINETTE, 1 SEPTEMBER 1779

My dear daughter, the portrait you have sent me shows her to be charming, strong and healthy and gave me great joy. I have it near me on a chair, not being able to put it out of my sight; I think she looks like the King.

I really must tell you of an anecdote which is being spread about and which I could not believe at first, but we hear from all sides that you are dominated by the duc de Guines and that you decide nothing without taking his advice. I have nothing against him, but his reputation of being very ambitious, obliges me to tell you of these rumours.

MERCY TO MARIA THERESA, 15 SEPTEMBER 1779

[Until recently the Queen was still taking walks]…in the evening on the terrace of the chateau. Despite the precautions taken to diminish the inconvenience of these night walks, there were still too many. Although, on these occasions, H.M. was always accompanied by her sisters in law, and attended by a number of ladies and of courtiers, it was not totally possible to keep back the crowds and bad company. They often approached too near to the royal family and exposed them to an undignified crush. These walks led to criticism in Paris; but finally the weather, become more cold and damp, no longer allows this type of amusement, and it ended a few days ago.

[EXTRACT FROM MME. CAMPAN 'MEMOIRS' [99]

I know for a certainty that the King spoke to M. de Maurepas, before two of his most confidential servants, respecting the risk which he saw the Queen ran from these night walks upon the terrace of Versailles, which the public ventured to censure openly, and that the old minister had the cruelty to advise that she should be suffered to go on; she

[99] Extract from Campan, vol I, p.244

possessed talent; her friends were very ambitious, and longed to see her take a part in public affairs; and to let her acquire the reputation of levity would do no harm.

M. de Vergennes was as hostile to the Queen's influence as M. de Maurepas. It may therefore be fairly presumed, since the Prime Minister durst point out to his King an advantage to be gained by the Queen's discrediting herself, that he and M. de Vergennes employed all means within the reach of powerful ministers in order to ruin her in the opinion of the public. (Soulavie in his book, 'Memoirs' writes: "It is known that in 1774, 1775, and 1776, M. de Maurepas stirred up private quarrels between Louis XVI and his wife on pretence of the Queen's inconsiderate conduct.")]

SECRET LETTER

What Y.M. was gracious enough to say in your last letter about the duc de Guines had the effect I had hoped for and foreseen on the Queen; this august princess was astonished that Y.M. was informed of a circumstance which she had considered a secret. I told the Queen it was incredible that she had this opinion about a matter which was very obvious, and which was occupying the attention of the court and town; that, far from such a favour remaining a secret, I was surprised it had taken so long to reach other courts. Fortunately, as on other similar occasions, the Queen's suspicions fell on the King of Prussia; this idea caused her to make a formidable outburst against the Prussian monarch and his ambassador.

MARIE ANTOINETTE TO MARIA THERESA, 15 SEPTEMBER 1779

It is true that the duc de Guines is part of my circle; but he is also part of the King's, and is treated well by him. I rendered him a service in the cruel business M. d'Aiguillon raised against him and it was natural that he would try to show his thanks. It is customary here for people to try to guess who is influencing us: I have experienced this too often over the past nine years to be astonished at it now.

My daughter is still very well. My dear mother's pleasure in her portrait shows me yet again all your love. I wish I could show you the extent of mine, and my gratitude! It would make you content.

MARIA THERESA TO MERCY, 30 SEPTEMBER 1779

Formerly my daughter believed my sister in law the princess Charlotte was responsible for telling me the news she did not want me to hear; now she believes it is through the King of Prussia I am informed. This suits us quite well.

MARIE ANTOINETTE TO MARIA THERESA, 14 OCTOBER 1779

My dear mother, we have decided not to go to Fontainebleau because of the expenses of the war, and also so that we can be quickly informed of the news from the army.

Our fleet could not engage the British and has achieved nothing at all; it is a lost campaign which has cost a lot of money. Worst of all is that there is illness on the boats which is causing havoc. The dysentery in Brittany and Normandy is also affecting the land army, which was meant to be taking sail: it is a depressing picture overall. The Spanish are also ill and this is cooling their ardour.

As I was overheated, I took some baths, and was purged the day before yesterday. I will be taking asses' milk while I am at Marly.

MERCY TO MARIA THERESA, 16 OCTOBER 1779

Although the Queen has always been received in an affectionate and satisfying way when she goes to Paris, she has not forgiven the public for the cold reception it has often given M. le comte d'Artois, and since that period, the Queen has almost totally stopped going to Paris.

SECRET LETTER

Sacred Majesty, [since your last letter]…the Queen, who had supposed that the duc de Guines was no longer ambitious, is now beginning to think she could have been wrong. I told her that the duc de Guines had just come back from a trip to see the duc de Choiseul, where they had planned some intrigue together. Chance had procured me some evidence about this and I explained it to the Queen in a way which left her astonished.

The comtesse Jules de Polignac has just abused her credit in the most shocking way to effect a favour for a comte de Vaudreuil, who is her very intimate friend, a fact which neither tries to disguise.

The latter's fortune is tied up in the French colonies, and he cannot gain access to it during wartime, therefore he is in difficulties. The comtesse Jules de Polignac knew of no other means of relieving him of this worry than by procuring him 30,000 livres per year from the royal treasury, for the duration of the war. The Queen was charged with making this request, and the King, with his usual obligingness, made no difficulties; they are agreed that this misplaced favour will remain a secret. In fact no one knows of this; but if people do learn about it, it will lead to complaints.

When the frightening news reached us of Y.M.'s fall, which, thank God, had no lasting effects, the Queen was so upset that even after two days, she trembled when she spoke of it to me.

MARIA THERESA TO MERCY, 1 NOVEMBER 1779

It seems to me that my daughter is too drugged, and these different milks and purges which they give her seem excessive to me.

MARIE ANTOINETTE TO MARIA THERESA,
16 NOVEMBER 1779

Orders have been given to disarm the fleet and bring the soldiers into winter quarters. The British will be harried by America and perhaps even by Ireland...[next year].

MERCY TO MARIA THERESA, 17 NOVEMBER 1779

The plan to disallow games of chance only held for a few days. For reasons of economy there were no plays, but it was decided to have gambling, which was worse than it has ever been before. The King of his own volition, began to play and lost 1,800 louis. The Queen lost about 1,200; but H.M. won back almost all this sum.

SECRET LETTER

Recently the duc de Guines was almost scornful to the Queen... [He wanted the Queen] to change many things at court, the Queen hesitated and the duc de Guines became cutting. This irritated the Queen, then Y.M.'s letter arrived...[After some reflection] the Queen herself decided to tell the duc de Guines that neither his views nor his advice were agreeable to H.M. and that she would be obliged if he did not raise these matters again but limited himself to enjoying the kindness and protection which the Queen was disposed to continue giving to him, provided he did not imagine he could direct her.

Apparently the comtesse de Polignac, his great friend, did not dare to support him at this point. No one knows the details, so please do not mention this to the Queen. The Queen wants to continue treating him kindly so that it will not seem she has suddenly stopped favouring him.

The King goes out of his way to please the Queen...[Recently he gave her all the money he had to put towards her debts, then when the King gambled] he could not pay his losses, so the Queen loaned him money and hopefully this will suffice to discourage him [in future]...The King

374

himself has decided to double the Queen's allowance. The director general of finances is very keen to show his zeal to the Queen and has eagerly seized this opportunity. However H.M has declared that so long as they are at war she does not want to accept the whole increase.

MERCY TO MARIA THERESA, 17 DECEMBER 1779

The due de Guines' fall from the Queen's favour, is becoming more and more obvious. The comte de Maurepas and all the ministers have been the first to talk of it. I was worried about how the comtesse Jules de Polignac would behave in this situation; but I have just discovered that she was suspicious, probably with good reason, of his sincerity.

What has happened to the duc de Guines may have encouraged the comtesse Jules de Polignac to reflect on the possibly transitory nature of her favour. She is now extraordinarily preoccupied with profiting from her present favour to secure a large fortune for her family. She has decided to procure, as an outright gift from the King, an estate with an income of one hundred thousand livres. The favourite has realized that she herself could not make such an exorbitant request: thus it was necessary to have her friends do so and M. le comte d'Artois was firstly charged with that commission, but other friends also joined their entreaties. However fond H. M. is of her favourite, she took fright at such an unreasonable idea; however she ended up adopting it and entered into discussions on the means of carrying it out.

It has been calculated that over a period of less than four years, all the Polignac family, without merit, and from favour alone, have already procured so many good positions that they receive about five hundred thousand livres in annual revenue. All the families who most deserve these favours complain about how they feel wronged by such a distribution of favours, and if they see yet another which is without precedent, the protests and the outrage will become extreme. There is even a risk of alienating the King with such incredible requests, and the Queen, who cannot ignore these truths, is tormented to excess. Because of what she deigned to tell us, the abbe de Vermond and I told her heatedly what we thought.

The minister of finance, sire Necker, despite his desire to please the Queen, made some very wise comments to her about this matter, which H.M. realized were appropriate and which she took well, although she did not yield on the principle, but agreed rather to reduce the exorbitance of her request. However this is the only disquieting point about the Queen's behaviour at present.

EXTRACT FROM LA MARCK'S CORRESPONDENCE WITH MIRABEAU [100]

As for the expenses which the Queen incurred because of the Polignac clan, they have been greatly exaggerated by the public. In fact, the comte and comtesse Jules de Polignac only received what was necessary to maintain a household which had for some time become that of the Queen, and sometimes that of the King. Also, when the Revolution occurred, they were in debt rather than rich.

---

[100] Extract from Bacourt (1851), vol 1, p.37, La Marck writing, in the Introduction.

1780

MARIA THERESA TO MARIE ANTOINETTE,
1 JANUARY 1780

My dear daughter, I cannot start the year better than by sending you my best wishes for the New Year, my chief wish being that you have a son, and that you have him this year. I am delighted at the mutual love and attentiveness between yourself and the King. I am not at all happy with the situation in America, nor that of the fleet. In the coming year you will have twice the forces against you that you have at present, as the resources of the British are immense and their fanaticism is incredible. You know what I would like as a good Frenchwoman and as mother of their dear Queen: peace.

MARIE ANTOINETTE TO MARIA THERESA,
15 JANUARY 1780

We are not discouraged and have every reason to believe that during the next campaign, we will have superior forces in America. M. de Guichen will leave shortly with a fleet of fifteen or eighteen ships, and three or four thousand soldiers.[101]

The weather here is very cold and unpleasant; there have been ghastly fogs here which have caused a general epidemic of colds; all Paris and Versailles is coughing. I was in bed for three days with a fever. Only the King and Monsieur avoided catching cold, and they looked after us all, as we were each in our rooms, unable to be up; even my daughter had a cold, but although she still has teeth coming through, she has not had a fever. I am still taking ipecacuanha tablets. I expect

---

[101] Marie Antoinette's great confidant, and possible future lover, the discreet Swede, Axel von Fersen, accompanied the French forces to America.

to take iron again next month and perhaps also be bled as a precaution.

My people have made an error; they forgot to send a keepsake which I hope will please my dear mother, with the last courier. The hair is from the King, my daughter and myself, the darkest is mine.

MERCY TO MARIA THERESA, 17 JANUARY 1780

Since the end of last month, the number of people at court has increased almost daily. There were few people at the Queen's first two balls, but by the third ball the number had increased and it was very successful, as probably will be those that follow. The Queen's kindness to everyone must add to the eagerness of the people to pay court to her. The Queen has decided to seriously occupy herself with restoring the former glory to Versailles and this will not take long, if the Queen does as she says she will. The two weekly suppers which have begun again in the private rooms, are attracting a lot of people; providing that favour does not influence the choice of people admitted too much, this is one method which can have a great effect – I told the Queen this and also asked her to prohibit card play for high stakes in her rooms, as this is feared by many people who do not wish to play beyond their means.

On New Year's Eve, the Queen received all the ladies from Paris who came to pay homage, between six and nine in the evening. In total there were 180 women. H. M. spoke to all and treated them with great kindness. The warmth in the rooms and the fatigue caused by this three hour session, obliged the Queen to go to bed.

Although the Queen is generally in good health, she is however subject to slight indispositions, which demand care to avoid becoming serious. The Queen catches cold very easily and often suffers from a weakness in her stomach. Lassone is going to give her iron to see if she becomes pregnant, as this method has worked for him before with others. He will try this when carnival time is over.

379

SECRET LETTER

You cannot imagine how people here have been pestering the Queen about an estate for the comtesse de Polignac. The comte de Maurepas has lent himself to their schemes. He went to the King, claimed this was the Queen's wish and forced his hand to some extent. After a series of manoeuvres, it was agreed that the comtesse de Polignac would receive four hundred thousand livres to pay her debts, the promise of an estate worth thirty five thousand livres in revenue, and eight hundred thousand livres in silver for her daughter's dowry.

They believe they can keep this favour secret, but it is more than probable that it will be known in time and will lead to public disquiet. The Queen realizes this and is pained as a result. The Queen told me, "The comtesse de Polignac has totally changed, and I do not know her any more." Perhaps you could mention to the Queen that "you heard rumours of an estate and millions to be given to the comtesse de Polignac; that Y.M. does not believe this, but you believe it necessary to let her know what is being said."

MARIA THERESA TO MARIE ANTOINETTE,
1 FEBRUARY 1780

It seems to me that Lassone is right to give you iron, which worked well for the Queen of Naples, and being bled cannot hurt. I could count on becoming pregnant when I was bled. They say that Polignac, solely because of her favour, has asked for the estate of Bitche. The public was surprised at this request, which seems to indicate avidity rather than attachment. They are even saying that you want to give her millions. I do not listen to these rumours, not believing them likely, but I think you should know about them, especially when the state has so many other expenses at present.

I hope that the future campaign will not be as costly and will be easier to win, but the British will have superior forces. They are making enormous preparations...[This] makes me worry for you both.

MARIE ANTOINETTE TO MARIA THERESA, 15 FEBRUARY 1780

I am too accustomed to the inventions and exaggerations of this place to be surprised at what they say about Mme de Polignac. It is quite usual here for the King to contribute to the dowry of people at court who are of good birth but not rich. The young Polignac is to marry the comte de Gramont, who is due to succeed to the post of captain of the guard. Her mother thought of the Bitche estate, but only for a moment, and as soon as she knew what it was worth, she was the first to tell me and gave up the idea. I am delighted to see that the King behaves in such a way that I am spared solicitation on behalf of my friend. He is totally convinced of her integrity and the nobility of her sentiments. He will be charmed to be able to do her a kindness.

The King has just published an edict to prepare the way for reforming his household and mine. This was tried unsuccessfully in the last two reigns. The King has the power and the good will, but it could result in new problems, as in the past. [Edit: it did]

MARIE ANTOINETTE TO MARIA THERESA, 16 MARCH 1780

My dear mother, I was bled and it was a total success. My health is very good just now, and I am again hopeful of becoming pregnant soon. I could not read what my dear mother told me about the Queen of Naples, without trembling; she is experiencing one appalling calamity after another. They say here that her little girl is quite ill and I am greatly afraid that her son will also catch smallpox; what is more, they say that it is the most virulent strain, which makes matters even worse. I pity her with all my heart and I can readily understand the anxiety a parent feels when her children are unwell. Thank God, I have not experienced this, as my daughter has not even had a slight fever since her birth. She will soon be weaned; she is so big and strong that she is taken for a child of two years.

She is walking alone, bends down and straightens up without being held, but she does not say much.

I must tell my dear and loving mother of how happy I was four days ago. There were several people in my daughter's room, and I had someone ask her where her mother was. The dear little child smiled at me and came to me holding out her arms, even though no one said a word to her. That was the first time she showed she recognised me; I must admit I was moved, and I believe I love her even more since then. But I realize I am talking about her at length; I know my dear mother will be kind and indulgent enough to excuse this chatter.

Last week we received the terrible news that an important convoy which we were sending to the West Indies had been lost. At first it was said that all the boats had been captured; now it seems certain that more than half have escaped. It was intended to have eight to ten thousand troops set sail for America at the end of the month, but I believe this news may postpone their departure. It is quite certain that we cannot risk this large convoy without being sure of the sea; it would be distressing to have to suffer more misfortunes yet again because of it; I must admit that I cannot think of this scenario calmly.

P.S. I have just opened my letter to tell my dear mother the good news which we have just been given. A convoy has arrived at Rochefort which is estimated to be worth more than thirty million.

MERCY TO MARIA THERESA, 18 MARCH 1780

This delay in our hopes for a pregnancy is even more upsetting as it is certainly not due to the former cause, and the King is living intimately with the Queen. The Queen has almost entirely given up horse riding, but it is not the same with many other amusements which occasion late nights and an almost continual restlessness: even Lent was not a time of repose at Versailles, as this year they have continued amusements, contrary to custom. Diane de Polignac, lady of honour to Mme Elisabeth, gave a ball. The Queen did not know about this, and means were found to have the King approve of it, and he even spent several hours there. It started at eleven in the evening and went on till eleven in the morning. All the royal family, apart from the aunts, was there. The ball was well attended, but it led to criticism, the most annoying of which is to suppose, although in error, that it is by such means that one can best please the Queen.

Yet another matter has caused outbursts in Versailles. Recent promotions in the military have just been made public, and most were made in accordance with the Queen's patronage. All the Polignacs played an important part, less in their own interests than their friends's; but these latter obtained far beyond what they could reasonably have wished. Although the Queen let herself be influenced by her usual kindness to her favourites, she did however try not to be unfair. The King lent himself to everything the Queen wanted. He made his own lists, which were changed several times according to the different intrigues at any particular moment.

SECRET LETTER

These last weeks have been quite distressing because of the majority of events which have taken place at Versailles. Other entertainments have been introduced at court which, because of their childish and noisy nature, are unsuitable to the contemplation normally associated with Lent, and even less to the dignity of the august people who participate in them.

These games are similar to blind man's buff, and culminate in the giving of a forfeit which is then redeemed by some bizarre penance, and the great activity which this occasions is often prolonged well into the night. The number of people from court as well as from the town who are admitted to these games, makes them even more subject to drawbacks; it is surprising to see that the King likes them and that he indulges in frivolities at a time as grave for the state as is the present. The Queen agrees that this must have a bad effect on public opinion. This august princess has no particular taste for these games, and lends herself to them from kindness; but the public unfairly attributes them to her, and they are generally deplored.

It seems that they intend encouraging the King to totally abandon business, and the comte de Maurepas himself is not exempt from suspicion in this project. It would be as pernicious to the glory of the young monarch, as harmful to the personal interests of the Queen if this happened, and I showed her all the possible consequences, in such a way that H.M. seemed astonished.

The Queen spoke to me of what Y.M. had said about the Polignac family. The Queen admitted that she was embarrassed to discuss this with Y.M., and had decided to acknowledge the dowry, but claim there were exaggerations, and add that such dowries were often given.

All Paris knows of the dowry of 800,000 livres given to the young Polignac, and they made this known themselves. The dowries given by the King sometimes, are payments of 6,000 livres; there is not a single example of a similar favour being granted.

You could [tell the Queen]...that it is said openly in Paris that a certain comte de Vaudreuil, apparently too closely linked to the comtesse de Polignac, has obtained through her agency 30,000 livres from the King.

[With regard to the Neckers]...I will tell them both what Y. M. has ordered me to say; they deserve such kindness, the husband because of his probity and his talents, the wife because of her exemplary virtues. [Edit: this is a reply to Maria Theresa's letter of the 3rd of March, in which she asked Mercy to tell the Neckers of her esteem for them. The Revolution changed this popular perception of Necker's so-called talents.]

MARIA THERESA TO MARIE ANTOINETTE, 1 APRIL 1780

I am very anxious about your affairs, as I believe the British are very skilful in that area [naval matters]...and no one can equal them.

Everything you tell me about your daughter delights me, and I can readily understand your feelings as a mother at everything she does. How touching it is! But we need a dauphin. Impatience is overcoming me, as my age does not leave me much time. The Queen, your sister, has lost her dear Marianne, saved her son so far, but a second daughter is quite ill with fever; in addition she is eight months pregnant. I am distressed about her situation.[102]

You have not replied to me about the matter I told you all the journals were discussing – the King's great generosity to the comtesse de Polignac in giving her a dowry of 800,000 livres for her daughter, an estate worth two million, and in addition paying her debts. There is a further story which I cannot believe, that a certain comte de Vaudreuil, who is claimed to be too intimately linked to this countess, obtained through her agency thirty thousand livres and an estate from the comte d'Artois, due to your intervention. I must warn you that this is causing a great sensation, and quite a bad one at that, with the public, [103] and abroad, especially when so many expenses at court are being reformed, which is entirely necessary and praiseworthy. But this excessive generosity makes these reforms seem more unpleasant and burdensome in comparison.

I could not remain silent about these stories which are affecting your reputation, as I am upset that, because of the kindness of your heart, you are letting yourself be blinded to the avidity of these so called friends, especially in the present circumstances. If I did not warn you, who else would dare? It has upset me to write this, but your total silence on this matter convinced me that the journals were not fabricating these issues, and that it was necessary to enlighten you on the facts. Nothing can better convince you of my love, and that I think only of your happiness, than this advice; I wish matters were not so. With love.

---

[102] Child mortality, even in royal families, was high. Marie Antoinette herself lost two of her four eventual children to illness, and then her remaining son died from ill treatment, after the deposition of Louis XVI.

[103] Only nine years later, when the Revolution began in 1789, Polignac and her family were so despised by the public, that they were obliged to flee France, as was the comte d'Artois. The Queen's life was similarly threatened, but she refused to abandon her husband and family.

MARIE ANTOINETTE TO MARIA THERESA, 13 APRIL 1780

My dear mother, the troops destined for the West Indies have embarked and are only awaiting a favourable wind, to leave port. May it please God that they arrive safely.

Weaning my daughter has not caused her any upset and she is still very well and absorbs me totally; I earnestly desire a companion for her, and I have more reason to be hopeful than ever.

I was delighted to see Joseph Kaunitz again [Edit: the son of Maria Theresa's secretary of state]. It is true that I would give everything to have a prince Kaunitz in this ministry, but unfortunately his like is not often encountered, and it is necessary to be able to recognise merit, as my dear mother does, to find such a man.

M. de Vaudreuil is a man of quality who has served the state well, and his relatives are distinguishing themselves in the present war. He has never asked for favours, and his fortune is such that he does not need money. He has many possessions in the West Indies, but is receiving nothing from them at present because of the war. The King gave him 30,000 francs, but he will only keep this until peace is made. He returned this to the King recently when the comte d'Artois gave him an estate.

I took no part in this; everybody here knows that M. de Vaudreuil is well enough liked by my brother, to need no other patron. I could say the same for Mme de Polignac in relation to the King; he is very fond of her, and although I am very grateful for any kindness he shows her, I do not need to ask for this. The gazette and story writers know more than I; I have not heard of an estate worth two million nor any other; if I knew more, I would tell my dear mother, and I will never try to avoid replying to you.

I wrote recently to the Queen of Naples; but because of her condition, I limited myself to expressing my worry about her health and my distress at the loss of her daughter.

What has most confirmed the comtesse de Polignac in her position, is that the King seems to have developed a sort of liking for her: he is grateful to her for having become an essential support to the Queen. He himself is becoming used to her company; when she is absent from Versailles, the monarch writes to her to let her know when her presence can be most agreeable or necessary to the Queen. In fact this same countess often influences the arrangements of the court. It had been decided that the court would go to Marly on the 5th, but this has not happened as the comtesse de Polignac, in her ninth month of pregnancy, has decided to go to Paris for her delivery, and the Queen, who wants to see her often, can more easily visit her from Versailles than from Marly.

The abolition of the office of general tax collector has caused much stir at court. The King's two brothers and the duc d'Orleans decided that this measure conflicted with their honorary right to nominate people to these positions in the provinces where they had exclusive rights. M. le comte d'Artois had a very lively discussion on this matter with the director general of finances, who replied firmly but respectfully. The young prince then had recourse to the Queen, all sorts of entreaties were used, but H.M. would not let herself be persuaded, and this instance, which has been preceded by several others which are similar, when M. le comte d'Artois' insinuations have also failed, prove that the Queen has resolved to limit her indulgence of her brother in law, who has abused her credit too often.

I must add that of all the King's ministers, the director Necker [104] is the one of whom the Queen has the best opinion

---

[104]The government deficit in the late 1780's was one of the factors which triggered the Revolution, as the aristocracy was, for the first time ever, asked to pay taxes, and they contested this outrageous request fiercely. The deficit was caused partly by the expenses of supporting the American insurgents, and possibly contributed to by the Queen's expenses, especially in the eyes of the public, who nicknamed her 'Madame Deficit' It is also believed that Necker mismanaged the finances, despite his high standing in the eyes of the court, in 1780, as above.

and whom she respects the most. He is the only person in a position of authority who knows how to have his reasons heard and accepted.

SECRET LETTER

Y.M.'s comments about the comtesse de Polignac and the comte de Vaudreuil have had a great effect. The Queen's first reaction was ill temper and a lively outburst against the writers who dared to spread such information...[I reasoned with the Queen], then she looked distinctly shamefaced and admitted these feelings to me with all her usual kindness and frankness. I do not know how this august princess will reply to you, but I presume that she will place some of the blame on the comte de Maurepas, and it is quite true that this old minister is very culpable.

It is true, as the Queen says, that the comte de Vaudreuil has given back the allowance, but it was the public outcry and not selflessness which forced this move. The Queen, by not replying to the remark about the intimate liaison between the comte de Vaudreuil and the comtesse de Polignac, seems to avow this tacitly.

MARIA THERESA TO MERCY, 30 APRIL 1780

Comte de Mercy-Argenteau, if we overlook my daughter's influence in less important matters, such as the recent promotions in the military, we will be able to concentrate on the important matters, which are more closely linked to our interests. Moreover, I am pleased my daughter was firm enough not to become involved in the dispute between the comte d'Artois and Necker, nor the claims of the comtesse de Brionne and her daughter princess Charlotte, for the prince de Vaudemont, nor the entreaties of the comtesse Polignac for the comte d'Adhemar. [Edit: these had all been mentioned by Mercy in his previous letter to Maria Theresa]

I firmly believe that the King, good as he is, is friendly to the comtesse de Polignac only in order to please my daughter. She was not slow to use this friendship in her reply to me about that woman. I will not reply about that matter, until you indicate to me that it is an appropriate moment.

MERCY TO MARIA THERESA, 17 MAY 1780

The Queen often spends her days at her chateau at Trianon and sometimes her evenings; then plays are held, and the King is regularly found there; only the inner court is admitted to these little entertainments; they begin by walks in the gardens until supper, after which everyone goes to the theatre, and what is most useful about this arrangement is that it is a diversion from games of chance.

SECRET LETTER

I am obliged to be very careful in what I say to the Queen about the comtesse de Polignac, and it is becoming very difficult to make useful remarks to her, if they conflict with her extreme liking for her favourite.[105] It is quite probable that the comtesse de Polignac, after her delivery, will have the title of duchesse.

MARIA THERESA TO MERCY, 31 MAY 1780

This repeated suspension of conjugal intimacy is not the sign of a lively passion between the two spouses. [Edit: Maria Theresa's marriage to Francis of Lorraine had been one of love. She fell in love with this prince (fortunately a suitable suitor) and insisted to her father that she would marry him. She did so. They had sixteen children.]

MERCY TO MARIA THERESA, 18 JUNE 1780

Sacred Majesty, [the court stayed at Marly for a week, while]...the comtesse de Polignac was confined, due to childbirth. The Queen went to see her every day.

---

[105] Such was the Queen's liking for Polignac, that the newssheets claimed that they were lovers.

During the stay at La Muette, the King visited the comtesse de Polignac; this is the only private house in Paris which he has entered since becoming King, and such distinctive treatment almost caused a greater sensation with the public than all the remunerative favours granted to the favourite.

The King has no other company normally than that of his family, and all his dangerous associates have no prolonged access to him. The Queen understands the importance of this very well. In this way H.M. thought of the little entertainments which she gives from time to time at Trianon, which have always been successful.

SECRET LETTER

The abbe de Vermond and I have allowed ourselves to make several representations about all the public outcries which have occurred recently. The Queen regards them as arising from envy and jealousy.

MARIA THERESA TO MERCY, 30 JUNE 1780

I can no longer conceal from you the worry I immediately felt when I heard of the frightening event which occurred to my daughter at the time of her delivery, and this terrifying thought recurs to me all the time. Could this incident possibly be the result of an assassination attempt?

MARIA THERESA TO MARIE ANTOINETTE, 30 JUNE 1780

This trip [Edit: by Joseph, to Russia] upsets me a lot and the future one [Edit: to Britain] will be even more distressing for me, especially after that horrifying riot, the like of which is unknown in civilised countries, which has just occurred. [Edit: Maria Theresa is alluding here to a riot directed against Catholics, which occurred in London on the 2nd of June] There can be found that greatly vaunted liberty, that unique legislature! But without religion or morals, nothing will endure.

We need a dauphin. Until now I have been measured, but eventually I will pester you. It would be murder not to give birth to more children from that line, as they say your dear little one is marvellously healthy and charming.

MARIE ANTOINETTE TO MARIA THERESA, 13 JULY 1780

I am longing to hear that the emperor has returned from his long trip. As for the other trip [Edit: to England], I hope he will consider very carefully before going to a country which is the decided enemy of all sovereigns [Edit: because of its parliament], and where the laws most necessary for peace and public propriety are negligible because of the spirit of liberty and independence. The recent riot made me tremble and gave me a lot to think about.

The capture of Charlestown [Edit: in America] is very annoying because of the resources it has given the British and their pride as a result; it is even more so because of the pitiful defence by the Americans; nothing can be hoped for from such incompetent soldiers.

MERCY TO MARIA THERESA, 15 JULY 1780

The Queen is more and more preoccupied with her country house [Edit: Trianon], she goes there almost every day, either in the morning or in the afternoon; H.M. is only accompanied by two or three people, except when she hosts entertainments for the King, to which she invites many people.

Madame, the King's sister in law, had the duchesse de l'Esparre as her dame d'atours. Unexpectedly, and without forewarning the duchesse de l'Esparre, Madame nominated a successor to her position and chose a comtesse de Balbi, who, due to improper and regrettable reasons, had just separated from her husband. [Edit: the comtesse de Balbi became Monsieur's mistress, or perhaps already was his mistress at this time.]

391

A successor who is nominated by someone other than the holder of the position, causes outrage to the latter, and the duchesse de l'Esparre did not hesitate to resign immediately...[Her relatives] tried to encourage the Queen to show some signs of disapproval, while Madame, on her part, used every possible means to persuade the Queen to show approval; but H.M. would not let herself adopt either part, and was so measured in her replies that neither could gain the slightest advantage.

SECRET LETTER

The comte de Maurepas is more than eighty years old and one way or another, he will not remain in his position for long. For a long time I have been asking the Queen to think of a future replacement for this prime minister. Because of the King's personality, and because of the way things are done here, it is evident that someone, no matter who, will acquire a major influence in politics, and it is especially important that this person should be carefully chosen by the Queen, and become her puppet. None of the reasons which I am continually presenting to the Queen has yet made much of an impression; but they are preparing the way, and it will be easier to develop this and put her ideas into practice when the right moment arises. I must submit to Y.M.'s profound insight to consider whether you judge it appropriate to suggest something about this in your letters.

When the Queen gave birth, I was in the bedroom near her bed and was very attentive to everything that was happening. Before the incident occurred and at the moment of occurrence, no one had touched the Queen except the midwife, the principal doctor Lassone, the principal surgeon Chavignac and the two first women of the bedchamber, Misery and Thibeau, all persons whose fidelity and integrity are so evident that it is totally impossible to suspect them.

Besides, the incident in question had a recognised cause, which was the abundance and vivacity of her blood. The midwife had insisted on a final bleeding which did not take place; he wanted the Queen to take a bath at the start of her pains, H.M. refused; when the vein was opened in the foot, the incident was over within seconds. It would be almost impossible for me to have been unaware of any indications of a criminal murder attempt, if such had occurred.

By an inconceivable fatality, it seems that from one day to the next, the Queen becomes less worried about not becoming pregnant, and when we sometimes succeed in fixing her attention and thoughts on such a major topic, this only lasts for a few moments.

MARIA THERESA TO MERCY, 31 JULY 1780

As it cannot be long before Maurepas will have to be replaced one way or another, it is important to start thinking now of choosing his successor, which is a matter which occupies the King of Prussia very much, as you know from the [Edit: intercepted] Prussian correspondence.

MARIA THERESA TO MARIE ANTOINETTE, 2 AUGUST 1780

Your outburst about the emperor's projected trip, agrees exactly with how I feel; but I must admit it amused me slightly to see you so adamant about that point. I am no less so, as for some years that nation [Edit: Britain] has been gaining influence everywhere; it is not possible to take too many precautions to forestall their influence in everything.

No appearance of a pregnancy yet, that distresses me: we absolutely need a dauphin.

MERCY TO MARIA THERESA, 16 AUGUST 1780

I mentioned in my previous very humble reports that the Queen had become much more eager to participate in the King's amusements, and this inclination is becoming a daily habit. The King quite likes a game called lotto. The Queen does not enjoy this game; it even bores her; however she is concerned to establish this game after supper, and H.M. plays it every evening until the King retires, after eleven o'clock.

The resignation of the duchesse de l'Esparre and Madame's granting of her position to the comtesse de Balbi, has been the cause of disputes at Versailles until now. The King showed he was displeased at this; Madame noticed this and as a result has not presented her new lady of honour to the King herself, as is the custom, and the comtesse de Balbi was received very coldly by the monarch when she came to receive the grandes entrees, which are a prerogative of her position. The Queen was a little less severe, but nonetheless she looked sufficiently serious to show that she did not approve of this change.

SECRET LETTER

Recently I found the Queen preoccupied and distressed at information she had been given. This information was that the newssheets concerning events at Versailles were now being printed in Dusseldorf, and that several exemplars had been sent to Vienna; that H.M. the emperor, when he left, had expressly ordered that these newssheets should be sent to him wherever he was, that H.R.H. Mme l'archiduchesse Marie [Edit: Marie Antoinette's sister], showed singular eagerness to procure these same newssheets, and that she seemed to amuse herself with all the disparaging little remarks against the Queen, which she found. H.M. added that she had asked the King to take measures to try to discover the sources of these newssheets and intercept them, and that the monarch had promised to do so.

I told the Queen that this information seemed to me to be the work of some intriguer, that if newssheets were printed in Dusseldorf, nothing was simpler than that they should reach Vienna and that H.M. the emperor and H.R.H. Mme l'archiduchesse Marie would know of them; but that it was shocking to dare to suggest that the monarch or his august sister would find pleasure in reading news which was unfavourable to the Queen and which could only excite their indignation. As the Queen enjoined me to silence, I would lose her trust if H.R.H. Mme l 'archiduchesse let it be known that she knew of this matter. I therefore leave it to Y.M. to decide how to resolve this matter.

MARIA THERESA TO MERCY, 31 AUGUST 1780

I will use the information you have given me about Delisle and the newssheets [Edit: Delisle corresponded with d'Artois and had given him the information about the newssheets], without compromising you with my daughter Marie.

MERCY TO MARIA THERESA, 16 SEPTEMBER 1780

For a month the Queen has only found interest and amusement in putting on two little plays in the theatre at Trianon. The King, who has attended the rehearsals very conscientiously, has shown how much he enjoys this type of entertainment. He shows his pleasure in them by applauding continually, particularly when the Queen is acting in her role.

A form of entertainment which is limited to such a small number of people is an even more marked indication of favour for these admitted, and consequently is a reason for jealousy and complaint in those excluded. The princesse de Lamballe, because of her position as superintendent, thought she could claim to be an exception, but this was not accepted. [Edit: the comtesse de Polignac's favour had increased while the princesse de Lamballe's had decreased, over the previous few years]

The Queen's ladies have claimed that, from established custom, there was no circumstance which should deprive them of the advantage of serving her, which was at present reduced only to appearing on Sundays and at special events at the Queen's toilette, and at the church services: these entreaties did not succeed, and have caused hostility [Edit: amongst the aristocracy] as a result and led to talk which has spread from Versailles to Paris.

The Queen has remained at Trianon all this week with the comtesse de Polignac, the duchesse de Guiche and the comtesse de Chalons. The King has gone there regularly every morning and returns in the evening. On Tuesday, the Queen came back to Versailles in the morning, so that the foreign ambassadors could pay court. The company [Edit: at Trianon] is slightly too restricted for this lively and demonstrative nation. The lack of opportunity to pay court could eventually diminish the desire to do so, and the custom. This year this was shown on the King's name day, when there was not even half the people who were at Versailles in previous years.

The comtesse de Balbi was persuaded to propose her sister, the comtesse de Cayla, as lady's companion to Madame, who agreed to this request. When Madame in turn made a request to present her new lady's companion, the King replied quite dryly that she had no doubt forgotten that she had to talk to him of this choice before deciding. However the presentation took place, but the King did not even glance at the person being presented. The Queen behaved in a similar manner, and Madame was doubly humiliated.

The King, who seems totally alienated from his sister in law, suggested to the Queen not to take supper at Madame's when Monsieur was not there. This little dispute will not last long. Madame has too much interest in this, and Monsieur, who is as politic as he is considered, will take charge of this in a capable way. The Queen likes peace and is naturally inclined to do whatever she can to obtain it or re-establish it.

SECRET LETTER

[With regard to the attempt to persuade the Queen to influence the choice of a successor to Maurepas]...H.M. believes that the King greatly dislikes, and is afraid of the idea of being led into making decisions; that he immediately suspects this when people talk to him of politics and that therefore it would be necessary to be cautious. I agreed, but as the King speaks to her about his ministers and the way they perform their duties, every day...[I believe that] if the Queen were to act appropriately, it is certain that she would decide the choice of a future minister.

MARIA THERESA TO MERCY, 30 SEPTEMBER 1780

I believe it would perhaps not be a bad idea if, after the comte de Maurepas' death, the King decided to govern by himself and not through some minister, assuming that he has sufficient talent and application to do so, and provided my daughter always maintains enough credit, and uses it well, in order to enjoy the King's confidence.

I regard the entertainments at Trianon as only fleeting, and have no worries about them, so long as no major problem arises as a result.

However displeased the King is with Madame, because of what happened with regard to Mme de Balbi, I believe the situation will be resolved. However it seems to me that it would have been more appropriate to prevent Madame executing her plan in favour of that woman.

MARIE ANTOINETTE TO MARIA THERESA, 11 OCTOBER 1780

My dear mother, my daughter's health has preoccupied me and worried me slightly for the past three weeks. She has been in great pain because several teeth have come through at the same time, and given her a fever. Lassone assures me there is no danger. The fever ended yesterday; God willing it will not recur! I was touched by the sweetness and patience of that dear little child in the midst of her suffering which at times was quite intense.[106]

We are going to Marly on the 13th; the company will be more numerous and consequently there will be etiquette, and on All Saint's Day, I will again hold court.[Edit: Mercy had prevailed on Marie Antoinette to leave Trianon and go to one of the country houses where it would be possible to invite more people than to Trianon.]

---

[106] The life of Marie Antoinette's daughter, Marie Therese, was to be one of great suffering. Her ordeal in captivity, when her father was deposed, was harrowing. See volume II.

EXTRACT FROM MME. CAMPAN 'MEMOIRS'[107]

The Queen's toilet was a masterpiece of etiquette; everything was done in a prescribed form. Both the dame d'honneur and the dame d'atours usually attended and officiated, assisted by the first femme de chambre and two ordinary women. The dame d'atours put on the petticoat, and handed the gown to the Queen. The dame d'honneur poured out the water for her hands and put on her linen.

One winter's day it happened that the Queen, who was entirely undressed, was just going to put on her shift; I held it ready unfolded for her; the dame d'honneur came in, slipped off her gloves, and took it. A scratching was heard at the door; it was opened, and in came the duchesse d'Orleans: her gloves were taken off, and she came forward to take the garment; but as it would have been wrong in the dame d'honneur to hand it to her she gave it to me, and I handed it to the princess. More scratching: it was Madame la comtesse de Provence; the duchesse d'Orleans handed her the linen. All the while the Queen kept her arms crossed upon her bosom, and appeared to feel cold; Madame observed her uncomfortable situation, and. merely laying down her handkerchief without taking off her gloves, she put on the linen, and in doing so knocked the Queen's cap off. The Queen laughed to conceal her impatience, but not until she had muttered several times, "How disagreeable! How tiresome!"

MERCY TO MARIA THERESA, 14 OCTOBER 1780

Mornings at Trianon resembled a country house, inhabited by private individuals. After lunchtime [many more people]…went to Trianon.

Immediately after the stay at Trianon, the comte Jules de Polignac was named a hereditary duke.

At the news of the death of the prince de Carignan, brother of the princesse de Lamballe, the Queen went to town to see the latter and spent some moments with her. That

---

[107] Extract from Campan, vol 1, p. 148

demonstration of kindness is the only one the superintendent has experienced for a long time; as she no longer has any credit, she only appears at court rarely.

SECRET LETTER

The Queen has been seriously thinking about a future successor to the comte de Maurepas and that is why she has decided to have the archbishop of Toulouse given the decoration which has just been promised to him. This prelate is the close friend of the abbe de Vermond; but I must render this latter the justice of stating that he is incapable of turning the Queen's trust to profit, for whatever reason. It is quite probable that the archbishop of Toulouse, because of the superiority of his talents, could one day be in the ministry, and as a result it would seem to be a good idea to make him a protege of the Queen.

It would no doubt be preferable for the King to be able and willing to forego having a prime minister, and if the Queen could decide to give him the necessary assistance, it would not be impossible for the monarch to govern by himself. It is certain that when the comte de Maurepas dies, the King will not want to replace him; but his lack of experience in politics, his difficulty in making decisions, and an infinite amount of reasons applicable only to this country, together mean that one or other of the ministers will influence the King, gain ascendancy, and perhaps, without having the title, will become prime minister in fact, and in this case what is desirable is that at least no one will have this position without the Queen's protection.

MARIA THERESA TO MERCY, 3 NOVEMBER 1780

I believe the greed of the woman who is now the duchesse de Polignac, and my daughter's indulgence, are so well established that there is no point in hoping for self restraint in either.[108]

My daughter does well to try to smooth over the quarrels with Madame, and not trust her character, or the firmness of the King, who shows discontent, but lets people do as they wish, which is a dangerous maxim in our position [Edit: a habit he continued in the Revolution – with disastrous results].

[The emperor's]…constant trips embitter my life and in the long run cannot honour him. As I must believe I am the reason for these absences, you can imagine how upset I am, and eventually I will not be able to endure them any longer. So long as I live, I will not permit changes to the government of the Netherlands [Edit: Maria Theresa's brother in law had just died and her daughter Marie was to be the governor in the Netherlands. Joseph's meddling very soon produced discontent in the Netherlands]; but I cannot believe that matters will continue as they are there, for long; my sorrows of all kinds are too great and increase every day, and I have no help or support; at my age that cannot be tolerated for long and my health will suffer.

MERCY TO MARIA THERESA, 18 NOVEMBER 1780

Of all the trips to Marly, the recent one was without doubt the one which was most ordered and dignified. The court observed the old customs, particularly in the salon, where lansquenet was played every evening.

The aristocracy of Paris was allowed to go to Marly, and as many people came as could be expected at a time when the war is keeping soldiers away. Those who were able to pay court were very pleased with the trip, and in that the Queen did

---

[108] La Marck, in his previously cited book, states: The Queen was often weary of the indiscreet requests made to her. Amongst those of her personal friends were many foreigners, such as the comtes Esterhazy, de Fersen etc., etc. One day I permitted myself to observe that her marked preference for foreigners could harm her in the eyes of the French. – "You are right," she told me sadly, "but they do not ask me for anything." (vol I, p.41)

as she had intended, which was to help people forget how they had been excluded from the trips to Trianon.

The dismissal of the minister for the navy produced a sensation at court. Those with ambitions in the war department became very active in order to grasp an opportunity which they felt was favourable to their plans, and because of this, the Queen's protection was anxiously sought. The comte d'Adhemar, French ambassador in Brussels, thought to show an interest in this, counting on the support of his close friend the duchesse de Polignac. The duchess supported him as well as she could; she became more and more pressing, even insistent, and a torment to the Queen, as it hurts her to resist her favourite's wishes; finally H.M. decided to tell her to abandon this idea, and the requests stopped. However they could merely be suspended, because the duchesse de Polignac now believes she can succeed in achieving whatever she wants, eventually.

Before going to Marly, the King spent two days at Compiegne with a retinue of young people. The company became slightly too licentious. The Queen, who became aware of this, showed her displeasure to those whom she knew had initiated these entertainments, which in any case held no interest for the King. It is essential that these pleasure parties are not repeated often if the Queen is not present.

SECRET LETTER

The dismissal of the minister for the navy was the result of an extraordinary intrigue, and I still have suspicions about this which I have only partly been able to verify. It is certain that the director general of finances [Edit: Necker] was the prime mover in this dismissal; but he would never have succeeded only using his own influence. He has always complained about the huge favours granted to the Polignacs. What he said to the Queen and to me, convinced me that he was opposed to the favourites, however I have learned that, on this occasion, these very favourites co operated totally with the director general, and in order to do so, they deceived the Queen as well as the comte de Maurepas. They used speed and secrecy to accomplish this.

401

The courier for October was about to leave when the Queen was suddenly assailed by the duchesse de Polignac and her friend, the comte de Vaudreuil, who endeavoured to persuade H.M. to speak to the King and convince him to sack sieur de Sartines and nominate the marquis de Castries to his post. In deference to her favourite, the Queen promised only to ascertain the King's opinion.

[When the abbe de Vermond and I heard, we spoke to the Queen]...She was already worried about what was happening, and decided to do nothing. The director general had an audience with the King, and with the Queen, at which she was noncommittal. The King said nothing as he wanted to wait until he had spoken to the comte de Maurepas. Then they were deceitful enough to tell the comte de Maurepas the supposed secret with which they had been entrusted, that the Queen had been given the King's word that he would dismiss sieur de Sartines and replace him by the marquis de Castries.

The old minister, who was at Paris and very weak because of his illness, decided to act in a politic manner and agree to an arrangement which he supposed it was impossible to change. When the King came to see him he agreed without hesitation to this change in the ministry. I have not yet discovered whether the lie told to the comte de Maurepas came from the Polignacs, or from other friends of the marquis de Castries, or from the director general, or from all. They have tried to spread the rumour that the Queen was responsible for the dismissal of sieur de Sartines; I did not hesitate to contradict this assertion, and gradually this rumour has stopped.

In recapitulating this to the Queen, she seemed astonished, but it is certain that this situation will make such an impression on the Queen that she will be very circumspect in future on similar occasions. It is a fact that the natural kindness of this august princess always inclines her to want to find excuses for the people she cares for.

With reference to H.M. the emperor's trip, I am afflicted by the painful thought that Y.M. is displeased by this, and if as a result, this were to have fatal consequences for Y.M.'s precious health, those of Y.M.'s faithful servants who are attached to your sacred person: and who are so with an infinitely pure zeal, would be totally overcome. May God preserve us from such a great misfortune and bless Y.M.'s glorious and salutary reign [Edit: it must be said that it was fortunate that Maria Theresa had time in November to go over her papers.]

MARIA THERESA TO MARIE ANTOINETTE, 3 NOVEMBER 1780

My dear daughter, yesterday I spent more time in France than in Austria [Edit: the previous day had been Marie Antoinette's birthday], remembering all the happy times in the past, which are now gone. The memories alone console me;[109]   I am very pleased that your little one, who you say is so sweet, is better.

I am glad that you intend resuming court life at Versailles; I know it is boring and empty; but believe me; if you do not, the drawbacks are worse, especially in your country, where the people are so impassioned. [Edit: Marie Antoinette did not resume court life with any consistency, thereby continuing to alienate the aristocracy] Like you, I would prefer winter to put an end to the emperor's trips; but he has decided to go to the Netherlands at the beginning of March and remain there for the summer. His trips increase in length every year, and that increases my distress and anxieties, while at my age I need support and consolation, and I am losing everyone I love, one after the other; I am overcome with it all.

For some weeks I have been tormented with rheumatism in my right arm, which is the reason why this letter is less well written than usual, and is why I will end now, assuring you of all my love.

---

[109] This letter is so sweet, that it is almost as if Maria Theresa foresaw the near future. It has been deliberately placed after the previous letter.

ACCOUNT BY MARIE-ANNE
(ELDEST DAUGHTER OF MARIA THERESA)

"Her Majesty's illness, as recorded in the autopsy, resulted from a hardening of the lungs, which, combined with the return of catarrh from which she had suffered for a long time, caused her great pain. She said that she felt as if her internal organs were hardening like a stone. At the same time she complained of a sensation of great internal heat, and latterly insisted on having her windows open both night and day. She incessantly asked for air. The doctors did not dare to have her bled, fearing dropsy, which seemed to be indicated by her pallor. Her illness began on the 24th of November; the return of her catarrh led to bouts of prolonged coughing, to which were added attacks of breathlessness, which had obliged her to rise from her bed the night before and she did not go back.

On the 24th, she spoke to us and the emperor, who thought there was no danger. However that morning doctor Storck had declared that the illness had become very serious. Having promised to give the empress prompt and sincere information at all times, he felt obliged to tell her towards evening that she should alert her confessor, and she did so, while saying to everyone that she did not believe she was in imminent danger, and that she was only doing this as a precaution. She thanked Storck, repeated her formal wish to be informed truthfully about her condition, declared that she did not want to see any other doctor, and expressed her desire not to be tormented by useless remedies.

On the 25th the empress had a very uncomfortable night; nevertheless H.M. sent for us in the morning to take breakfast with her, and spoke with such ease that it was difficult to guess that she was preparing for her final confession. The night of the 26th being equally unpleasant, H.M. wrote a note to the emperor telling him that she wanted to receive the Last Sacraments. The emperor, who was not yet worried, tried to dissuade her, but she would only agree to postpone Extreme Unction. The sad ceremony took place in the afternoon. The nuncio carried the Blessed Sacrament, and we accompanied it to the bedroom. The empress was kneeling on a prayer mat and wore a mourning veil, as on Good Friday. After communion, she rested for a while, then received us at six o'clock, with a gaiety which astonished us. Her breathing seemed slightly easier; but that did not last, and soon the breathlessness started again.

During the night of the 27th, she could not stay on her chaise longue, and had to sit in an armchair. The emperor, who was sleeping in an adjoining bedroom, was present for the first time during these distressing attacks of breathlessness, and from then he lost all hope.

The night of the 28th was so bad that it was feared H.M. would not survive. Storck warned her that it was time to receive Extreme Unction and at four in the morning they came to find us, while telling us that H.M. would dispense with our presence at the ceremony if we were afraid we would be too upset; but we all went and knelt around her. H.M. had a white cap on her head and was wearing a brown dressing gown which she wore to the end.

I bought this gown from her people after her death, and I regard it as a relic, and want to be wrapped in it when they put me in my coffin.

H.M. joined in her prayers with devotion; after the ceremony, she remained alone with her confessor for some time, then she saw us again. We were in a circle around H.M.'s armchair, she spoke to us for twenty minutes in a clear and intelligible voice; she thanked us for having loved her so tenderly, and told us the most touching things, while dissolving into tears. The emperor wanted to reply, but he could only sob, knelt beside his mother, received her blessing and kissed her hand.

Eventually H.M. told us: 'Go, it hurts me too much to see you.' The emperor alone remained; she spoke to him for a long time, gave him her blessing for her absent brothers and sisters, wrote a lot, disposed of some business, and gave him her last requests for her burial, arranging which prayers were to be said. She had neither the least fear nor the slightest scruple of conscience. She said: 'I have always been motivated by good intentions; I hope that God will be merciful towards me.'

Then she added: 'I have always wanted to die this way; but I feared that would not be granted. Now I see that all can be done with the grace of God.'

On the 28th, in the afternoon, she had suffered a bout of coughing accompanied by a feeling of coldness; she said: 'It is the gangrene, it will kill me within twenty four hours.' After a very bad attack of breathlessness, when H.M. came back to herself and saw that we were sitting beside her, inconsolable, she said to Storck: 'Is this the death throes?' – 'No,' he said, 'not yet.' – 'Then it is worse than this,' she continued. During this day and the night which followed, she suffered equally severe attacks. During one of these bouts she called out: 'Dear God! Will this end soon?' The prelate, who was beside her, believing that these words had been torn from her by the pain, recommended to her to be resigned. She replied: 'It is not for my sake that I wish my suffering to be over, it is for all of you. I am killing you; I can see how you are suffering.'

The night of the 29th was horrifying. H.M. had attacks of breathlessness during which more than once she almost died. When she came back to her senses, it seemed to us that she was ready to sleep; as she wanted to prevent herself sleeping, we advised her not to struggle; but she told us: 'Why do you want me to sleep when at any moment I could be called before my judge? I am afraid to sleep, I do not want to be taken by surprise, I want to see death coming.' After mass I spoke to her for half an hour. We spoke of unimportant matters: H.M.'s ideas were as clear as when she was in perfect health; her voice alone was hollow and faint, her face was very much changed and bore all the signs which precede death. After speaking privately to each of her daughters, she no longer wanted us in her rooms, as she did not want us to see her die. We went to the chapel.

In the course of her illness she had not wanted to take the medicines she had been given but had done so reluctantly; three hours before her death, Storck having brought her another potion, she said to him with a smile: 'I believe that this is meant to give me strength; therefore I will not take it.' Five minutes before her death, she rose abruptly from her armchair, took a few steps towards her chaise longue and collapsed. She was made as comfortable as possible. The emperor said to her: 'You are ill.' She replied: 'Ill enough to die.' She said to Storck: 'Light the mortuary candle and close my eyes, as that would be too much to expect from the emperor.' The emperor knelt beside her. We were sent for, but were too late."

MARIE ANTOINETTE TO JOSEPH, 10 DECEMBER 1780

I am overcome by this distressing news, and I cannot stop weeping as I write to you. My brother, my friend, you alone are left to me in a country which is and always will be dear to me! Be careful, look after yourself; you owe it to everyone. All that remains is for me to recommend my sisters to you. They have lost more than I have; they will be inconsolable! Farewell! I can no longer see what I am writing. Remember that we are your friends, your allies; love me. With all my love.

CHRONOLOGICAL TABLE

1754
(**AUGUST**) THE FUTURE LOUIS XVI BORN

1755
AXEL VON FERSEN BORN
(**NOVEMBER**) MARIE ANTOINETTE BORN

1765
(**DECEMBER**) THE FUTURE LOUIS XVI'S FATHER DIES, FOLLOWED SHORT TIME LATER, BY DEATH OF MOTHER.

1770
(**MAY**) MARRIAGE AT VERSAILLES OF MARIE ANTOINETTE (MA) AND DAUPHIN
(**JUNE**) VAUGUYON'S CABAL LYING TO KING TO DECREASE HIS LIKING FOR MA
(**AUGUST**) DAUPHIN SCORNFUL OF DU BARRY AND WHEN MA ASKS WHY HE LETS HIMSELF BE INVOLVED WITH THEM, REPLIES IS NECESSARY TO BE PRUDENT FOR SAKE OF PEACE
(**OCTOBER**) MERCY WRITES TO MARIA THERESA (MT), MA'S MOTHER, THAT DAUPHINE VERY CAREFUL WITH HER MONEY
(**NOVEMBER**) MERCY TELLS MT THAT VAUGUYON AND DU BARRY SPREADING LIES ABOUT MA IN ORDER TO LEAD PUBLIC ASTRAY
(**DECEMBER**) DAUPHINE'S KINDNESS TO INJURED POSTILION LEADS PUBLIC TO CONCLUDE SHE SECURED DECREASE IN PRICE OF BREAD

1771
MERCY WRITES – THRONE DEBASED BECAUSE OF MALICE OF DU BARRY'S CABAL, AND CONSEQUENTLY NATION PRODUCING SEDITIOUS WORKS.

1772
MERCY WRITES THAT DAUPHINE'S CHARACTER BECOMING WEAK, AND THAT SHE LETS HERSELF BE SUBJUGATED BY FEAR

1773
(**JANUARY**) DAUPHINE TELLS MERCY THAT FEARS HER HUSBAND'S APATHY
(**MAY**) MA'S OFFICIAL ENTRY INTO PARIS – RECEIVED RAPTUROUSLY. OTHER ROYALS JEALOUS OF HER POPULARITY

(AUGUST) MERCY WRITES THAT IF MA DOES NOT DOMINATE HER HUSBAND, SOMEONE ELSE WILL

1774

(JANUARY) FERSEN HAS LONG CONVERSATION WITH MA AT OPERA BALL. ATTRACTION BETWEEN TWO NOTICED.

(MAY) LOUIS XV DIES. MERCY ADVISES NEW QUEEN TO TAKE MEASURES TO HAVE PRICE OF BREAD IN PARIS FALL, AS PEOPLE EXPECT THIS FROM ADORED NEW QUEEN. MT UPSET – CHARACTER OF KING AND MINISTERS DO NOT TRANQUILLISE ME – MY DAUGHTER'S HAPPY DAYS OVER.

FERSEN LEAVES FRANCE

(JUNE) QUEEN TELLS MT THAT LATE KING LEFT HARDLY ANY MONEY.

(JULY) QUEEN INSISTS D'AIGUILLON DISMISSED FROM POST AS MINISTER FOR FOREIGN AFFAIRS. SOON HE IS FOUND TO BE INVOLVED IN ANTI- QUEEN AND ANTI-GOVERNMENT WRITINGS, BUT SUPPORTED BY UNCLE, MAUREPAS, A MINISTER.

(AUGUST) KING'S BROTHERS RESENTFUL OF NEW KING AND QUEEN. MT SHOCKED AT "ATROCIOUS" LIBEL ABOUT QUEEN. MERCY REPLIES THAT QUEEN KNOWN TO BE VIRTUOUS BY ALL, THEREFORE WOULD NOT BE HARMED BY LIBEL

1775

(MARCH) QUEEN NOT BEING RECEIVED SO WELL BY PUBLIC BECAUSE OF HER CONSTANT PLEASURE SEEKING.

(MAY) RIOTS IN PARIS BECAUSE OF PRICE OF BREAD

(JUNE) CORONATION. QUEEN WRITES OF "HAPPIEST DAY OF MY LIFE"

(JULY) MT UPSET BY MA'S LETTER IN WHICH REFERS TO KING AS "POOR MAN"

(AUGUST) BABY BOY BORN TO D'ARTOIS – HEIR TO THRONE

(OCTOBER) MT WRITES THAT KING SHOULD HAVE OPERATION

(DECEMBER) QUEEN WRITES THAT KING KIND AND STEADFAST, BUT AWKWARD.

1776

(JANUARY) D'ARTOIS GAMBLING FOR HIGH STAKES. QUEEN BUYING DIAMONDS

(FEBRUARY) MERCY COMPLAINS THAT KING ENCOURAGES QUEEN'S AMUSEMENTS

(MAY) MALESHERBES RESIGNS FROM MINISTRY BECAUSE OF QUEEN'S ANIMOSITY. TURGOT, POPULAR AND HONEST MINISTER, IS DISMISSED. QUEEN RESPONSIBLE, EXERCISING ASCENDANCY OVER KING. PUBLIC AWARE AND ANNOYED.

QUEEN LIES TO MOTHER ABOUT HER RESPONSIBILITY FOR THIS. QUEEN BORED. VERSAILLES DESERTED. D'ARTOIS ABOUT TO HAVE ANOTHER CHILD. QUEEN - NOT MY FAULT AM CHILDLESS. QUEEN SCOLDED BY MT. QUEEN ALMOST DAILY ATTENDING CHURCH, STOPS GOING TO PARIS FOR WHILE.

(JULY) QUEEN OWES MONEY BECAUSE OF DIAMOND PURCHASES

(AUGUST) QUEEN ADOPTS ORPHANED CHILD

(SEPTEMBER) MA SUFFERS FROM VAPOURS. MERCY – QUEEN'S INCOME MORE THAN DOUBLED, BUT DONATIONS TO CHARITY HAVE NOT. PUBLIC KNOWS OF QUEEN'S DEBTS.

(OCTOBER) MT WRITES – I PITY MY DAUGHTER, SURROUNDED BY LOW FLATTERERS, WITH NO HOPE OF SUCCESSION

(NOVEMBER) QUEEN PERMITTED BY KING TO PLAY PROHIBITED CARD GAME. MT UPSET THAT GAZETTES CRITICISING QUEEN

(DECEMBER) AT PLAY IN PARIS, QUEEN NOT ACCLAIMED AS MUCH AS USUAL

1777

(JANUARY) QUEEN'S DEBTS HUGE. KING AGREES TO HELP PAY THEM

(MARCH) PROHIBITED GAMES OF CHANCE START AGAIN BECAUSE OF COURT'S EXAMPLE. KING HAS TO RENEW PROHIBITION. HARDLY DARES TO TELL QUEEN. QUEEN ANNOYED AT RENEWAL OF PROHIBITION, AND IGNORES IT.

(APRIL/MAY) JOSEPH SENT TO FRANCE TO PERSUADE PROCRASTINATING LOUIS XVI TO HAVE REMEDIAL OPERATION. IS SUCCESSFUL

(JUNE) JOSEPH WRITES – QUEEN VIRTUOUS, LEFT HER WITH REGRET. MT WRITES TO MA – HOPES OF PREGNANCY AT LAST. ANGERS ME BECAUSE HAVING CHILDREN MEANS EVERYTHING TO YOU

(AUGUST) QUEEN'S DEBTS NOT BEING PAID. NO MONEY FOR CHARITY. PUBLIC ANNOYED

(NOVEMBER) QUEEN TELLS FRIENDS WOULD NOT BE BOTHERED IF KING TOOK LOVER, IF IT MADE HIM MORE PASSIONATE

1778

(FEBRUARY) JOSEPH'S EXPANSIONISM IN BAVARIA, CREATES STRESS FOR QUEEN

(SPRING) QUEEN FINALLY PREGNANT. FEELS IS A DREAM

(SUMMER) FERSEN RETURNS TO FRANCE. AGAIN ATTRACTION BETWEEN TWO, NOTICED BY COURTIERS.

410

(DECEMBER) SHORTLY BEFORE QUEEN'S LABOUR, LIBELS FOUND AT VERSAILLES. KING SAYS IS CAPITAL OFFENCE TO PRINT SUCH LIES. AUTHOR DISCOVERED, BUT NO ACTION TAKEN.
BIRTH OF DAUGHTER TO MARIE ANTOINETTE

1778 – 1789
FERSEN ABROAD, PARTICIPATES IN AMERICAN WAR OF IND-EPENDENCE, THEN TRAVELS WITH KING GUSTAV, BUT RETURNS PERIODICALLY TO FRANCE

1779
(FEBRUARY) KING AND QUEEN TO PARIS AFTER BIRTH. RECEPTION COOL
(APRIL) QUEEN HAD MEASLES. 4 MALE FRIENDS ALLOWED IN HER BEDROOM FROM 7AM TILL 11PM TO AMUSE HER. LED TO BAD JOKES. WHILE QUEEN RECUPERATING AT TRIANON, KING'S VALET TRIED TO TEMPT KING TO BEGIN AFFAIR. QUEEN HEARD ABOUT THIS AND ANXIOUS.
(OCTOBER) QUEEN DECIDES NOT TO GO TO FONTAINEBLEAU BECAUSE OF EXPENSES OF SUPPORTING AMERICAN WAR OF INDEPENDENCE.
(NOVEMBER) KING PLAYS A GAME OF CHANCE AS FAVOUR TO THE QUEEN, LOSES MONEY, AND CONSEQUENTLY HAS TO BORROW MONEY HE HAS LOANED TO QUEEN TO PAY HER DEBTS, BACK FROM HER.

1780
(MARCH) 8-10,000 MEN READY TO SET SAIL FOR AMERICA. PROMOTIONS IN MILITARY MADE ACCORDING TO QUEEN'S WISHES
(JULY) MERCY – BECAUSE OF KING'S PERSONALITY, EVIDENT THAT SOMEONE WILL DOMINATE HIM – SHOULD BE QUEEN'S PUPPET
(NOVEMBER) MT WRITES – KING SHOWS DISPLEASURE BUT LETS PEOPLE DO AS THEY WISH – DANGEROUS MAXIM. DEATH OF MT. MA WRITES TO JOSEPH – REMEMBER WE ARE YOUR FRIENDS. LOVE US

1781 - 1788
1781: BIRTH OF FIRST DAUPHIN (DIED **1789**); **1785**: BIRTH OF SECOND SON; **1786**: SECOND PRINCESS BORN (DIED 1787); PERIODIC RIOTS BECAUSE OF HIGH TAXES, PRICE OF BREAD, POOR HARVESTS.

1789

FERSEN RETURNS TO FRANCE AND DOES NOT LEAVE AGAIN UNTIL JUNE 1791, WHEN ESCORTS ROYAL FAMILY OUT OF PARIS IN ABORTIVE ESCAPE BID.

HASTILY CONVENED AND TEMPORARY, GATHERING OF STATES GENERAL, BECAUSE OF FINANCIAL DEFICIT (LATER CALL THEM-SELVES NATIONAL ASSEMBLY) – USURP POWER FROM KING AND MINISTERS – BEGINNING OF FRENCH REVOLUTION. DECLARATION OF RIGHTS OF MAN, BY NATIONAL ASSEMBLY.

1791

MERCY TO LA MARCK – WRITES OF KING & QUEEN "THOSE FOR WHOM WE ARE ACTING, WHO CANNOT UNDERSTAND, UNLESS EVERYTHING EXPLAINED TO THEM"

(JUNE) ROYALS ALMOST ESCAPE FROM FRANCE. ARRESTED NEAR BORDER. PROVENCE ESCAPES, AS DOES FERSEN, WHO WERE BOTH ORDERED BY KING TO TAKE OTHER ROUTES.

(SEPTEMBER) KING SWEARS IN ASSEMBLY TO UPHOLD NEWLY COMPLETED CONSTITUTION, PEOPLE JOYFUL, THEN RETURNS TO PALACE AND CRIES WITH MA. LATER THAT NIGHT SENDS COURIER TO VIENNA, ASKING FOR FOREIGN POWERS TO INVADE, AND RESTORE HIS POWERS. LA MARCK WRITES TO MERCY – "KING INCAPABLE OF REIGNING."

1792

(AUGUST) ALLIES INVADE FRANCE. ROYALS DEPOSED & IMPRISONED

(DECEMBER) KING PUT ON TRIAL

1793

(JANUARY) KING GUILLOTINED

(JULY) DAUPHIN REMOVED FROM QUEEN, AND 'CARED FOR' BY HARSH REVOLUTIONARY, SIMON.

(OCTOBER) MA GUILLOTINED

1794

(JANUARY) DAUPHIN NOW KEPT IN SOLITARY CONFINEMENT IN TOWER

(MAY) MARIE THERESE, ALSO ALONE IN TOWER, IN SEPARATE ROOMS, AFTER GUILLOTINING OF AUNT ELISABETH

1795

(JUNE) DAUPHIN DIES

(DECEMBER) MARIE THERESE RELEASED FROM TOWER

412

FROM AUGUST 1792 – AUSTRIANS AND PRUSSIANS INVADE FRANCE, ON LOUIS' INVITATION. LEADS TO PAN EUROPEAN WAR FOR MANY YEARS, IN WHICH MILLIONS OF EUROPEANS SUFFERED AND DIED. RISE OF NAPOLEON ETC.

INDEX OF MAIN NAMES

AIGUILLON: (DUC D') LOUIS XV'S FOREIGN MINISTER, NEPHEW OF MAUREPAS' WIFE. DISMISSED BY LOUIS XVI SHORTLY AFTER HIS ACCESSION, ON QUEEN'S INSISTENCE, BECAUSE OF HER JUSTIFIABLE SUSPICIONS OF HIS TREACHERY. SUSPECTED BY MERCY OF BEING RESPONSIBLE FOR THE SCURRILOUS WRITINGS AGAINST THE QUEEN, WHICH FIRST APPEARED IN 1774, AFTER HIS DISMISSAL. RALLYING POINT FOR THE DISAFFECTED, AND BECAUSE OF HIS POWERFUL CONNECTIONS, VERY DANGEROUS.

ANDLAU: (COMTESSE D') WELL KNOWN INTRIGUER. DISMISSED FROM COURT TWENTY YEARS BEFORE MARIE ANTOINETTE'S ARRIVAL, BECAUSE HAD PROCURED PORNOGRAPHIC BOOKS FOR MME ADELAIDE. AUNT OF POLIGNAC. AROUSED RESENTMENT BECAUSE SECURED PAYMENT FROM COURT. WAS BELIEVED WAS BECAUSE OF MARIE ANTOINETTE'S INFLUENCE

ARCHIDUCHESSE: (MADAME L') MARIE ANTOINETTE'S AUSTRIAN TITLE

ARTOIS: (COMTE D') YOUNGER BROTHER OF LOUIS XVI. MA'S CONSTANT COMPANION WHILST GAMBLING, ATTENDING OPERA BALLS ETC. LEFT FRANCE AFTER JULY 1789, BECAUSE OF THREATS TO HIS LIFE. BECAME FOCUS FOR DISENCHANTED ARISTOCRATS LEAVING FRANCE IN DROVES (EMIGRES), ALSO AFTER JULY 1789.

BARRY: (COMTESSE DU) LOUIS XV'S MISTRESS. RESENTFUL OF NEW DAUPHINE, AND SECRETLY PLOTTED AGAINST HER, BUT EVENTUALLY WON ROUND BY MERCY, WHO HINTED TO HER THAT OLD KING WOULD NOT LIVE FOR EVER, AND SHE WOULD THEN BECOME DEPENDENT ON MA'S GOOD GRACES.

CAMPAN: LADY IN WAITING TO QUEEN. SURVIVED REVOLUTION, AND WROTE MEMOIR

CHOISEUL: (DUC DE) LOUIS XV'S FOREIGN MINISTER. ARRANGED MARRIAGE OF MA AND LOUIS. LATER DISMISSED AND EXILED BY LOUIS XV, BECAUSE OF HIS SCHEMING. MISTRUSTED BY MT. TRIED TO MANIPULATE MA.

CREUTZ: (COMTE DE) SWEDISH AMBASSADOR TO FRANCE. REPORTED TO GUSTAVUS ABOUT ATTRACTION BETWEEN FERSEN & MA IN 1774: "IT IS NOT POSSIBLE TO BE MORE HONOURABLE THAN HE HAS BEEN." – THAT IS, FERSEN LEFT FRANCE, TO PUT A STOP TO GOSSIP ABOUT HIMSELF AND THE NEW QUEEN

DAUPHIN: CROWN PRINCE. LOUIS XVI'S TITLE BEFORE ACCESSION.

DAUPHINE : WIFE OF DAUPHIN

FERSEN: (COMTE DE) (FAMILY ORIGINALLY MACPHERSONS, FROM SCOTLAND) LOVER OF MARIE ANTOINETTE. FIRST MET MA IN JANUARY 1774. LEFT JUST AFTER SHE BECAME QUEEN IN MAY 1774. RETURNED WHEN SHE WAS FINALLY PREGNANT, IN SUMMER 1778. WROTE AT THAT TIME TO HIS FATHER "THE QUEEN ASKED ME TO COME TO HER PRIVATE ROOMS WEARING MY UNIFORM" AND "SHE IS THE SWEETEST AND MOST BEAUTIFUL PERSON I KNOW."

THEREAFTER TRAVELLED AROUND EUROPE WITH GUSTAVUS, AND FOUGHT FOR FRANCE IN AMERICAN WAR OF INDEPENDENCE, BUT PERIODICALLY RETURNED TO MA'S SIDE. REMAINED WITH HER FROM START OF REVOLUTION, IN 1789, UNTIL THE FAMILY'S UNSUCCESSFUL ATTEMPT TO ESCAPE FROM REVOLUTIONARY FRANCE, IN JUNE 1791, WHICH HE HELPED PLAN. HE SUCCESSFULLY ESCAPED.

FROM JUNE 1791, SPENT TIME TRAVELLING ROUND EUROPE, AS LOUIS XVI'S UNOFFICIAL AMBASSADOR, TRYING TO PERSUADE THE POWERS TO UNITE & INTERVENE IN FRANCE, ON BEHALF OF KING.

RETURNED TO PARIS IN FEBRUARY 1792 TO TRY TO PERSUADE MA TO LEAVE PARIS WITH HIM - SHE REFUSED. NEVER FORGAVE HIMSELF FOR OBEYING KING'S ORDER TO LEAVE ROYAL FAMILY, OUTSIDE PARIS, IN JUNE 1791.

AFTER JUNE 1792, AND IMPRISONMENT OF ROYALS, HIS GRIEF AND BITTERNESS BECAME AN OBSESSION

FOUQUIER-TINVILLE: PUBLIC PROSECUTOR FOR REVOLUTIONARY TRIBUNAL

GUEMENEE: (PRINCESSE DE) NIECE OF MARSAN, FRIEND OF QUEEN, 'INHERITED' POSITION OF GOVERNESS TO ROYAL CHILDREN FROM HER AUNT MARSAN. ENCOURAGED YOUNG QUEEN IN DISSOLUTE BEHAVIOUR.

GOLZ: (BARON DE) PRUSSIAN AMBASSADOR TO FRANCE. CORRESPONDENCE WITH PRUSSIA INTERCEPTED BY AUSTRIAN COURT.

GUSTAVUS: KING OF SWEDEN.

JOSEPH: EMPEROR OF AUSTRIA, RULED JOINTLY WITH HIS WIDOWED MOTHER, MARIA THERESA. REPEATEDLY OPPOSED MOTHER'S POLICIES. HIS EXPANSIONISM, AND MARIE ANTOINETTE'S SUPPORT OF THIS (ALTHOUGH RELUCTANT), WAS ANOTHER REASON FOR FRENCH DISLIKE OF MARIE ANTOINETTE.

LA FAYETTE: (MARQUIS DE) FRENCH HERO OF AMERICAN WAR OF INDEPENDENCE. AFTER REVOLUTION, ELECTED COMMANDER OF

415

PARISIAN NATIONAL GUARD. IN THAT POSITION, DOMINATED KING AND QUEEN, DURING 1790 AND 1791. THREATENED QUEEN THAT IF CAUGHT COMMITTING ADULTERY, SHE WOULD BE SEPARATED FROM KING AND IMPRISONED. LATER BECAME GENERAL AT FRONT, AND OFFERED TO ESCORT KING AND QUEEN OUT OF PARIS – THEY REFUSED TO LEAVE WITH HIM. UNDERSTANDABLY HATED BY QUEEN.

LAMBALLE: (PRINCESSE DE) MARIE THERESE. FRIEND OF MA. SISTER IN LAW TO DUC D'ORLEANS' WIFE. HUSBAND DEBAUCHED – DIED YOUNG.

LOUIS XV: GRANDFATHER OF LOUIS XVI. (LOUIS XVI'S FATHER HAD DIED FROM SMALLPOX.)

LOUIS XVI: HUSBAND OF MARIE ANTOINETTE.

MADAME: TERM CAN BE USED TO DENOTE HIGHEST RANKING PRINCESS

MALESHERBES: POPULAR AND HONEST MINISTER IN YOUNG KING'S REIGN. RESIGNED BECAUSE OF QUEEN'S ANIMOSITY. REPRESENTED KING AT HIS TRIAL. ENDURED HEROIC DEATH AS A CONSEQUENCE

MARIA THERESA: MOTHER OF MARIE ANTOINETTE, EMPRESS OF AUSTRIA

MARIE THERESE: DAUGHTER OF MA. BORN DECEMBER 1778

MARSAN : (COMTESSE DE) GOVERNESS TO FUTURE LOUIS XVI, HIS BROTHERS AND SISTERS. RETAINED ASCENDANCY OVER LOUIS XVI, WHEN ADULT. AUNT OF GUEMENEE & ROHAN

MAUREPAS: (COMTE DE) CHOSEN BY KING AS HIS CHIEF MINISTER AFTER HIS ACCESSION. WILY. DOMINATED KING. OPPOSED QUEEN'S POWER. SECRETLY SECONDED DANGEROUS NEPHEW D'AIGUILLON

MERCY: (COMTE DE) MARIA THERESA'S AMBASSADOR TO FRANCE. ADVISER TO QUEEN.

MESDAMES: COLLECTIVE TERM FOR LOUIS XV'S UNMARRIED DAUGHTERS – ADELAIDE, SOPHIE, VICTOIRE AND THE NUN, LOUISE

MONSIEUR: TERM CAN DENOTE HIGHEST RANKING PRINCE

NARBONNE: (COMTESSE DE) ADELAIDE'S LADY IN WAITING. INTRIGUER.

NOAILLES: (MME DE) MA'S LADY OF HONOUR

ORLEANS: (DUC DE) COUSIN OF LOUIS XVI. WIFE SISTER IN LAW TO LAMBALLE. JACOBIN & RIVAL FOR THE THRONE, DURING THE REVOLUTION. KNOWN AS DUC DE CHARTRES UNTIL DEATH OF FATHER.

POLIGNAC: (COMTESSE DE) FRIEND OF MA. HATED BY FRENCH BECAUSE OF FAVOURS EXTORTED FROM MA BY POLIGNAC'S FAMILY AND FRIENDS. LEFT FRANCE IN JULY 1789, BECAUSE OF THREATS BY REVOLUTIONARIES TO KILL HER.

PROVENCE: (COMTE DE) BROTHER OF LOUIS XVI. SUCCESSFULLY ESCAPED FROM FRANCE IN JUNE 1791, THEN JOINED YOUNGER BROTHER D'ARTOIS AND BOTH BECAME RALLYING POINT FOR EMIGRES. LOBBIED THE POWERS TO INTERVENE TO RESTORE ABSOLUTE MONARCHY. RESENTED BROTHER'S POSITION, AND ALSO RESENTFUL OF MA, WHO KEPT HIM POWERLESS, ON ADVICE OF MERCY, BECAUSE "CUT A BETTER FIGURE THAN OAF OF A BROTHER" (MT'S OPINION)

ROHAN: (PRINCE DE) LOUIS XV'S AMBASSADOR TO AUSTRIA. WAS EVENTUALLY REPLACED AFTER MA BECAME QUEEN, BECAUSE MT DISLIKED AND MISTRUSTED HIM, AND BECAME QUEEN'S ENEMY. NEPHEW OF KING'S FORMER GOVERNESS, MARSAN

ROSENBERG: ADVISER TO MARIA THERESA. RECEIVED LETTERS FROM MARIE ANTOINETTE WHICH SHOCKED MARIA THERESA.

TURGOT: FINANCE MINISTER IN LOUIS XVI'S EARLY REIGN. DISMISSED ON INSISTENCE OF QUEEN, BECAUSE OF PRESSURE FROM HER FRIENDS, WHO FEARED HIS FISCAL REFORMS WOULD COST THEM MONEY (IE. HE PROPOSED TAXING THE ARISTOCRACY, AND NOT SIMPLY EXTORTING MORE TAXES FROM THE PEOPLE – A NOVEL IDEA). IF HAD STAYED IN POST, COULD PERHAPS HAVE HELPED PREVENT BANKRUPTCY WHICH PRECIPITATED FRENCH REVOLUTION. MARIE ANTOINETTE WANTED HIM SENT TO THE BASTILLE

VAUGUYON: (DUC DE) LOUIS' GOVERNOR

VERMOND: (ABBE DE) SENT BY LOUIS XV TO VIENNA TO TEACH FRENCH TO THE BETROTHED MA. RETURNED WITH HER TO FRANCE AND CONTINUED TO WORK WITH HER AS TUTOR, THEN ADVISER. INFORMED MERCY OF MA'S DAILY DOINGS. MERCY IN TURN INFORMED MT. LEFT FRANCE AFTER OCTOBER 1789, BECAUSE SUSPECTED UNJUSTLY OF PRO-AUSTRIAN SYMPATHIES. OFTEN DESPAIRED OF MA

VRILLIERE: (DUC DE) BROTHER OF MAUREPAS' WIFE. MINISTER IN LOUIS XV'S CABINET AND ALSO IN THAT OF LOUIS XVI. WAS EVENTUALLY DISMISSED ON QUEEN'S INSISTENCE, BECAUSE OF HIS INCOMPETENCE, AND BECAME ANOTHER OF HER ENEMIES.

BIBLIOGRAPHY

Arneth, A. d'., & Geffroy, M. A. (1875). *Marie-Antoinette. Correspondance Secrete entre Marie-Therese et le Cte de Mercy-Argenteau avec les letters de Marie-Therese et de Marie-Antoinette.* Paris: Librairie de Firmin-Didot Freres.

Bacourt, A. de. (1851). *Correspondance entre le Comte de Mirabeau et le Comte de la Marck pendant les annees 1789, 1790 et 1791.* Paris: Librairie Ve Le Normant.

Campan, M. (1904). *Memoirs of the Court of Marie-Antoinette, Queen of France; with sketches and anecdotes of her private life, by Madame Campan, First Lady-in-Waiting to the Queen.* London: The Grolier Society. [Earlier edition published 1823]

Klinckowstrom, R. M. de (1877). *Le comte de Fersen et la cour de France.* Paris: Librairie de Firmin-Didot.

Rocheterie, M. de la. (1893). *The Life of Marie Antoinette.* London: James R Osgood, McIlvaine & Co.